Strategic Marketing

An Applied Perspective

Karel Jan Alsem
University of Groningen

**McGraw-Hill
Irwin**

Boston   Burr Ridge, IL   Dubuque, IA   Madison, WI   New York   San Francisco   St. Louis
Bangkok   Bogotá   Caracas   Kuala Lumpur   Lisbon   London   Madrid   Mexico City
Milan   Montreal   New Delhi   Santiago   Seoul   Singapore   Sydney   Taipei   Toronto

**McGraw-Hill
Irwin**

STRATEGIC MARKETING: AN APPLIED PERSPECTIVE

Published by McGraw-Hill/Irwin, a business unit of The McGraw-Hill Companies, Inc.,
1221 Avenue of the Americas, New York, NY, 10020. Copyright © 2007 by The
McGraw-Hill Companies, Inc. All rights reserved. No part of this publication may be
reproduced or distributed in any form or by any means, or stored in a database or retrieval
system, without the prior written consent of The McGraw-Hill Companies, Inc.,
including, but not limited to, in any network or other electronic storage or transmission,
or broadcast for distance learning.

Some ancillaries, including electronic and print components, may not be available to
customers outside the United States.

This book is printed on acid-free paper.

1 2 3 4 5 6 7 8 9 0 CCW/CCW 0 9 8 7 6

ISBN-13: 978-0-07-302586-5
ISBN-10: 0-07-302586-0

Editorial director: *John E. Biernat*
Publisher: *Andy Winston*
Sponsoring editor: *Barrett Koger*
Editorial coordinator: *Jill M. O'Malley*
Executive marketing manager: *Rhonda Seelinger*
Senior media producer: *Damian Moshak*
Lead project manager: *Christine A. Vaughan*
Lead production supervisor: *Michael R. McCormick*
Coordinator freelance design: *Artemio Ortiz Jr.*
Media project manager: *Joyce J. Chappetto*
Typeface: *10/12 Times New Roman*
Compositor: *Techbooks*
Printer: *Courier Westford*

Library of Congress Cataloging-in-Publication Data

Alsem, K. J.
    Strategic marketing : an applied perspective / Karel Jan Alsem.
      p. cm.
    Includes index.
    ISBN-13: 978-0-07-302586-5 (alk. paper)
    ISBN-10: 0-07-302586-0 (alk. paper)
    1. Marketing—Management.   I. Title.
  HF5415.13.A435 2007
  658.8'101—dc22

                                                2006013722

www.mhhe.com

To Dick Wittink (1945–2005), a great person and marketer

About the Author

Dr. Karel Jan Alsem   *University of Groningen*

Karel Jan Alsem (born 1957) is associate professor of marketing at the Faculty of Economics of the University of Groningen. He received a master of science degree in business administration (1981) and a PhD in marketing (1991) from the University of Groningen. His main research interests concern strategic brand management, marketing communications, and marketing planning. He has published papers in journals such as the *International Journal of Research in Marketing, Applied Economics,* and the *Journal of Market Focused Management*. He is the author of a Dutch book on strategic marketing planning, the market leader in business schools, which is now in its fourth edition. At the faculty he teaches MBA electives in marketing management, strategic brand management, and marketing communications, and he is the coordinator of the master of marketing program. He is also engaged in executive teaching and consulting on those topics. Students and professionals appreciate his motivating and clear method of education. As a branding expert, he is regularly asked for interviews in newspapers.

Dr. Alsem loves running and bird watching. He lives in Haren, a village near Groningen in the north of The Netherlands, with his wife, Cato, and his son and three daughters, Tom, Sophie (twins), Anne, and Floor.

Preface

This book describes the current thinking on strategic marketing from a how-to perspective. The theory of strategic marketing is presented in steps. Those steps can be followed to arrive at a strategic marketing plan. This book has a combination of five attributes that make it different from other marketing strategy books. First, it deals only with *strategic marketing*. Therefore, there are no separate chapters devoted to consumer behavior, market research, or marketing instruments [the 4 P's are put in one (albeit long) chapter]. The second attribute is the *process approach*. In presenting strategic marketing in steps, there is much attention to the logic of the different steps and the relations between them. Also, explicit attention is devoted to levels in a company. The third attribute relates to what we feel is important in marketing: customers and brands. A *customer and brand orientation* is followed throughout the book: in the analysis, in choosing options, in developing marketing strategy, and in implementation. The fourth attribute is that in many places in the book *strategic guidelines* are given: what to do and what not to do in marketing practice. Finally, there is much attention for *tools and techniques* that can be helpful in the planning process. In summary, this book combines an academic and applied approach of strategic marketing planning.

The book is primarily targeted at students with a basic knowledge of marketing. Thus, the relevant target groups are undergraduates in the third or fourth year and some MBAs. The book can be used in, for example, courses in marketing strategy or marketing management. The book can also be used in executive teaching and by marketing practitioners who are looking for academic support for their daily decision making.

The book consists of four parts including 12 chapters, with each chapter being a step in the strategic marketing planning process:

Part 1 Introduction and Market Definition

1. The strategic marketing planning process
2. Mission, value strategies, and market definition

Part 2 Situation Analysis

3. Internal analysis
4. Customer analysis
5. Industry analysis
6. Competitor analysis
7. Analysis of distribution and suppliers
8. From analysis to strategy

Part 3 Corporate and Marketing Decisions

9. Corporate objectives and corporate strategies
 10. Marketing objectives and marketing strategies

Part 4 Implementation

11. Objective and strategies for marketing instruments
12. Organization and implementation of marketing

Each chapter starts with key points and an illustrative case with questions. Throughout the text many examples are included, most of them in separate boxes, enabling readers to concentrate on the theory or the examples or both. Each chapter ends with a summary.

v

A complete Instructor's Manual with lecture notes, chapter outlines suggesting Power-Point slide use for various points in the lecture, a section of suggested cases and supplemental readings, and a section of discussion questions and answers to end-of-chapter material from the book can be found on the book's Web site, www.mhhe.com/alsem1e. A PowerPoint presentation for each chapter is also included on the Web site as well as other resources for the instructor's use in the classroom. Students will find self-grading assessments as well as learning objectives for each chapter.

This book tries to reduce the gap between strategic marketing theory and marketing practice. The main message is that you should keep asking yourself what effect your company's behavior has on potential customers. For example, you might ask, How does my amusing commercial score on brand recall? Or: Do more brand extensions reduce or increase customers' confusion? Things like this have to do with the attitude of the manager and also with the way the planning process is done. Both aspects receive attention in this book. The content of the book is the result of continuously wondering whether strategic marketing issues are and should be applicable in marketing practice. However, there is no "truth." Science by definition is a matter of "asking questions," and a field as young as marketing science is only at the beginning of the process of finding the "truth." It is my hope that the ideas in this book not only lead to better marketing decision making but also lead to the asking of better marketing questions.

I would greatly appreciate if you, as my customer, make me part of your ongoing needs and perceptions with regard to this book.

Karel Jan Alsem
University of Groningen
February 2006

Acknowledgments

The book is an updated and revised version of its Dutch counterpart, which is now in its fourth edition. First, I thank my Dutch publisher, Wolters Noordhoff, for permitting me to do this international version. Furthermore, I gratefully acknowledge the many marketing practitioners who have taken the brand and marketing communication courses at the Academy of Management of the University of Groningen for their insightful discussions. I also thank the many students who gave their comments on the book.

Regarding this international edition, I am first of all grateful for having the opportunity to have Professor Dick Wittink as my partner for this book. Unfortunately, in the middle of his admirable life he passed away, and so we could not jointly translate our inspiring discussions into text for the book. Nevertheless, I put several of Dick's ideas (such as the application of the work of Treacy and Wiersema) in the book. I also thank Dick's assistants for their detailed comments.

Second, I owe many thanks to Erik Kostelijk for preparing the starting cases and questions. He has been my "case partner" for many years, and I hope this will continue in the future. I also thank Jochem Meijer for preparing many of the small cases. I thank my publisher, McGraw-Hill, for publishing the book, and the McGraw team working on the book (Barrett Koger, Jill O'Malley, and Christine Vaughan) for their help and for being so patient. Finally, I would like to acknowledge the feedback I received from the following reviewers. Their thoughtful reviews are greatly appreciated.

Gordon Flanders
University of Minnesota

John Kozup
Villanova University

Wendy Moe
University of Texas at Austin

Kenny Chan
California State University at Chico

Chickery Kosouf
Worcester Polytechnic Institute

Finally, I thank two of my homes. My parent brands Daan and Ine Alsem-de Vreede are still going strong and gave and continue to give me a very solid base for developing my ideas. I thank my main cobrand Cato and my subbrands Tom, Sophie, Anne, and Floor for being inspiring and down-to-earth sparring partners in this current dynamic life.

Table of Contents

Introduction and Market Definition

1. The Strategic Marketing Planning Process

2. Mission, Value Strategies, and Market Definition

This book was written to bridge the gap between the theory and practice of strategic marketing. Current marketing theory describes how a company (or a brand) can implement the strategic marketing planning process and how strategic marketing decisions can be based on an analysis of the brand and the environment. Therefore, we will focus on the *activities* that must be carried out by a company within the framework of strategic marketing. These activities can be categorized as evaluation/ retrospective, analysis, planning (strategy development), and implementation (execution).

The book is divided into four parts. Part 1 describes the basic assumptions of the book and the marketing process. Part 2 is dedicated to evaluation and situation analysis. The basic assumption here is that without a thorough, systematic situation analysis, the success of a strategy is more a matter of luck than one of skill. Part 3 deals with the development of the strategy, with particular attention to brand decisions. Part 4 concerns the translation (e.g., into communication) and execution (implementation) of strategic decisions.

All marketing activities should be carried out with a single objective: to create value for the customer through a recognizable brand image. This objective (customer and brand) provides the basis for the description of the activities as well as practical advice. This book can be used for the development of a marketing plan and also as a guidebook for reexamining a company's marketing policy.

Part 1 begins with an overview and then moves on to the introductory phase of a company's marketing planning process. Chapter 1 provides an outline of the entire strategic marketing planning process that a company can follow to develop a marketing plan. This process is the common thread running through the book. Chapter 2 shows how to begin this process: mission, value strategy, and the identification of market boundaries. The value strategy sets the course by which a company will meet the customer's needs. Identification of market boundaries is necessary to make the transition to a deeper analysis of the products and target groups.

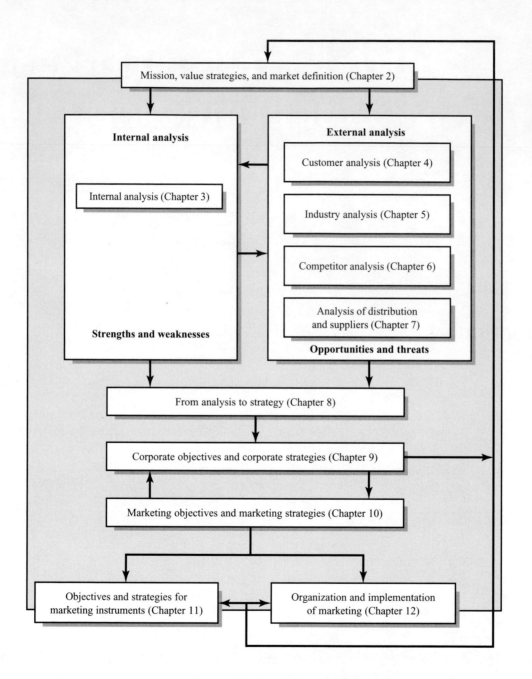

Chapter One

The Strategic Marketing Planning Process

Key Points in This Chapter

- Outline what marketing is and describe how marketing developed.
- Introduce value marketing (customer and brand) as the key to developing customers' relationship with a brand.
- Describe aggregation levels in organizations.
- Stress the importance of a sustainable competitive advantage.
- Summarize the strategic marketing planning process with an emphasis on doing one's homework to enable sound marketing decisions.

INTRODUCTION

Marketing theory and marketing practice have undergone an enormous development over the past 40 years. Marketing philosophy in the early twenty-first century is focused on two main themes: *customer value* and *brand equity*. Marketers ask themselves how they can respond to and anticipate the customer's needs as well as build and maintain a long standing relationship with the customer. Ultimately, they want to ensure that the brand plays a recognizable and trusted role in building customer loyalty.

This book covers the concept of strategic marketing from the customer and brand perspective. In addition, it demonstrates how to create and implement a marketing plan for a brand. In this introductory chapter we sketch an overview of that process and explain several concepts. First, in Section 1.1 we discuss the meaning of strategic marketing planning. In Section 1.2 we pay attention to developments in marketing philosophy up to the present. Different aggregation levels within a company play a role in the marketing planning process. We discuss those levels in Section 1.3. Section 1.4 goes into the concept of marketing strategy: targeting, getting a sustainable competitive advantage, and brand positioning. Finally, we describe what the strategic marketing planning process should look like in Section 1.5 and what a marketing plan looks like (chapter appendix). Since the structure of this book follows this planning process, Section 1.5 can be considered a summary of the book.

Introductory Case: Online Travel Companies Give the European Travel Industry Hope

After the Internet bubble burst, "dot-com companies" seemed to be in big trouble. But Brent Hoberman, the 34-year-old chief executive and cofounder of the London-based online travel service Lastminute.com remained an optimist. "We never gave up our dream of building Europe's largest e-travel business. The best motivation for our staff was to see new sales records every day. Any pessimism was wiped out by that."

In 2002, Lastminute.com sold $462 million worth of flights, hotel rooms, vacation packages, and even concert tickets over the Internet, a 107 percent increase from the previous year. The five-year-old company is now on the brink of breaking even, and analysts expect it to turn a modest profit for the year as a whole. Lastminute.com tries to adapt its strategy to the local market situation. This is done partly by buying smaller rivals who are already established in the market. Lastminute.com now serves eight European countries and has affiliates in four others.

Travel and the Internet turn out to be a perfect match. European online travel bookings rose 70 percent in 2002, reaching a total of $7.3 billion. For 2003, a growth of 50 percent is expected. That makes it the fastest growing segment in e-commerce and a beacon of hope for the troubled European travel industry. The overall European travel market fell 6 percent in 2002, declining to $180 billion.

Why such a surge now, especially amid weak economies and geopolitical anxiety? It's largely a reflection of Europe's fast-growing Internet penetration and the ensuing rush to online shopping. Also, e-travel has strong appeal in uncertain times as penny-pinching consumers comparison shop for the best deals. The shift to online sales, now just 4 percent of travel spending in Europe, will likely increase no matter what happens to other travel bookings. That's not to say online travel is crisis-proof. "If the travel industry fell 40 percent, everybody would be hit hard," Hoberman says. "But if it fell 20 percent, we'd see that as an opportunity."

Three companies are grabbing most of the online travel sales: Lastminute.com, Expedia, and Ebrookers. Ebrookers started out as a bricks-and-mortar travel agency. Ebrookers serves now 10 companies and is a top player in most, using a business model that blends the methods of traditional travel agencies with online sales. The company also runs a low-cost call center in India that allows customers to plan more complex trips with the aid of a flesh-and-blood agent.

European Online Travel Industry ($ Sales in Millions)

	2001	2002
European online travel sales	4,300	7,300
Expedia	Approx. 165	Approx. 400
Ebrookers	260	468
Lastminute.com	225	462

Expedia sold $440 million worth of products outside the United States in 2002—much of that in Europe—up a sizzling 146 percent from the year before. This U.S.-based company credits good software and the best online deals. "We claim our service has the widest selection and is the easiest to use," according to the senior vice president at Expedia Europe.

The latest capability, pioneered by Expedia, is a "dynamic packaging engine" that lets customers design their own personalized tours by picking and choosing among airlines, hotels, cars, restaurants, and activities—with package prices better than the sum of the parts. For conventional travel agents, already reeling as financially strapped airlines pare back commissions, such innovations promise to make life even more miserable. But for online brokers the flight is looking mighty smooth.

Source: *Business Week,* European edition, March 17, 2003.

Questions

1. Calculate the market shares of Expedia, Ebookers, and Lastminute.com for both 2001 and 2002.
2. Explain the growth of the European e-travel industry: Which trends have caused this market to grow?
3. Hoberman thinks that a fall of 20 percent in the European travel industry would present an opportunity for the e-travel industry. Do you agree with him? Explain why or why not.
4. Based on the information in this case, compare the strategies of the "big three" in the European e-travel business.
   a. Describe the strategy of each of the three companies.
   b. Which underlying competencies are used by each competitor to realize the needed competitive advantage?

1.1   STRATEGIC MARKETING PLANNING

Strategic marketing planning is increasingly important for companies for a variety of reasons. Some of these include:

- Companies increasingly are faced with a turbulent economic environment. In addition, technological developments have caused products to have increasingly shorter life cycles; therefore, their costs have to be recovered in a shorter time frame.
- Developments in information and communications technology since the 1990s are responsible for the growth of the global network economy.
- A third trend is that governments in many countries are striving to accommodate market forces. Even traditionally noncommercial organizations and markets such as postal services, energy, and health care are placing more emphasis on listening to the customer.
- Finally, consumers are becoming more independent, are learning more, and presumably are placing a higher value on simplicity and transparency.

On the one hand, these changes open up opportunities never before available. On the other hand, companies face increasing competition. As a result, more than before, companies need to respond to their ever-changing environment with increasing speed and more highly developed strategic plans. Strategic planning can also play an important internal role at a company by creating alignment. Strategic planning ensures that all employees are moving forward in the same direction.

1.1.1   Strategic Planning

Strategic planning is a way to take into account increasing uncertainties of today's marketplace. It consists of carefully analyzing the external environment and the company's internal possibilities and strengths. Based on this internal and external analysis, a company must formulate a list of objectives and a strategy to reach those objectives: what do we want to achieve and how do we want to get there? It is often helpful to formulate objectives and strategies for both the short term (less than one year) and the long term (2–5 years). Strategic planning has two important characteristics:

1. *An external orientation.* Strategic planning considers developments and interest groups in the *entire external environment* of a company. This includes not only the customers but also distributors, factors in the macroenvironment, suppliers, competitors, financiers, employees, and the general public.

2. *A long-term orientation.* In practice, strategies often are formulated for a period of two to five years. Those strategies should then be translated into short-term decisions for a period of a year or less. The short-term decisions are designated *tactical or operational decisions.*

With its choice of strategy, a company thus determines both the arena in which it wants to be active and the required resources for a longer period. Keep in mind, however, a strategy also should have a measure of flexibility. When it is necessary, the company must be able to change direction, for example, when there is an unanticipated action by a competitor. In reality, a company should at a minimum evaluate its long-term strategies annually and adjust them as necessary.

1.1.2 Strategic Management

Strategic planning is relevant to all the functional areas in a company, including marketing, finance, personnel, purchasing, and production. It is important that planning in the various functional areas be completely coordinated. For example, if the marketing department recommends entry into a new market with the goal of achieving a market share of 5 percent in three years, it is necessary that the other departments (new product development, production, purchasing, and finance) are also focused on that goal. Coordination and integration of decisions between the different functional areas in a company is the primary task of *strategic management.*

1.1.3 Strategic Marketing

While all functions of a company should be involved in the strategic planning process, this book focuses on the role of the marketing function. This means that we limit ourselves to the phases and components of strategic planning in which marketing plays a significant role. In this context, the focus is on creating strategies aimed at *markets,* in other words, all activities directed toward the stimulation, facilitation, and acceleration of sales. The next section is devoted to developments in strategic marketing, ending with our view of the marketing concept, which is the basis for this book.

1.2 TOWARD A MORE BALANCED MARKETING CONCEPT

1.2.1 Marketing Theory

Marketing can be interpreted in different ways[1]:

- As an *organizational culture* (the marketing concept or *marketing paradigm*): a set of values and beliefs that drives the organization to make a fundamental commitment to serving customers' needs as the path to sustained profitability.
- As a *strategy:* defining target markets and positioning product offerings.
- As *tactics:* the day-to-day activities of the four marketing instruments: product development, pricing, distribution, and communication.

These three meanings of marketing have been interpreted as a hierarchy in marketing theory. The top level (the marketing concept or marketing paradigm) defines the core content

FIGURE 1-1
Levels in Marketing Theory

of marketing. It stresses the main issues in marketing in general and provides a rough indication of what is important in the lower level: marketing strategy. Marketing strategy should give a direction to the lowest level: marketing tactics (Figure 1-1).

Marketing strategy deals with segmenting, targeting, and (brand) positioning (*STP*), raising the question of how to compete.[2] The issue of branding is discussed increasingly in the context of marketing strategy[3] and also in wider-ranging marketing textbooks.[4] Clear choices about the target group and brand positioning impose boundaries on a company's choice of the appropriate marketing mix (relationship with the lowest level). However, the relationship between the marketing concept and marketing strategy is somewhat ambiguous. The marketing concept focuses on the customer (the demand side), whereas marketing strategy mostly attempts to create a balance between the demand side (the customer) and the supply side (the brand identity) of the market. Therefore, the marketing concept should be updated by adding branding to the paradigm. Before describing our view of the marketing concept, we discuss developments in the marketing concept through the years.

1.2.2   Development of the Marketing Concept Before 2000

In the first edition of his textbook, Kotler (1967)[5] introduced the concept that companies must be both customer- and market-driven. In an influential paper, Day and Wensley[6] introduced the so-called *strategic marketing concept.* That concept is in fact an expansion of the "classic" marketing concept, which indicates that a company should use the wishes and desires of its customers as the basis for its actions, otherwise known as a "customer orientation". The strategic marketing concept states that a company should pay attention to:

- *Customers* (as in the classic marketing concept).
- *Competitors* (not just to be better but also perhaps to collaborate).
- *Long-term* relationships (including developing products for which there is a latent need and thus a potential demand).
- *Other interest groups* inside and outside the organization (such as distributors, employees, suppliers, financiers).

CASE 1-1
Anticipating Latent Needs: Flat Mania

The main reason for the sudden emergence of flat-panel TVs is that manufacturers smell a lucrative new market. As LCD screens in both desktop and laptop computers have become commonplace, margins have diminished. Televisions, however, use large LCD panels, which cost more to make but command far higher margins. Today's flat mania, says Scott McGregor, the boss of Philips Semiconductors, is "completely irrational" since a conventional TV can produce an image that is just as good at a fraction of the price. New entrants and established firms such as Motorola and Westinghouse, both of which stopped making TVs decades ago, are piling in. So too are computer makers such as Dell and Gateway, which already sell LCD computer monitors and are attracted by the larger margins in consumer electronics.

Source: "Thin Screens, Fat Margins," *The Economist,* December 20, 2003, p. 97.

These issues largely correspond to what is called "market orientation" in the current marketing literature.[7] Market orientation consists of three components:

1. *A customer-oriented philosophy (customer orientation)* would focus on the following questions: Does the company make reasonable promises, and is it able to keep those promises? Are customers treated as individuals? Is market research used concretely to determine the wishes and opinions of the target audience? If so, does that lead to actionable objectives for the company?

2. *A competitor-oriented philosophy (competitor orientation)*. Here a company asks: Do we have a lot of information about individual competitors? Is that information analyzed systematically and distributed throughout the organization? Does the company know when it should respond to actions of competitors and how it can differentiate itself from competitors? What are sustainable competitive advantages given the marketplace?

3. *Interfunctional coordination (integrated decision making)*. It is important to realize whether information is shared within the company are the strategies for various functional areas integrated? Are joint decisions made? Is the whole organization truly interested in its customers?

CASE 1-2 *Interfunctional Coordination at Dell*	No e-business conference is complete without a few slides on Dell's virtual supply chains and enviably slender inventory. Because Dell's suppliers have real-time access to information about its orders via its corporate extranet, they can organize their production and delivery to ensure that their powerful customer always has just enough of the right parts to keep the production line moving smoothly. By plugging its suppliers directly into its customer database, Dell ensures that they will instantly know about any changes in demand. And by plugging its customers into its supply chain via its website, Dell enables them to track the progress of their orders from the factory to the doorstep, thus saving on telephone or fax inquiries. Dell was pretty efficient before it started using the Internet, but now it is able to do even better by creating, as the jargon has it, a "fully integrated value chain."

Source: "A Revolution of One," *The Economist,* April 14, 2001, and "You'll Never Walk Alone," *The Economist,* June 26, 1999.

Over the years, the critical elements of the strategic marketing concept have shifted. In the 1980s, strong emphasis was placed on a competitor orientation. In the 1990s another component of the strategic marketing concept moved to center stage: the development of long-term relationships, especially with customers. In this context the focus is no longer on one-time transaction-oriented marketing but rather on *relationship marketing*.[8] Relationship marketing focuses on obtaining and sustaining a structural, direct relationship between a supplier and the customer. In this context of relations, Morgan and Hunt[9] theoretically and empirically show that *trust* is a key factor in relationship commitment. Due to the need to create direct (one-to-one) relationships, the use of databases increased. Therefore, relationship based marketing is sometimes called *direct marketing* or database marketing.

In the 2000s the shift continued with an increased attention given to customer value and services. *Customer value* is the value that users derive from products. In theory, this is the user benefit derived from product attributes minus the price and the effort made to obtain a product. In practice, customer value is determined by measuring not only customers' perceptions of product attributes but also their benefits as well as the goals they hope to attain by using a product.[10] The difference from the relationship philosophy of the 1990s is that at that time it was stated that companies should always strive for direct relationships as the way to provide customer value. Now the theory suggests that customers can receive customer value in various ways. In this context, Treacy and Wiersema[11] name three value strategies that can be summarized as customer leadership (*customer intimacy*), *product leadership,* and leadership in terms of convenience or price (*operational excellence*). Providing customer value is an important but insufficient condition for achieving customer loyalty. In addition, bonding and familiarity are necessary.

More recently Vargo and Lusch[12] argue that marketing be focused on *services*. In their view, marketers focus too much on products. Goods (tangible resources) are only distribution mechanisms for service provision. Put differently, companies should focus on value creation, on solving the "problems" of their customers. In building relationships with customers, intangible assets such as knowledge about customers and customer-friendly methods of dealing with complaints are highly relevant as well. These intangible competencies are embedded in the people working in a company. Only if all the people in a company are really interested in customers can that company really build relationships.[13] Thus, the service perspective of marketing is closely related to the relationship orientation.[14]

Hoekstra and associates[15] refer to the current marketing orientation as "the customer concept." It could be argued that the focus on customer value in effect represents a revival of the classic marketing philosophy. After all, the point of departure for classic marketing is that customers' wishes must be satisfied. This is essentially no different from stating that value must be provided to customers. This line of reasoning may be "not wrong". The most important factor here is that although fulfilling customers' wishes has been a basic principle of marketing for a long time, actual marketing practice appears to have lost track of customer satisfaction. There are many examples of situations in which customers are annoyed (e.g., telephone sales whether or not done under the guise of research), dissatisfied (user-unfriendliness of personal computers and cameras), and unhappy with bad settlement of complaints. Fournier and associates argue that it is important to avoid "the premature death of relationship marketing."[16] A central assumption of marketing should be that it leads to *win-win situations* for both the supplier and the customer. In essence, the emphasis on customer relationships can be translated into an increasing need to provide the customer with real "value."[17] Suppliers should strive primarily for customer loyalty: maintaining their most profitable customers. By contrast, in classic marketing suppliers focused more on attempting to recruit new customers.[18] Figure 1-2 summarizes developments in the marketing history.

| **CASE 1-3**
Customer
Retention:
HoustonStreet | Every day buyers from large utility companies and sellers from energy companies visit HoustonStreet Exchange, an online market that deals in wholesale electricity and gas, to haggle over the prices for the energy that heats and lights America's homes and offices. HoustonStreet knows it's hardly the only marketplace—online or off—that's vying for this kind of trading, and so it relies heavily on technology to build and retain strong one-on-one relationships with each of its customers. No interaction with a customer escapes the firm's centralized customer database, whether it's a HoustonStreet account manager calling on a buyer or a would-be seller seeking information from the Web site. Day by day, its copy of ON!contact Software's Client Management Software updates profiles and histories of each customer and all of the customer's interactions with HoustonStreet. Later, culling this data can help HoustonStreet managers evaluate their progress, make tactical marketing decisions, and plan strategic marketing moves.

Source: "Keep the 0010001 Happy," *Fortune,* Summer 2000, Technology Guide. |

Recently, Kotler and Keller[19] argued that marketing should better acknowledge that a broader, more integrated perspective is often necessary. Therefore, they introduced the *holistic marketing concept,* which consists of four dimensions: relationship marketing, integrated marketing, internal marketing, and socially responsible marketing.

FIGURE 1-2
Theoretical
Developments in
Marketing History

Period	Marketing	Emphasis On
Until circa 1980	Classic marketing	Customer wishes
1980–1990	Strategic marketing	Competitive advantages; long term
1990–2000	Relationship marketing	Direct relationships with customers and offering services
	Customer concept	Customer satisfaction and loyalty

In all of the marketing perspectives described above, no attention is devoted explicitly to building a brand identity. The next section focuses on this issue.

1.2.3   Branding, Core Competencies, and Customer Relations

In summary, the marketing concept focuses on the demand side of the market: customers. In marketing practice, and increasingly in marketing science, attention is being paid to what could be interpreted as the supply side of the market: *brands*. Branding theory[20] suggests that companies should try to create brands with *high name awareness* and *strong, favorable, and unique associations*. The idea of this cognitive approach to branding is that customers respond more favorably to the marketing instruments of a brand they know than to the marketing instruments of brands they do not know. Thus, it is helpful to have a clear, positive, and unique brand image. This holds true for product and service brands as well as corporate brands (where branding actually is the same as having a clearly defined reputation).

One of the key elements of effective brand management is consistency. This has two elements. The first is the need for a kind of "specialization": Brands and firms that do not clearly choose a strategy for brand positioning will not get into the customers' minds.[21] The second element is stability over time. It takes time to make customers aware of the brand identity, and so brand management is a long-term issue.

The issue of branding is strongly related to the *resource-based view* of the firm[22] and to the focus on *core competencies*.[23] These approaches suggest that the source of superior performance is the possession and development of distinctive and hard to imitate resources. This corresponds to the competitive advantage approach of Porter.[24] The resource approach appears to be supply-oriented, whereas the marketing concept is by definition demand-oriented. The question is how these two can or should be combined. Some authors argue that being too market-oriented can be disastrous[25] because customers may demand products or services that do not fit in with the core business of the firm. This also is true of branding: Customers may demand benefits that do not match the brand *identity*. And consumers appear to get used to innovations more quickly; this puts suppliers in a struggle to come up with more innovations (Figure 1-3).

Hooley and associates[26] suggest combining marketing and the resource-based view of the firm in what they refer to as resource-based marketing. In this approach firms base their

FIGURE 1-3
Innovation Spiral

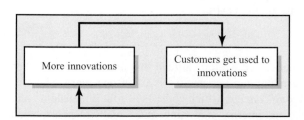

FIGURE 1-4
Marketing as a Balance between Customer and Brand

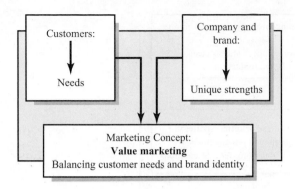

marketing strategies on an equal consideration of the requirements of the market and their ability to serve the market.[27]

1.2.4 Toward a New Marketing Concept

It increasingly is recognized that listening to the customer is not "everything," but this realization does not seem to affect current thinking about the marketing concept. In terms of the hierarchical meanings of marketing, if nothing is said in the marketing concept nothing about resources or branding, applying the marketing concept leads to the unbalanced guideline of strongly following customers' needs. Thus, the marketing concept can be augmented by stating that organizations should focus both on the customer and on *building a strong brand (or reputation)* (Figure 1-4). This adjusted marketing concept could be called *value marketing:* delivering customer value and building brand equity.

A manager should find a balance between the customer approach and the brand approach when selecting the company's positioning. In practice it can be noted that there are inadequacies on both sides of Figure 1-4. Because companies often reason too much on the basis of the supply perspective:

- Too little attention is paid to the customer: Does the customer really want this?
- Too little attention is paid to the brand personality: Are we making real choices and are we familiar to the customer? Without a choice a brand will not be recognized. Thus, the starting point of positioning should be a certain degree of specialization.

In the remainder of the book, both customer-oriented philosophy and brand-oriented philosophy will assume a central place.

CASE 1-4

Buick: Too Little Attention to Target Group Younger Buyers

Although many automakers chase after Generations Y and X, Buick is going after baby boomers—again. The General Motors Corp. brand has, since at least 1986, tried off and on to attract younger buyers, but without much success. The reason the brand hasn't succeeded in its mission to reach a younger demographic is that Buick didn't have the right models. Whereas GM sibling Cadillac has been able to attract younger buyers with new models in recent years, Buick really hasn't done anything to raise the antennae of young people. Research shows the median owner age across Buick's lineup is 70. The downside of brand loyalty is having your customers age with the brand and failing to attract new ones. According to *Automotive News,* the brand's peak was in 1984, when it sold 941,611 cars in the United States, giving it a 9 percent share of all cars sold that year. The marketer's total share slipped to 1.9 percent through October 2004 with 266,881 cars and trucks sold.

Source: Halliday, Jean, "Buick Sets Its Sights on Boomers with new Models," *Advertising Age,* November 29, 2004.

FIGURE 1-5
Value Marketing and
Marketing Strategy

1.2.5 Marketing as Strategy and Tactics

Based on the marketing concept outlined above, the marketing strategy and tactics are planned (Figure 1-5).

Marketing activities can be divided into four parts: analysis, planning, implementation, and control.[28] Examples of these activities are market research (analysis), decisions regarding positioning and communication (planning), execution of a campaign (implementation), and evaluation of results (control). We will focus in more detail on the activities of strategic marketing, employing the four-part division for this purpose.

Analysis within the framework of strategic marketing refers to analyzing potential customers (e.g., through market research), competitors, distribution structures and the suppliers, the industry structure and the macroenvironment (e.g., demographic developments), and internal factors as the company and the company's brand.

We interpret *planning activities* within the framework of strategic marketing as all decisions that are made as well as the documentation of those decisions in plans. In conducting planning activities, a company should be able to answer the following questions:

1. *Where (and when) to compete?* This refers to the choice of markets, positions, and periods.
2. *How to compete?* This refers to the choice of a sustainable competitive advantage, including positioning, target audience definition and segmentation, and determination of the objectives regarding the use of marketing mix elements.

This division into "where" and "how" is found increasingly in the marketing literature.[29] For example, the strategic marketing of a furniture manufacturer should focus on the following questions:

1. Where to compete?

   - In which markets do we want to be active in the future (cupboards, couches, tables or for final customers, offices, other companies, etc.)?
   - Which positions do we want to achieve in those markets within how many years?
   - How much money should we invest in the various markets?

2. How to compete?

   • Which competitive advantages should we strive to achieve (quality, cheapness, etc.)?
   • To which segments should we orient ourselves?
   • What are we striving for with the use of marketing mix elements?

These decisions show that strategic *marketing* planning is a very important component of strategic management. The choice of *markets* in which to be active is an extremely important decision for a company and therefore is at the heart of the corporate strategy. Proposals for and information about these decisions are provided by the functional area of marketing. In addition, it is clear that the components of strategic marketing mentioned above have implications for other functional areas. The sphere of activity of strategic marketing therefore cannot be separated from that of other functional areas. The fact that marketing plays such an important role in a company's strategic planning is related to the strong *external orientation* of both strategic planning and marketing.

Examples of activities relating to the *implementation* (execution) of these strategic marketing decisions are negotiating with top management about budgets (although this often takes place during the planning phase), motivating and managing the company's personnel, and involving and briefing the advertising agency.

In the framework of strategic marketing, *control* refers to items such as an analysis of the sales data and financial data, an evaluation of the results against objectives, and a check of the implementation of the decisions that were made.

All these activities are part of the strategic marketing planning process.

1.3 LEVELS WITHIN A COMPANY

There are companies that limit their activities to a single market, for example, a car manufacturer that produces small cars for one target audience. Many smaller or start-up companies also focus on a single market. However, many companies are active in *more than one market.* For example, Sara Lee/DE is active in various consumer markets, such as food and luxury foods and personal care items. However, even a small company such as a local restaurant can serve several markets, such as room rental, catering, and local dinners. To achieve clarity in the marketing planning process about what should be analyzed and what should be decided on, it is important to understand the levels within a company. Three levels can be distinguished (see Figure 1-6):

1. The company (or corporate) level.
2. The division and strategic business unit (SBU) level.
3. The product and marketing mix instrument level.

1.3.1 Company or Corporate Level

The company level is the "top" level. This level relates to the company as a whole. All the different products a company puts out on the various markets are collectively designated as the *product mix* or the *assortment*. For example, the product mix of Sara Lee/DE includes coffee, tea, beverage systems (warm and cold drinks for industrial customers), food, and rolling tobacco and pipe tobacco as well as items for the household and for personal care.

1.3.2 Division Level and Strategic Business Unit Level

A division is a somewhat autonomously operating unit within a company. A division may include several *product groups*. A product group (also called a product line, a product

FIGURE 1-6 **Aggregation Levels in a Company**

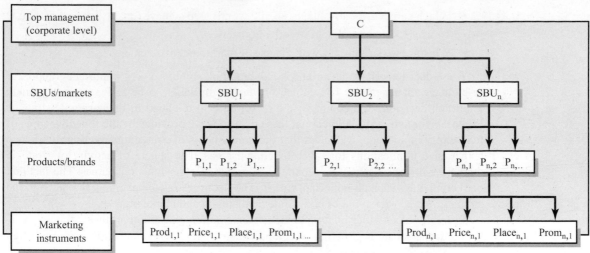

Note: This figure does not represent the way how marketing should be organized within a company; see also Chapter 12.

category, or simply a *category*) contains a group of related products. Examples of product groups are appetizers, internal transport, consultancy, foot care products, and men's clothing. In practice, a product group often is used for market definition, for example, the market for health insurance. Although the product group is only one of three dimensions in a market definition (the other two are customer groups and functions; see Chapter 2), product groups often correspond to markets. This book therefore makes this connection regularly.

A *strategic business unit* (also called a strategic product group) is concentrated on a single product group (and therefore usually on one market). Many companies employ SBUs. AKZO is an example: In that company all activities are classified into various business units to which sufficient authority has been delegated to allow for a fast and decisive response to market developments. At AKZO the various business units are grouped into five divisions. Another company where divisions and SBUs do not coincide is Sara Lee/DE. This company consists of two divisions, food and luxury foods, as well as household and personal care products. The division for food and luxury foods includes activities in the following markets: coffee, tea, beverage systems, nuts and snacks, rice, rolling tobacco, and pipe tobacco. Although there is often a difference between the division level and the SBU level, in the remainder of this book we do not distinguish between these levels because a division level can be regarded as a company level but one step lower. In practice, divisions often are smaller companies within a large company. Therefore, everything that is stated below about company objectives and strategies can be applied to division objectives and strategies. For example, company strategy often determines which financial resources are available for SBUs. If a division level exists between the company level and the SBU level, the division strategy determines the resource allocation for the SBUs.

For a company that is active in just one market, the company level and the SBU level coincide and the assortment is restricted to one product group.

1.3.3 Product Level and Marketing Mix Level

A product is an item (good or service) that is offered in a market. A product may be aimed at different target audiences. A combination of a product and a target audience is usually called a *product-market combination*. Sometimes different *varieties* of a product are presented in a market; for example, there may be differences in sizes or packets and flavors. A company often brings individual products into the market and supports them through the use of marketing mix elements. Typically, four categories of marketing mix elements are distinguished: product (composition, packaging), price, distribution (place), and sales promotion (e.g., advertising). Because marketing mix elements are applied to products, the marketing mix level corresponds to the product level.

1.3.4   The Position of the Brand

A brand is a word, name, symbol, letter, or picture (or a combination of these elements) used by a company to distinguish its products from those of the competition. The brand is the bearer of a reputation or image. From the perspective of the provider, a brand is also the manifest identity the product must embody. At which levels do brands play a role? The most obvious is the product level. A product almost always is offered under a brand name. Examples of products are Pampers diapers, ABN/AMRO student bank accounts, and Philips coffee makers. The brand designation has been associated with *products* for many years. Brand names at the product level are most visible in the consumable goods market: Every product has its own brand name. However, this is an understatement of the importance of brands. Brand names play a role not only at the product level but at all three levels in the company. Indeed, large conglomerates such as Unilever and Procter & Gamble rarely promote the name of the company to the consumer, but Unilever is still a brand in the labor and financial markets. Brands also are found at the intermediary division level: The manufacturers Van den Bergh Nederland and Iglo/Ola are also brands.

Sometimes brand names in the service and durable consumer goods markets are the same as company names (e.g., Philips, Ford). We will take a closer look at brands and brand levels in Chapter 10.

1.4   THE CORE OF THE MARKETING STRATEGY

It is important to make a distinction here between

- The corporate (or company) strategy (Section 1.4.1).
- The marketing strategy (Section 1.4.2).

1.4.1   Corporate Strategy: Direction of Growth and Value Strategy

At each of the levels mentioned above, decisions are made and strategies are outlined. The content of the decisions is different at the different levels. Thus, the chairperson of the board of directors (corporate or company level) does not spend time on advertising decisions (product level). Similarly, a product manager of a brand of margarine (product level) does not spend time deciding to invest more in diaper sales; that is a concern of upper management (company level).

A clear connection can be made between the strategic marketing mentioned in Section 1.2 and the levels described in Section 1.3. This connection is summarized in Figure 1-7.

The two main questions that must be answered at each level are:

- *Where are we going to compete?* In which markets, with which products, when, and to what extent?
- *How are we going to compete?* With what distinction?

The elaboration of both questions depends on the level.

At the company level, the question "Where will the company compete?" entails the following: The management of the company or division spends time on the establishment of

sometimes can achieve larger market shares than innovators do.[31] Pioneers therefore should take a flexible position and also attempt to learn from the experiences of followers.[32] To gain insight into the sustainability of its competitive advantage, a company might attempt to predict what the competition will do in the future. This is one of the objectives of competitor analysis.

CASE 1-5 *Leapfrogging in the Gaming Business*	Content is king in the game business, and hitting the shelves first would help Xbox bring out hot new games ahead of Sony and Nintendo Co., which says it will launch its next model when the new PlayStation comes out. PlayStation 2's early hits with such games as Gran Turismo 3: A-Spec and Grand Theft Auto 3, which were launched while Microsoft and Nintendo were finishing their consoles, put those rivals in a hole from which they've never emerged. That lead fed upon itself. Gamers bought PlayStation 2 because it had the best content, and developers made more games for it because it had the most users. If Microsoft can grab an early lead in the next round, it could displace Sony as gamers' top pick.

Source: Green, Jay, and Cliff Edwards, "Microsoft Plays Video Leapfrog," *BusinessWeek*, May 10, 2004.

The idea of a defendable competitive edge is closely linked to the concept of positioning. *Positioning* means determining the position of a brand in relation to the products of the competition in the minds of consumers: What image or associations does a company want to attach to the brand? Ries and Trout[33] describe positioning as the battle for the customer's mind. Positioning entails selecting the brand associations that

- Are *relevant* to buyers.
- Are *unique* to the brand.

If a brand successfully communicates the desired associations in such a way that the brand associations

- Are *strongly* anchored with the target group,

the three most important requirements for a successful brand have been met[34]: strong, relevant, and unique. Good positioning requires profound knowledge of the psychology of the customer. Another important requirement for positioning is the willingness to choose foci for goal-oriented positioning. A broad choice is no choice at all, as it is often said. The search process often comes down to choosing a single word with which a brand can distinguish itself. The choice of that word is difficult, essential, and subtle. It is difficult because general attributes such as quality, young, dynamic, and reliable typically do not distinguish a brand. A lot of brands want to be these things. It is also difficult because companies are often unwilling to choose; after all, if you have a single central message, "so many other good things are left unsaid." It is essential because this is the central choice in brand identity; that identity will be the basis of everything else. It is subtle because it requires a lot of creativity and empathy for the consumer and other parties in the environment to come up with the "right" word. An example of a brand that made a clear choice in 2005 is Philips (Simplicity).

CASE 1-6 *Unambiguous Choice for Philips: Positioning "Simplicity"*	The electronics conglomerate Philips has been working on this behind the screens for a year: equipment that can be operated with a single button, so to speak. Equipment whose instructions can be thrown in the dustbin before you read them. According to Philips, it is an ideal that consumers, who have been buried under new and advanced electronics for the past ten years, have been yearning for. The electronics company would now like to propagate the existence of simple devices. Therefore, the company is embodying the idea of simplicity in a new slogan: "Sense and simplicity."

Philips will spend 80 million euros in advertising over the next six months to spread this message around the globe. The current slogan "Let's make things better," which was launched in 1995, will disappear from all advertising.

The invention and production of devices that are simple to operate does not seem so simple. Video recorders are notoriously difficult to set. More recently, we have had operating problems with digital video or photo cameras. Or the computer itself—for many, the installation of new software poses an insurmountable raft of complications. The management of Philips found this out for themselves about six months ago when they all took wireless devices home with them one weekend to see if they could connect them by themselves. Hilarity ensued.

Philips created high expectations with the new campaign, states Andrea Ragnetti, executive director of marketing. "We are convinced that devices that are simple to operate are more important than ever before. This theme has become the mantra of such companies as Microsoft and Hewlett-Packard, which goes to show how important it is. We are the first to actually work on it. Even though it isn't easy."

According to Ragnetti, the new campaign is only a modest part of the enormous process needed within Philips to achieve the goal of simple devices. It will actually take a shift in culture, says Ragnetti. "But that kind of shift takes 20 to 30 years. We don't have that kind of time." Ragnetti says that the management of all company departments will be regularly checked to ensure that simplicity is being extolled as the guiding principle. "But it is already clear that the move from idea to reality needs a lot of reinforcement. This must be complete within two to three years."

On October 23, 2005, Philips took the unusual step of buying all advertising time in the popular U.S. TV program: 60 minutes." Costs: about $2 million. Goal: a quick building of awareness of the new Philips message "Sense and simplicity."

Source: a.o. NRC Handelsblad, 13 september 2004.

The concept of positioning sometimes is applied only with respect to communication. In this case, it's mainly about the slogan or "what interesting things we're going to say in the campaign this year." But brand positioning is a lot more than that: It is the focal point of all the activities related to the brand: production, personnel, purchasing, all marketing instruments, and so on (Figure 1-9; see also Case 1-6). After all, positioning is a promise to the client, and promises must be kept. This can be done only if everything has been set up to ensure it. It starts with the people who pick up the telephone, and it ends with the customer's level of satisfaction with the product. Thus, brand positioning serves not only an external function (a promise to the customer) but an *internal function* as well (for the employees). The communication of the brand positioning to internal target groups is called *internal branding*.

The concept of positioning is not significantly different from concepts such as desired reputation, identity, vision, and competitive edge. Since brands exist at different levels

FIGURE 1-9
Brand Positioning as a Control Mechanism within the Company

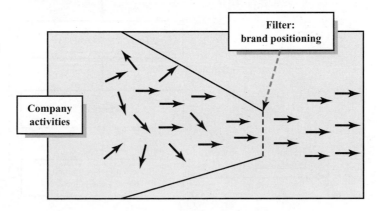

within a company, positioning also exists at different levels: at the company and product levels. At the company level, this concerns the reputation of the company, or "corporate identity," also known as "reputation." Philips's brand name is the same as that of most of its product names, and so the company identity is the same as that of all Philips products.

1.5   THE STRATEGIC MARKETING PLANNING PROCESS

1.5.1   The Importance of an Environmental Analysis

If a manager has a problem, there are two ways to arrive at a solution (Figure 1-10): provide a little support quickly or provide proper support a little more slowly. The first method is sometimes quite successful; a manager does not have to be an analyst to achieve success. In this book, however, we operate under the assumption that the probability for success is greater with better support. This "better support" lies in making use of a good system and good tools based on marketing theory and more and better knowledge because all the parties in the environment of the company are analyzed. The explicit formulation of alternatives is also a part of the better (more scientific) approach to practical management problems.

A "more scientific" approach to a marketing problem does not mean that the result will be less practical. A more holistic approach is needed for the final choice of a solution; this includes creativity, innovation, and a feel for the market. The "input" for this comes from doing one's homework. The way in which a company should go about doing its homework and subsequently translate it into targets and strategies makes up the content of the strategic marketing planning process. We will describe the overall setup of the process and then go into further detail about the parts of the process.

1.5.2   Overview of the Process

In the marketing literature, various authors[36] sketch the different steps a company may take to arrive at a strategy. Different authors use different ways to develop this process. Figure 1-11 indicates the steps that in our opinion a company should take in the planning process. In parentheses we have indicated the chapters in which the various steps are discussed further. In addition, we have indicated to which level in the company each

FIGURE 1-10   **Approaches to the Solution of Management Problems[35]**

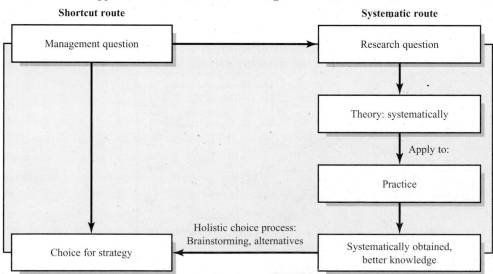

FIGURE 1-11 Overview of the Strategic Marketing Planning Process

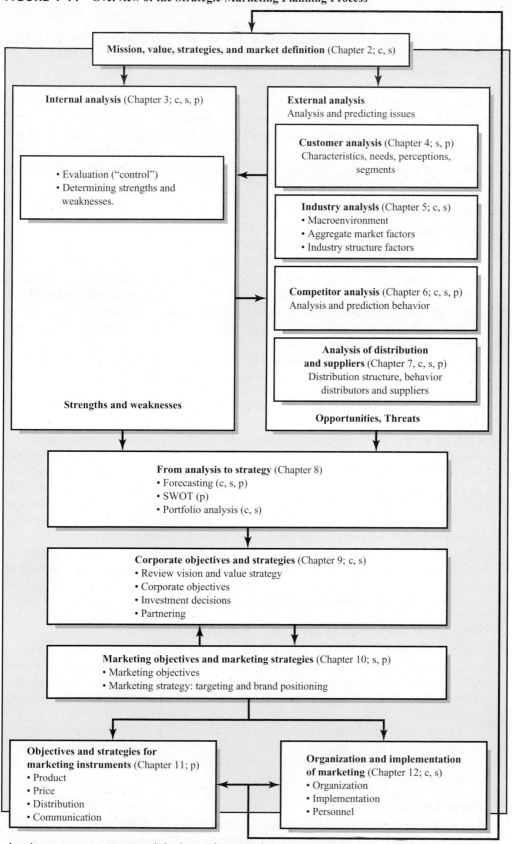

Levels: c = corporate, s = strategic business unit, p = product.

step applies (*c*ompany, *S*BU, or *p*roduct level). We will now clarify Figure 1-11, first globally and then in more detail. In the following chapters the various steps will be elaborated on further.

The global organization of the process is as follows: A combination of an *external analysis* (analysis of the environment) and an *internal analysis* (analysis of the company and the brand) form the basis for the formulation of objectives and strategies. The goal of the external analysis is to provide insight into the *opportunities* and *threats* that can be expected. The most important goal of the internal analysis is to determine the company's *strengths* and *weaknesses*. The combination of strengths, weaknesses, opportunities, and threats (SWOT) forms the input for the phase in which a strategy is chosen.

Situation Analysis (Part 2)

The situation analysis starts with a definition of the market and the current activities, including the company's vision and mission, and an evaluation of the results achieved so far. This first step usually provides a reasonable impression of potential problems (problem identification). The next step is to follow the various phases from the external analysis (predominantly at the SBU level and the product level) and the internal analysis (at all levels). These two components together form the *situation analysis*. Various authors prefer different sequences of phases in the situation analysis. We start with the internal analysis because we can ascribe the evaluation of the results to it. We basically consider the strengths and weaknesses of the company and the brand as preconditions for the development of the strategy. After all, financial attributes, management culture, company mission, and so on, cannot be changed overnight. This is also the case for the competition and organizational analysis in the external analysis: These factors also must be regarded as preconditions.

This does not apply to the most important target group: the *customer*. Marketing serves excellently as a method for "learning" target groups. In principle, the customer can be influenced in their perceptions and needs. Since in both theory and practice a lot of attention is paid to achieving value for the customer, the external analysis should start with an analysis of the customer. Insight into the wishes, satisfaction, and perceptions of customers and noncustomers (individual or otherwise) must be obtained continuously. This customer analysis is the source of a variety of information during other phases of the analysis. Subsequently, the other components of the external analysis are dealt with: an overview of the whole industry, followed by specific analyses of the competitors, distributors (or other intermediaries), and suppliers. Finally, a separate phase of strategic analysis occurs in which the results from the internal and external analyses are linked to one another. The first blocks are the analytical component of the planning process.

Decisions at the Company Level and the Marketing Level (Part 3)

After the analytical component, company objectives and strategies are chosen; these elements primarily answer questions dealing with where and when the company will compete. Because the analyses are often performed for SBUs (markets) and a company often is active in several markets, various situation analyses will form the basis for the company strategy.

If a new market is chosen, a new analysis should be performed. Subsequently, the marketing objectives and marketing strategies are chosen; the focus in this case is on sales goals as well as decisions about target audiences and brands. These decisions mainly determine "how the company will compete."

Implementation (Part 4)

The marketing strategy determines the choice of marketing mix elements. This is the marketing tactic, and it may be considered the marketing implementation.

Once the decisions have been documented in a marketing plan, the implementation is carried out. At this point, the organization of marketing and communication is also relevant. A manager also should pay sufficient attention to the employees. Without proper internal management, a good implementation is impossible.

1.5.3   Description of the Phases

Marketing Plan (This Chapter)

The marketing plan reflects the results of the strategic marketing planning process (analyses and decisions) and documents all the action steps for the coming year. This plan can serve later as a guideline for the evaluation of the results. It also fulfills a communicative role: Everyone in the company can read in the plan the direction the company wants to take and how it intends to achieve its chosen objectives. At the end of this chapter we include a layout of a marketing plan.

After the implementation of the strategies, an *evaluation* should take place: Have the objectives been achieved, and if not, what are the causes of this failure? This evaluation marks a new phase in the planning process. Therefore, in Figure 1-11 a feedback loop has been included from the last planning step back to the first steps (market definition and evaluation of results). The process outlined above should just be completed only periodically (e.g., once a year); instead, there should be a *continuous* internal and external analysis as well as an evaluation of objectives and strategies. The dynamic nature of the environment makes it too risky to treat planning as a merely periodic activity.

Strategic Marketing Planning in Practice

This book describes the different phases of the strategic marketing planning process. In doing so, we attempt to depict an ideal version of that process. The framework outlined here is in principle applicable to any company that is active in a particular market and is faced with competitors and customers. Such companies include producers of nondurable consumer goods (e.g., producers of food products) and service providers (e.g., banks). The framework can also be used by companies that are active in industrial markets (e.g., engineering offices); in that case, the customers consist of other companies. In addition, components of the process may be applicable to nonprofit organizations (e.g., Greenpeace, hospitals).

However, it would be an illusion to think that each company could or even should follow this process. Organizations and markets differ so substantially that some of the steps in the planning process may be less important for certain companies or may be followed in a different sequence.

Mission, Value Strategies, and Market Definition (Chapter 2)

There can be no situation analysis of a brand and a market until we get a picture of what the situation is: What are the market boundaries? For example, without an identification of market boundaries, the market share cannot be calculated. Is Coca-Cola active in the soft drink market or the "cola" market? This will have a strong influence on the size of the market share as well as the amount of competition. To determine this, we must examine the mission of the company. Typically, this is what statements on the market are based on. This should be considered a precondition for the development of a marketing strategy. From the positioning perspective (the core of the marketing strategy), it is also important to know which value strategy the company is following. The brand positioning should not be in conflict with that strategy. Finally, the current product-market combinations are brought into view and the market boundaries are specifically defined in terms of customer needs. At this point it is a matter of defining the current market: the market we are active in at the moment (what business are we in?).

Internal Analysis (Chapter 3)

The *internal analysis* starts with the question "What have the results been thus far?" This is the *"control"*: an evaluation of the results achieved. The desired results must be analyzed. These are the targets. Chapter 3 begins with a brief explanation of targets. The results of the strategy (and targets) can be measured as profit, sales, market share, and so forth; the choice of the unit of measurement depends on the way in which the targets were formulated. In addition to financial criteria, we look at *customer-oriented* standards such as customer satisfaction (the concept of the Balanced Scorecard will be discussed). This step provides an initial impression of where problems may lie. This analysis is carried out in as much detail as possible, that is, not only on the product and instrument levels but within those levels where possible, according to regions, customer groups (segments), varieties, and retailers. Then internal factors that are important for developing a new strategy are examined. For this purpose, the strengths and weaknesses of the company, the SBU, the product, and the marketing mix elements are determined. In this process, the perspective of the target audience is assumed as much as possible. The strengths and weaknesses are compared with those of competitors. If the strengths can be translated into added value of the products for customers, they provide a clue to sustainable competitive advantages (see Figure 1-5). If they threaten to create strategic problems, the weakness should be improved. This can be accomplished through internal improvement or through collaboration with competitors.

Chapters 4 through 7 discuss the external analysis.

Customer Analysis (Chapter 4)

The central assumption of this book is that the policy of a company should focus on creating optimal value for the customer. Maintaining a continuous "feeling" for the target audience therefore is essential. A good *customer analysis* (which includes potential customers) will provide that connection. More specific objectives for the customer analysis are to obtain insight into customers' attributes (Who are the customers? Can we distinguish separate segments? Which customers are the most profitable?), needs (the importance of concrete and abstract product attributes), and perceptions (How do they perceive the company's product and its competitors?). The customer analysis is implemented for an entire market (SBU level) as well as for individual segments and products (product level). The customer analysis also serves as a source of data for other phases in the situation analysis, and because of that, it is the core of the situation analysis. Therefore, there are straight lines to the competitor analysis (identification of competitors and determinants of success as well as the strengths and weaknesses of competitors), the distribution analysis (the brand's position at the retailer), the industry analysis (expected market growth), and the internal analysis (strengths and weaknesses of the brand).

Industry Analysis (Chapter 5)

After the customer analysis, the focus moves from "macro" to "micro": first an analysis of the whole industry and then a closer look at several interest groups within it, including competitors, distributors, and suppliers. A goal of the *industry analysis* is to identify potential opportunities and threats, especially from the macroenvironment. Another goal is to obtain an understanding of the attractiveness of the market. For that purpose, items such as the industry structure are analyzed. The attractiveness of the market has a strong impact on the objectives and investments that are determined for each SBU.

Three categories of factors are analyzed in the industry analysis:

1. *Macroenvironment* factors such as social-cultural and political developments.
2. *Aggregated market* factors, for example, market size and market growth.

3. Factors relating to industry structure, such as the intensity of the competition and the power of distributors.

Because it is especially important to gain insight into the *future* attractiveness of the market, this should include attempts at *forecasting*. In light of the uncertainty in the external environment of a company, it is advisable to define *scenarios* in this step, for example, scenarios regarding factors in the macroenvironment such as the economic situation. The analysis of industry structure takes place primarily at the SBU level, and it is done for the whole market. In addition, a company can research the attractiveness of specific segments.

Competitor Analysis (Chapter 6)

The goal of *competitor analysis* is to obtain insight into the likely future behavior as well as the strengths and weaknesses of the most important competitors of the company. The future behavior of competitors provides an understanding of potential opportunities and threats. A company should be familiar with the strengths and weaknesses of its competitors so that it can identify its own *relative* strengths and weaknesses (see Figure 1-5). A competitor analysis can be performed at all levels. At the product level, the most important competitors are the suppliers that focus on the same target audience as the company. The competitor analysis receives input at several points from the customer analysis (identification of competitors and their strengths and weaknesses).

Analysis of Distribution and Suppliers (Chapter 7)

After an analysis of the customers and the competitors, the other parties (interest groups) in the industry are critically analyzed. As was indicated earlier in the discussion of the strategic marketing concept, because of their growing power, distributors constitute an increasingly important interest group for manufacturers. It is becoming increasingly important to enter into partnerships with distributors, whether or not supported by systems such as *category management* (joint "management" of product groups).

A *distribution analysis* takes place at three levels: At the macro level, the focus is on the distribution structure; at the meso level, on the distribution of power within a single group of distributors, such as retailers; and at the micro level, on the behavior of individual distributors. At this stage, information from the customer analysis about purchasing behavior at and satisfaction with retailers can be integrated.

Suppliers are a final interest group that merits further analysis. A good relationship with suppliers means that purchasing can occur more efficiently and effectively.

Strategic Analysis Methods (Chapter 8)

After the external and internal analyses have been performed, the results of these two components are analyzed in relation to each other with the aid of strategic tools that have been developed for that purpose. Then, based on these strategic analyses alternative strategies are formulated.

The tools that are reviewed in this book are the following:

- *Forecasting.* Forecasts should be made of environmental factors such as market size (SBU level) and the behavior of the competition (levels of company, SBU, and product), as well as the results of the alternative strategies (especially product level: anticipated sales, market share, etc.). In this context various forecasting methods may be employed, perhaps in combination with scenarios.
- *SWOT analysis.* The SWOT analysis is the link between various analyses and the strategy phases. First, it is important to consider the different possibilities for the value

strategy. Next, we brainstorm ideas for the marketing strategy on the basis of a selection of strengths, weaknesses, opportunities, and threats. In this process, "'facts' are creatively translated into 'ideas.'" The SWOT analysis eventually produces a few different directions (options). Finally, the product manager comes to a decision about the desired strategy by dealing with the options with a number of selection criteria and preconditions.

- *Portfolio analysis.* The methodology of the portfolio analysis also provides a connection between the internal and external environments. A portfolio analysis compares the expected incoming and outgoing cash flows of different SBUs or brands. The results of this comparison are used to decide which SBUs or brands to invest more in and which to invest less in.

Company Objectives and Company Strategies (Chapter 9)

A first step in this analysis is a reevaluation of the company *mission:* Should the business of the company be modified? Subsequently, the *objectives* of the company are determined. The third step is choosing the *corporate strategy*. The corporate strategy embraces the choice and position of business units and brands. The fourth component is the competitive growth strategy: Does the company want to achieve growth

- Through its own development, that is, a position-strengthening strategy and/or
- Through a competition-decreasing strategy: through collaboration with competitors, takeover or merger with competitors (horizontal integration), or integration with suppliers or distributors (vertical integration)?

All three components of the company strategy commit both resources and people for a longer term and therefore typically are not changed significantly from year to year. Generally, these changes will be a matter of modification. We also emphasize here the interaction with marketing plans: The company decisions will receive input from the direction of the SBUs. Therefore, a feedback loop is included from the next planning step in the planning process (Figure 1-11).

Marketing Objectives and Marketing Strategies (Chapter 10)

After the formulation of company decisions, the objectives and strategies are chosen for marketing. The marketing objective is deduced from the SBU strategy. Marketing objectives are formulated per product, for example, growth of the market share of product Y to 34 percent in one year.

The *marketing strategy* includes the choice of the target audience (including segmentation) and the desired positioning of the brand. The marketing strategy forms the link between the company strategy and the decisions regarding marketing mix elements; therefore, this strategy is crucial. Without an explicit formulation of the marketing strategy, the use of the various elements of the marketing mix is aimless. The positioning of a brand is part of the value strategy of the SBU. The specific choice of the brand identity is a multiyear process that needs to be carried out on a long-term and consistent basis.

Objectives and Strategies for Marketing Mix Elements (Chapter 11)

Subsequently, the marketing strategy is translated into marketing tactics: decisions relating to the elements of the *marketing mix* (the four P's): product, price, place (distribution), and promotion (marketing communication). However, in the case of the marketing mix element "product," an important part of the strategic decisions has already been determined through the development of both the corporate strategy and the marketing strategy (such as brand decisions). In light of the great importance of communication in brand positioning, a relatively large amount of attention is paid to the communication planning process.

Implementation and Organization (Chapter 12)

Finally, the plans have to be converted into actions: the implementation. In many companies it is precisely in the implementation that things go wrong. It is important for the organization to adapt to the customer: to bring the customer in-house by using customer managers. All communication should be geared toward identity and preferably directed by a "reputation manager.". During implementation, it is important to provide support and guidance to the employees. Some useful tools are leadership, a clear vision, and employee incentives based on customer targets. There are a few planning tips at the end of the book.

Summary

Thinking on the basis of what the target groups want (the marketing concept) is becoming important for an ever-increasing number of organizations. The strategic marketing concept means that a company's primary point of departure consists of the wishes of the target audience; the company is customer-oriented, strives for competitive advantage, takes retailers and suppliers into account, and uses long-term planning. In recent marketing philosophy two other points have been added: the striving for customer satisfaction and value creation and the development of a brand personality. To accomplish this, a company should use a market-oriented focus, which includes, aside from customer orientation and competitor orientation, interfunctional coordination and decision making. Three levels play a role within a company: the entire company (upper management), strategic business units (product groups), and products. Brands play a role at every level. In addition to customer satisfaction, brand reputation is important in achieving customer loyalty. The brand positioning (desired brand associations) should be a balance between customer desires and the unique strengths of the brand. It is important to be willing to make a choice. Basically, the essence of marketing is that choices for customer values are made both at the company level (value strategy) and at the brand level (positioning), a kind of specialization. To make the best marketing decisions, it is best to use a systematic approach to knowledge acquisition. This book discusses the strategic marketing planning process. Starting from the chosen market definition and the evaluation of results, a situation analysis is performed: an internal analysis and an external analysis (customers, industry, competitors, distributors, and suppliers). The data obtained in this way are further analyzed via several strategic analysis methods, after which objectives, strategies, and a marketing plan are formulated. Finally, the plan needs to be implemented. Monitoring of the implementation and the results occurs through interim measurements. The evaluation results provide the input for a new planning process.

Appendix

Structure of a Marketing Plan

Figure 1-12 contains an overview of the components of a marketing plan. The various components largely parallel the structure of the strategic marketing planning process. It should be noted that the development of a marketing plan does not include company objectives or company strategies. A marketing plan essentially is developed for a single brand.

1. EXECUTIVE SUMMARY

The summary enables top management to review the core points of the plan quickly. The summary includes the most important conclusions from the SWOT analysis, the goals included in the plan, the chosen strategies, and the financial expectations. In the summary the

FIGURE 1.12   **Contents of a Marketing Plan for a Product or Brand**

Sources: Based on Dibb, S., L. Simkin, J. Bradley (1996), The Marketing Planning Workbook, Routledge, London, p. 162.

Component	Number of Pages
1. Executive summary	1–2
2. Introduction and background	2–3
• Company mission, company objectives, and SBU objectives	
• Market definition and product or brand background	
• Evaluation of results and conclusion about problem	
3. Situation analysis	6–10
• Internal analysis	
• Customer analysis	
• Industry analysis	
• Competitor analysis	
• Distribution and supplier analysis	
4. SWOT analysis	2–3
• Key issues (SWOTs)	
• Matrix-plus options	
• Choice of option (value strategy and/or brand positioning)	
5. Marketing objectives/expected results	1
6. Marketing strategy	2–4
• Target audiences	
• Brand or product positioning	
7. Decisions regarding marketing mix elements ("marketing programs")	6–10
• Objectives for marketing mix elements	
• Strategies and tactics for marketing mix elements	
8. Financial indicators and budgets	1–2
9. Evaluation criteria	1
10. Attachments:	10+
• Any further market data and information about past marketing activities	
• Any clarifications for the situation analysis	
• Scenario analysis and "contingency plans"	
• Timetable and schedule of activities	
• References	

arguments supporting the chosen strategy are very important. Although the summary should be short, it should be quite concrete.

2.   INTRODUCTION AND BACKGROUND

This part serves as general introduction to the marketing plan and a framework for decision making. The following components are included.

The first item is a description of the company mission and the company objectives as well as SBU objectives. It may be assumed that these objectives are considered an established fact for the product or brand. Subsequently, the market that is specifically applicable to the particular product is defined according to the dimensions discussed in Chapter 2. Without this definition it is not clear what the plan refers to. At this point it is also an option to describe the results of the identification of the competition (the first step in competitor analysis). The advantage of doing this is that it provides an idea of the market at the beginning of this section. Some background information about the product or brand is also included. After all, not every reader of the marketing plan will be familiar with the situation to which the marketing plan refers. Finally, a summary conclusion regarding the basic problem is provided. This forms the starting point for the plan. Therefore, it is included at the beginning. In the actual planning process; the conclusion regarding the basic problem is dealt with at a later stage (see Section 8.1).

Any available time series of various relevant variables (such as market shares and advertising expenses) can be attached as a "product fact book."

3. SITUATION ANALYSIS

The situation analysis is reviewed extensively in this book. Forecasts and/or planning assumptions for variables for the various components also may be included. This involves prognoses of variables such as macroenvironmental factors, market data, and competitor behavior. For variables for which no prognoses were made, the *assumptions* about future development should be provided. These assumptions should be defined as specifically as possible. For example: the assumptions for the next year are:

- Economic growth of 2 percent.
- Inflation of 4 percent.
- No reaction from competitor G will follow.
- No increase in excise duty will occur.
- Costs of raw materials will remain constant.
- Market demand will grow 5 percent.

The explicit description of assumptions is very important for the process of choosing objectives and for the later evaluation of the results (in the internal analysis). If the predicted results are not achieved, this may have been caused by an assumption that was not met; for example a competitor showed a reaction after all. In such a case an alternative strategy should be chosen (this is described in part 10 of the marketing plan).

In practice, the competitor analysis and the industry analysis are often described together.

4. SWOT ANALYSIS

The SWOT analysis and SWOT matrix form a summarizing description of the situation analysis and provide a starting point for strategies.

5. MARKETING OBJECTIVES/EXPECTED RESULTS

The results that need to be achieved in terms of sales, turnover, and market share are an important reason why a particular strategy is chosen. Objectives are often formulated for several years, for example, for a three-year period.

6. MARKETING STRATEGY

A brief indication of the marketing strategy is not sufficient here: Elements such as target audience personality, brand personality, and type of positioning should be described in detail. The line of reasoning that supports the choice of a particular strategy should also be described.

7.   DECISIONS REGARDING MARKETING MIX ELEMENTS

The plans should be translated in detail into *concrete programs of action for the upcoming year (year plans).* In this context, four questions should be answered: *What* exactly is going to happen? *When* will it happen? *Who* will do it? *How much* will it cost? A detailed development and assignment of responsibilities is important for a good implementation.

8.   FINANCIAL INDICATORS AND BUDGETS

Financial understanding is a very important component of the marketing plan. In this part the following financial indicators are described:

- The required budgets: budgets for sales promotion, sales expenses, research, product development, and so forth.
- The predicted expenses, revenues, cash flow, and profit; these predictions have been used at an earlier stage during the analysis of shareholder value.

This part is very important for top management, providing it with insight into the required investments and the extent to which the plan will contribute to the financial objectives of the company. The financial part therefore becomes the starting point for the negotiations between the manager who submits the plan and top management. To gain perspective on the *risks,* top management will always judge the "financial picture" in relation to the assumptions. Although an expected high profit is attractive, if there is great uncertainty about this assumption, it becomes an important minus. Top management will also attempt to estimate the payoff time, which is determined by issues such as the point when a profit will start to be made. If this point is too far in the future, the plan will not be considered very attractive.

9.   EVALUATION CRITERIA

To allow an evaluation of whether the plan will be able to meet its targeted goals during the course of a year, two subjects should be elaborated in this part. First, the objectives and budgets must be translated (differentiated) into regions, varieties, distribution channels, and periods within the year (for example, for each month or for each quarter). Next, the information that is needed for progress control should be indicated. In other words, the company needs to know which criteria will be used for the control and how they will be measured. These criteria depend on the objectives. Suppose the company wants to gain a market share of 5 percent in one year with the introduction of new brand X (marketing objective). This objective is translated as follows: On April 1 a share of 2 percent needs to have been achieved, on July 1 3 percent, on October 1 4 percent, and on December 31 the full 5 percent. Progress control occurs through Nielsen (scanning) data.

10.   ATTACHMENTS: ALTERNATIVE STRATEGIES AND TIME SCHEDULES

Especially in a strongly dynamic environment, it is advisable to have alternative strategies in case something "unexpected" (a contingency) occurs, such as the introduction of a competing product. These unexpected events may already have been analyzed in the scenario analysis. A "contingency plan" may be based on a strategy that was considered earlier but dropped. An attachment could describe which option should be chosen in which scenario. In addition, it should be indicated as specifically as possible *when* a particular scenario becomes relevant, for example, "when sales are more than 10 percent below the objectives" or "when the weighted distribution does not exceed 70 percent."

For easy reference and for monitoring afterward, it is important to include in the attachment time schedules with planned activities. For convenience, this could involve the use of a time frame.

Notes

1. Webster, F. E. (1994), *Market Driven Management,* London: Wiley.
2. Adcock, D. (2000), *Marketing Strategies for Competitive Advantage,* Chichester, UK: Wiley.
3. Aaker, D. A. (1991), *Managing Brand Equity: Capitalizing on the Value of a Brand Name,* New York: Free Press; Aaker, D. A. (1995), *Building Strong Brands,* New York: Free Press; Keller, K. L. (1993), "Conceptualizing, Measuring and Managing Customer-Based Brand Equity," *Journal of Marketing,* 57:1–22; Keller, K. L. (2003), *Strategic Brand Management: Building, Measuring and Managing Brand Equity,* 2nd ed., Upper Saddle River NJ, Pearson.
4. e.g. Kotler, Ph., and K. L. Keller (2005), *Marketing Management,* 12th ed., Upper Saddle River, NJ: Pearson.
5. Kotler, Ph. (1967), *Marketing Management,* 1st ed., Upper Saddle River, NJ: Pearson.
6. Day, G. S., and R. Wensley (1983), "Marketing Theory with a Strategic Orientation", *Journal of Marketing* 47(4):79–89.
7. Kohli, A. K., and B. J. Jaworski (1990), "Market Orientation: The Construct, Research Propositions and Managerial Implications," *Journal of Marketing* 54(2):1–18.
8. Gummesson, E. (1987), "The New Marketing—Developing Long Term Interactive Relationships," *Long Range Planning* 20(4):10–20; Gummesson, E. (1999), *Total Relationship Marketing—Rethinking Marketing Management: From 4 P's to 30 R's,* Oxford, UK: Butterworth-Heineman; Webster, F. E. (1992), "The Changing Role of Marketing in the Corporation," *Journal of Marketing* 56(10):1–17.
9. Morgan, R. M., and S. D. Hunt (1994), "The Commitment-Trust Theory of Relationship Marketing," *Journal of Marketing* 58:20–38.
10. Woodruff, R. B. (1997), "Customer Value: The Next Source for Competitive Advantage," *Journal of the Academy of Marketing Science* 25(2):139–153.
11. Treacy, M., and F. Wiersema (1993), "Customer Intimacy and Other Value Disciplines," *Harvard Business Review,* January–February, pp. 84–93.
12. Vargo, S. L., and R. F. Lusch (2004), "Evolving to a New Dominant Logic for Marketing," *Journal of Marketing* 68:1–17.
13. Gummesson, E. (1998), "Implementation Requires a Relationship Marketing Paradigm," *Journal of the Academy of Marketing Science* 26:242–249.
14. Grönroos, C. (1997), "Value-Driven Relational Marketing: From Products to Resources and Competences," *Journal of Marketing Management* 13:407–419
15. Hoekstra, J. C., P. S. H. Leeflang, and D. R. Wittink (1999), "The Customer Concept: The Basis for a New Marketing Paradigm," *Journal of Market Focused Management* 4:43–76.
16. Fournier, S., S. Dobscha, and D. G. Mick (1998), "Preventing the Premature Death of Relationship Marketing," *Harvard Business Review,* January–February, pp. 42–51.
17. Webster (1992 yes see note 8).
18. Reicheld, F. F. (1993), "Loyalty-Based Management," *Harvard Business Review,* March–April, pp. 64–73; Reicheld, F .F. (1996), "Learning from Customer Defections," *Harvard Business Review,* March–April, pp. 56–69.
19. Kotler and Keller (2005).
20. Keller (1993, 2003).
21. Ries, A., and J. Trout (1981), *Positioning: The Battle for Your Mind,* New York: McGraw-Hill.
22. Wernerfelt, B. (1984), "A Resource-Based View of the Firm," *Strategic Management Journal* 16:171–180.
23. Prahalad, C. K., and G. Hamel (1990), "The Core Competence of the Corporation," *Harvard Business Review,* May–June, pp. 79–91.

24. Porter, M. E. (1980), *Competitive Strategy,* New York: Free Press.

25. Day. G. (1999), "Misconceptions about Market Orientation," *Journal of Market Focused Management* 4:5–16.

26. Hooley, G., K. Möller, and A. J. Broderick (1998), "Competitive Positioning and the Resource Based View of the Firm," *Journal of Strategic Marketing* 6(2):97–115; Hooley, G., J. Saunders, and N. Piercy (2004), *Marketing Strategy and Competitive Positioning,* 3rd ed. Harlow, England, Pearson.

27. Hooley and associates (2004) show the relationship between marketing resources and market performance in a model that is based on the SPP model of competitive advantage of Day, G. S., and R. Wensley (1983), "Marketing Theory with a Strategic Orientation," *Journal of Marketing* 47(4):79–89: Sources of advantage leading to positional advantages (higher quality or lower costs), leading to better performance.

28. Kotler and Keller (2005).

29. See, e.g., Adcock (2000).

30. See, e.g., Porter (1980)).

31. Kerin, R. A., P. R. Varadarajan, and R. A. Peterson (1992), "First-Mover Advantage: A Synthesis, Conceptual Framework, and Research Propositions," *Journal of Marketing* 56:33–52; Bowman, D., and H. Gatignon (1996), "Order of Entry as a Moderator of the Effect of the Marketing Mix on Market Share," *Marketing Science* 15:222–242.

32. Christen, M. (2000), "Does It Pay to Be a Pioneer?" In: *Mastering Marketing,* Harlow, UK: Financial Times, Pearson Education, pp. 167–172.

33. Ries and Trout (1981).

34. Keller (2003) also names a fourth requirement: high brand awareness.

35. The idea for this figure comes from Erik Lanting with special thanks.

36. Kerin, R. A., V. Mahajan, and P. R. Varadajan (1990), *Contemporary Perspectives on Strategic Market Planning,* Boston: Allyn and Bacon; Aaker, D. A. (2005), *Strategic Market Management,* 6th ed., New York: Wiley; Ferell , O. C., M. D. Hartline, G. H. Lucas, and D. Luck (1999), *Marketing Strategy,* Orlando, FL: Dryden Press.

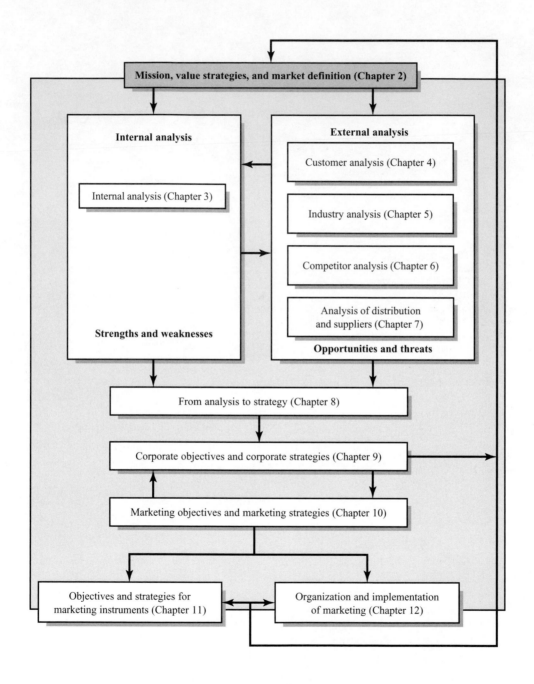

Chapter Two

Mission, Value Strategies, and Market Definition

Key Points in This Chapter

- Know the function and components of a mission and a vision.
- Be able to formulate a vision and a value strategy.
- Know how to define a market: components and guidelines.

INTRODUCTION

The first step in creating a marketing plan is to define the market. Without market definition, no analyses can be performed. A market definition for a brand should always be contained in the mission of a company. Therefore, the mission should be clear. This chapter starts with a section about the mission and the vision (Section 2.1). Within the vision the value discipline is important: Which customer needs does the company want to serve? We deal with value strategies in Section 2.2. After that, in Section 2.3 we discuss ways to define markets. Market definition is relevant at different levels in the organization.

Grazing at Starbucks?

There was a time when Americans sat down and ate real meals three times a day. Now, it seems, they never stop "grazing."

Unlike snacking, grazing isn't a matter of nibbling between meals. It replaces the meal. "The fundamental definition of a meal has changed. Today a meal can be a Diet Coke and a Snickers bar," says Kim Feil, division president at Information Resources, which recently released a survey on the eating habits of 2,000 American consumers. The study found the typical consumer eats 4.3 times a day and that many consumers eat 6 times a day. The study found that 35 percent of Americans eat two or fewer "square" meals daily. Nearly half eat between meals. Only 42 percent say they have "well-balanced" diets.

For a lot of people grazing has become a lifestyle. A typical Saturday eating regimen for many consumers might go something like this: 9 a.m., cappuccino and sandwich at Starbucks; noon, takeout salad from grocery bar; 3 p.m., hot pretzel and soft drink from concession stand at Target; 7 p.m., bowl of soup and half a sandwich at Panera Bread; 10 p.m., side of chili and Frostie from Wendy's. The only thing missing: a real meal.

Even McDonald's has noticed the increase in grazing. It hopes to test three-in-one restaurants soon that will be part restaurant, part coffee shop, and part bakery: a taste for every craving.

But why are all these people grazing?

- Tick, tick, tick. Time-pressed lives leave no time to cook. This leads to eating on the go.
- People spend more and more time in their cars, and cars are becoming mobile dining rooms.
- Click, click, click. A new generation is learning to surf and graze at the same time. A lack of structure in many teens' lives affects their eating habits. With an absence of family life, teens are looking for ways to fill the gap, such as snacks
- Smaller households. In the United States 60 percent of all households have two or fewer family members. In 1960, such households accounted for 40 percent of the population. Small households typically cook fewer meals.

The grazing trend is driving some restaurants and fast-food restaurants crazy, but it's the bread and butter for others, such as Starbucks.

Starbucks sells high-quality whole-bean coffees along with fresh, rich-brewed Italian-style espresso beverages and a variety of pastries and confections in its "coffee-bars." In the early 1980s Starbucks opened its first location in Seattle; by the end of 2002 there were almost 6,000 locations worldwide.

Starbucks' Mission Statement

"Establish Starbucks as the premier purveyor [supplier] of the finest coffee in the world while maintaining our uncompromising principles while we grow."

The following six guiding principles will help us measure the appropriateness of our decisions:

- Embrace diversity as an essential component in the way we do business
- Provide a great work environment and treat each other with respect and dignity
- Apply the highest standards of excellence to the purchasing, roasting and fresh delivery of our coffee
- Develop enthusiastically satisfied customers all of the time.
- Contribute positively to our communities and our environment
- Recognize that profitability is essential to our future success.

Starbucks is not just coffee. Some view Starbucks as the apostle of grazing. The chain took grazing to new heights by convincing millions of consumers that they can graze on a fancy, pricey espresso.

"Some people look at our beverages as meal replacements," says Dan Hurdle, vice president of retail food at Starbucks. The chain has 22 million visitors a week in the United States. Die-hard customers stop in an average of 18 times a month, and an average customer visits 5 times a month.

But serving meals at Starbucks has proved tricky. The company tested—and recently closed—four Café Starbucks eateries in the Seattle area. It seems folks don't come to Starbucks to eat meals but to graze. With that in mind, Starbucks has been trying out more food-on-the-go additions to the biscotti and pastry nibbles available with beverages. Many stores have a few sandwiches and salads part of the day.

Yogurt and fruit cups were recently added at many locations. And Starbucks is now testing Breakfast Savories. Call them fancy Egg McMuffins. These $2,95 breakfast sandwiches, with egg and cheese rolled into pastry, are available at 20 stores in the Seattle area. If they're a hit, the chain will roll them out nationally.

Sources: *USA Today,* April 24, 2003, p. B01; www.starbucks.com.

Questions

1. In this case study you can read the four reasons why grazing has become an important trend. Why is it important for companies like Starbucks to know the reasons behind this trend?
2. Suppose the marketing manager of Starbucks wants to use the information in this case as input for a strategic marketing plan.

   1. Which information in this case should be part of the customer analysis?
   2. Which information in this case should be part of the competitor analysis?
   3. Which information in this case should be part of the industry analysis?
   4. Which information in this case should be part of the internal analysis?

3. An organization can define its business in terms of the products it makes or the technologies it uses, but a business also can be defined in terms of the customer needs served by the company. What is the difference between a product-oriented and a needs-oriented business definition?
4. Read the mission statement of Starbucks.

   1. Is this mission statement defined in terms of the product or in terms of the customer needs served by Starbucks? Explain your answer.
   2. Which would you prefer: a product-oriented mission statement or a mission statement in terms of the customer needs served by Starbucks? Explain your answer.
   3. If you prefer that the mission statement be defined differently than it was in your answer to question 1, redefine the mission statement of Starbucks.

2.1 DEVELOPING A CUSTOMER-ORIENTED VISION

2.1.1 Mission and Vision

Many organizations have a *mission statement*. However, mission statements can be quite varied in their objective. On the basis of research on 59 large companies in Great Britain, Klemm and associates[1] classified missions into four different types:

1. *The pure mission.* This is a representation of the company's long-term objectives, based on the philosophies of top management. Here is an example from a publisher: "We want to make an increasing contribution to the information supply and the formation of public opinion in the UK."
2. *Strategic objectives.* This is a global representation of the company's desired direction and positions. Here is an example: "We want to become the market leader in the magazine industry."
3. *Quantified planning objectives.* These are the concrete objectives for a specific period. Here is an example: "Next year we want a profit 10 percent higher than this year's profit."

4. *Definition of the market (business definition).* This is a definition of the scope and activities of a company. Here is an example: "We publish newspapers and magazines."

This list shows that the missions formulated by companies can vary from very broad to very narrow. By way of an example, we provide here Shell's mission: "The objectives of Shell companies are to engage efficiently, responsibly and profitably in the oil, gas, chemicals, coal, steel and other appropriate businesses, and to participate in the search for, and development of other sources of energy. Shell companies seek a high standard of performance and aim to maintain a long-term position in their respective competitive environments."

The goal of a mission is threefold:

1. *Market definition.* The process of formulating a mission forces a company to reflect on its activities (asking what business are we in?). Thus, a mission statement is an important component of the strategic planning process.
2. *Employee motivation.* The second function of a mission statement is that it serves as an internal purpose of motivating employees. A mission should therefore lay out actionable objectives to help guide employees in their work.
3. *External image.* The third function is to create an outward image that allows the public to have a clear understanding of what you do. For that purpose, the identity of a company may be included in the mission, as well as, for example, its social objectives.

Corporate Image

According to the research by Klemm and associates, the *internal* function of a mission statement is especially important because it is meant to sell the philosophies and values of top management to the employees. An example of a very brief but also very motivating mission comes from a Japanese car manufacturer that for quite some time had the mission "beat Mercedes Benz." Research has also shown that companies are more likely to change their mission statement as a result of a change in management than as a result of a change in " market circumstances." Research has also shown that it is necessary to distinguish "mission" from "vision."[2] Formulating a brief, motivating vision that states what the organization aims to achieve in the future, is called a company's "strategic intent."[3]

Based on this analysis, it therefore may be argued that a mission has a real function only when it acts as a motivating force. Because in reality this is often not the case, it has been argued that companies should formulate *ambition statements* rather than *mission statements*. In this regard a distinction should be made between a vision and a mission. A mission is what a company is and does now, whereas a vision is what a company wants to achieve in the future. That vision acts as a motivating force. Figure 2-1 indicates which choices should be used as the basis for a strategic business plan. We let the mission be defined first so that it can be used to indicate what the company wants to achieve in the future (vision). We now discuss in more detail each of the components in Figure 2-1.[4]

FIGURE 2-1
Mission and Vision of an Organization

The mission: What are we doing now?

- Definition of activities
- Social mission (external and internal) and other dimensions of corporate image

The vision/ambition: What do we want to achieve in the future?

- Beliefs: explanation of what is important to the company
- Identity and positioning of the organization: value strategy
- Long-term goals

2.1.2 Mission

In this section we first discuss the mission component 'market definition', and then the component 'corporate identity'. The first mission component refers to the definition of current activities: What business are we in? A market definition may contain the following dimensions[5]:

- *Products* (customer technologies; we design systems that link client needs with the supply of information).
- *Customer groups* (segments; our target audiences are private individuals and companies in the United States).
- *Customer functions* (needs; we help our customers search for information more effectively and efficiently on the Internet).

The most obvious method is to define markets on the basis of the *products*: A market in that case consists of all the companieas that bring a certain product onto the market. For example, companies may be active in the beer market, the car market, the coffee market, the market for air travel, the market for personal computers, and so on. A disadvantage of defining markets on the basis of products is that this relates only to the supply side; it does not indicate for whom the products are intended, or who demands the product. As such, a market definition should include the *customers* as well. For example, beer may be manufactured for home use or for use in the catering industry or both. Personal computers may be intended for individuals, schools, or companies. A company can also differentiate its customers based on geography. Does the company serve only the national market or also the international market, and if it serves the latter, which countries? In short, a market defintion should describe the products as well as the customer.

Another disadvantage of using products to define a market is that it does not focus on the underlying *needs* of the customer for whom the product is intended. The danger in this case is that a company will overlook competitors that serve the same function for the customers (i.e., respond to the same needs) but with very different products.[6] For example, a gasoline company may use the product-oriented market definition "we sell gasoline" or the customer-oriented definition "we supply energy." In the second scenario, the company keeps the option to supply other products that meet the same need, such as natural gas. Thus, a market definition should be formulated not just in terms of products but also in terms of *functions for customers*.[7] A classic example of a product-oriented mission is provided by Swiss watch manufacturers, which for many years focused their market definition on manually produced precision clocks. The arrival of chip technology meant that they were surpassed by foreign manufacturers that could supply the same quality for significantly lower prices (digital watches). Only when sales of Swiss watches dropped dramatically did Swiss companies redefine the market on the basis of consumers' need "to know what time it is." Subsequently, those companies also started using new production methods and producing cheaper watches (Swatch).

CASE 2-1 *Digital Photo Technology Radically Shifts Market Shares*	From 2000 onward digital photography took an enormous flight. For consumers, digital photography is much more convenient than "classical" photography: One can immediately see the result, there is no need to print everything, and it is easy to handle photos on the computer. In the beginning, with 2- and 3-megapixel cameras, the quality was not comparable with that of classical photos. However, since the introduction of affordable 4-megapixel cameras, the quality was good enough. Since that time, classical photography has disappeared from the consumer market. Famous film producers Agfa and Kodak were not able to define new markets and dramatically lost share. Also, some retailers that changed too late to digital photography disappeared from the market. In the camera market, market shares changed enormously in favor of, for example, Canon, which positioned itself as a leader in consumer photography.

The other component of the mission is the *corporate image*. There are four dimensions of designing an external corporate image[8]:

1. *Product associations.* Companies can evoke associations that are strongly linked to the tangible or emotional values of the products and services they sell, such as Coca-Cola, Levi's, Ikea, Virgin, and BMW.

2. *Customer orientation.* This is related to the attitude of the direct contact staff: Is the company truly customer-oriented? This is an important dimension of the marketing concept, which was introduced in Chapter 1. For example, even in its logo, the Rabobank, a Dutch bank, literally puts the customer at the center; the question is how this is subsequently implemented in practice.

3. *Social responsibility ("values and programs").* Social responsibility is receiving a lot of attention. Three aspects of social a responsibility include: environmental friendliness, participating in social projects or worthy cases (through corporate giving), and maintaining important employee policies such as affirmative action and maternity leave.

4. *Credibility.* This is related to the extent to which consumers believe that a company is competent, trustworthy, and "nice."

2.1.3 Vision and Ambition

The vision is the 'dream of the entrepreneur'. It is the top management's view of a company and the role it plays in the market place. The vision originates to a large extent from the existing core competencies: What are we best at?

Visions may relate to three components (Figure 2-2):

1. *Opinions* about where the company believes the market is going (for example 'we believe that due to tempestuous communication technology developments, over the next five years consumers will develop a strong need for products that help them navigate the abundance of information online).

2. The *identity* of the company (our goal is to become the most innovative and best supplier of such products within five years); this will often be based on the core competencies of the company (see, for example, Case 2-2).

3. The *long-term goals* of the company (we want to become the largest supplier of such navigation products).

An important issue here is that the vision should contain a clear and motivating ambition with which the entire work force can identify. A vision should not be handed down to the staff as a straitjacket, but rather it is important that the company's leaders generate internal support for the vision. The ability to formulate a clear and challenging ambition is an important requirement for a *leader*. This principle is well known in politics: World leaders

FIGURE 2-2
Components of the Vision of a Company

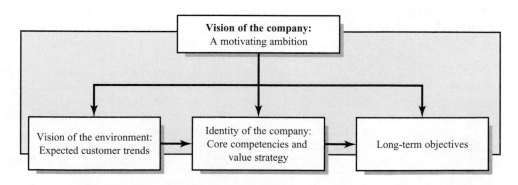

excel in conveying what they want. The same thing applies to organizations. A clear ambition is a strong tool for creating teams. However, in practice many organizations lack a challenging vision. In Chapter 12 we will return to this issue.

CASE 2-2 *The Core Competency of Volvo*	At Volvo, the main focus is safety. Its entire operational management is geared toward that goal. Company investments therefore are very closely related to safety. For example, at the end of the 1990s Volvo developed a completely new and unique testing hall to research and improve the safety of its cars. This testing hall is shaped like a cross so that side-impact crashes can be imitated. In the middle of the cross, the floor is a thick glass plate that allows measurements to be taken from below during the crash tests.

2.2 VALUE STRATEGIES

It was indicated in Chapter 1 that having a competitive advantage is essential. For the choice of such an advantage, the theory of Treacy and Wiersema[9] in regard to what they call *value disciplines* can be used with excellent results. First we will present this theory, and then we will compare it with the theory of Porter[10]; we will conclude with our own adaptation of the value disciplines (or value strategies). The Cases 2-3 through 2-5 provide the examples Treacy and Wiersema use.

CASE 2-3 *Choice of Value Discipline: Operational Excellence*	Price/Costco has vigorously pursued a strategy of operational excellence. Price/Costco, a chain of warehouse club stores, doesn't provide a particularly rich selection of merchandise: only 3,500 items, versus 50,000 or more in competing stores. However, as a customer, you don't have to spend much time deliberating over what brand of coffee or home appliance to select. Price/Costco saves you that hassle by choosing for you. The company's *Consumer Reports* mentality leads to a rigorous evaluation of leading brands and shrewd purchasing of the one brand in each category that represents the best value. Price/Costco follows an operating model in which it buys larger quantities and negotiates better prices than competing stores do. It carries only items that sell well. The company's information systems track product movement—and move it does. These data drive stocking decisions that optimize floor space usage. The place hums. It runs like a well-oiled machine, and customers love it.

CASE 2-4 *Choice of Value Discipline: Product Leadership*	Johnson & Johnson, an example of a company pursuing product leadership, continually pushes products into the realm of the unknown, the untried, or the highly desirable. It brings in new ideas, develops them quickly, and then looks for ways to improve them. The company has a focus on the core processes of invention, product development, and market exploitation. Furthermore, J&J can be characterized as having a business structure that is loosely knit, ad hoc, and ever changing to adjust to the entrepreneurial initiatives and redirections that characterize working in unexplored territory. Management systems are results-driven, measure and reward new product success, and don't punish the experimentation needed to get there. J&J's culture encourages individual imagination, accomplishment, out-of-the-box thinking, and a mind-set driven by the desire to create the future.

CASE 2-5 *Choice of Value Discipline: Customer Intimacy*	Cable & Wireless, a long-distance carrier, is a good example of a company that is better than most at building relationships that pay off in terms of repeat sales from loyal customers (customer intimacy). Company executives knew long ago that their long-distance operation couldn't compete on price with the Big Three: AT&T, MCI, and Sprint. Therefore, they attempted to differentiate themselves by providing the best customer support in the industry, along with direct sales consultation that gives salespeople intimate knowledge of what makes

its customers successful. The company holds out a big carrot to keep everyone focused on customer retention: It pays salespeople on the basis of how long a customer remains with the company. Salespeople thus don't hesitate to suggest that customers switch to more appropriate services, even if they bring in less money. The result: happier, more loyal customers.

Source of Cases 2-3 through 2-5: Treacy, Michael, and Fred Wiersema, "How Market Leaders Keep Their Edge," *Fortune*, February 6, 1995, p. 88–98.

In their frequently quoted article "Customer Intimacy and Other Value Disciplines," Treacy and Wiersema present three potential value strategies:

1. *Product leadership.* The development of innovative, value-added products; this strategy is employed, for example, by Procter & Gamble, which uses the basic assumption for all markets in which it is active that Procter brands will have the highest quality in their category and will be the best at fulfilling the customer need for which a product was made. Other companies that seem to choose product leadership are technologically strong companies such as Microsoft, Intel, Sony, and Philips.

2. *Operational excellence* (leader in low costs for the customer). This literally means to excel in the correct and efficient implementation of all corporate processes. This encompasses the idea that an "excellent production process" leads to the fact that the client has to minimize expenditure; thus, a low price is the most obvious way to comply with customer demands. Though this is not necessarily the case, "costs" can also be nonfinancial, such as the effort expended to buy the product (convenience). "Always delivering on time" also can be part of the strategy. With regard to this value strategy, standardization is important for a company, along with the achievement of economies of scale. This value strategy is chosen, for example, by the airline Easyjet, which saves costs in as many areas as possible (including the "service" en route: food is charged for) and therefore can compete at very low prices. Other companies that excel in operational excellence are McDonalds, Dell Computers (direct delivery through the Internet), Aldi, Ikea, and Wal-Mart. This value strategy deals explicitly with excelling in efficiency. In principle every company tries to keep its costs as low as possible and make the internal processes run as smoothly as possible (Philips, KLM, etc.); this does not mean, however, that these companies excel in creating low costs for the customer.

3. *Customer intimacy* (individual customer approach: "client leadership," or the best in relationship marketing). "Intimate" relations with the customer are achieved by supplying customized products and/or through a policy that is totally focused on attention to the individual customer and customer loyalty. Some companies follow this discipline, for example, Internet service providers such as Amazon.com and Bol.com, which know the preferences of individual customers and make appropriate offers (of books, compact discs, etc.) on the basis of those preferences. In business markets customer intimacy is normal as well: Personal contacts and products and services that are adjusted to individual customers (companies) are common in industrial markets. In small and medium-size enterprises an individual customer strategy seems to be applicable as well. Similarly, in service markets for consumers, there are possibilities for the implementation of customer intimacy. However, in the practice of marketing, many firms deal with sales instead of building relationships. In other sectors there are few providers that excel in this strategy, although some companies pay attention to individual customer care, for example, KLM with its frequent flyer program, through which loyal customers are rewarded with relevant offers. This does not mean, however, that the company excels in this area. Therefore, customer intimacy seems to be capable of offering a competitive edge in many sectors in the future.

Treacy and Wiersema suggest that every company has to make a basic choice to excel in one of these three disciplines: Which value does the company primarily want to support? This choice is decisive for the entire company management: production, staff, marketing, and so on. Furthermore, the other two value disciplines should be at an acceptable level. This condition is often omitted in the description by Treacy and Wiersema. However, it is very important, because these authors suggest that a company can excel in only one of the three disciplines once a minimum quality level of internal processes (operational "excellence") has been achieved. In fact, at first all three should be at an acceptable level; only thereafter can a company excel in one of them. A company therefore should have "its things in order" in the fields of innovation, efficiency, and customer orientation before it tries to excel in one of them. Furthermore, these authors suggest that expectations from customers should not only be met but exceeded. This can be done, for example, by offering unsolicited service.[11]

Other Frameworks

Treacy and Wiersema's arrangement has similarities to the generic competitive strategies of Porter.[12] Product leadership strongly corresponds to Porter's strategy of differentiation. Operational excellence appears to be similar to cost leadership but actually is substantially different. Cost leadership is an internal strategy that includes an emphasis on cost reduction, whereas operational excellence starts from the perspective of a customer who wants convenience or a low price. The third strategy is the focus strategy. The strategy of customer intimacy may be interpreted as a farther-reaching form of segmentation: The company does not necessarily orient itself necessarily toward a small segment but instead toward individual customers. Porter's recommendations correspond fairly well to those of Treacy and Wiersema: A company should focus on one of the three options. Treacy and Wiersema also state that focusing is important, but they add that an adequate level in the other two disciplines is also required. Since their framework is really customer-oriented, it is strongly preferred to that of Porter.

Comments on the Treacy and Wiersema Model

We will add three comments on the theory of Treacy and Wiersema:

1. *The brand image is not explicitly included.* In the model of Treacy and Wiersema no clear space has been created for companies or products that distinguish themselves on the basis of brand image. For example, in the market for soft drinks and beer, the difference based on brand image is demonstrably the most important. In our opinion, this could be interpreted as a type of product leadership in which the image excels, and the company should in fact excel by using the means of communication. In this way a company such as Coca-Cola is also a product leader. Although it has been proved during taste tests that Pepsi and Coca-Cola are appreciated more or less equally, the market share of Coca-Cola is remarkably greater. Coca-Cola is apparently very good at image building.

2. *There is a relationship with segmentation.* Segmentation is the subdivision of the market into subgroups and the subsequent taking of the differences in the wishes of those groups into account. In the case of leadership in efficiency, the smallest degree of segmentation can be expected. In case of product leadership, segmentation is more likely, and customer leadership is to be viewed as "complete segmentation." Clients are served individually.

3. *The Treacy and Wiersema model applies to companies, divisions, or strategic business units (SBUs).* Both in the systems of Porter and Treacy and Wiersema, it is justifiable to ask whether they apply to the whole company. Can different value strategies be chosen within one company? Hendry suggests that Porter's concept should be applied at the level of SBUs.[13] When we extend this to the system of Treacy and Wiersema, we conclude that within an SBU one value strategy should be chosen but that between SBUs

FIGURE 2-3
Value Strategies

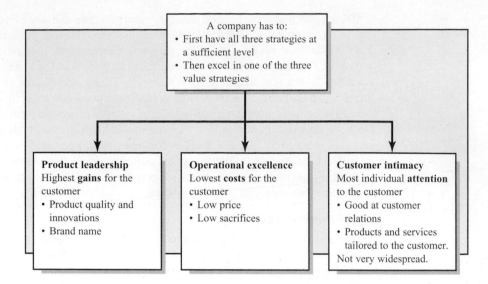

different value strategies are possible. The clearest way to do this is to choose one value strategy for a complete company, but if there are more or less autonomously operating divisions or SBUs within a company, differences in value strategies are imaginable.

Figure 2-3 summarizes the division of value strategies and our recommendations. Is it even possible to formulate a vision before doing a situation analysis? Is an organization capable of making decisions about the future if it has not completed an extensive situation analysis? We consider the vision more or less as a given for the marketing planning process. This is related to the level at which these issues are relevant: Formulating a vision is a task for top management ("the leader"), whereas the strategic marketing planning process is related to separate markets and SBUs. If, for example, a company did not clearly choose a value strategy, it still would be necessary to do this after the situation analysis. We will return to this issue in Section 8.2.

The recommendation to define a mission and vision applies to both *for-profit* and *non-profit* organizations. For nonprofit organizations, the implementation of some of these components will be more challenging than is the case in for-profit organizations. In this context we want to focus especially on the choice of long-term goals (a component of the vision) and the market definition (a component of the mission). In for-profit organizations, choosing a long-term objective typically does not present a problem. Financial goals (profit, share price, market share, etc.) usually are the guiding principle. For nonprofit organizations such as hospitals, other health-care organizations, environmental groups, government agencies, and sport organizations, it is a different matter. In those cases it is not always clear beforehand which goal should be achieved. This creates a problem as soon as a nonprofit organization decides that it wants to become more "customer-oriented" and create a marketing plan. For which target audience does the organization want to achieve something? If there is no clarity about this, it will be difficult to "do marketing." Therefore, two questions are important: Who is the relevant target audience? and What do we want to achieve with that target audience? Since objectives of nonprofit organizations typically are not expressed in terms of sales, variables such as the number of members, customer satisfaction, visit frequency, the number of complaints, and length of membership may be used.

Until now, we have discussed the role of a mission statement at the corporate level. In practice, missions also occur in individual divisions of a corporation. For example, both

General Electric and its division NBC have separate mission statements. Since a division, like NBC, often is considered a separate company, all the same strategies we have discussed at the corporate level will apply to the division or SBU level.

In summary, in the long term each company should choose a value strategy to excel and should communicate it internally and externally in the ambition statement. Choosing a value strategy has consequences throughout the organization and also provides guidelines for the marketing instruments and for doing market research. A manager should organize all these activities in a consistent and integrated way.

2.3 MARKET DEFINITION

2.3.1 Market Definition at the SBU Level

For convenience, in Chapter 1 an SBU was defined around a specific market or product category, for example, the SBU salad dressing, children's clothing, student accounts, or travel insurance. This definition implies that an SBU is not always concretely visible as an organizational unit within a company.

A market definition at the SBU level occurs in a similar manner as it does with the mission: according to the dimensions of products, target audiences, and needs. However, there are two differences between the company level and the SBU level. First, because marketing plans are determined at the SBU level, the market definition at that level needs to be as concrete as possible, whereas vaguer terms may be used for the mission. Second, the market for an SBU by definition is smaller than that of a company; the "sum" of all market definitions of the SBU will in theory correspond to the market definition of the entire company.

The definition of customer need has a direct impact on the *range of the competition*. After all, a competitor is by definition a supplier that can satisfy the same customer need. Therefore, the manner in which that need is defined determines the competition. In that regard, not only the concrete needs are important but also associated product characteristics, such as prestige and status. These values can also be used for the market definition.

We illustrate the use of the dimensions at the SBU level through an example (Figure 2-4). The SBU "jam" of a manufacturer researches the possibilities for the three different dimensions. The *need* that is addressed is defined concretely in this example; it is the need for sandwich fillings. Alternative needs are cake filling and components for desserts. Potential *customer groups* are home users, the catering industry, the health-care industry, and company cafeterias. Alternative *customer technologies* (associated with the need for sandwich fillings) are jam, peanut butter, sandwich spread, cheese spread, cheese, and sliced meat. Within these dimensions the following market definition is chosen: "We provide for the need of home users to have sandwich fillings by making jam." In Figure 2-4 it should be noted that in principle the definition is constructed for the level of the final customers (consumers).

| **CASE 2-6**
Market
Dimensions in
Sport Markets | Organizations in sports markets (clubs, associations, stadiums, etc.) have to deal with two target groups: spectators and viewers and advertisers (sponsors). The "product" sport is "a battle." The special aspect of this "product" is that it is not stable. The course and outcome are always unsure. There are two kinds of sports marketing: marketing of sports and marketing through sports (sponsoring). Organizations that deal with the marketing of the "battle" (sports) might best apply the planning concepts that are described in this book. In that case it is important to sell the company's own product as well as possible to viewers and advertisers and to build up relationships with those target groups. In the case of marketing "through sports," the main issue is communication. Sponsors can use the "medium" sports to realize brand targets (brand name, image) and to build up their own relationships (for example, invite customers to sky boxes). |

FIGURE 2-4 Market Definition for a Manufacturer of Jam

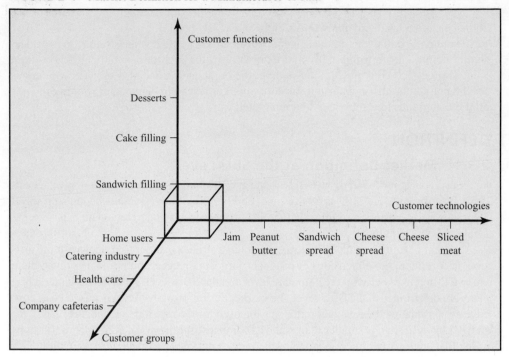

The use of these three dimensions not only is important for defining the current market, it also allows for a structural approach to considering potential growth directions during the process of company decision making. The four well-known growth strategies as defined by Ansoff[14] (see Section 9.3) can be linked directly to the axes in Figure 2-4. The relationships between the dimensions of the market definition and Ansoff's growth strategies are shown in Figure 2-5.

Figure 2-5 shows which growth strategy is applicable for a certain combination of changes in market dimensions. For instance, if the goal is to grow within the existing three dimensions, it is a matter of market penetration. The same thing applies if only the customer function is changed. Growth that occurs exclusively in the dimension of customer groups implies market development, whereas growth that exclusively involves expansion of the product dimension (that is, for the same needs and customers) is called product development.

Change in the dimensions of customer groups and products means diversification. In the case of related products that cover the same needs, this is called related diversification. If other needs are also addressed, it is called unrelated diversification. Figure 2-5 may serve as a checklist for generating growth options. The process of creating options is addressed in the section on the SWOT analysis in Chapter 8. Final decisions about growth directions are made after the situation analysis during the process of creating a company strategy. Therefore, in Chapters 9 and 10, we return to growth strategies.

2.3.2 Market Definition at the Product or Brand Level

Aside from a market definition at the SBU level, a more detailed definition can be helpful for brands during further analyses. Concretely, this may involve a segmentation of two of the three previously mentioned dimensions: target groups and products and services. For this purpose, all products are listed. This should be a relatively quick procedure for

FIGURE 2.5 Market Dimensions and Growth Strategies

Growth along Dimensions				
Customer Function (Needs)	Customer Groups (Segments)	Customer Technology (Products)	Growth Strategy According to Ansoff	Example of Jam Producer
−	−	−	Market penetration	Price reduction of jam
+	−	−	Market penetration	Emphasize another application: jam as cake filling
−	+	−	Market development	Sell jam to catering industry or abroad
−	−	+	Product development	Produce peanut butter for consumers
−	+	+	Related diversification	Sell peanut butter abroad
+	+	+	Unrelated diversification	Produce fruit juices or ready-made pizzas

− = "no change"; + = "change."

companies that produce goods, but for suppliers of services it is more challenging: What are the products of a bank, for example? A second step is the description of the different target audiences (customers) of the organization. An obvious distinction is between private customers (final customers) and companies (business markets). However, it is also possible to segment further within those groups on the basis of various segmentation criteria ranging from general background characteristics (age, type of business, store chain, etc.) to more product-specific variables such as heavy versus light "users" or price buyers versus quality seekers. Third, it should be indicated which combinations of products and target audiences are currently relevant for the organization. Figure 2-6 contains several worksheets that may be used. Segmentation is discussed further in Chapter 6.

An advantage of overviews such as the one in Figure 2-6 is that they can be used as the basis for subsequent analyses.

2.3.3 Market Definition and New Activities

Defining the market (at the levels of the company, the SBU, and the product) before doing the situation analysis seems to imply that this definition is not influenced by the results of the situation analysis, but this is not the case. For example, if there are very negative

FIGURE 2.6 Worksheets for Defining Product-Market Combinations

Matrix of Product–Target Audience Combinations	Target Audience 1	Target Audience 2	Target Audience 3	Target Audience 4	Target Audience . . .
Product 1					
Product 2					
Product 3					
Product 4					
Product . . .					

Mark each section with a "x" if that combination exists for the organization.

FIGURE 2-7
Signals for New
Activities

Component of Situation Analysis	Signal
Internal analysis	Core competencies: possibilities for extensions
Customer analysis	Unfulfilled customer needs to be determined from problems with existing products
Industry analysis	Substitute products and expected developments in macroenvironment
Competitor analysis	Competitor activities outside the "own" existing market
Distributor and supplier analysis	Distributor experiences in other categories

developments in the market for newspapers and magazines in which a publisher is active, that could be a reason to revise the publisher's mission (e.g., being active in the consumer market of the media) and to become active in the supply of information for companies. In that case, the question *"What should our business be?"* (supply of information for companies) is answered differently than is the question *"What business are we in?"* (consumer market of the media). This clarifies the relationship with the vision once again: The vision is the difference between the current market and the desired market.

However, if there is a difference between the current field of activities and the intended activities, this means that the new field (in the example, supplying news via the Internet) also should be analyzed to determine whether the new markets are attractive.

Finally, it may be asked whether ideas for new activities will even appear on the radar screen if the company analyzes only the existing markets from the perspective of the existing SBUs. In this regard, both during the SWOT analysis and during the reconsideration of the mission, the company needs to pay explicit attention to signals that indicate opportunities outside the scope of current activities (Figure 2-7).

In summarizing the material above, the following steps can be taken in the process of market definition and mission formulation:

1. Start with a definition of the market in which the company is currently active.
2. Complete an external analysis of the environment. This should include an analysis of the opportunities and threats outside the existing market.
3. On the basis of the external (and internal) analysis, determine whether there is a reason to become active outside the existing market; in other words, define the desired market.
4. If this is the case, complete a new external analysis with the changed market definition. This is necessary because a different market definition also involves a different competitive situation and different market growth. With a broader market definition, the number of competitors will be higher.

After the external analysis has been performed again, the company should determine whether the chosen market is still considered attractive. If it is, the planning process will be continued. This process is summarized in Figure 2-8.

In short, the phases "definition of the (current) market," "external analysis," and "formulation of company decisions: definition of the desired market" are completed until the company perceives no further reason to change the market definition. In practice these steps are usually completed only once or at most twice: first for the current market and then for a more broadly defined market.

FIGURE 2-8
Market Definition
and External Analysis

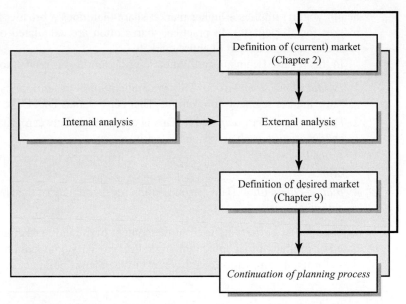

Definition of (current) market
(Chapter 2)

Internal analysis

External analysis

Definition of desired market
(Chapter 9)

Continuation of planning process

Here is an example that will clarify Figure 2-8.

Suppose a manufacturer uses the production of toy trains for a current market definition and mission. An analysis of the toy train market indicates that sales are decreasing. An important cause of this situation appears to be the growth of computer games. An important reason for the growth in the market for computer games is strong technological developments that have made it possible to bring these games onto the market for relatively low prices. Based on this assessment, the manufacturer must make an important choice: either leave the mission unchanged and attempt to maintain the sales level of toy trains through marketing efforts or adapt the mission and decide to enter the market for computer games. The choice of whether to adapt the mission depends, among other things, on the situation in the market for computer games. Therefore, the manufacturer completes an additional external analysis specific to the market for computer games. This analysis shows that there is very strong competition in this market. Therefore, the manufacturer decides not to alter the mission but attempt to restore the company's sales of toy trains by focusing more on the target audience of fathers.

In reality the situation analysis is often repeated when a company is considering whether to become active abroad. In that case, in the second round the foreign market should be analyzed.

2.3.4 Importance of a Market Definition

In the article "Marketing Myopia" Levitt[15] warned against a market definition that is too supply-oriented. In relation to the mission, Section 2.1.2 discussed the example of an overly narrowly defined, product-oriented market definition among producers of Swiss watches. It is of vital importance how broadly or narrowly a manager defines the market. With a broad definition, there will be many competitors. If a company restricts its business to a niche (narrow market defition), the number of competitors will be low. Thus, there is a direct relationship between the market definition and the number of competitors: Setting the boundaries of a market actually is the same as *defining the competitive set.*[16] This also implies a direct relationship with the concept of market share. Since the market share is calculated over the designated market, a limited market definition (e.g., the market for health yogurt) implies a higher market share than does a broader market definition (the market for all yogurts). In practice, shares often are calculated on the basis of market segments rather than that of entire markets.

In this regard, Lehmann and Winer describe four levels related to competition[17]:

1. *Product form competition.* This is competition between brands that are aimed at the same market segment, for example, Diet Pepsi versus Diet Coke.
2. *Product category competition.* This is competition between products with comparable characteristics, such as various soft drinks.
3. *Generic competition.* These are products that address the same consumer needs, such as drinks.
4. *Budget competition.* This is competition for the money of the consumer, as in food and entertainment.

The market definitions used in the context of annual marketing planning usually are based on product form competition or product category competition. Chapter 5 will discuss these forms of competition in the context of the identification of competitors.

Summary

To be able to perform a situation analysis and make strategic decisions, it should be known in what market the company operates and which value strategy the company pursues. Within these constraints the marketing strategy is developed. The market definition is related to the mission, and the value strategy is related to the vision. Organizations can best be directed if there are a clear mission and a common vision. A vision pertains to the future: What does top management consider important? Which identity should the organization have? and What are other long-term goals? The corporate identity can be formulated in terms of a value strategy: product or brand leadership, operational excellence, or customer intimacy. A company should be sufficiently good in all these areas and should try to excel in one. A clear and differentiating vision is necessary to motivate personnel and attract and retain customers. In the mission, the market for the organization is defined. At the SBU level, a further market definition occurs, based on the dimensions of products, needs, and target audiences. The market definition chosen at that level forms the starting point for the situation analysis. At the level of the product or brand, the dimension of target audiences may be further disaggregated to obtain a more precise definition of product-market combinations. A market definition should be demand-oriented and not too small in order to avoid overlooking important competitors and new market developments.

Notes

1. Klemm, A., S. Sanderson, and G. Luffman (1991), "Mission Statements: Selling Corporate Values to Employees," *Long Range Planning* 24(3):73–78.
2. Hooley, G. J., A. J. Cox, and A. Adams (1992), "Our Five Year Mission—To Boldly Go Where No Man Has Been Before . . ." *Journal of Marketing Management* 8:35–48.
3. Hamel, G., and C. K. Prahalad (1989), "Strategic Intent," *Harvard Business Review,* May–June, pp. 79–91.
4. Partly based on a Dutch book by Krijnen, H. G., and A. Greven (2000), *Strategisch ondernemerschap,* Groningen: Wolters-Noordhoff.
5. These dimensions are comparable to those used by Abell (1980). Abell uses the designations customer technologies, customer groups, and customer functions.
6. Levitt, T. (1960), "Marketing Myopia," *Harvard Business Review,* July–August 1960.
7. Abell, D. F. (1980), *Defining the Business: The Starting Point of Strategic Planning,* Englewood Cliffs, NJ: Prentice-Hall; Abell, D. F., and J. S. Hammond (1979), *Strategic Market Planning,* Englewood Cliffs, NJ: Prentice-Hall.

8. Keller, K. L. (2003), *Strategic Brand Management: Building, Measuring and Managing Brand Equity,* 2nd ed. Englewood Cliffs: NJ: Prentice Hall; see also Dowling, G. R. (1994), *Corporate Reputations,* Melbourne, Australia: Longman Professional.

9. Treacy, M., and F. Wiersema (1993), "Customer Intimacy and Other Value Disciplines," *Harvard Business Review,* January–February, pp. 84–93.

10. Porter, M. E. (1980), *Competitive Strategy,* New York: Free Press.

11. See also Vargo, S. L., and R. F. Lusch (2004), "Evolving to a New Dominant Logic for Marketing," Journal of Marketing 68:1–17, who even posit that the marketing concept should be focused on services. See also Chapter 1.

12. Porter (1980).

13. Hendry, J. (1990), 'The Problem with Porter's Generic Strategies', *European Management Journal,* 8, p. 443–450.

14. Ansoff, H. I. (1957), 'Strategies for Diversification', *Harvard Business Review,* vol. 35, September–October, p. 113–124.

15. Levitt (1960).

16. Lehmann, D. R., and R. S. Winer (2002), *Analysis for Marketing Planning,* New York: McGraw Hill Companies, 5th edition..

17. Lehmann, Winer (2002, p. 21)

Situation Analysis

In this part the components of the situation analysis are reviewed. A thorough situation analysis forms the basis for well-thought-out objectives and strategies. We start the situation analysis with an internal analysis, including a review of the company's results. The external analysis starts with a customer analysis (Chapter 4). This reflects the importance of insight into the wishes and perceptions of the target audience. Another reason for starting with an analysis of the target audience is that it becomes the source for other components of the situation analysis. After the customer analysis, the next step is providing an overview of the whole industry (Chapter 5). Then we review several parties within the industry more carefully. Chapter 6 focuses on competitor analysis. Chapter 7 considers distributors and suppliers. Part 2 concludes with a discussion of several important analytic methods that can be used to form a link between analysis and strategy (Chapter 8).

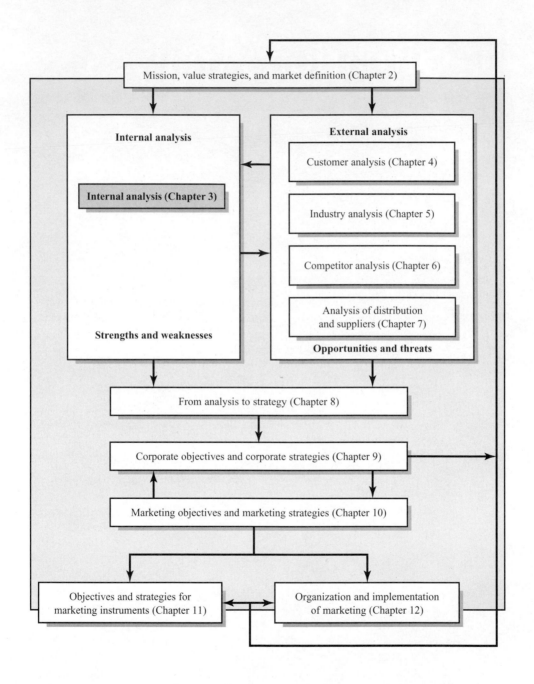

Chapter **Three**

Internal Analysis

Key Points in This Chapter

- Know how to define objectives for a company.
- Recognize the importance of applying customer-oriented objectives.
- Be capable of analyzing a brand's performance.
- Apply appropriate frameworks for a strengths-weaknesses analysis.
- Know how to assess a company's marketing effectiveness.

INTRODUCTION

In Chapter 2, the market was defined and a company's value strategy and other ambitions were reviewed. In this chapter, a company's strengths and weaknesses are analyzed in an internal analysis. When these elements are compared with those of competitors, insight is developed into the company's relative strengths and weaknesses—relative in relation to the competition. In Chapter 8 these relative strengths and weaknesses are contrasted with the corresponding opportunities and threats. However, before going into the strengths-weaknesses analysis it is important to get a feel for how the brand is performing. Thus, a detailed analysis of the brand's performance with respect to its objectives is needed. This is the "control" phase of the planning process, which is the starting point of the process.

This chapter is organized as follows. Section 3.1 starts by describing how objectives should be formulated and which objectives can be chosen (the balanced scorecard). In this stage it is not yet possible to formulate objectives; what is needed is a review of the current objectives. Section 3.2 presents a framework for a performance analysis. Sections 3.3 through 3.5 are devoted to the core part of the internal analysis: the strengths-weaknesses analysis. Since the company's brand and those of the competitors eventually are compared, it is not surprising that the structure of this part of the internal analysis is similar to the structure of a competitor analysis. Concretely, in the internal analysis, two of the five phases of the competitor analysis are performed: determining the current strategy (section 3.3) and a strengths-weaknesses analysis. For the strengths-weaknesses analysis we use the model that Day and Wensley (1988) (hereinafter abbreviated as DW) constructed for the concept of competitive advantage.[1] Therefore, we guide the analysis of the company's strengths and weaknesses in the context of searching for a competitive advantage. The DW model is presented in section 3.4, after which we translate it (section 3.5) into an analysis of strengths and weaknesses at the level of both the organization and the brand.

Diesel

The clothing brand Diesel, 25 years old, is growing turbulently. Owner Renzo Rosso says: "We have made jeans into a fast fashion article." A farmer's son, Rosso started the brand for Genius, the mother company of, for example, the Replay brand. He chose the name Diesel because it is a word that sounds the same in most languages. In 1985 he took over the company. At that time Diesel had a turnover of 2.5 million euros per year. By now this has become 660 million euros; even in the difficult aftermath of September 11, 2001, the company, based in the Italian town of Molvena, kept growing.

"And we could easily become even larger if we would produce cheaper pants. But we are the most expensive and most luxurious jeans brand in the world," says Rosso. "And I would like to keep it that way; it is a very pleasant position. I don't want to become the next Levi's or Gap."

Diesel indeed expands only with more expensive labels. It took over the young, fashionable brand Dsquared[2] as well as the house of the avant-garde designer Martin Margiela. Furthermore, there is the DieselStyleLab, Diesel's own fashion brand, whose collection is presented during the New York fashion week, and 55dsl, the snowboarding line. Under the name Diesel, apart from jeans (starting price 85 euros) and other clothes, accessories, perfumes, underwear, children's clothing, and now jewelry are being sold. The last idea came from Rosso himself ("I said: 'Let's do something with jewelry; that is such a dull market'"). Rosso still looks after the design department intensively. That department is of crucial importance for Diesel: The company has to be capable to "create" new fashion continuously.

"In the old days you had fashion, and you had jeans. Those you wore for a couple of years. Diesel changed that. We were one of the first brands that experimented with washings and ripped jeans. We turned jeans into a fast fashion article. Also, the extremely successful models are being taken out of the collection very quickly. As soon as there is a new collection, suddenly you don't fancy those old pants anymore, and you have no idea why."

Until the early 1990s the brand grew steadily. Then it began advertising as well, using the now world-famous ironic "Successful Living" campaign.

Since 1996 Diesel has opened more than 50 of its own stores, starting with a 1,400-square-meter "cathedral" in New York. Almost 30 percent of the sales now come from Diesel's own stores. In the meantime the number of other sales outlets has been reduced by half. As Rosso explains: "In that way you enable the sale of more difficult goods."

The great danger remains, though, that Diesel will become as mainstream like, for example, the archetype Levi's, which it has surpassed in some areas. "As a brand you have to be a world brand, but I want to hide as much as possible that we are a multi-national company," Rosso says. "Individuality is still the sex appeal of the brand." That's why every shop is designed in a different way and sells different goods. Furthermore, the brand distributes, just like almost every large sports and jeans brand in recent years, so-called limited editions. One of the latest inventions: the Greengrocer, dungarees with stains on the butt that appear to have been created because "strawberry fingers" were wiped on it. Starting at $200 and for sale only in New York.

Source: *De Volkskrant,* 'Diesel should not become the next Levi's or Gap', September 8, 2003, p. 6.

Questions

1. Which value discipline (Treacy and Wiersema, see chapter 2) has been chosen by Diesel? Explain your answer.

   a. What do you think is the competitive advantage of Diesel?
   b. What is the source of this competitive advantage?
   c. What is an important key success factor in the jeans industry, according to this case?
   d. What is the relationship between key success factors and the competitive advantage of a company? Demonstrate this relationship in the case of Diesel.

2. What is Diesel's marketing strategy?
3. Use the information in the case to identify the strengths of Diesel.
4. Marketing theory prescribes that a strategy should be developed after an extensive analysis of the market in which the organization operates. However, some companies seem to focus on their core competencies without adapting their strategies to the environment.

   a. On the basis of the information in this case, one could say that Diesel is an example of a company that focuses mainly on its core competencies. Explain why.
   b. Is Diesel really a company for which the concept of a situation analysis is irrelevant? Explain your answer.

3.1 OBJECTIVES

3.1.1 Requirements for Objectives

Formulating an objective has a number of functions. First, within the company it serves as a guideline for what the company wants to achieve. Thus, it has, among other functions, a communicative or motivating function: Everyone knows what is being pursued. A second function of an objective is that it is a tool for the planning process: An objective is a standard for determining whether a strategy has succeeded. If the objective has been achieved, the company can be satisfied and perhaps continue in the same vein, but if the objective has not been achieved, the strategy probably should be altered.

In light of these functions, an objective should meet five requirements, summarized by the acronym SMART:

1. *S*pecific
2. *M*easurable
3. *A*mbitious
4. *R*ealistic
5. *T*imed

Specific relates to being precise about what the company is going to achieve.

Measurability means that it is possible to document whether the objective was achieved. The objective therefore should be expressed in measurable variables and preferably be quantitative—expressed in numbers. In practice, objectives often are used that are not quantitative, such as "achieving a high market share," "a reasonable profit," "continuously being able to offer good quality products," and "a good work atmosphere." Although it is not objectionable per se for a company to have qualitative objectives, the company should realize that such objectives cannot play a role in the planning process. At most they serve a motivating function, but even in that role the question remains whether management has achieved the objectives: For example, how does a company know that "a good work atmosphere" exists?

Ambitious means that the objectives should not be set too "low." If the level of aspirations is set too low, it will lead to a reduction in the motivation to perform.

However, the objective should be *realistic*. It should be reasonably possible to achieve it. An objective such as doubling the market share in one year may be challenging and ambitious but is typically not feasible. This leads to the unnecessary situation in which every strategy will in effect "fail." The need to be realistic also has to do with relevance for the person or department for which the objective is defined. That person or department should be able to influence the chosen objective.

Finally, an objective should be defined for a specific *time period*. If this does not happen, it is difficult to determine the moment when it is possible to check whether the objective was achieved. If the planning horizon is longer than one year (e.g., three years), it is prudent to indicate a time line so that interim evaluations are possible. For example, the objective might be: We want to achieve the following market share development with new product X over the next three years: year 1, 10 percent; year 2, 12 percent; year 3, 14 percent.

The acronym SMART is well known and often differently described. For example, the *A* is also used for "achievable" (resembling realistic) and the *R* for "relevant." In addition, other conditions are mentioned, for example, clear, challenging, and customer-focused. We return to the issue of choosing customer-oriented objectives in the next section and in Chapter 12.

In summary, an objective should be quantified, include a time frame, and be ambitious but realistic.

3.1.2 The Balanced Scorecard

In making both decisions (prioritization and value definition), the method of the balanced scorecard as developed by Kaplan and Norton[2] may be helpful. This method means that in joint deliberations involving lower management, middle management, and top management, measurable objectives are developed for four fields: *customer satisfaction, efficiency, innovation,* and *finances*. Case 3-1 describes a company that uses the balanced scorecard. We then review the measures mentioned above.

CASE 3-1
Balanced Scorecard

Many organizations have benefited from the balanced scorecard (BSC) since Robert Kaplan and David Norton introduced the concept in 1992. These organizations excel at implementing Kaplan and Norton's principles of the strategy-focused organization. Hilton, Mobil, and UPS stand out because of the ways they applied the following principle: Make strategy everyone's job. They used a variety of means to apply this principle:

1. Large town meeting–style employee gatherings for executives to provide initial promotion of and education about the BSC in a question-and-answer forum.
2. Inexpensive, broad-based impersonal communiqués such as posters, paycheck stuffers, brochures, newsletters, and intranet postings.
3. Formal and intensive training sessions that target top management and then all employees.

Source: Pforsich, Hugh, "Does Your Scorecard Need a Workshop?" *Strategic Finance* 86(8), p. 31–35.

Financial Goals

Nearly every company sets *financial goals*. Those goals may be defined in terms of profit, gross margin, cash flow, share price, and so on. Some financial measures may be stated in absolute or relative terms, for example, in relation to sales (profit margin) or to invested capital [return on investment (ROI)]. Ultimately, financial measures are the main criteria for judging a marketing plan. For this reason, every marketing plan should be accompanied by a forecast of revenues and profit. In chapter 12 we will provide an example of this.

Setting financial goals, however, is one-sided. Kaplan and Norton state that it is also important to develop goals in relation to the building blocks of, for example, profit. Those building blocks include costs and revenues. Revenues in turn are influenced by customer perceptions of the quality and the degree of innovation of the company. Kaplan and Norton argue that formulating goals related to costs, customer-oriented measures, and innovation will provide a more balanced interpretation of the objectives.

Customer-Oriented Goals

Aside from financial goals, customer-oriented goals may be developed. Such goals are also called *marketing objectives*. They may include the following:

- "Hard" goals such as sales, turnover, and market share.
- More underlying ("softer") goals such as:
  - Customer satisfaction.
  - Customer loyalty or brand loyalty, which is measured on the basis of interviews and/or analyses of data regarding purchasing patterns.
- Perceived quality or other image aspects of the brand: "How does the customer perceive the company's brand and that of competing products?"
- Number and content of complaints.

Customer satisfaction and *customer loyalty* are strongly related but are not identical.[3] The pursuit of customer satisfaction and customer loyalty is receiving a lot of attention; this can be explained by the increased focus on value management. Customer loyalty has two dimensions: a *behavioral dimension* (this could be measured as the share of the brand or the company in the category purchases of the customer: the "market share" of the customer) and an *emotional dimension* (the attitude of the customer toward the brand, which is measured through questionnaires).

Internal Goals

This dimension relates to functioning effectively and efficiently in the internal environment. The goals in this context relate to *efficiency* and the *employees*. Measures for efficiency include the following:

- Turnover in relation to investments.
- Turnover rate.
- Accounts receivable.
- Liquidity.
- Overhead costs.

Measures for employee satisfaction include the following:

- Work atmosphere and morale.
- Personal development.
- Staff turnover.
- Use of sick leave.
- Turnover per employee.

Setting goals for employees is becoming more important in practice. This is related to the insight that customer satisfaction can be achieved only when everyone in the organization, especially the direct-contact staff, operates in a customer-friendly fashion.

Innovation Goals

According to Kaplan and Norton, innovation is the basis for success. Only companies that introduce new products regularly are relatively successful. In this regard, the extent to which a company learns from prior experiences also plays a role. Measures in this regard could be the percentage of successful product introductions, the turnover from new products, and the number of concrete new product plans that are being developed.

Evaluation of the Balanced Scorecard

The essence of the balanced scorecard is that measurable objectives are formulated within each of these categories and that each manager is held responsible for one or more of those objectives. This has the advantages that the planning and control processes are closely linked and that the motivation of managers to achieve the objectives is increased. In addition, the formulation of collective measurable objectives makes an important contribution to increasing *team spirit*. It has been said that the process of setting measurable objectives is the most important tool for turning a group of individuals into a team. The balanced scorecard is therefore an important instrument for the implementation of strategies (see also section 12.2).

However, a problem here is the implementation of the method. It requires a large and very detailed information and control system: Every measure needs to be quantifiable, which means that a large amount of detailed data must be collected both internally and externally. Another problem is flexibility: If it becomes clear that certain objectives (e.g., sales) will not be achieved and this is accepted by management, all measures should be updated again.

The danger of a fully implemented balanced scorecard is that a company will become too *internally focused* instead of being focused on the customers. Especially in organizations that are "naturally" oriented to measuring and accounting (companies in financial services), the control mechanism may receive more attention than the company's ultimate goal: the customer.

Figure 3-1 shows an elaboration of the BSC. In the vision, long-term goals for financial growth, customer satisfaction, costs, and innovation are formulated. If top management finds stimulating customer orientation and brand building important and realizes that this may bring in additional investments, the financial goals can be put somewhat lower and the customer-oriented goals higher. Subsequently, the long-term goals are made more specific for the short term. Thus, "elevating customer satisfaction" is translated into "enhancement of brand image," "elevation of frequency," and "elevation of customer satisfaction." Then, with all of these factors, it is indicated how they should be measured. In this way the enhancement of the brand image is measured by the percentage of people from the target group who associate the brand with the identity characteristic "bold." Finally, the numerical goals are indicated. This is done after consultation between top

FIGURE 3-1   **Example of Balanced Scorecard with Elaboration of Customer Part**

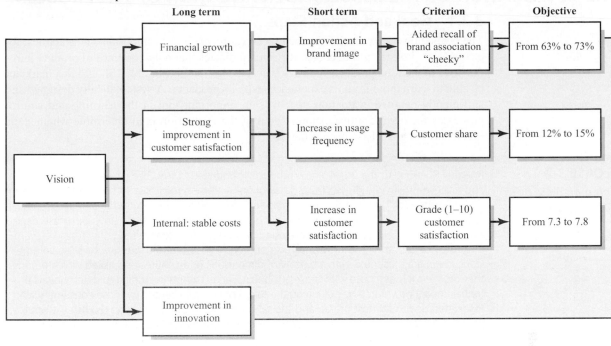

management and middle management, during which the goals are assigned to certain managers.

The importance that is placed on the different areas and the interpretation of that placement will depend on the chosen *value strategy*. With operational excellence, more emphasis will be put on the costs and customer-oriented criteria will be important, though not in detailed form; instead, an aggregated form will be used. With product leadership, innovation is very important, and with customer intimacy, certain client criteria will be very important, for example, how long customers want to remain customers of the company (brand loyalty). Figure 3-2 shows some relationships between value strategy and the four areas of the BSC.

FIGURE 3-2   **Relationship between Value Strategy and Relevance of Objectives**

	Financial Objectives	Customer Objectives	Efficiency Objectives	Innovation Objectives
Operational excellence	Very relevant in short and long term	Especially total measurements	High importance	Less importance
Product leadership	Of importance	Of high importance, attitude, measurements of the perception of innovations	Less important, especially in the long term	Most important
Customer intimacy	Of importance	Of high importance: deaggregated (individual) measurements, lifetime value, etc.	Less important, especially in the long term	Of importance

3.2 EVALUATION OF THE RESULTS: IDENTIFICATION OF THE PROBLEM

3.2.1 Goal and Action Steps

The evaluation of the results obtained so far (*control*) is very important. This applies, for example, to product introductions. Research indicates that only one-third of product introductions in the food products industry succeed. How is this possible? Shouldn't a marketer be able to learn more from its experiences with its products? A systematically designed and sufficiently detailed evaluation system is an important tool in the learning and control processes for organizations. Another goal of the evaluation is to determine whether the previously set goals have been achieved.

CASE 3-2 *Importance of Evaluating Results*

Roughly 80–90% of the 30,000 new products introduced in the US each year eventually fail, and are eventually withdrawn from distribution at tremendous cost to both manufacturers and the trade. All too often the positioning for new products does not address real consumer needs, focusing instead on less-salient benefits that do not ultimately drive purchase decisions. VNU's AC Nielsen BASES developed a method for determining the most relevant attributes of a brand. The new analytical approach links brand attributes to sales volume. Consumers are presented with a battery of dimensions or attributes and asked which brands they most closely associate with those attributes. Each attribute is studied to determine its potential impact on volume by examining the sales volume contributed by those consumers who associated it with the test brand, and the sales volume among those who did not. Attributes with smaller differences in volume contributed by these two groups are generally less important in driving purchase behavior.

Source: AC Nielsen, *Facts, Figures & the Future* (monthly e-publication), March 2003.

In this section we present a systematic approach to the evaluation process, using the sequence of action steps shown in Figure 3-3. Each of the phases is reviewed in the following sections.

3.2.2 Comparison of Results with Objectives

During the evaluation process, those factors (variables) should be examined to indicate which objectives were formulated in an earlier phase. Following the logic of the previous section (balanced scorecard), we note that four categories of objectives may be distinguished:

1. Financial (e.g., profit).
2. Customer-oriented (e.g., sales, customer satisfaction).
3. Internal (efficiency).
4. Innovative.

Objectives may be formulated at the level of:

- The company (or division).
- Brands and products: marketing objectives.
- Elements of the marketing mix.

FIGURE 3-3
Phases in the Process of Evaluating Results

1. Comparison of results with objectives: successful or not?
2. Detailed analysis of customer-oriented variables: diagnosis and identification of the problem.
3. Process evaluation: Was the implementation done well?

FIGURE 3-4
Summary of
Objectives

Level	Company	Brand or Product Marketing	Marketing Mix Elements
Type of goal			
Financial	Yes	Possible	No
Customer-oriented	If company profiles itself to customers	Yes	Yes
Internal	Yes	Possible	No
Innovative	Yes	Possible	No

Relationships exist between the types of objectives and the levels. These relationships are shown in Figure 3-4, which indicates which goals will exist in practice. For each of the objectives that were set in the past, it needs to be determined whether it has been achieved. If there are no measurable objectives available from earlier phases, this phase will be limited to choosing the variables the company wants to analyze. This entails choosing one or more of the categories and levels and the specific variables within them.

3.2.3   Detailed Analysis of Customer-Oriented Variables

A detailed analysis of results is especially useful for the category of customer-oriented measures. The level of detail for the analysis of customer data depends on the availability of data. A large number of data are available for the market for food products. We first discuss analyses that may be performed with these data and then conclude this section with several remarks about branches other than those of daily use goods (fast-moving consumer goods).

For the markets for food products, the following sales developments may be analyzed:

1. *Market* developments: sales developments for the entire market and for market segments (varieties).

2. Analysis of the manufacturer's *brands:*

   • Developments for each brand total and for packaging units.
   • Regional differences in brand developments.

3. *Competitor* analysis:

   • Identification of the largest competitors.
   • Sales developments of competing manufacturers.

4. Position of manufacturer's brands and competitor brands at the various *retail* organizations as well as developments over time (analysis of sales and distribution).

5. Sales developments at retailers with and without *promotions* (provides insight into effects of promotions).

If data from household panels or sales figures for customers from the company's own database are available, additional sales analyses may take place that are disaggregated by target audiences.

These detailed analyses are required because it is difficult to assign causes on the basis of aggregated data. For example, a slight growth in sales may appear not to be an unfavorable result, but it may in reality be a combination of strong growth in region A and stabilization or even a decline in region B. This would lead to the conclusion that there are problems in region B, such as disappointing distribution.

A careful analysis of the market share may also give indications of problems.[4] Is it a case of a decrease or an increase? For a market share analysis, the market definition is crucial (see section 2.2). With a smaller market, the market share automatically becomes "larger."

A useful tool for market share analysis is the *Parfitt-Collins analysis*.[5] This type of analysis divides the market share of a brand into the product of three components:

1. *Degree of penetration.* This is the percentage of households that have ever bought the product.
2. *The percentage of repeat purchases.* This is the degree to which, after the purchase of a brand, the same brand is purchased again.
3. *The usage intensity index.* This is the degree to which buyers of the brand use more or less of the relevant product group.

For example, if these three components assume values of 10 percent (penetration), 40 percent (repeat purchases), and 1.5 (usage intensity), the market share will be 6 percent. The development of these separate components provides better insight into potential problems than does the progress of the market share as a whole.

The Parfitt-Collins analysis often is used in combination with awareness measurements. The following indicators are then relevant: percentage of people who know the brand (*awareness,* spontaneous or assisted), percentage of people who are considering the brand (*consideration set*), percent trial purchases (*trial*), and percent repeat purchases (*repeat*). The size of the various percentages and especially the differences between them form an important starting point for the formulation of objectives for the elements of the marketing mix. For example, a low awareness and a relatively high *trial* lead to the conclusion that the communication should be intensified. A low *trial* may be related to a price that is too high or distribution that is too limited. A low *repeat* is more closely related to the performance of the product itself.

Although less detailed, careful analyses are possible in other areas. The most important data limitation outside the markets for fast-moving consumer goods (FMCGs) is that the data typically are not collected centrally and therefore no solid competitor sales data are available. However, each company may document its own sales in detail and may also perform customer research through research agencies. It is important to ensure that data collection is long-lasting and consistent. As long as a company's own sales data or measures of customer satisfaction are used instead of market share, many organizations are able to measure and analyze results in detail.

In this discussion, customer-oriented measures were analyzed at the level of brands and products. In practice, financial analyses increasingly are performed at the product level. For assortment decisions, it is very important to know to what extent the various products contribute to the profit. The biggest problem in such analyses is the allocation of fixed costs to products. For this purpose, methods in the field of *activity-based costing* (ABC) should be applied. We will not discuss this point further in this book.

3.3   SUMMARY OF THE STRATEGY

Before it can be determined whether a company is moving in the right direction, it should be made clear what the company actually has in mind: What were the intended results (objectives), and what was the intended strategy? This needs to be determined because if the destination and the current course are not known, how can that destination and that course be changed? If a marketing plan that meets all the requirements has been created within the company, answering these questions should be simple.

However, quite often there is no marketing plan or it is too limited or too vague. Issues that are sometimes underdeveloped include objectives (not specific and/or not for the marketing mix, such as communication) and the marketing strategy (choice of target audience and desired positioning). It sometimes is said that strategy often can be determined only afterward as being the "common denominator of a number of relatively consistent actions by a company." In short, companies are often "unconsciously" kept on a certain course. Without making a statement about the desirability of this situation, we believe that the identification of the company's strategy should be a first step in the internal analysis. In effect, this step is comparable to one of the first steps in a competitor analysis, where the objectives and strategies of a competitor are determined through observation.

A strategy may be identified by observing and analyzing the a company's elements of the marketing mix over a longer period. Which product varieties exist? What is our price in relation to that of the competitors? Do we use price promotions? Do we often react to competitors, and if so, to which ones? What is the margin policy toward distributors? What do we communicate to our target audiences? Has the content of our communications been consistent over time? The answers to questions such as these typically make it possible to indicate the marketing strategy: Who do we actually target, and what image do we project?

3.4   COMPETITIVE ADVANTAGE AS AN ANALYTIC MODEL

The most important goal in identifying strengths and weaknesses is to find a potential *competitive advantage*. In a well-known publication, Day and Wensley divided the concept of competitive advantage into three components. The DW model is ideally suited as a framework for completing a strengths-weaknesses analysis for a brand and therefore will be used as an outline in the rest of this chapter.

Figure 3-5 shows the elements of a competitive advantage. A competitive advantage consists of three components:

1. *Sources of advantages:* strengths at the company level that may lead to
2. *Positional advantages* in terms of a higher customer value of the brand or lower costs in comparison to the competitors, which may lead to
3. *Better results* by the brand in terms of, for example, higher brand loyalty, which in turn may lead to a higher market share.

For a company to maintain its competitive advantage, the better results should be used to strengthen the strengths. After all, because the competition does not sit still, the company will lose its competitive advantage if it does nothing.

The three components of a competitive advantage are closely related to the factors that determine success in an industry. In fact, the strengths that lead to better results in an

FIGURE 3-5
**The Elements
of Competitive
Advantage**

Source: Day and Wensley
(1988).

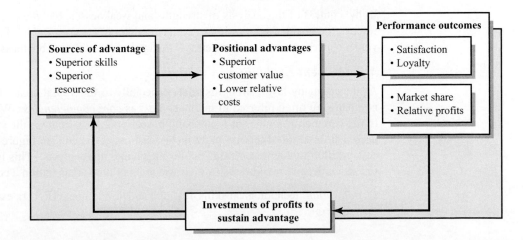

industry may be interpreted as being the factors that determine success. We will now discuss the three components of the competitive advantage in more detail (see Figure 3-5).

Sources of Advantages

A competitive advantage should always be based on the strength of a company. These strengths may arise from better skills (such as strong marketing skills) and better resources (such as financial resources or means of production). A source of advantage does not automatically lead to a positional advantage (the next phase). A company needs to focus on turning a strength into a positional advantage.

Positional Advantages

Day and Wensley mention two possible categories of positional advantages: a higher value for customers and lower relative costs. These two advantages were also mentioned in regard to the framework of Treacy and Wiersema in Chapter 2 (product leadership and operational excellence).

Results

If a company has translated its strengths into positional advantages, the next step is to make this visible (i.e., communicate) to its target audience. It is also important that the competition not react. Otherwise there no longer will be an advantage. This is often a problem: Maintaining an advantage in relation to a competitor is sometimes possible through a patent or through a takeover and/or collaboration, but often it is not possible. If the company succeeds in translating the positional advantage to the target audience, there will be satisfied customers, and that helps build brand loyalty. This in turn will lead to a higher market share and, if the investments are not higher than the additional proceeds, produce higher profits.

3.5   IDENTIFYING COMPETITIVE ADVANTAGES

3.5.1   Overview of Methods

Day and Wensley present various methods that may be helpful in identifying competitive advantages or strengths (along with weaknesses) of the company and the brand. Those authors classify those methods on the basis of two criteria: the element of the competitive advantage to which a method relates and whether the method is competitor-oriented or customer-oriented (Figure 3-6). We discuss the strengths-weaknesses analysis at the company level (sources) and then at the brand level (positional advantages and results).

3.5.2   Analysis of Strengths and Weaknesses at the Organization Level

In the context of the analysis of strengths and weaknesses, by "the organization level" we refer to the visible organization or company that creates the product. For purposes of convenience we ignore here the intermediate level of the strategic business unit (SBU).

Management Evaluation

At the company level, strengths relate especially to functional areas. The core skills of a company are often referred to in this context as *core competencies*.[6] We devoted attention to the core competencies of a company in section 2.1. To analyze the strengths and weaknesses at the level of the company, a checklist may be used [see Figure 3-7, which is from Aaker (2005), who presents this list for the competitor analysis.[7] This list relates to potential strengths and weaknesses of the various functional areas within a company:

- *Innovation:* technological skills, research and development (R&D), expenditures, patents, and so on.

FIGURE 3-6 **Methods for Identifying Competitive Advantages**

Source: Day and Wensley (1988).

	Competition-Oriented	Customer-Oriented
Determining sources: strengths at the company level	• Management evaluation of strengths and weaknesses • Marketing audit • Comparison of the application of resources by competitors	
Indicators of positional advantages: costs or higher customer value of the brand	• Cost analysis of competitors with value chain • Experience curves of competitors	• Analyses of customer attitudes with direct choice models, conjoint analysis, Multi Dimensional Scaling (MDS)
Identifying factors that determine success	• Comparison of successful versus nonsuccessful companies • Analysis of added value in value chain	
Measuring the results of brands	• Market share • Profitability	• Studies of customer satisfaction • Brand loyalty • Relative market shares (in relation to biggest competitor) in segments

- *Production:* added value, capacity, and so on.
- *Financing possibilities:* in the short term, in the long term, possibility for financing through the parent company, and so on.
- *Management and organization:* quality of top management, organization structure, company culture, and so on.
- *Personnel:* motivation, customer orientation.
- *Marketing:* customer orientation of top management and staff, product quality, width of the product line, strength of the advertising agency, and so on.

The strengths and weaknesses mentioned in Figure 3-7 are not independent of one another. For example, the attitude and motivation of the staff strongly depend on the quality of top management and the organization structure, and that motivation also has an influence on the creativity and the innovative capacity of the company, and so on.

CASE 3-3 *Premier Farnell: Strength by personnel*	The distribution company Premier Farnell believes that the only real source of sustainable competitive advantage is talent. With this in mind, it recognizes that it is through training and development programs and effective communications that employees become better equipped to deal with the challenges its business throws at them. To enable its employees to deal with those challenges, it is investing heavily and continually in the training and development of people at all levels of the organization. Training includes a leadership development program for its top 150 leaders, a managerial skills program for first-line managers and supervisors, and an online learning center that is open to all employees for self-paced learning. To keep employees informed about the business, the firm issues a quarterly newsletter and an electronic bulletin about the group's financial performance and conducts monthly face-to-face business briefings. It says there is anecdotal evidence that employees are more enthusiastic and engaged in the future of the organization. **Source:** "Investing in People Award: Premier Farnell," *Electronics Weekly,* November 24, 2004, p. 27.

FIGURE 3-7
**Potential Strengths
and Weaknesses
(Sources of
Advantages) at the
Company Level**

Source: Adapted from Aaker
(2005), p. 68.

Finances and access to capital

- From the operational activities
- From resources available in the short term
- Possibilities for attracting net assets and debt capital
- Willingness of "parent company" to finance

Marketing

- Customer orientation
- Product quality
- Width of the product line
- Segmentation
- Distribution
- Relationship with distributors
- Quality of the sales promotion
- Representatives
- Service

Innovation

- Technical product superiority
- New product possibilities
- Research and development
- Technologies
- Patents

Production

- Cost structure
- Flexibility in production
- Means of production (machines, etc.)
- Access to raw materials
- Vertical integration
- Production capacity

Management and organization

- Quality of top and middle management
- Knowledge of the market
- Company culture
- Organization structure
- Strategic objectives and plans
- Company qualities
- Planning system
- Staff turnover
- Quality of strategic decision making

Staff

- Attitude and motivation of staff
- Customer orientation

We end this section by discussing the following aspects of the measurement of strengths and weaknesses: the analysis of financial strengths, the marketing audit, and the issue of constraints in developing strategies.

Analysis of Financial Strengths

In relation to the analysis of the financial position of the product and the company, the well-known financial ratios may be calculated and analyzed in relation to the following:

- *The liquidity.* This is the extent to which a company can meet its ongoing financial obligations; it is measured, for example, through the current ratio (current assets/current liabilities).
- *The financial structure (solvency).* This is measured, for example, through the debt ratio (debt capital/total invested capital).
- *The activities.* These activities include the turnover rate of the inventory (sales/inventory) and the average credit term of creditors (average amount receivable/sales per 365 days).
- *The profitability.* This is measured, for example, through the gross or net profit margin or the profitability of the net assets (net profit/net assets).

Marketing Audit

Measuring the quality of the marketing department is the subject of a marketing audit: an independent "investigation" of all marketing activities in the company or the SBU. Put differently, the question is whether the company is truly customer-oriented. This involves an evaluation of the following:

- The extent to which a company is operating in a market-oriented fashion: Do clearly formulated objectives and strategies exist? Do the objectives and strategies explicitly take environmental factors into account? Do the strategies actually relate to environmental factors? How do customers perceive the company and its products?
- The knowledge that the company has of the environment: What does the company know about developments in the macroenvironment, about factors related to industry structure, about competitors, and about customers?
- The analysis the company has made of the environment: Is market research being performed? Are predictions being made? Is there a regular strategy evaluation? Is there a marketing information system?

To perform a marketing audit, a checklist can be used. Figure 3-8 shows the *marketing effectiveness review instrument* developed by Kotler.[8] For each question a maximum of two points can be scored; the total score provides an indication of the level of marketing effectiveness.

Constraints

Financial and management strengths may not only present a source of advantage but also serve as constraints within which strategies have to be developed. For example, strategies should be financially feasible and fit within the "culture" of the company. There is little use in recommending a strongly innovative strategy if the company is not ready for such a strategy from an organizational perspective. We will discuss preconditions during strategy selection in section 8.2.

FIGURE 3-8
**Marketing
Effectiveness Review
Instrument**

Source: Philip Kotler,
"From Sales Obsession to
Marketing Effectiveness,"
Harvard Business Review,
November–December 1977,
pp. 67–75. Reprinted with
permission.

Customer Philosophy

1. Does management recognize the importance of designing the company to serve the needs and wants of the chosen markets?
2. Does management develop different offerings and marketing plans for different segments of the market?
3. Does management take a whole marketing system view?

Integrated Marketing Organization

4. Is there high-level marketing integration and control of the major marketing functions?
5. Does marketing management work well with management in research, manufacturing, purchasing, logistics, and finance?
6. How well organized is the new product development process?

Adequate Marketing Information

7. When were the latest market research studies of customers, buying influences, channels, and competitors conducted?
8. How well does management know the sales potential and profitability of different market segments, customers, territories, products, channels, and order sizes?
9. What effort is expended to measure and improve the cost-effectiveness of different marketing expenditures?

Strategic Orientation

10. What is the extent of formal marketing planning?
11. How clear and innovative is the current marketing strategy?
12. What is the extent of contingency thinking and planning?

Operational Efficiency

13. How well is the marketing strategy communicated and implemented?
14. Is management doing an effective job with its marketing resources?
15. Does management show a good capacity to react quickly and effectively to on-the-spot developments?

3.5.3 Strengths and Weaknesses at the Brand Level

Benchmarking

Benchmarking is a comparison of a company's achievements with those of competitors. In effect, this is an attempt to learn from competitors. Three of the methods mentioned by Day and Wensley relate to this topic:

1. Analysis of the *application of resources* by competitors and the results of that application (e.g., a lot of advertising or a little, emphasis on quality or price, emphasis on innovation or not, etc.).
2. *Cost analysis* of the competitors: Which costs and margins are achieved in which phase of the total logistic and production route (value chain)?
3. What does the *experience curve* of the competitors look like? This curve indicates the connection between cumulative sales (what the company has produced and sold until now) and average cost per unit of the product.

A comparison of the resources and costs of a competitor with those of the company provides insight into the company's strength or weakness in that area. For example, if costs are relatively high, it will be difficult to achieve a competitive advantage in this regard.

Customer Analyses

A manager obtains insight into strengths and weaknesses at the brand level largely through the customer analysis. The goal is to know how the customer perceives the brand (attitudes). In the context of value thinking, using a customer perspective in the analysis of strengths and weaknesses is relevant. Whatever the customer thinks is the reality with which the manager has to deal. Performing customer analyses will be discussed in Chapter 4. At this point, suffice it to say that measurements of perceptions are important.

Summary

The most important goal of an internal analysis is to provide insight into the performance and the company's strengths and weaknesses. During the evaluation an inventory is made of which goals are achievable for the different levels and whether the goals that were set have been achieved. The principle of the balanced scorecard states that besides financial goals, other, underlying goals should be measured: criteria on innovation, efficiency, and customer satisfaction. Subsequently, customer-oriented criteria are subjected to a detailed analysis to obtain insight into possible problem areas. Before the determination of strengths and weaknesses, it should be clear what actual marketing strategy (target audience and brand positioning) has been used until now. Subsequently, an analysis of strengths and weaknesses is performed, based on the components of the concept of competitive advantage. This model distinguishes sources of advantages (especially at the organization level), positional advantages (at the brand level), and results (at the brand level). At the organization level, strengths or weaknesses may be identified through evaluation of the strengths and weaknesses in the various functional areas (completing a marketing audit). At the brand level, benchmarking (comparison with competitors) may be helpful. Another source is customer analyses, which have the advantage that the analysis of strengths and weaknesses is by definition performed from the perspective of the customer.

Notes

1. Day, G. S., and R. Wensley (1988), "Assessing Advantage: A Framework for Diagnosing Competitive Superiority," *Journal of Marketing* 52:1–20.
2. Kaplan, R. S., and D. P. Norton (1992), "The Balanced Scorecard—Measures That Drive Performance," *Harvard Business Review*, January–February, pp. 71–79; Kaplan, R. S., and D. P. Norton (1993), "Putting the the Balanced Scorecard to Work," *Harvard Business Review,* September–October, pp. 134–142.
3. Oliver, R. L. (1999), "Whence Customer Loyalty," *Journal of Marketing* 63:33–44.
4. Hulbert, J. M., and M. E. Toy (1977), "A Strategic Framework for Marketing Control," *Journal of Marketing* 41:12–20.
5. Parfitt, J. H., and B. J. K. Collins (1968), "Use of Consumer Panels for Brand-Share Prediction," *Journal of Marketing Research* 5(2):131–145.
6. Prahalad, C. K., and G. Hamel (1990), "The Core Competence of the Corporation," *Harvard Business Review,* May–June, pp. 79–91.
7. Aaker, D. A. (2005), *Strategic Market Management,* 7th ed., Hoboken, NJ, Wiley, p. 72.
8. See Kotler, Ph., and K. L. Keller, (2005), *Marketing Management,* Upper Saddle River, NJ: Pearson Education, pp. 720–721

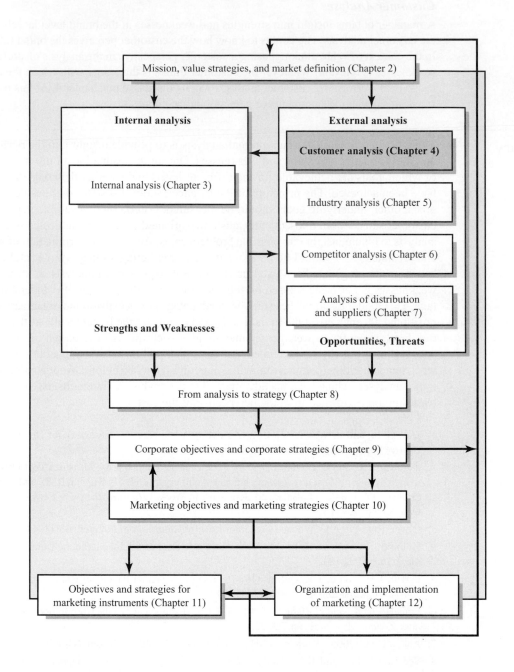

Mission, value strategies, and market definition (Chapter 2)

Internal analysis

External analysis

Customer analysis (Chapter 4)

Internal analysis (Chapter 3)

Industry analysis (Chapter 5)

Competitor analysis (Chapter 6)

Analysis of distribution and suppliers (Chapter 7)

Strengths and Weaknesses

Opportunities, Threats

From analysis to strategy (Chapter 8)

Corporate objectives and corporate strategies (Chapter 9)

Marketing objectives and marketing strategies (Chapter 10)

Objectives and strategies for marketing instruments (Chapter 11)

Organization and implementation of marketing (Chapter 12)

Chapter Four

Customer Analysis

Key Points in This Chapter

- Know the goals of and steps in customer research.
- Know the relevance and process of segmentation.
- Apply basic models in measuring customer perceptions.
- Know the advantages and limitations of qualitative and quantitative research.
- Be able to build sources of individual customer data.
- Be able to trace secondary sources of customer data.

INTRODUCTION

Recent developments in the marketing concept have placed greater emphasis on the idea that the creation of customer value should be a company's central focus. That is the reason the external analysis starts with an analysis of the target audience. This chapter is structured as follows. In section 4.1 the phases in a customer analysis are outlined. Section 4.2 is dedicated to segmentation. Sections 4.3 and 4.4 deal with the analysis of customer perceptions. First several helpful models are described (section 4.3), and then a framework for analyzing customer perceptions is outlined. Section 4.5 briefly reviews individual customer data. Section 4.6 provides some guidelines for primary research, discussing both qualitative and quantitative research. Finally, section 4.7 is dedicated to secondary existing data sources that are available for customer research. The relevance of some of the parts of this chapter depends on the chosen value discipline. For example, for a company competing on customer intimacy, individual customer data (section 4.5) are relatively more important. Segmentation is most relevant for product leadership and in a sense also for operational excellence.

Marketing to Mom

The adoption of digital cameras has been similar to that of other technologies, such as personal computers. When they were introduced, personal computers tended to attract males who were interested in the new technology. However, as personal computers reached the mass market, their sellers emphasized applications for mothers and for families, such as recipe storage, gift card design, and interactive learning games. Digital cameras also changed their focus as they entered the mass market. Now digital camera users are primarily those who are traditionally the most photoactive—women and parents of young children—and so camera manufacturers and retailers are focusing on the ability to use digital cameras to preserve memories.

Typically the keepers of the family photo album, women tend to print a greater proportion of the digital images they save and are more likely to indicate that it is important to make prints of digital images. Households with young children are more likely than average to indicate that it is important to make digital prints. Women and the parents of young children are also more likely to use online photo services and self-service imaging kiosks to receive prints of their pictures. Overall, the photo industry has seen a rise in the i-Mom, a technologically savvy digital camera user who takes full advantage of new technology for sharing images electronically while still making prints for the family photo album.

Digital-Still Camera Sales

During the life cycle of a technology, new products are considered to have reached the mass market after achieving 22 percent penetration (the figures in this case refer to the U.S. market). In 2003, digital cameras surpassed that mark, with 27.7 percent of households owning a digital-still camera, or roughly 33 million households.

In 2003, 51.6 percent of all digital-still cameras purchased were additional cameras. Although the majority are being purchased as an additional camera, a full 18 percent are being purchased as a replacement for a conventional film camera, up from 15.8 percent in 2002. Some consumers are replacing a digital camera with a new one, usually a camera with more options or a greater number of megapixels. In all, 9.1 percent of households purchased a camera for this reason. The rest—21.4 percent—purchased a digital-still camera as their first camera.

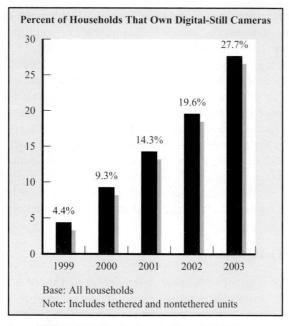

Percent of Households That Own Digital-Still Cameras

Base: All households
Note: Includes tethered and nontethered units

Source: 2000 DMA Digital Imaging Consumer Survey, 2001–2004
PMA Camera/Camcorder, Digital Imaging Surveyes.

Profile of Digital-Still Camera Users

Digital cameras are no longer used and purchased only by the early adopters, who mostly were tech- and gadget-minded men. Although these early adopters have not stopped using digital cameras, they are no longer the primary customers. Women and young parents are increasingly becoming active digital camera users and purchasers.

Thus, marketing digital cameras and related technology to women is one of the keys to the continued success of digital imaging.

Women are the primary picture takers in most households and are generally regarded as the keeper of the family photo album. Women also typically take more pictures than men, no matter what type of camera they use.

In roughly half of all households that own a digital-still camera, a woman is the primary user. In comparison, women are the primary users in 74 percent of households that own 35-mm point-and-shoot cameras and in 70 percent of households that own Advanced Photo System cameras. As digital technology continues to penetrate the mass market, the female-to-male ratio for digital camera users will more closely resemble that of film camera users, who are predominantly female.

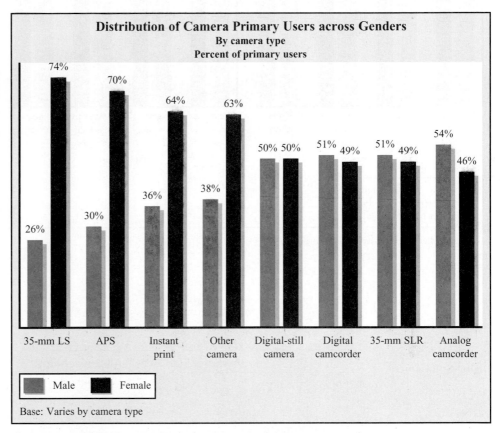

Distribution of Camera Primary Users across Genders
By camera type
Percent of primary users

Base: Varies by camera type

Source: 2004 PMA Camera/Camcorder, Digital Imaging Survey.

Reasons for Using Digital Cameras

Digital-still camera owners are using their cameras in the same way they have always used traditional analog cameras: to preserve memories. This is now the main reason for using a digital-still camera over sending photos by e-mail, which in the past was the main reason for using such a camera. More than 75 percent of households cite preserving memories as their main reason for using a digital-still camera, compared with 65 percent of households that use a digital camera to send photos by e-mail.

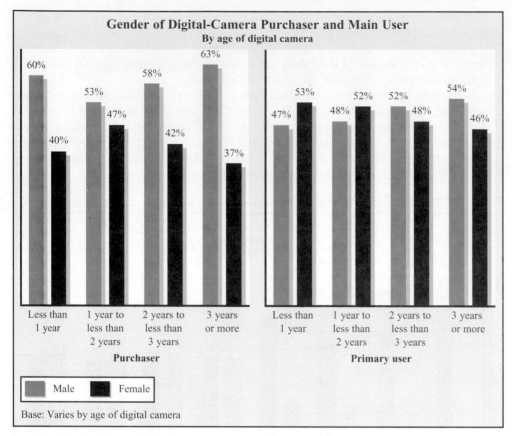

Source: 2004 PMA Camera/Camcorder, Digital Imaging Survey.

Reasons for Using a Digital-Still Camera

Source: 2004 PMA Camera/Camcorder, Digital Imaging Survey.

	All Households	Female	Male
To preserve memories	75%	80%	76%
To send photos by e-mail	65%	71%	65%
To share later with others	65%	70%	65%
For pure enjoyment	56%	57%	56%
Like to take photographs	43%	48%	41%
To use in a computer for hobby	29%	29%	33%
To give away as gifts	17%	17%	17%
To master the skills involved	12%	12%	14%
To create an artistic impression	11%	11%	13%
To use photos for business	10%	10%	12%
To use photos in computer for business	9%	9%	10%
To earn income on a moonlighting job	2%	2%	3%
To earn income for regular job	1%	1%	1%
Other	6%	6%	8%

Notes: Based on households that owned digital-still cameras in 2003. Multiple responses allowed

Digital Printing Habits

In 2003, roughly 63 percent of all households that owned a digital-still camera made prints of some of their digital images. Both men and women had a similar likelihood of printing their digital images. With digital cameras increasingly becoming cheaper, especially those with a lower number of megapixels, they are quickly becoming more affordable for young parents, who tend to take a lot of pictures. These parents want to save memories of their children's births and birthdays, sporting events, and so on, and so they are taking more pictures in general and are more likely to make prints of those images.

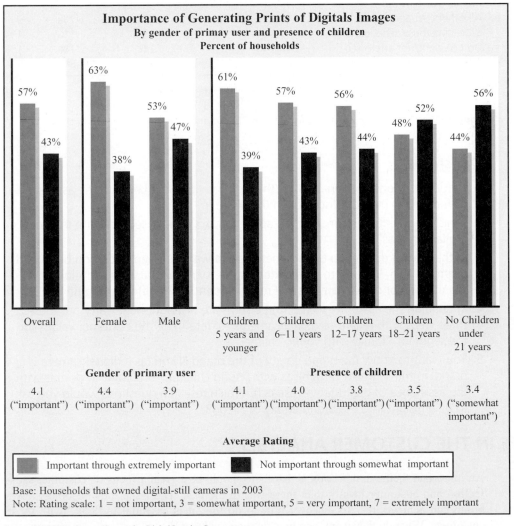

Importance of Generating Prints of Digitals Images
By gender of primay user and presence of children
Percent of households

	Overall	Female	Male	Children 5 years and younger	Children 6–11 years	Children 12–17 years	Children 18–21 years	No Children under 21 years
Important through extremely important	57%	63%	53%	61%	57%	56%	48%	44%
Not important through somewhat important	43%	38%	47%	39%	43%	44%	52%	56%

Gender of primary user / **Presence of children**

| 4.1 ("important") | 4.4 ("important") | 3.9 ("important") | 4.1 ("important") | 4.0 ("important") | 3.8 ("important") | 3.5 ("important") | 3.4 ("somewhat important") |

Average Rating

▨ Important through extremely important   ■ Not important through somewhat important

Base: Households that owned digital-still cameras in 2003
Note: Rating scale: 1 = not important, 3 = somewhat important, 5 = very important, 7 = extremely important

Source: 2004 PMA Camera/Camcorder, Digital Imaging Survey.

What Would Be Required for You to Print More of Your Digital Camera Images?

Source: 2004 PMA Camera/Camcorder, Digital Imaging Survey.

	All Households	Female	Male
If you could print out the images in a high-quality format on your own printer	44%	45%	41%
If printing digital camera images at home becomes easier and less time-consuming than it currently is	41%	42%	40%
If the price of digital processing were comparable to that of processing a roll of film	25%	23%	26%
If the price of digital camera memory cards were lower than it currently is	21%	21%	18%
If you could take digital camera memory cards to any local photo-processing outlet and get them processed into prints just like film	17%	16%	17%
If operation and usage of digital still cameras became more simple	17%	17%	15%
If you could e-mail pictures to the store or upload to the store's Web site for pickup later	15%	17%	12%
If you were not required to leave your digital camera memory card at the store	9%	9%	8%
All other cost comments	7%	7%	9%
More time/busy schedule	1%	1%	1%
Do not want/not interested	1%	1%	1%
All others	7%	8%	5%

Notes: Based on households that owned digital-still cameras in 2003. Multiple responses allowed

Source: Photo Marketing Association International, "Marketing to Mom: Mom in the Digital Era," www.pmai.org.

Questions

1. Carry out a consumer analysis for the digital camera market with the assistance of the six W's method discussed in this chapter.
2. Which segmentation variables are applied in this case to segment the market for digital cameras?
3. In the book a distinction is made between forward segmentation and backward segmentation. Indicate to what extent these two segmentation techniques for the market for digital cameras will result in identical or differing segments.
4. In defining the customer values, three steps are distinguished. Carry out these three steps with regard to digital cameras to determine the customer values for the segment "family with young children."
5. You want to know the brand equity of the brand Nikon (as a digital camera brand) in the segment of families with young children. You want to do this with the assistance of quantitative research. Which research questions would you ask to gain insight into the brand equity of Nikon?

4.1 PHASES IN THE CUSTOMER ANALYSIS

An important theme in this book is that there should be a greater focus on customer satisfaction and customer loyalty than there was in the past. The issue thus becomes how a brand can achieve this. To discover how to do this, it is essential to "talk" with those customers. What do they want, and how do they see "you"?

This chapter provides a structure for conducting a customer analysis. A customer analysis ("market research") is not the only source for insight into customers' wishes. The largest problem in market research is that it is difficult for people to indicate what they might like in the future. People typically underestimate their future needs. Data from a customer analysis therefore should not be used as a direct guideline for action but should be interpreted and subsequently combined with other sources. With that in mind, we now consider what may be called the most important phase of the situation analysis.

Customer research can be used for different purposes. A distinction often is based on the type of research[1]:

- *Exploratory:* qualitative research.
- *Descriptive:* quantitative research (surveys and observation).
- *Causal:* experiments.

This distinction is clear but does not indicate with what kind of data are required.

Another way to subdivide the customer analysis is by the kind of information sought, for example, the six W's[2]:

1. *Who* are our current and potential customers?
2. *What* do our customers do with our products (use situations)?
3. *Where* do our customers purchase our products?
4. *When* do our customers purchase our products?
5. *Why* and how do our customers choose our products (e.g., perception of brands and products and needs)?
6. *Why* do potential customers *not* purchase our products?

This division is very useful, but it is limited by the fact that no distinction is made between the different strategic goals of the customer analysis. A customer analysis has various potential usage situations, and each situation requires that different information be collected.

There are four usage situations or goals of the customer analysis:

1. Use for segmentation and choice of the target market (Chapter 10).
2. Use as a basis for strengths and weaknesses research (Chapter 3) and positioning decisions (Chapter 10).
3. Use to check achieved results (Chapter 3) and to measure the effects of marketing mix elements (Chapter 11).
4. Use to identify competitors (Chapter 6).

Each of these goals requires specific information (the division by questions) and a specific research approach (the division by research method). Figure 4-1 summarizes this. The first three of these goals are discussed in detail in this chapter.

4.2 SEGMENTATION RESEARCH

A *segment* is a group of potential customers. Research into segments relates to the first dimension of the marketing strategy: the choice of the target market (*targeting*). A group of customers may be considered a segment if the following four conditions are met:

1. *Homogeneity/heterogeneity.* Within a segment the response to a marketing activity should be as homogeneous as possible, and between segments it should be as heterogeneous as possible.

FIGURE 4-1   **Goals of the Customer Analysis**

Goal of Customer Analysis Is Information for	Required Data from Primary Research	Type of Research	Research Discussed in
1. Segmentation and choice of target market	Who, what, where, when, why	Quantitative	Section 4.2
2. Positioning and strengths and weaknesses	Value hierarchy and customer satisfaction: why, why not?	Qualitative and quantitative	Sections 4.3 and 4.4
3. Analysis of results (control) and research on effects	Why, why not, e.g., brand awareness, brand associations, customer satisfaction	Quantitative	Sections 4.3, 4.4, and 11.6
4. Competitor analysis	Who, what, why, why not: chosen brand and competitors	Quantitative	Section 4.2

2. *Sufficient size.* Segments that are so small that profitable exploitation is impossible are not meaningful.

3. *Measurable/identifiable.* The customers in segments should be identified in one way or another so that results and strategies can be linked to concretely described segments. In addition, without identification it is difficult to estimate the size of a segment.

4. *Accessible.* To use the elements of the marketing mix, especially distribution and promotion, it is essential that the segment be accessible.

Only quantitative research can provide insight into these conditions. This type of research involves collecting a large quantity of data from a large number of people and then attempting to identify groups of consumers that meet these requirements (segments).

In this process, the segmentation analysis is divided into three phases:

1. *Collection of the data.* First, tools such as in-depth interviews and group discussions with customers are used to obtain as much insight as possible into the motivations, attitudes, and behavior of the customers. With this knowledge, a questionnaire is created that is administered to a large group of customers. For consumer markets, this process has to include data collection about three categories of segmentation variables: personal (geographic, demographic, psychographic), product behavior and brand attitude. (Figure 4-2). Figure 4-3 includes an overview of segmentation variables for business markets (industrial markets).

The data mentioned in Figures 4-2 and 4-3 may be considered the minimum background data collected from customers.

2. *Analysis of the data.* Based on the collected data, segments should be deduced. This process can occur in principle in two ways (Figure 4-4):

   a. *Forward segmentation (a priori segmentation).* Customers are classified on the basis of personal characteristics (for consumer markets, the first category of variables mentioned in Figure 4-2); subsequently, differences between groups in terms of product and brand (behavioral) characteristics are examined.

   b. *Backward segmentation (segmentation based on behavioral differences).* This process starts with groups of customers that demonstrate different behavior in relation to the product or brand variables for example by having different preferences (benefits); subsequently, a search is made for general (personal) characteristics that can be used to describe the groups.

FIGURE 4-2
Most Important
Segmentation
Variables for
Consumer Markets[3]

Category	Sub Category	Variables
A. Personal (general)	1. Geographic data	• Region • Province, municipality • Degree of urbanization
	2. Demographic data/ socio-economic data	• Age • Gender • Family size • Family phase • Religion • Race • Income • Profession • Education • Social status
	3. Psychographic data	• Lifestyle (Activities, Interests, Opinions) • Personality • General values
B. Product (category)	1. Benefits	• Benefits sought = product-specific values • Importance of product characteristics (price, quality, taste etc.)
	2. Purchasing behavior	• Role in decision-making process (Initiator, Influencer, Decision Maker) • Buying process • Buying/Shopping behavior
	3. Usage behavior	• User status • Usage situations • Values in usage situations • Usage amount (light, medium, heavy users)
C. Brand	1. Brand awareness and attitude	• Towards own brand: —stage in purchasing process (awareness, attitude, intention, purchase) • Towards competitive brands —evoked set
	2. Brand associations (perceptions)	• Own brand —strength —relevance —uniqueness • Competitors' brands —considerations
	3. Brand loyalty	• Behavior —customer share (share of wallet) —switching behavior • Emotional —recommendation: ambassador, fan

FIGURE 4-3
Segmentation
Variables for
Business Markets

Source: Bonoma, T.V., B.P.
Shapiro (1983), Segmenting
the industrial market,
Lexington, MA: Lexington
books.

Category	Variables
Demographic	• Industry sector • Company size • Location
Usage variables	• Technology (required technology at the customer level) • Usage status (heavy user, light user, none) • Customer capacities (need for service)
Purchasing approach	• Purchasing organization (centralized, decentralized) • Power structure (technically oriented, financial, etc.) • Types of relationships (strong, weak) • Purchasing policy (leasing, service, systems, etc.) • Purchasing criteria (quality, service, price, etc.)
Situation-related factors	• Urgency of delivery • Applications of delivered product • Size of order
Personal characteristics	• Degree of similarity to supplier • Risk attitude • Supplier loyalty

FIGURE 4-4
Segmentation
Approaches

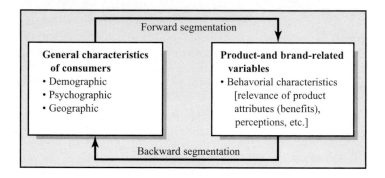

The behavior analysis is often based on differences in the importance customers attach to certain product attributes (benefits). This form of segmentation therefore is called *benefit segmentation*. The major advantage of benefit segmentation is that if segments are discovered, at a minimum the condition of homogeneity/heterogeneity has been met: There is a direct relationship to purchasing behavior. This means that different products and varieties can be developed for the different benefit segments. Because of this, benefit segmentation increasingly is used in practice.

Typically, two analysis techniques are used for benefit segmentation: factor analysis to reduce the data set to a smaller number of factors and then cluster analysis to create segments that are as differentiated from one another as possible. In doing this, the researcher should indicate the "behavior" variables on which the search for a cluster should be based.

3. *Description of the segments.* Subsequently, a profile is created for each discovered segment, based on the scores for the examined variables. The focus is on identifying the most distinguishing characteristics of the segments, and for identification

purposes, each segment is given a name. Since markets change, the segmentation phases should be repeated regularly. Case 4-1 contains an example of segmentation research. Once target markets have been defined, media are used to reach a certain target market.

CASE 4-1 *Segmentation* *Applying* *Psychographics:* *The VALS Tool*	VALS is a marketing and consulting tool that helps businesses worldwide develop and execute effective strategies. The VALS system identifies current and future opportunities by segmenting the consumer marketplace on the basis of the personality traits that drive consumer behavior. The main dimensions of the segmentation framework are primary motivation and resources. Consumers are inspired by one of three primary motivations: ideals, achievement, and self-expression. Consumers who are motivated primarily by ideals are guided by knowledge and principles. Consumers who are motivated primarily by achievement look for products and services that demonstrate success to their peers. Consumers who are motivated primarily by self-expression desire social or physical activity, variety, and risk. Different levels of resources enhance or constrain a person's expression of his or her primary motivation. Based on this logic, VALS places U.S. adult consumers into one of eight segments: innovators, thinkers, achievers, experiencers, believers, strivers, makers, and survivors. **Source:** SRI Consulting Business Intelligence (SRIC-BI); www.sric-bi.com/VALS.

Segmentation is an important subject in marketing literature not only because of its strategic importance but also because it is a quantitative subject on which a lot of empirical research can be carried out. At this stage we will not elaborate on the statistical methods of segmentation, but these methods are becoming more "flexible" all the time. Using these methods, it can be taken into account that one person ends up not in one but in two segments. This links up with the fact that people can have different preferences at different moments. Also, there are more methods all the time that enable segmentation in spite of missing data, for example, when people do not fill out a questionnaire completely.

A general finding appears to be that segmenting from product-connected variables produces better results than does segmenting from the background characteristics of people, such as age. The reasons for this include the following:

- People's behavior is becoming less "predictable."
- In each user situation, the preferences of people can differ strongly.
- Within households, individual members can have very different preferences.

The backward segmentation method should be given preference. In all cases it is necessary to collect data on behavioral and background characteristics of a large number of potential customers.

4.3 MODELS OF CUSTOMER PERCEPTIONS

Before a setup for research on customer wishes can be established, it is important to have an idea of what customer wishes in fact are. Three models are suitable here: the *multiattribute attitude model,* the middle-target *chain of meanings,* and, for service markets, the *SERVQUAL model.* These three simple models should be viewed as "conceptual models" that can be the basis for a research method. A comprehensive model does not exist. Each manager has to choose for himself or herself which aspects he or she finds important to research.

FIGURE 4-5
The Multiattribute
Attitude Model

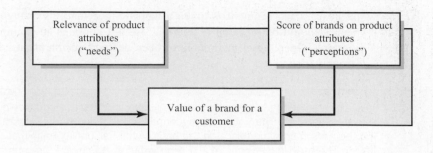

4.3.1 Multi-Attribute Attitude Model

The name of the *multiattribute attitude model* makes it seem more complex than it actually is (see Figure 4-5): This model just shows that the value (the "use") a customer extracts from a product is determined by the *importance* that customer attaches to certain product characteristics (for example, he or she attaches a lot of value to the price) and the *score* of a brand on those characteristics (a high price therefore leads to little "use"). The name of the model means that a combination of *many characteristics* leads to a total judgment (*attitude*). Viewed "mathematically," it could be said that if the importance of all characteristics is combined (multiplied) with the scores on all those characteristics, some sort of total use can be obtained. Figure 4-6 shows a calculation example. The total mark ("use") shop A receives from the customer is 6.7.

FIGURE 4-6
Calculation
Example with the
Multiattribute
Attitude Model

Characteristic	Importance (%)	Score for Shop A (mark)	Importance × Score
Price level	40	7	2.8
Variety of selection	20	8	1.6
Friendliness of staff	20	5	1.0
Freshness of products	10	6	0.6
Cleanliness of shop	10	7	0.7
Total	100		6.7

The multiattribute attitude model assumes that a product can be classified into separate characteristics and that it is possible to name those characteristics. In practice this is not always easy. Emotional ("brand") characteristics are especially difficult to group in the model. Furthermore, the importance people give to characteristics is strongly linked with their deeper motives and with the user situation. For buying daily consumer goods, for example, a customer may find the price more important than he or she does when doing Christmas shopping.

4.3.2 Model of Customer Value

Both limitations are taken into account in the model of the product characteristics shown in Figure 4-7. The model is a combination of two other models that have a lot in common: the goal-means chain of meanings ("means-end chain") and the customer value model. Both names for the model shown in Figure 4-7 can be used.

The essence of the model is that it is important to know the *motivation* of people to buy products. For instance, people buy a yogurt dessert because of its low fat content (attribute); they find that important because it keeps them slim (consequence); in turn, that is important

FIGURE 4-7
Model of Customer
Value, or Means-End
Chain

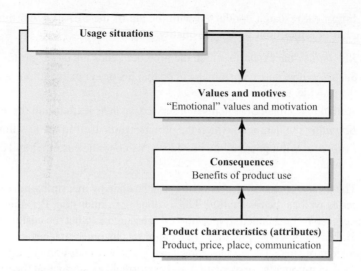

because it makes them appreciated in their environment (value or motivation). The same dessert may be bought in the summer because of its fresh taste. In that case there is a difference in motivation, depending on the season. The higher values are often the basis for adding emotional characteristics to the brand by means of communication. The customer value model is hierarchical. "Lower" benefits serve to satisfy "higher" goals.

4.3.3 SERVQUAL Model

When measured in terms of product value, in many countries services represent a larger category than do physical products. The model discussed above can also be used in services contexts. Nonetheless, a well-known model of *service quality,*[4] has been developed. The *SERVQUAL (service quality)* model is shown in Figure 4-8.

The central issue in using this model is that the quality of service is defined as the difference between the expected service and the realized service. When there is a gap between the two, there is not optimum quality. The idea of this model is to give customers what they want. When there is a gap, the gap can have different reasons. The model explores this by showing a number of other (not shown in Figure 4-8) gaps, such as the difference between what management thinks the customer wants and what the customer really wants.

FIGURE 4-8
Model of Service
Quality: SERVQUAL

Source: Parasuraman,
Zeithaml and Berry (1985).

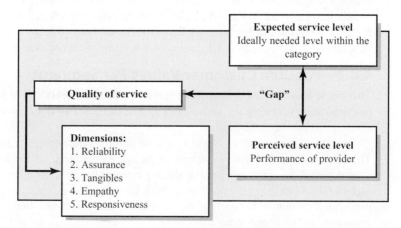

Empirical research conducted with the aid of the SERVQUAL model has identified a number of dimensions of service quality:

1. *Reliability:* the extent to which the provider keeps his or her promises.
2. *Security:* how sure a customer can be that his or her expectations are being met (trust in the provider).
3. *Tangibility:* all tangible items of a service, such as leaflets and the atmosphere in a bank.
4. *Empathy:* the degree to which the provider puts itself in the position of the customer.
5. *Response:* willingness of the provider to listen to the customer and do what the customer wants.

The measurement of service quality can be done by measuring the *expectation* of the customer as well as the *realization*. This is done per dimension. Per dimension, different subaspects can be questioned. Expectation is measured as what the customer would *ideally* want apart from the specific provider; for example, a customer attaches great value to the fact that a provider of financial services shows that it knows the customer (aspect of empathy).

Both components—expectation and performance—show that the model originates from the multiattribute attitude model in that a *demand* (importance in general in the category) and a *score* (of the specific brand) are identified.

Finally, one must take into consideration the fact that the demands people have toward brands and the performance of those brands are not separated. The more customers have frequent and long-term good experiences, the more their demands increase. This is a difficult issue because it means that the wishes of customers are never stable and that customers constantly have to be "taught" what they can and cannot expect. This also stresses the importance of innovation. At a certain moment people get used to something new, and then something else that is new has to be presented to them.

4.4 RESEARCH INTO CUSTOMER VALUES

4.4.1 Introduction

The classic way to do a needs assessment is to ask customers the following:

- What they consider important: the importance of product characteristics.
- How well the various brands meet those needs: how they score on the desired characteristics.

Such research, which often is done quantitatively, is implicitly based on the multiattribute attitude model described above. In this section we sketch an action plan to achieve insight into customer values while taking into account the shortcomings mentioned above.[5] Figure 4-9 represents the phases of this plan. The analysis of target audiences was discussed in section 4.2. In sections 4.4.2 through 4.4.4, the other three phases will be discussed.

4.4.2 Possible Customer Values Per Segment

This phase serves to uncover as many relevant values as possible. The research in this phase is explorative (drawing up an inventory) and therefore is done in a qualitative manner. Three steps can be distinguished.

First, the most important *usage situations* in the product category should be determined. This may include different locations (at home, recreational, at work), different points in time during a day, different periods during the year (holidays, vacation), differences in social environment (alone, with family, with visitors), and so on. The following phases are performed separately for each of the most important usage situations. For example, beer is consumed at home and in bars.

FIGURE 4-9
Structure for
Research on
Customer Values

Phases	Components
1. Determination of target audiences (see also section 4.2)	
2. Determination of possible values per target audience (qualitative research)	• Usage situations: Where and when is the product category used? • General values per usage situation: What is important in that situation, and why are you in that situation? • Product-specific values per usage situation: What is important in those cases in the product category?
3. Determination of importance of values(qualitative research)	• Importance of general values (general needs): How important is . . . ? • Importance of product-specific values (product-specific needs): How important is . . . ?
4. Performance of brands regarding values (consequences, benefits) and distinctiveness (qualitative and quantitative)	• Satisfaction: perceptions of brand performances, reasons why or why not Scores and distinctiveness regarding general values: To what extent is brand X a brand that possesses the abstract characteristic . . . ? • To what extent is that a distinguishing feature? • Scores and distinctiveness regarding product-specific values: To what extent is brand X a brand that possesses the tangible characteristic . . . ? To what extent is that a distinguishing feature?

The second step is to gain insight into what people find important in a general sense in the usage situation: the *general values*. For example, one might ask: What do you consider important in going out or in a the café? Quietness, chatting with friends (no noise, disco)? The third step involves looking for the consumers' *product-specific values,* in other words, which product characteristics consumers consider important in that situation.

CASE 4-2
Needs of a Specific Target Market

The Latino Minority

With around 39 million people, Latinos have overtaken African Americans as the largest ethnic minority in the United States. This has attracted the attention of politicians and academics, but for the most part American businesses have been slow to react. One reason in the past may have been the belief that Latinos were the poorest segment of the population and could be ignored as consumers—a view increasingly at odds with the data. The Latino population not only is the largest minority, it is growing, and Latinos are getting richer. Among American firms, only banks seem to have awakened to this potential. That has left a huge opportunity for Mexican firms, in particular, to go north to find the growth that eludes them in a stagnant home market. Mexican television program makers have an edge over their rivals because of the comparatively accentless brand of Spanish that Mexicans speak. The Mexican-American population also seems to be happiest with its own brands of food and drink.

Source: "Opportunity knocks," *The Economist,* August 24, 2004, p. 59.

The steps may be completed by using separate questions, but it is also possible to start from product-specific values to gain insight into general values. In doing this, a company attempts to determine the entire customer value hierarchy ("ladder") at once. A well-known technique that can be used for this purpose is *laddering*. This is a technique that completes the value hierarchy from the bottom to the top by continually asking the customer for the meaning of what he or she considers important: Why do you find that important, and so on? To discover as many "ladders" as possible, it is advisable to review different usage situations explicitly with the customer (*grand tour technique*).

The only issue that is not clarified with qualitative research is the *extent* to which various phenomena play a role. For this purpose, the following phases should be completed.

4.4.3 Importance of Customer Values and Conjoint Analysis

The importance a customer attaches to a certain value makes a statement about that customer's needs. What does he or she want? This question is directly relevant to identifying a sustainable competitive advantage. A competitive advantage can be obtained from a characteristic that customers consider important. A characteristic that is perceived to be important may be a factor that determines success in a market.

To determine the importance of values, it is necessary to distinguish between general values and product-specific values. Product-specific values are related to desired consequences (*benefits*) of product characteristics. For example, one might ask: How important is peace and quiet to you when you are going out (general value)? and How important is it that the café you visit uses your preferred brand (product-specific value)?

Direct Methods

One way to research the importance of dimensions is to ask directly about that importance (with or without a scale technique, e.g., a four-point scale ranging from very important to unimportant). However, a direct method of asking about importance has two disadvantages. One is that customers often indicate that they consider everything important and that they are not forced to take the interaction between product characteristics into account (e.g., quality and price). The second disadvantage is that customers have a tendency to think concretely: Tangible product characteristics are often mentioned as being important, whereas in reality abstract image aspects are often decisive. Therefore, it may be better to use indirect methods such as conjoint analysis.

Conjoint Analysis

Conjoint analysis is a method that is used to define the *importance* of product characteristics. This does not take place by asking for it but by deducing it from the choices consumers make in a simply designed experiment. Figure 4-10 shows how this process works. The basis is that a product consists of a bundle of characteristics. For example, the value (the "use") of a cake for a person is defined by five characteristics (step 1). From each of those characteristics possible levels, which are realistic in practice, are defined for the experiment (step 2), for example, the taste (nice, neutral), the price ($1 or $2), the color (yellow or brown), the freshness (fresh or not fresh), and the brand name (Hostess or Twinkies). Through conjoint measuring a manager tries to find out how important these characteristics are. Then new characteristics can be included. When the analyses have included a large number of people, the differences between groups of consumers can be viewed (benefit segmentation).

Subsequently, a number of so-called products are defined, and every product is defined as a combination of characteristics (step 3: "profiles"). For example, it may be determined that cake 1 has a nice taste, has a high price, is brown, is not fresh, and is from Hostess, whereas cake 2 is medium tasty, has a low price, is yellow, is fresh, and is from Twinkies. This is done until a certain amount, for example, 18 cakes, has been categorized. It is not necessary to use all possible combinations (in the example, these could amount to 32), but

FIGURE 4-10
Structure of Conjoint Analysis

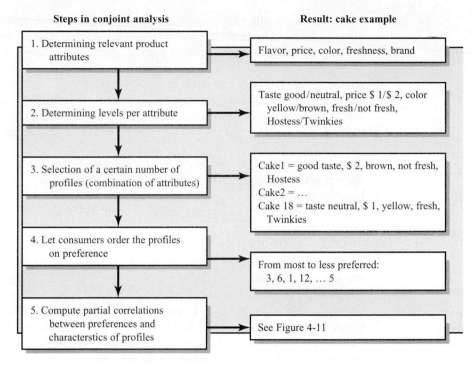

Steps in conjoint analysis | Result: cake example

1. Determining relevant product attributes → Flavor, price, color, freshness, brand

2. Determining levels per attribute → Taste good/neutral, price $ 1/$ 2, color yellow/brown, fresh/not fresh, Hostess/Twinkies

3. Selection of a certain number of profiles (combination of attributes) → Cake1 = good taste, $ 2, brown, not fresh, Hostess
Cake2 = …
Cake 18 = taste neutral, $ 1, yellow, fresh, Twinkies

4. Let consumers order the profiles on preference → From most to less preferred: 3, 6, 1, 12, … 5

5. Compute partial correlations between preferences and characterstics of profiles → See Figure 4-11

with the help of schemes developed especially for this purpose, a selection can be made.[6] The only thing the consumer has to do is sort the cakes according to his or her preference (step 4). For this purpose it can be useful to place a card on every product, with or without a suitable image. The consumer then can sort the cards. Using statistical software (for example SPSS Statistical Package for the Social Sciences) the preferences of respondents are statistically explained by the structure of the profiles. Per respondent (or group of respondents), it is then calculated how important the consumer found each of the characteristics, for example, taste 35 percent, price 20 percent, color 5 percent, freshness 10 percent, brand 30 percent (for a possible outcome, see Figure 4-11). Data for larger groups of consumers can be used for segmentation, product decisions, and price decisions.

The advantages of conjoint analysis are the simple questioning (the choice process of customers is imitated) and the fact that the interaction between characteristics is included (respondents have to consider implicitly which characteristics they consider the most important). Conjoint analysis is used extensively in both marketing theory and practice, with a wide range of applications.[7]

FIGURE 4-11 **Possible Result of Conjoint Analysis, Example Cake for One Respondent**

	Taste		Price		Color		Freshness		Brand Name	
	Level	**Score**	**Level**	**Score**	**Level**	**Score**	**Level**	**Score**	**Level**	**Score**
	Good	60*	$1	40	Yellow	10	Fresh	25	Hostess	30
	Neutral	10	$2	10	Brown	5	Not fresh	15	Twinkies	15
Difference between highest and lowest scores	50		30		5		10		15	
Importance	45%†		27%		5%		9%		14%	

*Means that level "tastes good" of attribute "taste" delivers a score of 60. The measurement scale is not of vital importance; what counts are the relative differences between levels.
†Computed as 50 divided by the sum of all differences (110).

The results of either the conjoint analysis or the direct needs assessment are appropriate for *segmentation*. After all, this phase creates insight into what customers consider important, and that is an excellent basis for segmentation (see section 4.2).

In choosing respondents, the question is whether only existing customers should be researched or whether potential ones should be included. An argument can be made for either choice. Researching only the preferences of existing customers fits with the pursuit of customer relations. However, a brand cannot ignore the fact that new customers need to be attracted on an ongoing basis, and so research into potential customers is also important.

Researching existing customers has the advantage that customer preferences can be integrated into a client information system. When a client has been a client for a while, the importance of values can be deduced from the purchasing behavior of users. Section 4.5 will discuss the specific problems associated with collecting individual client data.

4.4.4 Brand Perceptions and Multidimensional Scaling

How well or how badly do we provide the desired customer values? This question may be researched in a qualitative manner but also in a quantitative manner: How do we score and how does the competition score on characteristics and benefits? In effect this involves measuring brand perceptions. Here a comparison is appropriate with the measurement of what Keller calls brand equity. According to Keller, brand awareness and brand associations are the sources of brand equity.[8] These sources should lead to results such as satisfaction, brand loyalty, and market. To know whether a brand is successful and why, it is therefore important to measure the sources and results of brand equity. The measurement of brand associations can be done through qualitative or quantitative methods.

Qualitative methods are:

- The *direct association* method: With what do you associate brand A?
- *Projective techniques*: indirect methods such as indicating matching photographs or describing the brand as a person with a character. This method is suitable for measuring the psychosocial (abstract) characteristics of a brand and offers important information for the purpose of choosing brand positioning.

Another goal of qualitative analysis is to gain insight into the satisfaction of consumers and especially into the underlying causes of the extent of that satisfaction. Talking with consumers about what they think of the brand and why is often an eye-opener for managers. As will be explained in section 4.6, qualitative research does not require a great number of respondents to obtain a fairly complete picture of the thoughts and feelings of customers (and noncustomers). In cases in which a company decides to not perform quantitative research, qualitative research becomes even more useful and can be used separately for making strategic decisions.

Qualitative methods can also be divided into direct and indirect methods. Direct methods use, for example, statements for which a respondent is asked to indicate on a ranking scale the extent to which he or she agrees. Ranking scales such as five-point scales ranging from completely disagree through completely agree that force the respondent to choose a position are called *Likert scales*. Keller distinguishes three characteristics of brand associations: strength, relevance, and uniqueness.[9] Each of these three characteristics can be measured (Figure 4-12). Figure 4-12 also indicates how brand loyalty can be measured.

Brand Awareness

Measuring spontaneous brand awareness can be done only in verbal interviews. Assisted awareness can be measured by asking in different ways the extent to which a respondent knows the brand.

FIGURE 4-12
Measuring the
Sources and Results
of Brand Equity

Variable	Example Question
Brand awareness	
• Top-of-mind awareness (TOMA)	Name the first . . . brand you can think of. Name as many other brands as you are aware of.
• Spontaneous	I know what brand A looks like. Agree or disagree I can easily remember several characteristics of brand A.
• Aided	Agree or disagree
Brand associations	
• Strength	How well do you think the following statement fits with brand A? Brand A is young. Does not fit at all . . . Fits very well.
• Relevance	How important is it to you whether a brand in category X is young? Unimportant . . . Very important
• Uniqueness	To what extent do you think the young character of brand A is distinct from other brands? Not differentiated . . . Very differentiated
Brand loyalty	
• Behavioral component	Customer share: market share with the customer
• Emotional component	I consider myself to have brand loyalty for brand A. Agree . . . Disagree Brand A is my first choice. Agree . . . Disagree I recommend brand A to my friends Agree . . . Disagree

Brand Associations

The *strength* of a specific association may be measured for individual respondents and for an entire group. At the individual level, a question may be asked about how well an aspect fits with a brand, or a statement can be presented for which the respondent needs to indicate on a scale the extent to which he or she agrees with it. The percentage of people who find a characteristic suitable is also a measure of the strength of an association.

The *relevance* of a characteristic was discussed in section 4.4.3. Questions may be asked about its importance. The *distinctiveness* of an association may be examined directly. In addition, associations with the most important competitor may be asked about, after which the researcher can compare the brands' scores with the competitors' scores.

Brand Loyalty

This measure is receiving a lot of attention in the literature because it fits well with the pursuit of real customer satisfaction. It is generally advisable to measure two dimensions in gauging brand loyalty: a *behavioral* component and an *emotional* component.[10] The behavioral component may be measured through the customer share: the share of the customer category purchases that is related to the brand, in other words, the market share at the client level. The emotional component can be measured through statements such as "I recommend brand A to my friends."

Indirect quantitative methods for measuring brand perceptions are used for *perceptual mapping*. Perceptual maps are, especially in the case of positioning and communication decisions,

FIGURE 4-13
Example of Multidimensional Scaling: Joint Space with Attributes, Tobacco Brands

Source: Zwart (1992)[11].

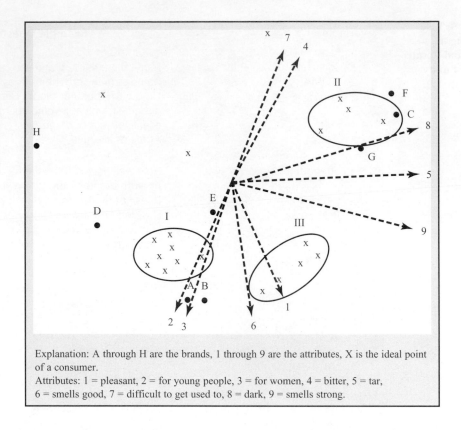

Explanation: A through H are the brands, 1 through 9 are the attributes, X is the ideal point of a consumer.
Attributes: 1 = pleasant, 2 = for young people, 3 = for women, 4 = bitter, 5 = tar, 6 = smells good, 7 = difficult to get used to, 8 = dark, 9 = smells strong.

important and easily understood research methods. In this technique, brands are placed in a coordinate system in which the axes represent, for example, conservative/dynamic, tough/feminine, or other brand personality characteristics (see the overview of brand values in section 10.3). Figure 4-13 includes an example. Sometimes groups of consumers (segments) are placed in such maps. A valid method for obtaining such perceptual maps is the technique of *multidimensional scaling (MDS)*. In MDS, brands, characteristics, and ideal points (wishes) of users are conveniently arranged in one figure through the use of a statistical method that employs simple questions for respondents to answer. Figure 4-13 includes an example of a "*joint space*" for the market for rolling tobacco. The figure demonstrates that tobacco brands C and F score the highest on the characteristic of femininity, whereas brand A has a young and feminine image. The image of brand A is quite similar to that of B. If brand A wants to grow at the expense of B, it should position itself differently, for example, more "cozy" (in the direction of characteristic 1). An advantage of this strategy is that there is a segment of smokers that desires a brand that is strong and cozy (segment III), but no such brand exists.

MDS has several important advantages as a research method. First, the results of MDS (graphic representations of the positions of brands) are easily understood, making it an excellent *communication tool* for positioning decisions. Second, MDS makes it possible to use *more than two dimensions*. The dimensions on which people judge a brand are placed in the figure as vectors. Third, the positions of the brands in the coordinate system space are "hard"; that is, they have been calculated according to a *quantitative method*. This differentiates MDS from many of the other qualitative methods used to place brands in spaces. Fourth, the method of data collection in MDS is *true to life*: Respondents are asked to compare brands as a whole with each other just as they do in a shop, and only afterward are the characteristics placed in the figure. This means that MDS is an indirect method in which the respondents do not have to indicate what they consider important, yet this can be

FIGURE 4-14
Brand Images of Detergent Brands

Source: Leeflang (2003)[12].

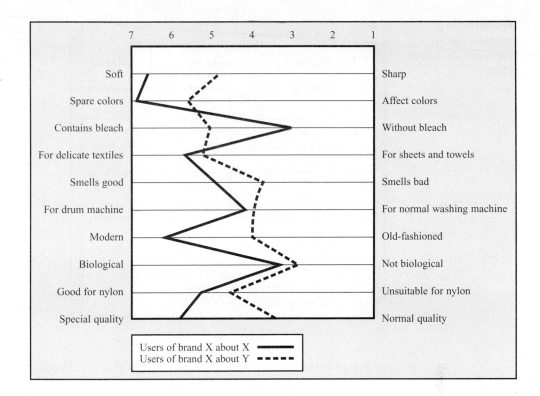

determined afterward by the researcher on the basis of the results. Reliable MDS results can be obtained even with a small number of respondents, and the results are also suitable for *segmentation* into, for example, usage versus nonusage.

A simple tool that represents both tangible and abstract brand characteristics in a conveniently arranged manner is the *semantic differential:* a graphic representation of brand scores on various characteristics. With the data collected in the research described earlier, such a figure is easy to construct. Figure 4-14 shows an example. Conducting measurements such as those shown in Figures 4-13 and 4-14 creates insight into the *strengths and weaknesses* of a brand. At this point it is very important to distinguish between *customers* and *potential customers*. Potential customers (i.e., noncustomers) often perceive a brand differently than customers do. An answer to the question "Why don't potential customers purchase our product?" is important for attracting new customers.

CASE 4-3

Difference in Perception between Customers and Noncustomers

California is no paradise for Wal-Mart. It's a rich market, but not all communities want the retailer. Wal-Mart Stores has faced a barrage of criticism for being too big, too powerful, and too willing to shave a penny off its costs at the expense of workers' well-being. In a reaction to that criticism, its 2004 ad campaign painted the chain as a friend of local communities and a rich source of opportunity and good benefits for workers. A recent Wal-Mart-financed study by the nonprofit Los Angeles County Economic Development Corp. found that southern California consumers could save at least $3.76 billion a year, or $589 per household, if Wal-Mart grabbed a 20 percent share of the grocery market. And the savings would create more jobs than Wal-Mart might destroy, the study contended. However, opponents scoff at the chain's "consumer choice" rhetoric. They say Wal-Mart creates costly urban sprawl, displaces small businesses, and drives down living standards with its low wages and benefits.

Source: Zellner, Wendy, and Peter Burrows, "California Is No Paradise for Wal-Mart," *Business Week Online*, March 4, 2004.

FIGURE 4-15
Summary of Main
Customer Research
Phases

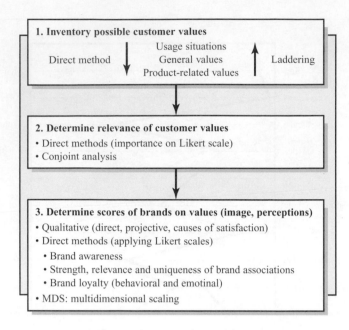

Figure 4-15 summarizes the main phases in customer research.

4.4.5 Tracking

Tracking generally refers to the frequent and consistent quantitative measurement of variables related to objectives. In light of the importance of client-oriented goals, the measurement of client-oriented variables is important. A number of client-related measures are shown in Figure 4-9: the sources of brand equity. In addition, tracking usually includes advertising variables and variables that Keller[13] designates as the results of brand equity, such as purchasing intention, customer satisfaction, and brand loyalty.

Figure 4-16 includes a summary overview. In section 11. 5 (on communication decisions) we will revisit the issue of tracking.

4.4.6 Future Customer Values

Research into customer values is valuable but does not generate direct insight into what customers will consider important in the future. However, that is more important than

FIGURE 4-16
Variables in Tracking
Research

Description of target audience	General background characteristics: geographic, demographic, and psychographic characteristics Product-specific characteristics (e.g., purchasing behavior)
Communication responses	Communication awareness Communication attitude
Brand responses	Brand awareness Brand associations (strength, relevance, differentiation)
Marketing responses	Customer satisfaction Brand loyalty

knowing the current situation. To arrive at *prognoses* for customer values, the following steps can be taken:

1. Aside from customer research, consult *sources about trends* in customer wishes such as sellers, researchers, consultants, and other experts.
2. Analyze the tracking data and attempt to (statistically) *link* any changes in customer values to factors such as economic fluctuations and social-cultural developments.
3. Discuss the data from the customer analysis, the other sources, and the company's self-analysis in *brainstorming sessions* to arrive at prognoses collectively.

Finally, research into customer values can easily be connected to the value strategies of Treacy and Wiersema that were discussed in earlier chapters. Those value strategies are in effect three ways to provide customer value. Research among customers must indicate which value or combination of values (innovative products, cheap products or convenience, direct relationships with customers) will have to be chosen in the future.

4.5   INDIVIDUAL CUSTOMER DATA

In this section, we will focus first on the possibilities and limitations of individual customer data and then on the process of selecting customers.

4.5.1   Possibilities and Limitations

As was indicated in Chapter 1, the concept of creating direct relationships with customers (*customer intimacy*) has received a lot of attention since the 1990s. This value strategy implies and requires that a company have insight into customer preferences at the individual level and then respond to those preferences. Although this subject receives a lot of attention in both theory and practice, its implementation is challenging. The biggest problem is obtaining and maintaining a sufficiently rich *database of client data*. In section 4.2 we stated that ideally, the following types of client characteristics should be measured: geographic, demographic (and socioeconomic), psychographic, product related and brand related (behavioral). Obtaining *geographic* data ("NAR data": name, address, residence) is not a problem: Names can be obtained through a sales promotion that requires sending in a coupon or through direct sales. Obtaining *demographic and psychographic* data is a bit more challenging but can be done if the client is prepared to complete a questionnaire. Such a list should be completed annually since people's lifestyles and habits may change. The most challenging problem is to gain insight into *behavior-related variables:* customers' preferences and purchasing and usage behavior. It is possible to ask for preferences through a questionnaire, but preferences change quickly and it is difficult to indicate future preferences. On a practical level it is inconvenient to request data regarding purchasing and usage behavior from customers continuously. However, those data are of essential importance because insight into individual preferences and the company's response to those preferences gives the customer the feeling that the supplier knows him or her and therefore has a relationship with him or her.

The seriousness of the problem of obtaining individual client data depends to a large extent on the distribution channel that is used. For purchases that are made directly from the supplier (through the Internet or by telephone), registration of individual purchasing behavior is not a problem. In addition, companies such as Amazon.com have insight into customer-indicated preferences. Based on those interests and the analysis of customer purchasing behavior, Amazon.com has a fairly precise insight into customer preferences in the areas of books and CDs. However, such suppliers are a minority: Purchases made through e-commerce still account for only a small proportion of total market sales. Another limitation is that nothing is known about the extent to which customers purchase at competitors. In practice, this makes it very difficult to calculate the *customer share*.

For suppliers whose sales still occur through regular retail, obtaining good databases is even more challenging. In this case, agreements with retailers may be required to obtain customer purchasing data. However, for those retailers, creating a customer base is less challenging because they have direct contact with customers. This group of companies therefore has better opportunities for database marketing.

Another big challenge in using individual client data is *privacy*. In many countries, there is resistance to the use of individual personal details and household details. In practice, there are two systems for protecting individual client data: opt-in and opt-out. *Opt-in* means choosing to participate and includes the fact that people have to give explicit permission for the use of data (e.g., active agreement with a customer card); *opt-out* means choosing to "leave" and implies a tacit assumption that personal data may be used unless objections are made (a passive agreement, for example, reacting to a coupon action). In practice, opt-out occurs more often than opt-in. As a result of the privacy problems mentioned above, it is argued that customers need to be asked for explicit permission. In this context the term *permission marketing* is used: You can start a direct relationship with the customer only if he or she has explicitly given his or her permission (therefore, this is a type of opt-in). When they sign up for such a card, customers have the option of giving their names and giving permission for their individual data to be used for other purposes. The willingness of customers to participate in one-on-one programs can be increased by, for example, providing a discount in exchange a win-win situation).

All in all, it is difficult to obtain and maintain data about individual preferences and purchases. Since that is an important component of the value strategy of *customer intimacy,* it sets limitations to the applicability of this strategy.

4.5.2 Customer Selection

For companies that are able to obtain customer-level data regarding purchasing behavior, several tools are available to analyze those data. We will discuss two: the customer pyramid (Figure 4-17) and customer portfolio analysis.

The customer pyramid is a framework that places potential customers in an order. This arrangement may be based on annual sales per customer. It is likely that for customers a similar 80–20 rule exists as exists for products: Twenty percent of the customers may be responsible for 80 percent of sales. Of course, this is a fairly arbitrary rule of thumb and it is equally likely that another proportion applies, but the meaning is clear: A small number of

FIGURE 4-17
Customer Pyramid

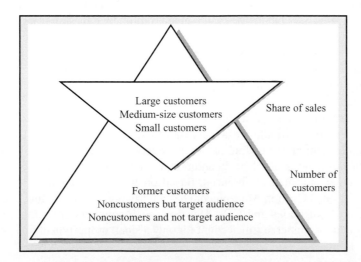

customers is responsible for a large amount of sales. Farther down the pyramid we find medium-size and small customers, former customers, not or never customers, and finally non–target audience persons. When customers are arranged in order, the next issue is the characteristics the various groups possess. Why is a large customer large and a small customer small? Why have some customers left? Why are some members of the target audience not customers at all? Figure 4-17 can be a tool for choosing the target audience and the value strategy. In theory, the best strategy would be one that involves as strong a flow-through as possible from the bottom toward the top, but there are three different possibilities:

1. Turning a noncustomer into a customer.
2. Maintaining customers.
3. Increasing sales to customers.

Each of these strategies requires a different approach. In the context of relationship marketing it is often stated that maintaining customers is four times cheaper than making new customers. However, it is unwise to ignore new customers. Without growth the client base will decrease.

CASE 4-4 *Customer Selection*	Thanks to the Internet, many opportunities for customer discrimination are emerging. The most obvious example is airlines. Airline Web sites now discriminate in extraordinarily refined ways, setting fares that may vary not just by class but by the date of booking and the time of the flight. Some manufacturers are starting to do the same thing: Dell charges different prices for the same computer on its Web pages, depending on whether the buyer is a state or local government or a small business. Such discrimination is being extended to other parts of the economy. JSTOR, a nonprofit organization that makes available online back numbers of scholarly journals, analyzes the electronic data it accumulates to charge libraries and academic institutions different fees that depend on use and circumstances. **Source:** "They're Watching You," *The Economist*, October 18, 2003, p. 77.

Another tool that may be useful in this context is *customer portfolio analysis*. Each customer is classified on the basis of two characteristics:

1. The extent to which the customer is a "heavy user" in the product category: the potential *size of the customer.*
2. The share of the brand sales in the customer's category purchases, in other words, the market share at the customer level (*customer share*).

The first criterion addresses the potential and/or expected attractiveness of the customer; the second addresses the customer's current attractiveness. The classification of customers may facilitate the strategy choice process. It depends on the product category whether a brand's management is able to determine the potential size of a customer. How should the category usage of a beer drinker be determined or that of a bank customer or a purchaser of a personal computer? Historical time sequence analysis seems to be required in this case.[14]

4.6 PRIMARY RESEARCH

Primary data are data that the organization collects by itself through fieldwork (market research). For an extensive discussion of market research, refer to the literature.[15] Here we pay attention to several points. In doing market research, the following choices have to be made:

1. *Choice of the target audience (who?).* For which target audience or audiences should the research be performed? This question largely determines the remainder of the structure.

2. *Desired information and choice of quantitative or qualitative research (what?).* We will focus on this in section 4.6.1.

3. *Structure (how?):*
   - Data collection
   - Sampling
   - Method of questioning. This component will be discussed in sections 4.6.2 and 4.6.3.

4.6.1 Qualitative or Quantitative Research

As is always the case in market research, there are in principle two possible ways to do research: quantitative and qualitative. By definition, *quantitative research* is performed on a larger number of people. The large-scale approach allows the drawing of "harder" conclusions than is the case with qualitative research; after all, the results are stated in percentages. Another advantage is that differences between subgroups in the target audience (segments) can be made visible, for example, differences in satisfaction between youths and older people or between different types of companies (an "explanatory" goal). Because the type of fieldwork done for quantitative research (written, telephone, or Internet) requires a structured approach, such research is most appropriate for "factual" research, that is, descriptive research. It is not the primary goal of quantitative research to provide insight into the "why" of certain results.

Qualitative research consists of personal (face-to-face) interviews with individuals ("in-depth interviews") or groups (group discussions, focus groups). Qualitative research can be used as an independent source or may be performed before quantitative research as a source of inspiration and/or a pretest of a questionnaire. Qualitative research provides answers regarding, for example:

- *Strategic market description.* How can we describe the various target audiences in terms of wishes, needs, and behavior?
- *Consumer decision-making behavior.* Why does the consumer buy one product and not another?
- *Customer satisfaction.* How satisfied are our customers, what makes them satisfied, and how can we increase that satisfaction?
- *Communication research.* How is our draft advertisement understood and evaluated, and to what extent is the reader inspired to take action?
- *Idea generation.* Which potential wishes and motives exist in a product field, and what possibilities exist for responding to them?
- *Development of products and concepts.* How can we ensure that our new services and products have an optimal fit with the wishes and needs of customers (physical product, packaging, promotion, distribution)?
- *Development of a quantitative questionnaire.* Which themes are relevant in relation to a specific market or a specific product, and what words do respondents use to describe aspects?

These subjects indicate that qualitative research is often *diagnostic* or exploratory in nature.

The decision to do quantitative versus qualitative research should not be based primarily on the idea that quantitative research may by definition be more reliable than qualitative. More important is the question of what *type of information* a company wants to obtain. If the organization, as part of its customer satisfaction research, wishes to obtain insight into the percentage of people from the target audience who are or are not satisfied with the

FIGURE 4-18
Research Phases

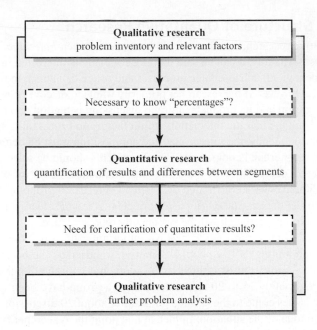

product as well as the relationship with the composition and backgrounds of the target audience, a quantitative approach is required. However, a company should realize that such research will not provide information about the *causes of any dissatisfaction*. Information about those causes typically can best be obtained by checking the written comments of respondents (e.g., at the end of a questionnaire). In that way, the most important complaints become clear. However, that involves an incidental inventory of problems, which is in effect qualitative in nature. If a company wants to know why dissatisfaction exists and how the company can address it, a qualitative approach is appropriate.

Figure 4-18 contains the ideal choice in this regard: first qualitative, then potentially quantitative, and again qualitative. Customer research always starts with qualitative research, in which a first inventory of potential problems is obtained and information is collected for structuring the quantitative research. Such research may be followed by quantitative research to gain insight into whether goals were achieved, the extent to which certain problems exist, and differences between groups. Subsequently, a deeper qualitative analysis may be performed for target audiences to determine the cause or causes of any problems and perhaps to propose potential solutions to respondents. Of course this is possible only if sufficient resources are available. If resources are limited, at a minimum some qualitative research will be required, because even a small number of discussions with customers provides insight into problems and potential solutions. Following are two examples.

By talking with just a few customers, a large telecommunications business discovered that customers did not consider the various subscription options to be as simple as the managers had expected. A bank allowed some customers to try its technically clever Web site. It turned out that the customers failed to understand many of the options: The Web site had been created far too much from the perspective of the business and not sufficiently from the perspective of the customer.

Once it has been decided which type of research is the most appropriate, decisions should be made regarding the further structure as well as the size and composition of the sample. We will flesh out these subjects first for qualitative and then for quantitative research.

4.6.2 Structure of Qualitative Research

In qualitative research, a choice should be made between *individual* interviews and *group* interviews. Generally, it can be said that if a company is interested in people's personal, individual behavior (such as choice processes and usage behavior), individual discussions are preferable. However, if the researcher primarily wants to discover how "people" think about the organization and its products, a group discussion is a good choice. A group discussion has the advantage that the interaction within the group brings more issues and ideas to the surface. Subsequently, the sample size and composition must be determined. The composition is the most crucial component: The respondents should be selected carefully according to the relative composition of the entire target audience. If, for example, 30 percent of the target audience consists of women over age 60, a research group of 20 people should have 6 women older than age 60. Using the "correct" method of selecting respondents guarantees that the qualitative research will be sufficiently representative.

A related point is the *sample size*. An important criticism about qualitative research is that research among "a few people" sometimes is used as the basis for an organization's strategic decisions. However, this may be countered with the fact that research shows that after approximately 15 to 20 respondents from a group have been questioned, hardly any other new issues come to the surface. Thus, after about 20 discussions, the researcher has a fairly good idea of the situation. In fact, at that point the researcher typically also has a reasonable impression of the extent to which issues are important to the target audience.

The normal recommendation for group discussions is to interview relatively *homogeneous groups*. This might include several customer groups as well as one or more groups of noncustomers (potential customers) and perhaps some former customers. A frequently occurring problem in market research is that only existing customers are questioned. However, the results of such research are by definition not representative for the entire potential target audience because existing customers typically view the organization in a more positive light than do customers who use its competitor. Assuming that every organization does not exist only for the benefit of its customers but is also interested in potential customers, this means that *noncustomers* should also be questioned. In terms of the size of groups for group discussions, six to eight people per group is considered appropriate in most cases. The number 15 to 25 respondents applies to each of the groups to be researched about which the researcher wants to make statements. If the researcher wants to examine the differences between, for example, male customers, female customers, and noncustomers, the numerical guideline should be applied three times. If the minimum of approximately 15 people per group is used and a choice is made to have group discussions involving around 8 people per discussion, in this example at least six group discussions have to be organized.

In terms of the method of data collection, open questions are used in which the interviewer needs to ensure that all subjects will be discussed. One cannot ignore the danger of *interviewer bias:* contaminated answers that result from the influence of the interviewer. To obtain information that is as pure as possible, face-to-face research requires expert questioning. Thus, the power of qualitative research lies in *"creative listening."*

4.6.3 Structure of Quantitative Research

Three types of data collection are in principle possible for quantitative research: by *telephone, written* (mail), or by *Internet.* The advantages of research by telephone include a faster, higher response rate and the possibility of clarification of answers. A disadvantage is the limited length of the questionnaire. The advantages of a written questionnaire are the possibility of using a longer questionnaire and the relative ease with which a large number of people can be reached. However, the response rate is often very low (for consumer research, often no more than 15 percent). Research via Internet is very popular and combines two advantages: speed and many questions possible. A disadvantage is a possible task of representivity. Quantitative research demands a completely prestructured multiple-choice questionnaire.

Because a mistake or vagueness in a questionnaire cannot be rectified, it is essential to ensure that the questionnaire has been extensively tested beforehand until test persons no longer indicate any confusing items (after they have been explicitly asked about confusing items).

In terms of the *sample size,* the statistical reliability of the results increases to the extent that the sample size increases, but this is not a direct relationship. Without going more deeply into the formulas that can be used to calculate the margins of error for responses, it can be stated as a rule of thumb that a minimum of 100 respondents must be obtained for each target audience to be researched. Assuming an expected response rate of 20 percent, this means that for a written research project, at a minimum 500 questionnaires should be sent out per group.

CASE 4-5 *Using Quantitative Data to Profile the 55+*	The 2000 U.S. Census counted approximately 60 million people 55 years of age and older. The number of people in this age group is expected to double by the year 2030 and will constitute 33 percent of the U.S. population. Segments exist within the large elderly market that require different marketing strategies. Research conducted at the Center for Mature Consumer Studies during the last 15 years has amassed evidence of the superiority of a segmentation model known as gerontographics. The gerontographic segmentation analysis has provided the following four older consumer segments: —*Healthy hermits.* These are individuals in relatively good health yet somewhat withdrawn socially (20 million). —*Ailing outgoers.* These are individuals in relatively poor health yet determined to remain socially active (18 million). —*Frail recluses.* These are inactive individuals who usually are burdened with health problems. They spend most of their time at home and are concerned with personal and physical security (18 million). —*Healthy indulgers.* These are relatively wealthy people who are focused on making the most of life (7 million). **Source:** Moschis, George P., Danny N. Bellenger, and Carolyn Folkman Curasi, "What Influences the Mature Customer?" *Marketing Health Services* 23(4), 2003, p. 16–21.

More important than the sample size is sample *composition.* If the composition of the group of people who have participated does not resemble the target audience in terms of characteristics relevant for the research project (the composition is not representative), the results are unreliable. Therefore, it is very important to check afterward whether the requirement of representation has been met. If the response group deviates from the target audience, additional respondents should be obtained or so-called reweighing should be applied during the analysis.

4.7   SECONDARY SOURCES OF CONSUMER DATA

In many countries market research agencies collect quantitative data that are very important in the context of consumer marketing. Two types of data sets (and agencies) can be distinguished:

1. Agencies that collect quantitative data, including *consumer purchasing behavior.*
2. Agencies that are involved in collecting data on households (such as prosperity and lifestyle) for *direct-marketing objectives.*

FIGURE 4-19   Databases of Nielsen, GfK, and IRI

	AC Nielsen and IRI Retail Panel	GfK Consumer Panel
Variables	• Sales • Price • Distribution • Promotions	Sales Price Characteristics of consumers
Shop types	• AC Nielsen and IRI: supermarkets, gas stations, tobacco shops • AC Nielsen: drugstores/perfumeries, wine shops, pet stores, media	Fast-moving consumer goods Consumer durables
Periodicity	• Varies by channel from weekly to bimonthly	Weekly
Aggregation level	• Per brand or variety	Per brand or variety
Number of data	• Tousands of shops	Tousands of households

In this section we discuss these sources. Although the specific agencies may differ, in many countries comparable data are collected.

4.7.1   Sales Databases

Disaggregated data are especially available for fast moving consumer goods ('food'). There are three large, international databases that contain information such as sales data for food products in markets: the databases of *AC Nielsen (retail panel),* the *IRI retail panel,* and the *GfK household panel.* Figure 4-19 gives an overview of the contents of these databases. All three databases are available in many countries. The market research companies can provide the data and can also perform analyses for a brand to provide insights, in for example the effects of sales promotions or price changes. Because of the similarity in what they offer, the competing databases Nielsen and IRI shop panel have been put into one column.

All three databases contain data about sales and prices of products. Both shop panels also measure the distribution spread. Gfk's household panel also includes data about consumer background characteristics such as age, gender, income, region, and media consumption. An advantage of this system is a potential linkage to consumer characteristics. Another advantage is that the consumer data can be used to trace brand loyalty as well as "switching behavior": the extent to which consumers switch back and forth in purchasing certain brands. Such data are very important for the identification of competitors.

An advantage of the shop panel data from AC Nielsen and IRI is the availability of distribution and promotion data. This may provide a manufacturer with insight into potential bottlenecks. In addition, both agencies provide data on promotions. Since in the retail panels, some tousands of shops participate, while in the consumer panel tousands of households participate, the number of transactions in the retail databases is much larger.

In both shop panels the data are collected through scanning in shops. By *"scanning"* we mean methods that register electronically (via a bar code) the purchases made in a shop. Scanning data collected in shops at the cash register are used to build databases that are based on a panel of shops. Scanning data have the advantage that the data usually are collected at the disaggregated level in terms of the time (weekly or even daily data) and the products (by variety). In the past, AC Nielsen collected sales data bimonthly (based on inventory and purchasing in shops), but because of the more detailed time-related information available with current scanning data, these days short-term effects of promotions also can be detected. With the use of bimonthly data, the effect of an action often could not be observed (see section 11.5.7).

4.7.2 Direct Marketing Databases

In Chapter 1 we indicated the increasing importance of direct relationships with customers, especially for organizations that choose customer intimacy as a value discipline. An important tool in this regard is tailored *direct communication* (direct mail). Individual databases can be used for direct marketing but also for issues such as target audience selection and location research. The most effective method is to collect data from customers "yourself." For example, an advertisement in a daily newspaper may contain a coupon that customers can fill in (including their names, etc) to get a discount. This is a valuable source for a database for a brand.

However, a manager can also buy data. Some market research companies build large databases of *individual households*. These so-called *individual segmentation systems* contain information at the household level about, for example, family composition, age, hobbies, interests, characteristics of possessions, purchasing plans, and media behavior. Such sources may contain data from millions of households. One of the purposes for which these data can be used is to find the best-responding components from a database and create a lifestyle profile of the potential customers. It is also possible to determine at the household level who belongs to the target audience, based on a description of the profile of the target audience. Companies can also gain better insight into the characteristics of the target audience by analyzing the data available in the database on the company's existing customers.

In many countries these "ready-made" individual databases are collected. For example, in Europe companies such as Cendris and Wegener DM have large databases of consumer households. In the UK, the Wegener database contains 42 million individuals, 12 million of which are lead-to-purchase and lifestyle records that are continually updated with information collected in the UK's largest opt-in survey programme. In the US, Claritas' PRIZM is a well known database; PRIZM defined 14 segments of households, applying income (low, medium, high) and lifestyle variables (urban, suburban, second city, town and country). Actually individual segmentation databases can answer three questions: what are they like, where can I find them and how can I reach them?

Summary

Customer analysis is composed primary of research (market research) and secondary research (existing sources). Primary customer analysis has four goals. The first goal is to provide a foundation for segmentation. Identification of segments takes place through the analysis, based on large-scale quantitative research, of which groups of consumers or customers demonstrate similar preferences or similar usage behavior and subsequently a description of those groups on the basis of the characteristics that are the most distinctive. The discovered segments form the basis for decisions that will later be made regarding the target audience (targeting). The second goal of customer analysis is to provide the information required for making positioning decisions. For this purpose, insight has to be gained into the value hierarchy of customers: What are the goals for which customers use the products (usage situations)? What do they generally consider important in those situations (general values)? What do they consider important in products (product-specific values)? What are the achievements of our brand on those general values (abstract brand characteristics) and on the product-specific values (desired product characteristics, benefits)? and To what extent are those achievements distinctive? This component provides insight into the strengths and weaknesses of a brand. Aside from insight into the value hierarchy, a manager needs to know the extent of customer satisfaction. One measure in that regard is brand loyalty. Brand loyalty has a behavioral component (market share at the customer level, or *customer share*) and an emotional component ("real brand loyalty," which can be measured through statements such as "I recommend brand X to my friends"). In these research phases, qualitative methods such as laddering are used and quantitative research also takes place. Both types of research are performed for customers and noncustomers.

The third goal of customer analysis is to provide information for the testing of client-oriented objectives. For this purpose a number of measures, such as customer satisfaction and brand achievements, should be repeated regularly (tracking). The fourth goal of customer analysis is to gain insight into how customers perceive the competition. Customer research does not address customers' future values directly. For that purpose, other sources have to be consulted.

A company that has individual client data regarding the preferences and purchases of customers is able to make a selection of the most profitable customers on the basis of customer pyramids and customer portfolio analyses. This fits with the pursuit of relationships with customers.

Secondary data sources that may be used for markets for fast-moving consumer goods include the databases of Nielsen, IRI and GfK. These databases contain weekly data regarding sales, price, distribution, and promotions. GfK also has data regarding customer characteristics. Other important secondary sources, especially for direct marketing, are individual segmentation systems.

Notes

1. Malhotra, N. K. (2004), *Marketing Research: An Applied Orientation,* 4th ed., Upper Saddle River, NJ: Pearson Education.

2. Ferell, O. C., M. D. Hartline, G. H. Lucas, and D. Luck (1999), *Marketing Strategy,* Orlando, FL: Dryden Press.

3. Connie Schenk is gratefully acknowledged for her suggestions for this table.

4. Parasuraman, A., V. A. Zeithaml, and L. Berry (1985), "A Conceptual Model of Service Quality and Its Implocations for Future Research," *Journal of Marketing* 49:41–50.

5. This is based on Woodruff, R. B., and S. F. Gardial (1996), *Know Your Customer: New Approaches to Understanding Customer Value and Satisfaction, Cambridge,* MA: Blackwell, but we have made several changes.

6. This concerns so-called fractional designs: overviews of combinations of profiles with a given number of attributes and levels per attribute.

7. Cattin, P., and D. R. Wittink (1982), "Commercial Use of Conjoint Analysis: A Survey," *Journal of Marketing* 46:44–53.

8. Keller, K. L. (1993), "Conceptualizing, Measuring and Managing Customer-Based Brand Equity," *Journal of Marketing* 57:1–22.

9. Keller's "favorability of a brand association" (second issue) is discussed here as relevance.

10. Morgan, R. P. (2000), "A Consumer-Oriented Framework of Brand Equity and Loyalty," *International Journal of Market Research* 42(1):65–78.

11. Zwart, P.S. (1992), *Methoden van Marktonderzoek,* Leiden: Stenfert Kroese, 4th ed, pp. 250–252.

12. Leeflang, P.S.H. (2003), Marketing, Groningen: Wolters Noordhoff, p. 207.

13. Keller (1993).

14. For more advanced methods for determining the profitability of customers, refer to the overview by Mulhern, F. J. (1999), "Customer Profitability Analysis: Measurement, Concentration, and Research Directions," *Journal of Interactive Marketing* 13:25–40.

15. See Malhotra (2004) for a more extensive discussion.

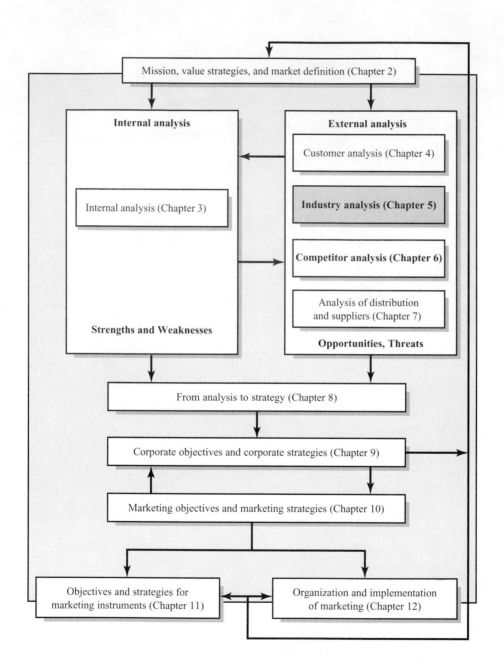

Chapter Five

Industry Analysis

Key Points in This Chapter

- Know the differences between and the goals of an industry analysis and a competitor analysis.
- Know the components of an industry analysis.
- Realize that a Porter analysis is only part of an industry analysis, which in turn is part of an external analysis.
- Be able to perform a macroenvironmental analysis for a company.
- Know how to assess the attractiveness of a market.

INTRODUCTION

This chapter will review the industry analysis. The most important goal of this type of analysis is to gain insight into *opportunities and threats* from the perspective of the industry and the macroenvironment as well as insight into the *attractiveness of the market* in which the organization operates. Insight into the attractiveness of the market is important in regard to issues such as determining the investment level. Section 5.1 discusses the concept of industry analysis in relation to the concept of competitor analysis; these two concepts are strongly related. In Section 5.2 the goal and structure of an industry analysis are outlined. We then review the various phases of the industry analysis. Section 5.3 focuses on the analysis of the macroenvironment. The so-called aggregated market factors (including the product life cycle) are reviewed in Section 5.4. In Section 5.5 the factors related to industry structure (including the five competitive forces identified by Porter) receive attention. Finally, Section 5.6 explains how the results of the entire industry analysis can be summarized into conclusions about market attractiveness.

Because an industry analysis reviews not just the existing suppliers but also potential ones as well as parties that are not operating in the market directly, this chapter uses the term *industry analysis*. In this regard we are giving a broader meaning to that concept than is done in daily usage, where it typically refers to a group of businesses that produce or trade strongly related products, such as the house construction industry, the garment industry, and the shoe industry.

Barbie versus Bratz

Barbie was a dream in every way—not only for young girls who wanted to place themselves in the dream world in which Barbie, with Ken at her side, lived but also for the manufacturer, Mattel, which had for years, thanks to Barbie, a dominating market position in the segment of fashion dolls.

However, that dream has been rudely disturbed. For decades the position of the now 45-year-old Barbie was inviolable until the U.S.-based company MGA Entertainment introduced Bratz in 2001. The Bratz line consisted of five dolls dressed in hipper-than-hip clothes strongly pacing on platform soles. They looked as if they had just walked out of an MTV video clip. The packaging reads: "Hip dolls for girls with a passion for fashion." The march of Yasmin (as Pretty Princess, the leader of the group), Cloë (the cheeky blonde), Jade (cool and sexy), Megyan (extremely bold), and Sasha (completely hip-hop) seems almost unstoppable.

U.S. sales of all types of dolls totaled about $2.7 billion in 2003. Since 2000 this figure has more or less been stable, but that does not mean that no movements take place within the doll market. Mattel's share of the U.S. fashion doll market has dropped from 75 percent to about 60 percent since 2000. The multiethnic girls of Bratz, with their remarkably large eyes, hold 30 percent of that market.

The world of girls' dolls has become a real fighter's market. Mattel and MGA Entertainment are involved in a fierce battle. Mattel, in addition to Barbie also the producer of, for instance, Fisher Prince and Hot Wheels, has become quite concerned. In the second quarter of 2004 the worldwide sales of Barbie dropped 13 percent. The doll with the ideal figure was doing worst in the United States, with a sales slump of 15 percent.

Meanwhile, the margins on the sweet candy princess are decreasing. In an attempt to reduce the damage, Mattel has been adding more and more expensive accessories to the Barbie packages.

The Changing Toy Market

The toy branch is a stable market. This partly has to do with the stagnating economy. Demography also plays a role: Especially in the United States and Europe, birthrates have been declining for years. Furthermore, the sector has to deal with the fact that children grow up more quickly. Whereas the Action Man line used to be sold to boys in the age group six to nine, it now is sold to children four to seven years old. Boys age of eight and nine are forever lost for the toy branch. They play mainly play with computers and games.

The "rejuvenation trend" is also an explanation for the success of Bratz. Many girls age 9 to 10 are simply not interested anymore in the pink world of Barbie and Ken. Bratz chose a different approach. With hip clothing, the latest fashion is followed—very contemporary. And there are five cool boy dolls as boyfriends for the Bratz girls. "In that age category girls in real life are not thinking about boys yet, but they are through those dolls. The world that they will enter in a moment is being acted out now. That's what it's all about with fashion dolls," according to a spokesperson from Bratz.

Ken Dumped

How did Mattel react to the megasuccess of the bold Bratz? After the failure of the first quick me-too operations under the name Flava's, the company introduced the My Scene collection: a series of dolls that look strikingly like the Bratz girls. Mattel also has followed a second track. After long hesitation and an apparently happy marriage of 43 years, Ken was put aside to make room for a hipper image of Barbie and a new friend: Blaine, a sturdy Australian surf dude.

At Bratz they don't really care: "My Scene cannibalizes especially the Barbie sales, and Barbie herself is more a playing doll in the traditional meaning of the word. Bratz dolls have another function. They are more fashion dolls. Precisely that fashion aspect makes Bratz attractive for older girls."

Through that stretching of age, the potential target group for dolls has become larger. This suits the manufacturers of Bratz well. "Toys seep slowly down the age demography. You always see that with fashionable products. Older children start to play with it, and younger ones subsequently pick it up. But before you know it the older ones think of it as something for the little ones. For us the challenge is to keep things relevant, exciting, and full of aspiration exactly for those eight- to nine-year olds. Otherwise they phase out completely to makeup, fashion, and mobile phones."

The role of parents is also an important influence in the toy branch, especially with the more expensive toys. Both Bratz and Barbie cost at least $25 to $30. Parental approval is necessary for this price category. Parents often decide on the basis of one of the following criteria:

- Does the toy have a good price-quality relationship?
- Is it informative and fun?
- Did I play with it myself in the past?

Especially on the last criterion Barbie has a clear advantage. Bratz in turn reacts skillfully to melting mothers by introducing a nostalgia flashback fever line.

Finally, there is a very different threat to the doll market: imminent limitations in advertisements aimed at children. Especially in a number of European countries, severe rules are already applicable.

Source: "Can Mattel Save Barbie?" Parija Bhatnagar, http://money.cnn.com/2004/10/18/news/fortune500/mattel_barbie.

Questions

1. Segment the toy market on the basis of the information in this case. Which segmentation variables play a role here?
2. Which four competition levels do you know? Show per level the competition for Barbie.
3. What are the strong and the weak points of Bratz compared with Barbie?
4. Analyze developments in the fashion doll market with the aid of the product life cycle. Apply the life cycle concept to both the product group level ("the doll market") and the brand level (for Bratz and Barbie).
5. Which developments in the macroenvironment are affecting the doll market according to the case? Try to show whether these developments represent an opportunity or a threat.
6. Assess the fashion doll market with the aid of the business model of Porter.
7. How do you view the future of the fashion doll market? Explain your predictions.

5.1 COMPETITIVE ANALYSIS: INDUSTRY AND COMPETITORS

The question "What is competition?" seems redundant. After all, everyone knows the answer. However, we need to focus briefly on this concept since in the literature there has been a tendency to classify more issues and parties under the designations *competition* and *competitor analysis*.

The concept of competition can have two meanings:

1. The *extent of competition* (rivalry, competitive struggle in a market: How strong is the battle in a market for the favor of the customers; in other words, how intense is the competition?).
2. The *individual competitors:* the collective name for all the competitors of a company.

FIGURE 5-1
Components of
Competitive Analysis

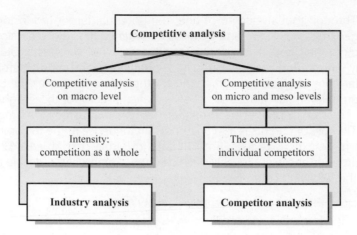

Because of these two different meanings of the concept of competition, a competition analysis consists of two components[1]:

1. An analysis of the intensity of the competition in a market; this component of the analysis is included with the *industry analysis.*
2. An analysis of the behavior of individual competitors: this is known as *competitor analysis.*

The most important difference between the two components is that a competitor analysis examines individual competitors, whereas in an industry analysis the competition as a whole is analyzed (Figure 5-1). In other words, the industry analysis is a competition analysis on the macro level, and the competitor analysis can be seen as a competition analysis on the micro (and meso) level.

Another difference between the competitor analysis and the industry analysis is that completely different aspects of the competition are examined. In competitor analysis, the focus is on analyzing and predicting the behavior and reactions of competitor A, competitor B, and so on. For that purpose, the strengths and weaknesses of the competitors are portrayed. In industry analysis, the focus is on the competitive forces in a market, for example, the division of power among sellers or the negotiation power of suppliers. In this regard, Porter's model of five competitive forces is often used.[2]

5.2　GOAL AND STRUCTURE OF THE INDUSTRY ANALYSIS

5.2.1　Goal

One of the components of the industry analysis is an examination of the market structure: How large are the various suppliers? Is there a strong power concentration? Are the products similar to each other, or does the customer perceive significant differences? Although these kinds of questions are interesting in and of themselves, a company needs to consider beforehand what should be done with the answers. If no clear goal for the analysis is formulated up front, many issues may be examined in great detail without a clear link to strategy formation. That would mean that the "homework" was done for nothing.

In terms of the industry analysis, there are two explicit goals. We want to gain insight into the following:

1. The *attractiveness of the market.*
2. *Opportunities and threats* from the perspective of the *industry* (e.g., from macroenvironmental factors).

The conclusions with regard to market attractiveness are especially important for the formulation of growth strategies and marketing objectives for the market that is being analyzed. For example, a finding that the market is relatively attractive (e.g., due to expected growth) is more likely to lead to a decision to invest and to the formulation of ambitious growth objectives than is the case if the market is found not to be attractive (e.g., saturated). This demonstrates that the industry analysis has a strong relationship with the *portfolio analysis*. After all, the portfolio analysis also is done to determine the investments for each product-market combination. Obtaining insight into potential opportunities and threats is a logical component of the strengths, weaknesses, opportunities, and threats (SWOT) analysis. The opportunities and threats will be juxtaposed in a later phase with the strengths and weaknesses to arrive at potential strategies.

5.2.2 Structure

An industry analysis examines all factors that may influence market attractiveness. These factors can be divided into three groups:

1. *Macroenvironmental factors.* These are factors over which the various suppliers in a market have little or no influence, such as government decisions.
2. *Aggregated market factors.* These are factors that are related to market demand and directly determine the attractiveness of a market, such as market growth.
3. *Industry structure factors.* This are factors that determine the intensity of competition in a market, for example, the distribution of the "power" in a market: the concentration.

These factors are summarized in Figure 5-2.[3] The combination of the three categories in Figure 5-2 determines the attractiveness of a market. In the analysis, the main issue is to observe changes over time and ideally to make a prognosis.

FIGURE 5-2
Components of the Industry Analysis

Macroenvironmental factors

- Demographic
- Economic
- Social-cultural
- Technological
- Ecological
- Political-legal (government)

Market factors

- Market size
- Market and submarket growth and phase in product life cycle
- Sensitivity to economic and seasonal trends

Industry structure factors

- Profitability
- Threat of new entrants
- Bargaining power of customers
- Bargaining power of suppliers
- Intensity of competition
- Threat of substitute products

5.3   MACROENVIRONMENTAL FACTORS

We include in macroenvironmental variables the variables that a company and other suppliers in the market cannot control or can control only to a limited extent. Figure 5-2 shows the categories of such factors that can be distinguished ("DESTEP factors"): demographic, economic, social-cultural, technological, ecological, and political-legal. In the context of the industry analysis, these factors are important because:

- In most cases they influence all the businesses in an industry.
- They directly influence market size and therefore market attractiveness.
- They may influence other functional areas in a company, such as personnel and production.

In this classification of macroenvironmental factors, a process of *mutual influence* may exist between the different categories of factors. For example, political decisions regarding income distribution may lead to changes in economic factors. A social-cultural development such as increasing environmental awareness is linked with a more strict environmental policy and with technological developments that lead to products that are more environmentally friendly.

For each factor, the first step should be determining the influence it had in the past. For factors that are quantifiable, such as economic and demographic developments, causal models may be used (see Section 8.1). Subsequently, the manager should indicate how much influence is expected in the future, but to be able to do this, the macroenvironmental factor itself should first be predicted. For this purpose, a number of forecasting methods may be used (see Section 8.1). For each category that will be discussed below, we will review the content, the data sources, and the predictability. We conclude with several general points about the macroenvironmental analysis.

5.3.1   Demographic Factors

The literal meaning of *demography* is "description of the people." Therefore, it relates to characteristics of the population. Demographic factors include the following:

- The size of the population in an area.
- The age distribution of the population.
- The number and size of households.
- The degree of urbanization of the population in an area.
- The composition of the population.

A well-known example of a demographic development in many modern countries is the *aging* of the population: an increase in the percentage of elderly people. This has negative consequences for companies that bring products onto the market for babies, such as diapers. However, a positive consequence exists for markets for the elderly, such as trips for older people and magazines aimed at the elderly.

| **CASE 5-1**
Aging | Europe is aging much faster than the United States is. Europe faces a daunting demographic challenge. The expansion of the European Union from 15 to 25 countries in 2004 increased its population from 380 million to 455 million—way ahead of America's 295 million. Yet by 2050 the United States will have almost caught up: If forecasts prove correct, there will be 420 million Americans, compared with 430 million Europeans. Europe's rapid aging will inflict economic pain. Even as numbers of workers fall, the numbers of people dependent on them will rise. Looming ahead is a big rise in spending not only on pensions but also on health and long-term care. The demographic challenge facing Europe may be even greater than most projections |

suggest. Population aging, although a demographic problem, requires an economic rather than a demographic solution. Europe still has much work to do to make the labor market and pension reforms that are needed to counter the adverse effects of its aging population.

Source: "Old Europe," *The Economist*, October 2, 2004, p. 49–50.

Other demographic developments in some countries include a decrease in population growth and decreasing household size. In most countries there are central statistical agencies that maintain detailed data, which are accessible on the Internet, regarding both past and predicted demographic developments. Although demographic developments are important issues for marketing, their effects appear gradually and in the long term.

5.3.2   Economic Factors

Economic factors are important for many companies because these variables influence the extent to which consumers are likely to purchase certain products. Examples of these variables include the following:

- The economic situation, measured via:

  - Volume of world trade:
  - Gross national product
  - Economic index
  - Consumer confidence index

- The purchasing power of consumers, measured via:

  - Paid wages and salaries;
  - Consumer expenditures
  - Consumer credit
  - Size of social security payments

- Other variables, such as:

  - Price level of family consumption
  - Unemployment
  - Exports
  - Energy prices

The influence of these variables on market demand varies with the market. In general, because of their luxury nature, durable consumer goods are more sensitive to changes in economic developments than are fast-moving consumer goods. Economic developments typically do not have an important influence on the market demand for fast-moving consumer goods, but there may be a shift in demand. For example, an economic recession will have a positive influence on cheaper brands, such as a store's own brands.

Data about past economic developments are available in detail at national agencies that collect statistical data. In contrast to government-related factors, economic factors can be predicted with reasonable accuracy for the not too distant future. This is the case because economic factors typically involve long-term trends that do not change drastically at any single point in time. However, in the longer term (more than a year ahead) economic variables (especially economic cycles) are difficult to predict.

An advantage of predicting economic variables is the fact that a company does not have to do it on its own. Annually, various general economic businesses, both national and international, publish prognoses for various macroeconomic variables. Since economic trends are strongly influenced by political developments, economic expectations can change drastically. However, as was indicated above, this typically is not the case and developments occur in accordance with trend lines.

5.3.3 Social-Cultural Factors

Social-cultural factors relate to issues such as people's way of life, opinions, and standards in a society. They include a large number of divergent developments, such as the following:

- Social changes within the family household such as:

  - Marrying at a later age
  - The increasing role of women in the labor process
  - An increase of the role of men in the household
  - Delayed childbearing
  - Changes in the upbringing of children

- The increase and revaluation of leisure time.
- Increasing attention to health (eating habits, sports).
- Increasing environmental awareness and attention to nature.
- Growth of subcultures.
- Changes in media use (increase in television watching time).

These factors may have important implications for marketing. For example, new and/or growing markets have come into being for leisure products, fast meals, "healthy" eating, environmentally friendly products, and so forth. Social-cultural trends are relevant not just for product development but also for communications. For example, in advertising promotions an increase in "house fathers" can be observed.

Partly as a result of several of these social-cultural and demographic developments, two trends have been noticeable over the last few years. First there is the so-called *individualization trend*. This means that an increasing number of people are creating their own worlds in which they pay as little attention as possible to other people. A strategic implication of this trend is that within a single family, different people make their own purchasing decisions, and so it is possible to find in one family several versions of a durable consumer good such as audio equipment.

CASE 5-2	**McDonald's Continues to Address Health Trend**
Social-Cultural Development	The image-reliant fast-food category is expected to dole out its annual billion dollars in prime-time network advertising as the top burger chains work to get their newfound identities cooking. McDonald's is entering year 2 of its successful "I'm Lovin' It" campaign. The biggest brand in all the land isn't going to stray too far from the formula that helped it rebound: Its fast-paced vignettes touting new salads and sandwiches will pepper prime time throughout the fall season. Familiar faces such Serena and Venus Williams and Yao Ming, among others, will flash their winning smiles as the chain continues to make its menu more health-conscious. The chain has even crafted an active lifestyles campaign called "It's What I Eat and What I Do." The fast feeder's ads attempt to promote the ideas of eating fight and keeping active to both parents and kids.

Source: Hein, Kenneth, "Fast Food," *MediaWeek*, April 25, 2005, p. SR18.

A second trend is a decreased ability to observe a link between consumers' characteristics and their purchasing behavior. For example, items such as a winter sports holiday, holidays by air, and a second car are no longer accessible only to consumers with high incomes. A related development is that the purchasing behavior of many consumers appears to be increasingly capricious. One moment the consumer is driving an expensive car, and the next he or she is buying a cheap pair of jeans or eating junk food. The implication of all this is that it will not always be easy for a company to convert a specific social-cultural development into a concrete opportunity.

Some national agencies maintain information about past and future social-cultural factors. In addition, newspapers and magazines often observe social-cultural trends in an early phase. A number of market research agencies also explicitly collect information on the various ways of life. For example, in the Netherlands the market research agency Trendbox has been registering a large number of social-cultural developments for several years. Since some trends might also be relevant in other countries, here are a few examples:

- Environmental awareness has decreased steadily since 1991; women have more interest in the environment than men do.
- People are becoming less "conservative." For example, women's emancipation is increasing: An increasing number of people think that even in families with children, the woman should be able to work.
- People are becoming less "impulse-oriented" and more focused on the future. An example is that concern about a financially secure future is increasing steadily.
- People receive less and less pleasure from television commercials.
- The interest in fresh and do-it-yourself meals has decreased strongly. Convenience is increasingly important (see Case 5-2).
- The consumer is becoming more price-conscious.

Case 5-3 describes the main food trends in the US.

CASE 5-3

Emerging Top Food Trends in U.S. and Abroad

Food trends once primed to focus on families are reshaping as baby-boomers become empty-nesters, and health-related products are booming worldwide. This is according to this month's issue of Food Technology magazine (April 2005) and its cover story, Top 10 Global Food Trends. Food Technology is published monthly by the scientific society Institute of Food Technologists.

Health became a key driver to the world's food marketplace in 2004 and do-if-yourself doctoring is one of ten major trends shaping today's consumer choices, according to the article. The Top 10 Food Trends are:

1. **Quick Fix**—Time to prepare food is still at a minimum, so a limited number of side dishes are prepared with entrees and ease of preparation is a major factor in eating at home.
2. **Drive-and-Go**—Takeout service at full service restaurants is growing, and the combination of stress with a sense of entitlement is leading consumers' drive for more upscale foods.
3. **Inherently Healthy**—More people are eating more fruits, vegetables, grains, nuts and yogurts.
4. **Fancy**—The premium foods market is projected to grow to nearly $100 billion before 2010. Wine and liqueurs are finding their way into crackers and drinks, and products for cocktails are hot.
5. **Farm-Friendly**—Foods deemed to be closer to the farm are capturing consumers' dollars.
6. **Layered Flavor**—Layering flavors is sending sales of food such as cheeses, condiments and ethnic foods soaring. Exotic fruit flavors such as starfruit, dragonfruit and Kaffir lime continue to grow.

7. **Grazing**—Seven million vending machines are in the U.S. with 100 million daily customers and more healthy fare to choose from. The low-carb snack category is falling, but smaller portion sizes are gaining and gourmet snack selections are strong. Health-oriented fun kid snacks will be well received.

8. **Low-, No- and Reduced**—With low-carb interest waning, consumers are returning to watching their fat and calorie intake. Low-fat tops the many health claims consumers now seek out.

9. **Do-It-Yourself Doctoring**—Shoppers are trying to manage or treat conditions through diet. Whey peptides are playing a role in Europe in beverages formulated to reduce blood pressure. IFT's new Functional Foods Expert Report details the promise bioactive components in new products can have on health. (See www.ift.org/ExpertReport.)

10. **Global Gangbusters**—Convenience and ready-meals are accelerating worldwide. Fresh, chilled, ready-to-eat products are emerging domestically and dominate the United Kingdom, commanding 25% of the food market, excluding beverages. More flexible packaging (e.g. pouches) is appearing. A majority of Southeast Asians eat take-out at least once a week, even more than Americans.

Source: Institute of Food Technologists, J.N.Klapthor, *Emerging top food trends in U.S. and abroad*, http://www.ift.org/cms/?pid=1001255, April 13, 2005.

5.3.4 Technological Factors

Technological developments can have far-reaching consequences. The development of cars, computers, personal computers, video games, microwave ovens, fax machines, the Internet, and mobile telephones has led to important shifts in living patterns and consumption patterns. However, less sweeping developments such as the introduction of instant soup, instant coffee, and compact laundry detergent can present important opportunities or threats. Technological developments are important not just from the marketing perspective but also for other functional areas in the company, such as production, logistics, and information processing. In the context of marketing applications, it often is stated that a new technological finding ("technological push") is interesting only if it is accompanied by sufficient interest in the market ("market pull").

The rate of technological development has increased over the last few years. Partly as a result of that, product life cycles are becoming shorter: The time until a new, better product is developed is getting shorter. Since basic technological research typically is very expensive, it is becoming increasingly important for companies to be the first in the market with a product. Only in that case will there be sufficient time and market potential for the company to be able to recover the development costs of a product. If a competitor is earlier, part of the market already has been supplied and the company no longer has the important image of being "the first."

In contrast to other macroenvironmental factors, a company can partially influence technological developments by itself, for example, through a strong research and development program. Influencing other macroenvironmental factors is generally not possible. Information sources about technological developments include specialized magazines.

5.3.5 Ecological Factors

Ecological factors ("physical environment") includes the weather and the availability of natural resources. Except in the very short term, the weather is by definition unpredictable. However, that is not a reason to leave this factor out of a macroenvironmental analysis. It can be very important to know the past impact of the weather on the sales of a product. After all, the sales progress must be controlled for the influence of the weather to gain insight into other factors that have had an influence. The "average" weather (the climate), for example, the average temperature, should be used as the basis for making prognoses. Weather-related data are maintained by national agencies and can be found on Internet.

In the last few years, limitations with regard to natural resources and issues such as environmental pollution and climate change have come to the fore. They have become such important external factors that they have to be taken into consideration in a macroenvironmental analysis. A related factor involves energy prices, which we have included with economic factors.

Related problems such as the spread of diseases can be included with ecological issues. For example, animal-related diseases (such as avian flu) obviously have a direct impact on people's consumption habits, but indirectly they also lead to increased attention to health issues.

5.3.6   Political-Legal Factors (Government)

Factors such as environmental policy, media policy, subsidy schemes, employment policy, monetary policy, and political developments abroad may present, either directly or indirectly, threats to or opportunities for a company. This influence may be limited, but it also may represent a "trend break" in the development of a market. An obvious example of an important political development in this context is the opening of Eastern European markets several years ago. Another example is a change in duty for certain products.

The influence of government regulation on the companies in a market depends to a large extent on the specific market and a company's ability to respond to the regulation. For example, the many environmental regulations that have been enacted represent threats to environmentally unfriendly products such as diesel fuel but opportunities for environmentally friendly products such as liquefied petroleum gas (LPG).

Newspapers are an obvious source of information about government decisions. Many journalists closely watch political issues. In terms of the possibility of *predicting* government decisions, the results of political deliberations typically are difficult to foresee. However, political decisions are often made in a reaction to other developments in the environment (such as environmental policy decisions), and this provides a point of departure for predictions.

CASE 5-4 *Influence of the Government*	The European Commission ruled in March 2004 that Microsoft had abused its dominant position in the European software market. The company paid a 497 million euro fine in the summer of 2004, but it has not acted on two orders to change its business practices. The commission ordered that Microsoft make room for rival programs by offering a second version of its Windows operating system without the Media Player program. It also instructed Microsoft to license secret information inside Windows to rivals so that they could produce server software that works with Windows, which operates more than 95 percent of personal computers around the world. **Source:** *The New York Times,* May 24, 2005, section C, p. 4.

It is useful to follow politics closely to the extent that it is relevant to the company and to keep one's ear to the ground by networking in the hope of becoming aware at an early stage of any potentially important government decision.

In the United States, many companies consider the government so important that specific officers have been appointed to "spot" the behavior of the government and use it for deducing potential opportunities and threats.

5.3.7 Points of Interest for the Macroenvironmental Analysis

In the analysis of all these macroenvironmental factors, three points of interest should have a central focus.

Opportunity or Threat

The influence of an environmental factor on a company depends on the ability of that company to respond to the development, that is, on the company's relative strengths and weaknesses. Therefore, it is impossible to state a priori whether a specific development is an opportunity or a threat. For one company it may be an opportunity; for another one it may be a threat. If it is a threat, a company can still attempt to turn a threat into an opportunity by applying as many resources as possible so that it can respond to the development.

We return to this issue in the discussion of SWOT analysis in Chapter 8. In the attempt to make a distinction between opportunities and threats, it is helpful to define an opportunity as a development that has a positive influence on a company's performance *if the company does not change its strategy.* Applying this condition enables one to classify environmental issues in terms of opportunities and threats.

Continuous Analysis

As a result of the importance of making a timely response to developments in the macroenvironment and, where possible, being the first responder, a company should take care to be open for signals from the environment that indicate the start of a new trend. In this context the term *environmental scanning* has been used: the continuous scanning of the environment. Especially for larger companies it can be advisable to assign someone to this task.

The environmental scanning should be limited to potentially relevant factors. A complete macroenvironmental analysis is impossible and unnecessary: Instead, it can be focused on the most important factors in the external environment, about which a company should collect data continuously. These factors should be designated not only for the macroenvironmental analysis (e.g., demographic trend A, economic trend B, government factor C) but also for the customer analysis (e.g., segments A and B) and the competitor analysis (e.g., competitor A and potential competitor B).

Forecasting and Scenarios

Many developments in the macroenvironment are very difficult to predict. In reality, many predictions do not prove to be true or do so many years later (or earlier). Specialized agencies also produce new prognoses regularly. To be able to cope with this uncertainty during the planning process, it is advisable to define *scenarios* for the most important factors. A scenario is a description of a potential environmental situation, for example, a disappointing economic climate or, for a drinks manufacturer, a total prohibition on advertising for alcoholic drinks. A scenario may also be defined in relation to the competition; for example, the competitor reacts or does not react (see also Chapter 6).

In practice, typically no more than two scenarios are defined: a pessimistic one and a most probable one. In addition to a pessimistic variation, an optimistic scenario could be defined. After all, events can turn out to be disappointing but can also be better than expected. If events turn out better than expected, perhaps the planned strategy needs to be modified. However, in reality, the optimistic scenarios are often omitted because of cautiousness.

Defining a scenario is meaningful only if it also includes guidelines for how the company should react in that situation. For this purpose, the marketing plan may include an attachment that describes an alternative plan to be used for the pessimistic scenario. Such an alternative plan is also called a *contingency plan* and is accompanied by "standards" (limiting values of variables) that indicate when the plan becomes current. The most likely scenario then becomes the basis for the marketing plan.

All scenarios should be realistic. A pessimistic scenario is not the same as the assumption that *everything* will go wrong. For example, it is extremely unlikely that simultaneously with disappointing economic growth, a competitor will introduce new, better products while energy prices rise and the government enforces important limitations on advertising.

As was indicated above, macroenvironmental factors may have a direct impact on total market demand. In the next section we discuss aggregated market factors.

5.4 AGGREGATED MARKET FACTORS

In the previous section we reviewed the various categories of macroenvironmental factors: demographic, economic, social-cultural, technological, ecological, and political-legal variables (*DESTEP factors*). As was indicated, each organization should attempt to stay informed about developments in these variables. Each potential change or trend may present an opportunity or a threat. In the context of macroenvironmental analysis it sometimes is argued that threats do not exist. Each potential threat can be turned into an opportunity if the organization makes an effort to respond to that specific development. For example, a publisher of youth magazines does not have to consider the reduction in the number of youths and the increase in the number of elderly people as a threat if it is able to bring a magazine for older people onto the market.

A macroenvironmental analysis is also very important in terms of an industry analysis, since developments in the macroenvironment may have an important influence on the attractiveness of a market. This influence works largely through total market demand. For example, in the case of the publisher of youth magazines, the reduction in the number of youths will have a negative impact on the market size (readers of youth magazines), whereas the aging trend will have the reverse effect on the markets for products and services for elderly people. In this way we arrive at an analysis of the aggregated market factors.

Aggregated market factors are variables that are defined in terms of the total market demand (the primary demand or the size of the market). This involves the following variables:

- The potential market size.
- The expected market growth and the phase in the product life cycle.
- Sensitivity to economic and seasonal trends.

5.4.1 Market Size

The *size of the market* is important because larger markets are more *attractive* than smaller markets. After all, large markets have more sales possibilities, making it easier to recover the costs of investments. In addition, a larger market offers more opportunities for segmentation, such as searching for niches. Larger markets also attract more competitors, and that has a negative influence on the attractiveness of a market.

Another reason for determining market size is that it may be used to indicate the *meaning* of a certain market share. For example, a market share of 1 percent in the market for laundry detergent will lead to a lot more sales than will the same market share in the market for liquid detergents. This implies that it is important to define a market clearly: Without precise *market definition,* it is unclear what the various analyses in the strategic marketing planning process are referring to. In this context, the manager can choose a broad or a narrow market definition. With a broad definition, the market share will be relatively low and the number of competitors will be large. With a narrow definition, the reverse applies. This may give the impression that a manager can easily "manipulate" the company's market share by choosing another market definition, but that is not the case. The market definition is based on strategic choices: Which customer groups does the company serve, and who are the most important competitors?

In the analysis of the size of the market, a distinction must be made between the *served* market and the *potential* market. The served market is the current market; the potential market is the maximum of what would be feasible, for example, with a 100 percent distribution of the product and a strong sales promotion. Determining the potential market requires the application of forecasting methods (see Section 8.1). Data about total market demand for food products are collected by agencies such as AC Nielsen and IRI. For other markets, data from trade associations should be used.

5.4.2 Market and Submarket Growth and Product Life Cycle

Market growth is also an important criterion for the attractiveness of a market. In addition, *growth in submarkets* should be identified.[4] Strong market or submarket growth implies that even with a stable market share, increasing sales may be expected. However, even if the aggregate market size declines, there may be opportunities:

- If market sales decline, competitors may leave the market and the firm may become dominant.
- If aggregate market sales decline, there may be submarkets that grow, and so a disaggregated market analysis is needed.

Market growth is so important that this factor has been included as *the* market characteristic in the portfolio analysis of the Boston Consulting Group (see Section 8.3). Aside from current market growth, *expected* market growth is important. Therefore, predictions of market growth need to be made. In making prognoses, the concept of the *product life cycle* may be used because the phase in the life cycle in which the product happens to be helps determine the expected future development.

Many products have a life cycle. After the introduction and sales growth come stabilization and then decline. An important reason for this cycle is that as time goes by, other, better products come onto the market, after which sales of the "old" product start to decline. The life cycle of a product is typically depicted with a graph that shows the course of sales over time. It is often assumed that this curve is S-shaped and that five phases can be distinguished (Figure 5-3).

In the *introductory* phase, sales are growing slowly: There are only a few consumers who know or use the product, and distribution is limited. In the *growth* phase, sales are increasing

FIGURE 5-3
Example of a Product Life Cycle Curve

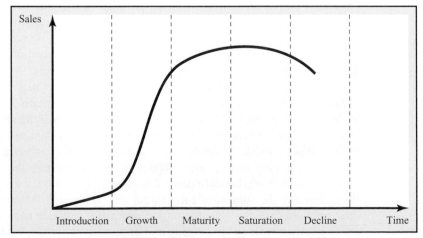

at an ever more rapid pace: The product catches on, distribution increases, and an increasing number of consumers are buying the product. In the *mature* phase, sales are still increasing but the rate of growth is starting to slow down: There are not many "new" consumers anymore. In the *saturation* phase, sales start to decline slowly, after which, in the *decline* phase, sales drop sharply. In these later phases the function of the product is taken over by other products.

The concept of the product life cycle may be applied to product groups, brands, and varieties. At this point we are discussing the life cycle of a *product group,* for example, personal computers. Therefore, the focus is on the market as a whole. In that case, the implementation of the elements of the marketing mix will differ by phase. For example, brands in the growth phase of a market can grow by focusing on the market potential, whereas in the saturation phase growth should be pursued by taking sales away from competitors (increasing market share) or through innovation. Brands and varieties can also have a life cycle, as in the case of Colgate toothpaste and Ariel Liquid laundry detergent. It has been argued that in the introductory phase of a brand, the brand values to be communicated should be mostly tangible, whereas in later phases, the emphasis can be more on emotional characteristics.

However, the strategic implications of the life cycle concept are not always clear. A market in the growth phase appears attractive but also draws competitors. Often in growth markets, the number of suppliers becomes too large in relation to the final market size. This leads irrevocably to the downfall of a number of the suppliers. A product in the mature or saturation phase appears less attractive, but in these phases there may be segments that are still experiencing growth. If the most appropriate segmentation strategy is chosen, sales growth of the company's own brand is still possible. This shows that the life cycle of a product or brand should not be taken as a *given* because a company can influence and even lengthen this cycle. Through the choice of a good marketing strategy, a product or brand in the saturation phase can still offer many possibilities for remaining profitable or becoming profitable again.

5.4.3 Sensitivity to Economic and Seasonal Trends

Markets in which sales are very sensitive to economic or seasonal trends are less attractive than markets in which this is not the case. After all, more uncertainty regarding sales and/or larger fluctuations mean that a company needs to have a great deal of flexibility. Sensitivity to economic trends occurs especially with luxury goods, which are often durable consumer goods. Sales fluctuations within a year that result from sensitivity to seasonal influences may occur with many products, such as drinks, travel, and sports products. A company that is active in several markets can attempt to reduce uncertainty regarding total sales through a careful choice of product-market combinations (a portfolio decision).

5.5 FACTORS RELATED TO INDUSTRY STRUCTURE

Factors related to *industry structure* are factors that determine the intensity of the competition in a market. An analysis of the intensity of the competition is important because a market is less attractive to the extent that the competition is more intense. Strong competition leads to increased marketing activity (promotional campaigns, intense advertising efforts), which increases costs; therefore, the average profitability of these companies is relatively low.

Since the profitability of companies is in the end a central point in the industry structure analysis, an attempt should be made to obtain more insight into profitability (Section 5.5.1). Subsequently, factors that have an impact on average profitability should be examined. For this purpose, the industry model of Porter (1980) may be used (Section 5.5.2).

FIGURE 5-4 **Industry Structure**

Source: Porter (1980).

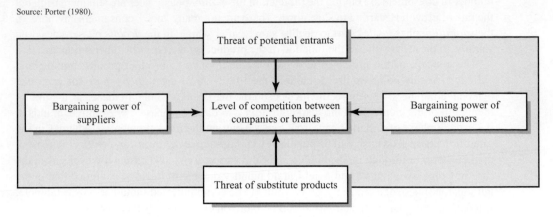

5.5.1 Profitability

There may be significant differences between the profitability of various brands in a specific market. Also, there typically are large differences in profitability between markets. Factors that determine profitability include the manufacturing process, the cost structure, and the competition. In an industry structure analysis, the task is to gain as much insight as possible into profitability. In addition, the *variability* of profitability is important: the extent to which profitability fluctuates over time. This represents an indication of the risks in a specific market. In markets with relatively high fixed costs, a decline in demand will lead to a stronger decline in profit than is the case in markets with relatively low fixed costs.

In practice, it is not easy to gain insight into the average profitability in a market. Although companies publish data about expenditures and revenues in their annual reports, these data are never broken down by products and/or markets. Mostly such data are considered extremely strategic and confidential. The average profitability in a market therefore typically must be estimated on the basis of impressions.

5.5.2 Industry Structure According to Porter

In *Competitive Strategy,* Porter (1980) creates a link between the industry structure and competitive strategies.[5] He argues that five factors ("competitive forces") have an influence on the competition structure in an industry (Figure 5-4). In Porter's model, the central industry factor is the intensity of competition between existing suppliers in a market.

External Factors

The intensity of the competition is determined by external and internal factors. Figure 5-4 shows the *external* factors. This relates to the threat of new competitors (potential suppliers and substitute products) and the negotiation power of suppliers and buyers (distributors and final customers). If these "threats" are strong, the intensity of the competition will be relatively strong and the average rate of return of companies will be relatively low.

The threat exerted by each of these four factors depends on a number of underlying factors. The *threat of new suppliers* is strong when:

- Entrance barriers are low because of:
- The absence of economies of scale
- Limited communication intensity

- There is little product differentiation.
- There is easy access to distribution channels.

In many markets for consumer goods there is little physical product differentiation, but because of that situation there are intense communication efforts. A new product or a new brand can be successful only if an appropriate corresponding communications budget is available. This also increases access to the distribution channels: Distributors prefer brands for which the manufacturer is engaged in intensive sales promotion.

The *threat of substitute products* depends on the broadness of the market definition on which the analysis is based. If a narrow market definition is assumed, there are a relatively large number of substitute products.

The *power of suppliers and/or buyers (distributors)* is strong when:

- Their power is strongly concentrated.
- They are not very price-sensitive.
- There is little product differentiation (presence of alternatives).

In the food industry in some countries, buyers (distributors) have strong power because of their concentration. As a result of various fusions and mergers, only a few purchasing combinations are responsible for a large share of sales in the food industry. In other countries, that power is much smaller. Especially in the less developed grocery markets in, for example, southern Europe, there are many smaller distributors and therefore these buyers have less power.

It is clear that for manufacturers, the power of buyers is an important factor. The increased concentration in some countries has led to the development of the *account management* system by manufacturers and a greater emphasis on collaboration with distributors.

This demonstrates that in the context of Porter's model, it is important to analyze the *distribution structure*. The market structure of the distribution chain determines the power of the distributor and consequently determines the influence of this factor on market attractiveness.

Aside from the power of distributors, the power of final customers (consumers) is increasing because of the Internet. Through the Internet, consumers can bundle their powers and extract price reductions (or conduct campaigns via Web sites, for example, involving complaints about suppliers or the government). Conversely, suppliers can easily organize auctions on the Internet for which principles such as "highest bidder" and "the lowest" may be used.

Internal Factors: The Supply Structure

Aside from the factors mentioned above, the intensity of the competition between existing suppliers in a market is determined by a number of underlying *internal* factors. These are factors that directly determine the *supply structure* of a market. These factors are not shown in Figure 5-4 but will be discussed below. First, we discuss four elements that determine the supply structure: the number of suppliers, the degree of product differentiation (together these two dimensions determine the market form), concentration, and collaboration.

The market form determines the number of suppliers and the extent to which suppliers and products differ from one another.

1. *The number of suppliers.* A larger number of suppliers in principle leads to a larger degree of competition.
2. *The degree of product differentiation.* This is the extent to which suppliers and products differ from one another. In terms of the degree of product differentiation, if consumers perceive few differences between the offered products, the competition is more intense.

As a result of the ever-increasing rate of technological development, in many markets products appear increasingly similar to one another.

3. *The degree of concentration of suppliers.* With a strong concentration, it is easier to make market agreements and the competition typically is less intensive; this is also the case if the number of competitors decreases. This relationship does not always apply. If a company merges with a competitor (which increases the concentration), the larger company can apply more resources to the competition battle. The relationship between concentration and competition is therefore not unequivocal and depends on the company that is conducting the analysis. For example, with a merger the competition for the merging partners will decrease by definition, whereas for the remaining suppliers the competition may increase.

The degree of concentration can be measured by graphing the collective market share (*concentration ratio*) of the largest two (CR2) or four companies (CR4) and analyzing it over time. An increasing concentration ratio indicates a more one-sided distribution of power in the market. Partly as a result of the importance of internationalization, the concentration in various markets has been increasing, for example, in sectors such as banking, insurance, and the airline industry.

4. *Collaboration within a market.* The existence of market agreements or other forms of collaboration between competitors has an influence on the organization of the market and therefore on the degree of competition.

Figure 5-5 provides an overview of the possible market forms.

The dimensions mentioned above constitute the supply structure of the market. In addition, several other elements have an influence on the competitive behavior of suppliers:

• *The development of the primary demand (market size).* In a shrinking market, sales growth can be achieved only at the expense of the competitors. Many markets are saturated, and so this factor generally leads to strong competition.

• *The proportion of fixed and variable costs.* If the fixed costs in the industry are relatively high, a company will have to fight harder to recover those costs.

• *The minimum scale required for capacity expansion.* In industries in which the production capacity can be expanded only in large leaps because of the optimal scale of the production unit, competition will be more fierce.

• *The surplus capacity.* The larger the surplus capacity, the fiercer the competition.

• *The strategic effort of companies.* If a company conducts its main activity in a certain industry, it will be more dedicated to the competitive battle than will a company that only has a sideline in that industry.

• *Uncertainty in regard to the production technology.* If the production technology is new or still is being developed, the competition will be more intense.

FIGURE 5-5
Market Forms

Homogeneity of the Products	Number of Suppliers		
	Many	**Few**	**One**
Homogeneous	Full competition	Homogeneous oligopoly	Monopoly
Heterogeneous	Monopolistic competition	Heterogeneous oligopoly	Monopoly

- *Exit barriers.* This refers to all the factors that make it difficult for a company to end loss-making business activities: The higher the exit barriers are, the longer companies will continue with activities that lose money and the stronger the competition will be. Exit barriers may include the following:

  - *Social factors:* The legally required procedures regarding mass layoffs and the resistance of employees who are in danger of losing their jobs present very important exit barriers.
  - *Strongly specialized assets:* The liquidation value of a strongly specialized machine is often significantly lower than the utility value.
  - The *connection of a certain product to other products,* for example, through the collective use of fixed means of production (buildings, machines, etc.) or because of the desire to carry a full assortment or as a result of the image of the company (removing a product from the market will have a negative impact on the share price).
  - *Emotional factors* such as attachment to a certain product.
  - *Government support:* Government support for companies in trouble may present an exit barrier.

For a company that is considering entering a market, one of these factors deserves special attention: *entrance barriers.* An analysis of entrance barriers is important not only to be able to determine the threat of potential suppliers but also to be able to determine which barriers the company has to overcome to enter the market. For a company that is considering entering a market, high entrance barriers obviously count as negative factors. In contrast, for companies that are already active in a market, high entrance barriers are a positive factor because they limit the threat of new entrants.

5.6   DETERMINING MARKET ATTRACTIVENESS

Completing an industry analysis serves two goals:

1. Obtaining insight into opportunities and threats from the perspective of the industry.
2. Obtaining insight into the attractiveness of the market.

To summarize an industry analysis, first the observed opportunities and threats are listed. Once a company has researched the attractiveness of a market by means of the factors listed in Figure 5-1, trying to arrive at summarizing conclusions may present a problem. After all, what should the conclusion be if some factors are interpreted positively and others are interpreted negatively? This problem can be solved through the assumption that a high score on one factor can compensate for a low score on another factor. With this assumption, it is possible to calculate a summarizing "score" that is based on a *weighted factor scoring method.*

Suppose a manufacturer of ice cream is considering the production of candy bars. To research the attractiveness of the market for candy bars, the manufacturer examines the factors listed in Figure 5-6. The management rates each factor with a score on a scale ranging from 1 (very unattractive) to 5 (very attractive). In this example, a large market exists. This leads to a score of 5 for the factor market size. However, there is also intense competition. Therefore, that factor receives a score of 1. Subsequently, each factor receives a *weight* that is based on the importance (as assessed by management) of that factor for the attractiveness of the specific market. Because in different markets there are different *determinants of success,* these weights may differ by market. In addition, in the weighting process it matters how important management considers a factor to be. For example, one company may consider growth important, whereas for another profitability is the most important factor.

In the example, the factor of market growth is considered the most important (weight 0.20). When all the factors have been multiplied by their weights and summed, we arrive at an attractiveness score of 2.95.

The next issue is how this score should be interpreted. Is 2.95 high or low? The interpretation depends, among other things, on whether the company that is doing the analysis is already active in that market. A company that is already active in the market could compare the results with those from a *previous period.* That would provide an answer to whether the market is becoming more or less attractive and why. A potential entrant, as in the example, could compare the results with *another market,* for example, the market for sandwich fillings: The market with the higher score is the most attractive for entrance. In addition, the potential entrant needs to balance the score against the *height of the entrance barriers:* What problems need to be overcome to enter the market? A different market with a lower attractiveness score but with lower entrance barriers may be preferable. After all, the entrance barriers can be interpreted as the "price" that has to be paid to enter a market.

Obviously, the factor scoring method described here is *subjective.* The biggest challenge is determining the appropriate weights for the individual factors. In addition, it is assumed that a low score on one factor may be compensated for by a high score on another factor. However, it is not unthinkable that a company requires minimum values for certain factors, for example, minimum required market growth.

An important advantage of the use of the factor scoring method in the industry analysis is that it provides a well-organized summary of the results of the entire analysis. A systematically implemented and well-organized depiction of the industry analysis is very important not just for the company's analyses but also for internal communication within the company.

In Figure 5-6 the macroenvironmental factors from Figure 5-1 have not been included specifically. The reason for this is that these macro factors are included in the interpretation of the attractiveness of the market through their impact on market size and market growth. The method of summarizing the industry analysis in Figure 5-6 allows a direct link with the *portfolio analyses,* in which several factors are considered (see Section 8.3). The fact is that in the context of such "multifactor portfolio analyses," the kind of analysis in Figure 5-6 is very common.

FIGURE 5-6   **The Calculation of the Attractiveness Score of the Market for Candy Bars (1 = unattractive; 5 = very attractive)**

Factor	Weight	Assessment	Score	Value
Aggregated market factors				
Market size	0.15	Large	5	0.75
Market growth/phase in product life cycle	0.20	Saturated	2	0.40
Sensitivity to economic and seasonal trends	0.05	Limited	4	0.20
Industry structure factors				
Profit margin	0.15	Fairly high	4	0.60
Threat of new entrants	0.05	Limited	5	0.25
Negotiation power of customers	0.10	Strong	2	0.20
Negotiation power of suppliers	0.05	Limited	4	0.20
Intensity of competition	0.20	Very heavy	1	0.20
Threat of substitute products	0.05	Fairly strong	3	0.15
Total	1.0			2.95

Summary

The goal of the industry analysis is to obtain an impression of future opportunities and threats from the perspective of the industry as well as changes in the attractiveness of the market in which a company is active. The attractiveness or expected profitability of a market is determined by the intensity of competition. The more intense the battle, the less attractive the market. The degree of competition in turn is determined by three categories of factors: developments in the macroenvironment (such as demographic and social-cultural trends), aggregated market factors (such as the phase in the product life cycle), and factors related to the industry structure (such as the intensity of competition). The analysis of the macroenvironment is an important source of opportunities. If a company is able to respond quickly to a social-cultural development, it may achieve a competitive advantage. The attractiveness of a market and its submarkets should be determined by evaluating all these underlying factors and, based on this evaluation, determining an attractiveness score. By assigning weights to each of the examined factors and summing the various values, a company will arrive at an attractiveness score that may be compared with the scores for other markets or with the score for a previous period. Since trends in the industry may include large degrees of uncertainty with large consequences, a manager can define scenarios with respect to the main trends.

The information from an industry analysis regarding the attractiveness of a market is important for determining both objectives and the appropriate investment level of the organization in that specific market (corporate strategy; see Chapter 10). The information about possible opportunities and threats can be used in determining the marketing strategy.

Notes

1. This distinction was introduced by Alsem, K. J. (1991), in his dissertation *Concurrentie-analyse in de marketing (Competitive Analysis in Marketing,* Groningen,. Netherlands, University of Groningen, Faculty of Economics.
2. Porter, M. E. (1980), *Competitive Strategy,* New York: Free Press.
3. Partly based on Lehmann, D. R., R. S. Winer (2002) *Analysis for Marketing Planning,* New York: McGraw-Hill, 5th ed.
4. See also Aaker, D. A. (2005), *Strategic Market Management,* 7th ed., New York: Wiley, Chapter 5.
5. Porter (1980).

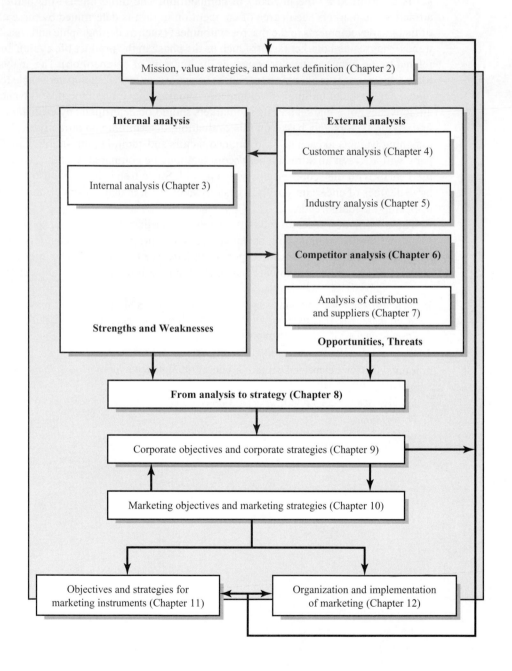

Mission, value strategies, and market definition (Chapter 2)

Internal analysis

Internal analysis (Chapter 3)

Strengths and Weaknesses

External analysis

Customer analysis (Chapter 4)

Industry analysis (Chapter 5)

Competitor analysis (Chapter 6)

Analysis of distribution and suppliers (Chapter 7)

Opportunities, Threats

From analysis to strategy (Chapter 8)

Corporate objectives and corporate strategies (Chapter 9)

Marketing objectives and marketing strategies (Chapter 10)

Objectives and strategies for marketing instruments (Chapter 11)

Organization and implementation of marketing (Chapter 12)

Chapter **Six**

Competitor Analysis

Key Points in This Chapter

- Know the steps of a competitor analysis.
- Be able to identify competitors by using the appropriate methods.
- Assess competitors' strengths and weaknesses on the corporate and brand levels.
- Know which qualitative and quantitative data sources can be used.in a competitor analysis.
- Put it all together in making a forecast of a competitor's strategy and reactions.

INTRODUCTION

A competitor analysis can be thought of as a competition analysis at the micro level: The behavior of individual competitors is analyzed with the ultimate goal of predicting the competitors' actions and reactions. It is important to maintain a clear structure in a competitor analysis. Without structuring, the problem may arise, as it often does in practice, that large amounts of data are collected about competitors without deducing the relevant *information* from the data.

Section 6.1 describes the goal and structure of a competitor analysis. The first phase in a competitor analysis is identification of the competitors. Section 6.2 discusses the methods that may be useful in that process. Sections 6.3 through 6.6 outline the other phases of the competitor analysis. Section 6.7 reviews a number of data sources that may be used. In practice, in a competitor analysis mostly qualitative data are used.

Toys 'R' Us

Every child in New York and the surrounding area knows it. For Barbie, race cars, Lego, and a "unique" shopping experience, you have to be at Times Square, Manhattan. There you find the ultimate Toys 'R' Us. A real Ferris wheel turns right in the middle of the shop, and a bit farther in there's a roaring dinosaur eight meters tall: a tourist attraction within the magnet that the circuslike square is for visitors from all quarters of the world. The mega shopping mall is a Valhalla for children and a hell for most parents. For the thousands of daily passers-by it is hard to imagine, but it is not unlikely that this toy paradise will no longer exist in a couple of years.

It is as if McDonald's would stop making hamburgers, but Toys 'R' Us is serious. In the beginning of 2004 the management pointed out in a short statement that the toy sector is being separated from the baby business. In a remarkable subordinate clause, "the possible sale of the worldwide toy business" is mentioned. A company says something like that only when there are really such plans.

Toys 'R' Us, in which the "R" in the logo is playfully turned around, became the leader in the toy market in the 1990s. Every self-respecting city in the United States got a fancifully colored store. The new law of Toyland was simple: For balloons, Power Rangers, and everything in between you had to be at Toys 'R' Us. But like many other sectors, the company has suffered over the last few years from the competition of discount chains such as Wal-Mart and Target. They are growing fast and sell literally everything in their efficiently equipped stores.

These chains' conquest of the American toy market, in which annually around $27 billion is turned over, has gone fast. The reason: extremely low prices, a wide assortment under one roof, and far-reaching power over the suppliers. In 1994 Toys 'R' U.S. was the market leader, with a share of over 20 percent. Now Wal-Mart is leading with the same percentage, and Toys 'R' Us has dropped to 17 percent.

The self-assured toy king lived in style. The splashy flagship store on Times Square was opened in 2001, with an optimistic profit expectation. The almost 700 other shops in the United States got hip new designs. Toys 'R' Us achieved its leading position in the 1990s by dealing ruthlessly with competitors by threatening to overtake them, by having low prices, and by keeping an iron grip on the supplying companies: exactly the same thing Wal-Mart is now doing.

Possibly Toys 'R' Us was so busy with its own positioning at the top that the discount competitors simply were not seen. In 2003 its profit tumbled to $88 million, after reaching $279 million in 2000, while sales of more than $11 billion remained steady. In 2003 it was decided to close 146 Kids 'R' Us shops (children's clothing), and 3,800 jobs were lost. Toys 'R' Us shares were worth around $16 each at the end of 2004; the peak was $40 around the turn of the century.

Of course the recession and the events of September 11, 2001, played a role. Because of the economic downfall, parents paid less for dollhouses and cuddly toys. Because of the 9/11 attacks tourism was hit, and that was especially important for the New York branch on Times Square. Because of a harbor strike in 2002 the shipping costs of the suppliers rose drastically. However, those factors also applied to the competitors.

There is one branch that does bring in money: Baby's 'R' Us. Those shops are aimed at young parents and their smallest kids, and apparently there is growth in that sector. Although this department constitutes only 15 percent of the company, half the profits are made there. In the first quarter of 2004 profits rose $11 million to $63 million, whereas the toys branch and the Internet shop lost money during the same period.

Wall Street analysts were initially enthusiastic about a possible closing of the toys branch. The sale of the real estate would by itself bring in a couple of billion. In that way a smaller, more focused, and financially perfectly sound company would appear.

But Wal-Mart watches well and learns fast. In several branches it is experimenting with special baby departments. If Wal-Mart is going to offer a qualitatively reasonable product at the usual rock-bottom price, Baby's 'R' Us will have to fear the worst. One expert dared to adopt a straightforward pessimistic outlook. Retail business consultant Burt Flickinger said what he had to say in various media. By chance he came across the baby corner of a Wal-Mart. "The mothers poured in. It looks like this is going to mean the very early death of Baby's 'R' Us."

Toys 'R' Us is therefore wisely taking a little more time to watch the developments. Because sales always peak in December, the company said that until Christmas no shops or branches will be closed down. "Our customers should know," senior official John Eyler said recently, "that we will deal with our toy branch with new energy." That's for the future to show.

Sources: www2.toysrus.com; *De Volkskrant*, August 23, 2004, p. 6 .

Questions

1. a. What was the target of Toys 'R' Us in the 1990s?
   b. Which strategy do you think was used to reach that target?
2. a. With respect to competition, four levels can be differentiated. Identify those four levels from the Toys 'R' Us viewpoint.
   b. According to the information in the case, which competition level constitutes the greatest threat to Toys 'R' Us? Explain your answer.
3. Describe the strategy that Wal-Mart used in 2003 during "the battle for the toy market."
4. Which are the strong and weak points of Toys 'R' Us?
5. Why was Toys 'R' Us been hit hard by the recession, 9/11, and the harbor strike, whereas Wal-Mart seemed to profit from those developments?
6. What would you advise Toys 'R' Us to do, taking the situation as described in the case into account? Explain your answer.

6.1 GOAL AND STRUCTURE OF THE COMPETITOR ANALYSIS

A competitor analysis examines *individual competitors*. Opportunities that may be expected from competitors typically are found in the weaknesses of those competitors. Those weaknesses provide starting points for the company's competitive advantages. The extent to which competitors are threatening the company depends on their objectives and strategies. If a competitor is satisfied with its position and has no new plans, there is relatively less danger to be expected. However, a competitor that wants to grow and starts an active competition battle for that purpose, with new products and intensive advertising efforts, presents an important threat to the company.

Therefore, the objectives of the competitor analysis are to obtain insight into:

- The *strengths and weaknesses* of the competitors.
- The *future behavior* of the competitors.

The strengths and weaknesses of competitors are compared with the company's own strengths and weaknesses to understand the extent to which the company is strong or weak in relation to the competitors. For example, a company's strength has little strategic value if the competitors have the same strength. However, a weakness is less serious if all the competitors have the same weakness. Therefore, the goal is to determine the company's *relative* strengths and weaknesses.

An understanding of the expected behavior of competitors provides indications for opportunities and threats caused by competitors. In terms of the future behavior of competitors, a distinction can be made between the "autonomous" expected behavior of the competitors—what they are planning to do on their own initiative—and possible reactions of competitors to the company's strategies.

In performing a competitor analysis, two approaches may be chosen. The first is to consider the competitor as a *"rival,"* another supplier that does battle for the favor of the customers and therefore should be "fought." Until the end of the 1980s this approach was the most common. The goal was to beat the competition, and the competitor analysis therefore was aimed at identifying the weaknesses of the opponent. By placing a company's strength against those weaknesses, the company could achieve a competitive advantage. This approach to competitor analysis is still relevant, but since the start of the 1990s another approach has been gaining ground. In this approach, the company considers its

FIGURE 6-1 **Framework for a Competitor Analysis**

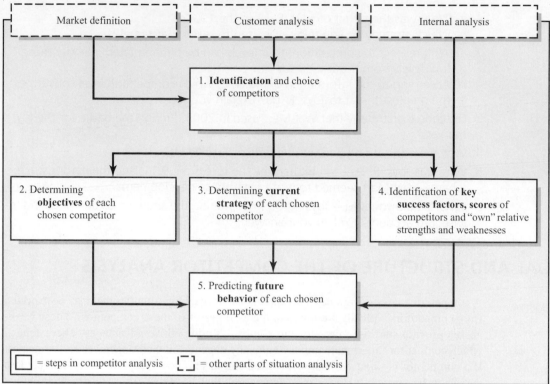

competitors as future *collaboration partners*. Partly as a result of the trend toward internationalization that was mentioned earlier in this book, in many industries survival is possible only through collaboration with competitors, not through attempting to beat them. Examples of industries in which collaboration has taken on an increasingly important role are the airline industry, the banking and insurance industries, the printing and allied trades, and the computer industry.

The concept of a competitor as a future partner is in line with increasing attention to relationship marketing. This is sometimes referred to as *relationship marketing at the macro level:* maintaining relationships with competitors.[1] Relationship marketing at the micro level refers to relationships with customers. In terms of the practice of performing a competitor analysis, this means that the analysis should be focused not only on searching for weaknesses of the opponent (to gain a competitive advantage for the company) but also on searching for starting points for collaboration. An opportunity presents itself when the competitor has an interesting strength in an area where the company has a weakness, and vice versa.

Five phases may be distinguished in a competitor analysis (Figure 6-1):

1. Identification and choice of competitors.
2. Objectives of competitors.
3. Current strategies of competitors.
4. Identification of factors that determine success and the strengths and weaknesses of competitors.
5. Prediction of the strategies of competitors.

Phases 4 and 5 of this process provide the information mentioned in the description of the objectives of a competitor analysis (strengths and weaknesses, future behavior). We will now discuss each of the five phases.

6.2 IDENTIFICATION AND CHOICE OF COMPETITORS

In terms of a definition of what a competitor is, it may be another supplier that potentially fulfills the same need of the target audience. On the basis of this definition, the question of who the competitors are therefore depends on the definition of the need. That definition is connected to the market definition. Does Coca-Cola's top management consider that the company is active in the market for colas or the market for soft drinks or in the market for luxury items?

6.2.1 Competition Levels

In regard to competition, four levels can be distinguished:

1. *Product form competition.* This is competition between brands that are focused on the same market segment, for example, Diet Pepsi and Diet Coke.
2. *Product category competition.* This is competition between products with comparable characteristics, such as various soft drinks.
3. *Generic competition.* This competition between products that respond to the same needs of consumers, such as drinks.
4. *Budget competition.* This is competition for the money of the consumer, such as food and entertainment.

Figure 6-2 includes several other examples of competition at these four levels. In moving from product form competition toward budget competition, the market definition broadens and, consequently, the number of competitors increases. Therefore, a direct relationship exists between the definition of the market and the identification of the competitors. Because of this, there is also a relationship with the marketing decisions: Different product characteristics should be emphasized at the different competition levels. For example, if a manufacturer of low-priced video recorders chooses the product form level of competition in Figure 6-2, the competitors are other low-priced video recorders and the manufacturer should emphasize why its video recorder is better than the other cheap recorders. However, if the manufacturer chooses the product category level, the manufacturer should position itself in relation to all other video recorders, for example, through price. On the generic level, the advantages of the video recorder over other equipment should be pointed out to the consumer. On the budget level, the company might communicate why using a video recorder is more interesting than other leisure activities.

The choice of the competition level therefore is clearly connected to the market definition. The market definition in turn is determined, among other things, by two related factors:

1. The *planning level* in the company: company level, business unit level, or product level.
2. The *planning period:* Is it a matter of short-term plans (a year or less) or longer-term plans?

FIGURE 6-2
Examples of Competition Levels

Competition Level	Low-Alcohol Beer	Low-Priced Video Recorder	Chinese Restaurant
Product form	Low-alcohol or alcohol-free beer	Low-price video recorder	Chinese restaurants
Product category	Beer	Video recorders	Restaurants
Generic	Drinks	Audio and video equipment	Eating at home
Budget	Drinks, food, entertainment	Durable goods, vacations	Food, drinks, entertainment

FIGURE 6-3
Relationship between Aggregation Level, Planning Horizon, Market Definition, and Competition Level

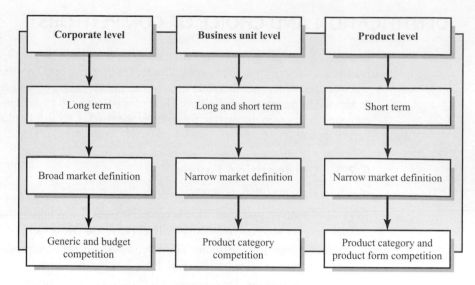

Figure 6-3 shows the relationship between these two factors. To the extent that a *higher* aggregation level in the company is involved, the planning period usually becomes *longer,* the market definition *broader,* and the level of competition *higher*. For example, at the company level issues such as collaboration with potential partners play a role. That is a long-term issue that requires a broad market definition and therefore a high level of competition. After all, potential partners do not need to be active only in the direct market of the company but may also be active in adjacent markets. At the product level the annual short-term planning is relevant; this involves, for example, the daily threat of directly competing products and brands (product category competition and product form competition).

6.2.2 Methods for Identifying Competitors

The methods that can be used for identifying the competitors include competition-based methods and customer-based methods. In *customer-based methods,* data regarding the demand side of the market are used: The competition is analyzed from the perspective of the customers. For example, customers may be asked which product or brand they would purchase if the preferred product or brand were not available. A *competition-based approach* means that the company identifies the competition on the basis of data about the competitors, for example, by examining which competitors follow a strategy similar to the one used by the company.

In general, competition-based methods are suitable for identifying the competition at the *company level,* whereas customer-based methods are appropriate for identifying competing *products*. We will review two competition-based methods and then three customer-based methods. We will conclude this part of the chapter with a brief discussion of the advantages and disadvantages of both categories of methods.

Competition-Based Methods

Two competition-based methods can be distinguished:

1. Management opinion
2. Strategic groups

Management Opinion By using his or her experience and knowledge of the market, a manager can often make a reasonable estimate of the identity of current and future competitors (management opinion). As needed, the manager also can consult the company's representatives, distributors, and other internal experts. A tool that can used for this purpose is the division of competitors into companies that:

- Bring the same *products* onto the market.
- Serve the same *customers* (markets and/or segments).

The most *direct competitors* are companies that supply the same products to the same markets. More *indirect competitors* are companies that supply the same products but focus on a different market. Companies that serve the same market but sell other products may be designated as *potential competitors*.

Strategic Groups A second competition-based way to identify competitors is to divide the suppliers in a market into *strategic groups*. A strategic group is a group of companies that employ similar strategies. A company can develop insight into how these groups are composed by determining which strategies the suppliers in a market have chosen, that is, by examining the choice of a target audience and the positioning as well the implementation of the elements of the marketing mix: product quality, assortment, price setting, distribution spread, use of representatives, and the communications mix. Furthermore, the strategies relating to other functional areas are important, such as the extent of research and development (R&D) efforts, production, purchasing, and finances.

CASE 6-1
Strategic Groups in the Clothing Market

At Polo Ralph Lauren's inception more than 30 years ago, fashion industry experts of almost every stripe criticized the company. Lacking creativity in design, how could Ralph Lauren charge such high prices? Lauren's lack of fashion was its greatest strength. Ralph Lauren built on the decisive advantages of the two strategic groups that dominated the high-end clothing market: designer haute couture and the higher-volume but lower-priced classical lines of Burberry's, Brooks Brothers, Aquascutum, and the like. Ralph Lauren has built its brand in the space between these two strategic groups, but it did not do that by taking the average of the groups' differences. Its designer name, the elegance of its stores, and the luxury of its materials capture what most customers value in haute couture; its updated classical look and price capture the best of the classical lines. By combining the most attractive factors of both groups, Polo Ralph Lauren not only captured share from both segments but also drew many new customers into the market.

Source: Kim, W. Chan, and Renee Mauborgne, "Creating New Market Space," *Harvard Business Review,* January–February, 1999, p. 83–93.

The concept of strategic groups simplifies the identification and choice of competitors. After all, the competition will be strongest within strategic groups. If there is a large number of competitors, a company may place the most emphasis on its own strategic group. The other strategic groups may then be analyzed as a whole. In practice, sometimes all competitors or groups of "small competitors" are defined as a strategic group; in this case the company makes the assumption that those small competitors all use strategies that are more or less comparable (this often is not the case).

Customer-Based Methods

We distinguish three customer-based methods:

1. Direct identification research with customers.
2. Brand switching.
3. Positioning research.

Direct Identification Research with Customers The most direct and simple method to identify the competition via customers is to ask *directly* who the competitors are, for example, by asking questions such as "Which other similar products do you know?" and "Which products did you also consider buying?" (for an example, see Case 6-2). Insight into the most direct competitor may be obtained by asking, "If your preferred brand was no longer available, which brand would you buy?" A disadvantage of such questions is that the extent to which the opinion of the interviewee is actually a reflection of his or her behavior is uncertain. The simplicity of this method is an important advantage.

CASE 6-2	**The Shampoo Market Analyzed**
Identification of the Competition through Direct Customer Research	Based on the question of which brands are being considered, NIPO, a Dutch market research agency, arrived at the following classification of the shampoo market: 1. The niche brands, which are more chic brands that focus on the top of the market: Guhl, Henna Plus, Elsève, Revlon. 2. Brands that are also oriented toward skin care products: Sanex, Nivea, Zwitsal. 3. Brands that are oriented toward the use of active ingredients and the health and condition of the hair ("feed the hair at the root"): Organics, Pantène Pro-V. 4. The "normal" well-known brands: Andrélon, Schwartzkopf, Palmolive. 5. Solution-oriented brands (e.g., used against dandruff or shampoo and conditioner combined into one product): Head & Shoulders, Wash & Go. **Source:** *Nieuws Tribune,* November 14, 1996.

A variation on asking a direct question is to make a connection with product usage. In approaches that entail *product usage associations,* users of the product are asked to name all usage situations or applications. Then they are asked to name suitable products for each application. Other product users are then asked to indicate how suitable each product is for each usage situation. Finally, the products may be clustered on the basis of similarity of suitable applications. An advantage of this method is that it is possible to gain insight into less direct forms of competition, such as generic competition.

Brand Switching A more advanced customer-based identification method uses data about the extent to which customers switch between brands (brand-switching data). The advantage of this method is that it uses *behavioral data*. The data usually are collected through the use of panels of households. The assumption is that a high degree of brand switching indicates a strong similarity and therefore strong competition. For example, if it is observed that many households switch regularly between brands B, D, and E, it is concluded that those brands are competitors of one another. A disadvantage of these data is that they usually refer to households ("families"), leaving it unclear *who* actually buys the product. Because of this, there is the possibility that the switching behavior is not caused by similarity but is done because different family members with different preferences make the purchases.

A solution to this problem is to register the purchases made by individuals. This is being done increasingly. For example, the increasing use of cash cards allows the retail industry to register who makes certain purchases. If these data can be combined with data on the purchases of articles that have been collected through scanning (reading bar codes), a detailed "brand-switching" analysis is possible. In Chapter 4 we discussed developments in scanning. Brand-switching analysis is suitable only for fast-moving consumer goods, and as a result of the lack of data, it cannot be used for service and industrial markets.

Positioning Research It is also possible to obtain insight into the competitive situation in a market through a more indirect method of customer-based research: so-called *positioning research*. This method often uses multidimensional scaling (MDS) techniques. With research of that kind, customers are asked to compare the products or companies they know on the basis of similarity and/or preference. Using these data and software especially developed for the purpose, it then becomes possible to represent the different products in relation to each other graphically in a multidimensional space (a "perceptual map"; see Chapter 4). Products that are located close to each other are close competitors. In addition, positioning research produces other important strategic information, such as information about the image of the company's product and that of the competitors.

6.2.3   Choice of Identification Method

In practice, competition-based methods are used the most frequently. This is also the simplest technique: A company forms a judgment on the basis of its own market knowledge and is not required to perform additional fieldwork. However, competition-based methods have an important disadvantage: They are based on the assumption that what the company thinks about the competition actually corresponds to the perceptions of the customers. The danger is that a company may perceive certain businesses as being competitors, whereas in reality the customers do not consider those businesses in that light, and vice versa. This danger does not exist when a customer-based approach to identifying the competition is chosen.

Suppose national educational institute A wants to identify its competitors. Based on an analysis of the course catalogue and the target audience of other institutes, management concludes that three other national educational institutes (B, C, and D) are the current competitors. On the basis of this analysis, management also concludes that a fourth national institute (E), which currently offers other courses, may be considered a potential competitor. Then management uses a questionnaire to examine how customers perceive this issue. The students are asked to indicate which other institutes they considered in addition to A. This questionnaire shows first of all that among the other national institutes, only B and C are mentioned frequently. Some other questions lead to the discovery that because of its high prices, students do not consider D comparable to A. In addition, regional institutes are often mentioned. Thus, in contrast to management's perceptions, D is apparently not a direct competitor, according to the customers. However, the customers indicate that regional institutes are competitors.

From this example it may be concluded that during competitor identification, a company should choose a customer-based approach. However, a customer-based approach has two limitations. First, it is difficult to gain insight into *potential* customers and *indirect* competitors. After all, customers know only the existing products and are not aware of competitors that have not yet entered the market. Second, customer-based methods typically have to be performed at the level of brands and products. That is, customers often do not know the suppliers of products. These limitations imply that customer-based methods are especially well suited to *short-term planning*. After all, in the short term it is unlikely that new competitors will enter the market, and the analyses therefore can be limited to the product or brand level. However, for longer-term planning, both the company level and potential competitors also need to be considered. The competition-based methods are especially appropriate for this purpose.

Therefore, it is advisable to choose both a customer-based approach and a competition-based approach for the identification of competitors. In this way, the company will put into practice what Kotler articulated many years ago: "learn how your customers view your competitors rather than how you view your competitors."[2]

6.2.4   Choosing the Competitors

If, with the aid of the previously discussed methods, the competitors have been identified, the next issue is whether a detailed behavioral analysis must be performed for all possible competitors. In practice this is not necessary, and it usually is not feasible. It also is not possible to perform a separate behavioral analysis of all *potential competitors*. Therefore, the manager needs to choose the competitors that merit the most attention in the chosen market. But which one is the most important? The largest one or the one that is most similar to ourselves? And which one will be important in the future? Because these questions in principle will be answered in the subsequent analysis, it seems impossible to make a choice beforehand. A solution to this chicken-and-egg problem is to perform a global competitor analysis and then examine a number of competitors more closely.

For the first selection of competitors, two factors are important: market share and *similarity* with the company's product or the company. It is advisable to consider the competitors that are largest as well as those which have comparable products or focus on the same target audience.

6.3 OBJECTIVES OF COMPETITORS

In the second phase of the competitor analysis, an attempt is made to deduce the *objectives* of the most important competitors. This involves two aspects:

1. What does the competitor want?
2. How much does the competitor want it?

The first aspect is related to the competitor's *growth direction:* Does the competitor want to maintain its market share or increase it? If it wants to increase its market share, does the competitor want to grow with the aid of existing or new products and with existing or new customers? The second aspect is determined by the "commitment" of the competitor: the extent to which the competitor is involved with the product or market. Both aspects together determine the effort and aggression with which a competitor is active in the market. The largest threat may be expected from a competitor that is very involved with a market and wants to grow in that market. However, a competitor that "only" wants to maintain its market share but strongly wants to maintain it also presents an important threat.

Indications of what the competitor wants may be obtained in the following ways:

1. *Comparison of the objectives of the competitor with the current results*. A difference between desired and achieved market share leads to an expected growth strategy.
2. *Application of a portfolio analysis to the competitor*. Assuming that the competitor also uses a portfolio analysis, a company can perform its own analysis of the position of the competitor's strategic business units (SBUs) and products in a portfolio model and use it to deduce the competitor's most logical portfolio decision (investments and growth direction).
3. *Determining how important a product is for the competitor*. This can be measured in terms of sales, profit, or number of employees.
4. *Studying the competitor's use of the marketing mix over time*. For example, a price reduction together with an increase in advertising expenses may indicate that the competitor is pursuing growth, and this might present a threat to the company's product. In contrast, a competitor's minimizing of marketing efforts might indicate a harvesting strategy, which means attempting to maximize profit. This type of competitor typically presents less of a threat in the long term.

6.4 CURRENT STRATEGIES OF COMPETITORS

In an attempt to discover the expected strategy of a competitor, the first step is to examine the competitor's *current strategy*. This involves, among other things:

- The *marketing strategy:* the choice of the target audience (segments) and the chosen positioning.
- The use of the *marketing mix.*

Insight into the marketing strategy is obtained by observing and analyzing the elements of the marketing mix. Typically, a company will examine the competitor's use of the marketing mix and use that information to deduce its marketing strategy. An understanding of the *segments* targeted by the competitor can be obtained through market research (who are the customers of the competitor?) as well as through indirect methods such as the media choice and advertising messages of competitors. The choice of distribution points also makes a statement about the choice of a target audience. Analysis of the target audiences defined by competitors is important to avoid segments with intense competition, whereas segments with little competition present an opportunity.

Insight into the *competitive advantage* pursued by the competitor can be provided by the competitor's advertising campaigns. It is fair to assume that each company will communicate its supposed strength to the customers. Therefore, a detailed analysis of the contents of the competitor's communications is very important. In Section 6.7 we review tangible data sources that may be used for the analysis of the competitor's strategy.

CASE 6-3 *Strategy of a* *Competitor*	By pushing for market-share gains through a price war, Dell has presented its competitors with a true lose-lose dilemma. One possible response is to try to maintain market share by pricing against Dell. The problem here is that because of its business model advantage, Dell can stand in the deep end of the pool forever. A competitor wading down there probably will run out of oxygen before too long. Currently, Gateway is the only player that has followed this path, and understandably so. As the only other large player with a completely direct strategy, Gateway is best equipped to ride out the war. The other possible response, the one that has been chosen by IBM and Hewlett-Packard, is to declare the price war "irrational." The problem here is that along the way you lose market share and Dell continues the tear that led it to become the number one maker of personal computers in the world. Sitting out the war is as dangerous as entering it, and that is precisely why Dell's decision to push the pedal during these tough times is so remarkably shrewd.

Source: Gurley, J. William, "Why Dell's War Isn't Dumb," *Fortune*, July 9, 2001, p. 134–136.

6.5 FACTORS THAT DETERMINE SUCCESS AND STRENGTHS AND WEAKNESSES

In this phase, three questions should be answered:

1. Which resources and skills are important in this market; in other words, what are the *determinants of success?*
2. What are the *strengths and weaknesses* of the competitors?
3. What summarizing *conclusions* can be drawn?

6.5.1 Identification of Key Success Factors

To avoid having to determine all possible strengths and weaknesses during a strengths-weaknesses analysis of the competitors, it is useful to determine which resources and skills are the most important in a particular market: the key success factors. For this purpose, the factors that determine success in a market should be identified, that is, the resources or skills that have a large influence on the results of a company. "Result" in this context may refer to relative costs, customer loyalty, market share, profit, and so on.[3] In other words, the focus here is on the strengths that lead to a better than average result. If a company possesses those strengths, it has an advantage relative to its competitors. Examples are for a manufacturer of food items, an efficient physical distribution; for a manufacturer of televisions, low labor costs; and for an insurance company, a good relationship with agents.

To be able to operate successfully, knowledge of the factors that determine success is very important for a company. As a starting point for the identification of these factors, a checklist similar to the one used for an internal analysis may be employed (Figure 3-7). Next, the question is which factors from that schedule are the most important. The following questions may be useful in this regard:

1. *Why* are successful companies *successful* and unsuccessful companies unsuccessful?
2. What are the most important *motivations* of customers? What do customers consider important?
3. Which phase in the production process creates the highest *added value,* and which phase creates the highest costs?
4. What are the *entrance barriers* in the industry and between segments in the market?

A method that is related to the first question involves doing a comparison of successful and less successful companies. By comparing the characteristics of successful and less successful companies in its own industry, a company can develop an understanding of the characteristics that are responsible for success. To arrive at reliable conclusions, sufficient data must be available. Because this is often not the case or only partly the case for a company's industry, such an analysis often has to be performed qualitatively and the conclusions are only indicative.

To answer the second question, a customer analysis should be performed. The goal is to discover what customers consider important. The simplest method is to ask directly how important customers consider certain product characteristics (attributes) to be. To prevent respondents from answering that they consider everything important, methods have been developed that take into account the "trade-off" between characteristics. In this regard a suitable analysis method is *conjoint analysis* (see Section 4.43).

A method that is related to the third question is an analysis of the *value chain* as it applies "on average" in the industry. The activities that on average contribute the highest added value are factors that may determine success. In addition, the phases with the highest costs are the most likely candidates for pursuing cost advantages.

The fourth question implies that the *entrance barriers* should be analyzed. The factors that make it difficult for a potential supplier to enter into the market (e.g., obtaining the technology required for making the product, achieving a high degree of distribution, executing an intensive advertising campaign) are typically very important in the industry.

Based on the preceding analyses, for each factor a company can indicate its importance in the industry (see the first column in Figure 6-4).

6.5.2 Determining the Strengths and Weaknesses of Competitors

The next step is to determine for each of the factors in Figure 6-4 the extent to which the chosen competitors are strong or weak in that factor. For this purpose a great deal of mostly qualitative data have to be collected, and in that process interviews with various "experts" (representatives, customers, researchers, etc.) will be an important source. In Figure 6-4 a short description and designation may be added to each of the characteristics of competitors. Note that in this figure the strengths and weaknesses may apply to both the corporate level and the brand level of a competitor. Information regarding the brand level can be collected through marketing research.

6.5.3 Determining Relative Strengths and Weaknesses

In light of the large amount of information that a strengths-weaknesses analysis of the competitors may produce, it is important to summarize this information adequately. A manageable method is to summarize the essentials in *a score chart* (Figure 6-5), which may be limited to the *key success factors*. Strengths and weaknesses can be summarized on two levels: the corporate

FIGURE 6-4   Potential Key Success Factors and Strengths and Weaknesses of a Company or Brand

Characteristics	Importance in Industry	Competitor A Competitor A	Competitor B	Competitor C	Other Competitors*
Marketing and market position					
• Customer orientation					
• Product quality					
• Market knowledge					
• Relationship with distributors					
• Sales promotion					
• Service					
• Market share					
• Brand loyalty					
• Brand awareness					
• Customer satisfaction					
Innovation					
• Technology					
• R&D expenses					
• Patents					
Production					
• Resources					
• Means of production					
• Personnel					
Financing					
• "Cash flow"					
• Parent company					
• Current position					
Management					
• Flexibility					
• Entrepreneurial quality					
• Staff turnover					

*This might also be assessed for a strategic group.

level and the brand level. Figure 6-5 may also be used for an explicit comparison of the organization with the competitors. For that reason, the "scores" of the company's own brand are added; they are obtained from an internal analysis of strengths and weaknesses (Chapter 3).

FIGURE 6-5   Scores on Key Success Factors of Competitors and a Company's Own Brand
(1 = very weak; 5 = very strong)

Characteristics	Competitor A	Competitor B	Competitor C	Group of Small Competitors	"Own" Company or Brand
Customer orientation	2	4	4	4	4
Unique and strong brand image	1	4	3	4	3
Innovation	4	2	4	3	2
Quality	4	3	4	2	2
Finance	5	3	4	2	5

From Figure 6-5 it is easy to deduce the following:

- *The strengths and weaknesses of competitors.* For example, it turns out that competitor A is not good at marketing but does have good products, whereas more or less the reverse is true of competitor B; competitor C is good in both and thus seems to be the main threat.
- *The relative strengths and weaknesses of the firm.* The firm's brand image is not very strong but its product quality deserves attention, which should be feasible because of the firm's strong financial position.

A more specific form of comparison of the organization with the competitors is called *benchmarking*. Benchmarking (sometimes called "cheating") is best described as searching for best practices. By comparing operational processes in the company with those in other companies, one can gain insight into the company's performance and therefore also into starting points for improvement. These operational processes may range from administration and production to a comparison of commercial performance. This comparison may be made with competitors but also with nondirect competitors. Case 6-4 provides an example of benchmarking.

CASE 6-4 *Benchmarking*	The World Bank, multinational companies, and software suppliers have announced plans to store the definitions of thousands of business processes in an online database. The proposed benchmarking service, which is backed by companies that include Shell Oil, the consumer goods firm Procter & Gamble, the U.S. Navy, the analyst firm Gartner, and IBM, could help information technology (IT) directors compare the performance of their IT systems and business processes with those of other companies. The business processes covered by the plans include supply chain, financial management, IT, customer service, marketing, and sales efficiency. The companies and organizations involved in the project are working with the American Productivity and Quality Center to create a standard set of thousands of measures of business processes, ranging from the cost of processing a customer order to reducing wastage on the factory floor. **Source:** Huber, Nick, "Global Companies Join Plan for Online Business Process Database," *Computer Weekly*, June 1, 2004, p. 24.

6.6   EXPECTED STRATEGIES OF COMPETITORS

Identifying with Competitors

In the previous phases, an answer was provided to the questions of who the most important competitors are and what the objectives, current strategies, and strengths and weaknesses of those competitors are. In the last phase of the competitor analysis, those elements should be used as a basis to answer the question of what the competitor is going to do in the future. In addition, this process should include an attempt to predict how the competitors may react to the strategies formulated by the company. In this phase, the assignment is therefore to draw a "conclusion" about the expected behavior of the competitors that is based on all previously collected information. It is therefore important to identify oneself with the competitor.

It is not easy to make tangible predictions in this phase. Among others, *subjective forecasting methods* will have to be used: methods through which, in one way or another, "experts" generate prognoses that are based on the available information. Concrete methods that may be used for this purpose are *Delphi research* (attempting to arrive at a prognosis through several rounds with experts within the company) and *role playing*. In a role play, people are assigned the roles of market parties and everyone is required to create a plan based on his or her own objectives (which by definition are conflicting; not everyone's market share can grow). Armstrong has demonstrated that this forecasting method often creates good predictions of competitors' behavior.[4] As with the analysis of other environmental factors, it may be useful to define *scenarios* here; for example, the competitor does or does not react to our strategy.

Importance of Customer Orientation

Finally, it is important to take into account the importance of the customer. Some firms are so strongly directed toward competitors that they seem to forget the customer. Academic research on price reactions of U.S. retailers shows that brands often *overreact* to competitors' actions.[5] This may lead to a competitive battle that is bad for all brands.

CASE 6-5 *Price Reactions*	With the Wal-Mart and Target price war during the 2003 holiday selling season discounters reinforced the idea that many toys can be purchased for less than specialty toy stores charge, and that has taken a toll. Already, two major toy-selling chains, F.A.O. Schwarz and Zany Brainy, have essentially disappeared after FAO Inc., their parent company, declared bankruptcy. Two others—Toys 'R' Us and KB Toys—have seen their business fall off. The industry is dominated by discounters such as Wal-Mart Stores and Target. Their relentless price cutting and focus on drawing attention to only the most popular toys have pushed the major specialty retailers to the wall. Toy sellers and their suppliers have attempted to reverse the trend. However, global sales fell 2 percent in 2004, and many toy manufacturers are so unsure of their ability to grow by selling toys that they are branching out into candy, furniture, apparel, and other areas. **Source:** Hays, Constance L., "More Gloom on the Island of Lost Toy Makers," *New York Times*, February 23, 2005, Section C, p. 1.

6.7 DATA SOURCES

Collecting data about competitors is sometimes called "competitive intelligence" or "business intelligence." In effect, all this means is that a company tries to collect as much data about the competitors as it can in as inventive a way as possible. This may range from requesting university research reports to buying up an employee of the competitor. We offer no opinion about how far the creativity should be allowed to go in this regard.[6]

In practice, several publicly accessible sources can be used. A distinction can be made between three types of sources:

1. What *other market parties* say about the competitor, for example, customers, suppliers, its own representatives, and financial institutions.
2. What competitors say about *themselves,* for example, in annual reports, lectures, press releases, personnel advertisements, and advertising expressions or through "bought-up" employees of competitors.
3. What *third parties* say about the competitors, for example, articles in newspapers and magazines, consumer organizations (product tests), industry studies, research reports, and universities.

It is important to collect all the data about the competitors that are being gathered in a company and to make the data accessible to others in the company. Only in that way is it possible to arrive at a coherent picture of the current and expected behavior of the competitors. To bring this about, two conditions must be met:

1. The *responsibility* for the competitor analysis is concentrated in one person. This person can ensure that the correct analyses are performed and that all data are gathered in one place.
2. There is a well-functioning *marketing information system*. Such an automated system should store not just the data about the company but also the data about its competitors. Everyone in the company should have the ability to request the most current data about the most important competitors and also to enter his or her own "news items."

In addition to qualitative data, there are several *quantitative* data sources. The most important data source is the internal marketing research of the firm. A company can and should investigate customers' perception of the competitors. In some countries there may also be secondary quantitative data sources about the competitors. In Section 4.6 we discussed the AC Nielsen, IRI, and GfK files that include data regarding sales, prices, and distribution of fast-moving consumer goods and some other product categories as well. Here we discuss sources for advertising data.

Detailed data about the marketing mix element of *advertising* are collected in many countries. An example is TNS Media Intelligence, whose tracking technologies collect advertising expenditure and occurrence data, as well as select creative executions, for more than 2.2 million brands across 19 media in 23 countries. Another example of a company providing media data is VNU's Nielsen Media research. Case 6-6 provides an impression of the kind of information available from various Nielsen businesses (including sales data, see also section 4.7.1).

CASE 6-6

Data from Nielsen Media Research: A Multi Dimensional Look at 'American Idols'

The fourth season of "American Idol" premieres on Tuesday, January 18 on FOX. Information from several VNU businesses provide a multi-dimensional look into the program's impact on the entertainment industry.

TV Ratings (Nielsen Media Research)

For the 2003–04 broadcast season, American Idol on Tuesdays tied as the #1 most-viewed show, with 25.7 million average viewers, and was the second-highest rated program with a 14.9% household rating. For the past three premieres of the 'American Idol' season, the highest average ratings for the premiere have come from the Atlanta market. The Atlanta market has finished as the number one market for each premiere of the show with an average household rating of 26.4%. In 2004, 'American Idol' occupied 23 spots among the top-30 viewed telecasts among Kids 2–11. The January 28 telecast was the third most-viewed telecast among Kids 2–11 for the calendar year.

Ad Expenditures (Nielsen Monitor-Plus)

Ad expenditures have increased more than 290% since the show first aired in the summer of 2002. The average cost per 30-second spot has increased by more than a 110%. The top advertiser for all three seasons so far has been the Ford Motor Company spending more than $60 million in total. Coca-Cola was the second-highest advertiser last season spending more than $9 million.

Product Placement (Nielsen Product Placement)

For the 2004 season, Coca-Cola products dominated the show with the most total branded occurrences, which are a combination of audio and visual mentions, according to Nielsen Product Placement. The top Coca-Cola products included regular Coke with the top branded occurrences overall, Vanilla Coke (3rd) and C2 (5th). AT&T Wireless received the second-most branded occurrences and Ford Autos & Trucks was fourth.

Album Sales (Nielsen SoundScan)

To date, the former contestant whose albums have sold the most is 2003 runner-up Clay Aiken. Aiken's combined album sales is more than 3.6 million copies with his debut album "Measure of a Man" selling more than 2.7 million copies. The 2002 winner Kelly Clarkson's combined album sales are more than 3 million, and her debut album, "Thankful," sold more than 2.1 million copies.

Internet Traffic (Nielsen//NetRatings)

The 'American Idol' Web site consistently draws significant traffic, according to Nielsen//NetRatings, the leading Internet audience measurement service, averaging three million unique visitors during the peak of each season. During the past two seasons, traffic peaked during the month of May, with 3.0 million unique visitors in 2004 and 3.3 million visitors in 2003. The first season of the show saw a spike in August 2002 with more than three million unique visitors.

Book Sales (Nielsen BookScan)
Along with the albums and singles released from the show, a few books have been released as well. Two of them are from judges of the 'American Idol' show—Simon Cowell and Randy Jackson. Simon's book, "I Don't Mean to Be Rude, But...: Backstage Gossip from American Idol & the Secrets that Can Make You a Star," has sold more than 11,000 copies since its release in December 2003.

Source: New York, January 18, 2005, News Releases from Nielsen Media Research, www.nielsenmediaresearch.com

As was noted before, a limitation of the quantitative data sources mentioned here is that they relate primarily to markets for consumer goods. This implies that conducting a competitor analysis in the service or industrial markets requires a greater amount of ingenuity than is the case for consumer markets. Nonetheless, even for such markets an adequate competitor analysis is possible through the involvement of the appropriate people and the structured collection and processing of data.

Summary

The goal of a competitor analysis is to obtain insight into the strengths and weaknesses of the most important competitors and their expected strategies. The combination of those two issues, linked to the company's own strengths and weaknesses, determines whether a competitor should be considered a rival or a future partner. The answer to the question of how many competitors a company has depends on the level at which the competition occurs for the target audience: at the budget level, the generic level, the product category level, or the product form level. In the context of the annual marketing plan, the last two levels are usually considered. Next, the most important competitors at the chosen level should be identified. It is important to perform that identification process from the perspective of management but also to examine how the target audience perceives the competition (market research).

Subsequently, for the most important competitors the company will determine their current strategy and objectives and their strengths and weaknesses. These issues may apply to the corporate level (e.g., a competitor's customer orientation) and the brand level (e.g., the brand's associations and customer satisfaction regarding the competitive brand). Finally, all the information about a competitor becomes the input for a brainstorm session or role-playing setting in which a forecast is made of a competitor's strategy and possible reactions to the firm's strategies. Data regarding competitors are to a large extent qualitative in nature. Quantitative data regarding sales and advertising are sometimes collected by research agencies, and a firm's internal marketing research is also an important source of information on competitors.

Notes

1. Christopher, M., A. Payne, and D. Ballantyne (1991), *Relationship Marketing,* Oxford, UK: Butterworth Heinemann.
2. Kotler, Ph. (1984), Interview in *Marketing News,* September 14. 1984, p. 22.
3. Day, G. S., and R. Wensley (1988), "Assessing Advantage: A Framework for Diagnosing Competitive Superiority," *Journal of Marketing* 52:1–20; see also Chapter 3.
4. Armstrong, J. S. (2002), "Assessing game theory, role playing and unaided judgment," *International Journal of Forecasting,* 18 (3), 345–352.
5. Leeflang, P. S. H., and D. R. Wittink (1996), "Competitive Reaction versus Consumer Response: Do Managers Overreact?" *International Journal of Research in Marketing* 13(2):103–119.
6. For an overview of the way in which American companies interpret the concept of "competitive intelligence," refer to Taylor, J. W. (1992), "Competitive Intelligence: A Status Report on US Business Practices," *Journal of Marketing Management* 8:117–125.

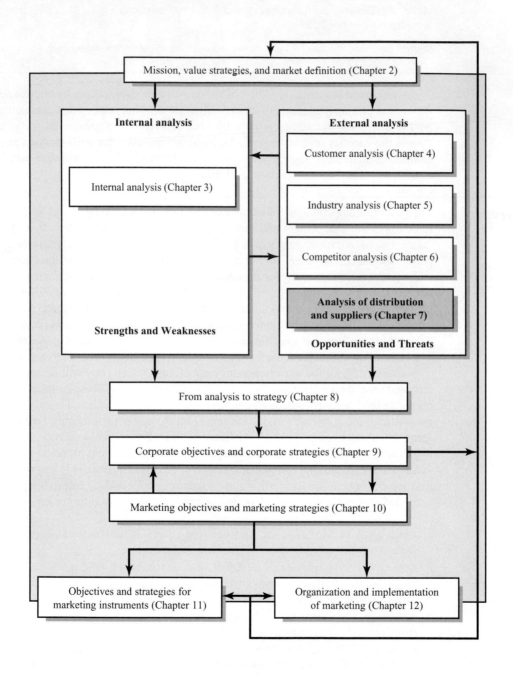

Chapter Seven

Analysis of Distribution and Suppliers

Key Points in This Chapter

- Know aggregation levels in the distribution analysis.
- Be able to analyze the distribution structure in an industry.
- Assess the role of disintermediation.
- Be able to analyze the distribution intensity by applying different criteria.
- Know the steps in an individual distributor and supplier analysis.

INTRODUCTION

With the increased focus on the strategic marketing concept described in Chapter 1, the purview of marketing has been broadened from customers to include other interest groups within and outside the company. Two interest groups play a central role: competitors and distributors. Chapter 6 discussed competitor analysis. This chapter focuses on the distributors. In addition, it pays attention to suppliers.

The importance of a thorough distribution and supplier analysis lies in the opportunity to gain advantages from good relationships with those parties. Consumers seem to be becoming more critical and are placing more emphasis on simplicity, and so a competitive edge can be gained through a good channel strategy (e.g., as a component of operational excellence). A good relationship with suppliers can serve as the foundation for high quality products which is the key focus in a strategy of product leadership. Section 7.1 focuses on the structure of the distribution analysis, after which Sections 7.2 through 7.4 flesh out the distribution analysis on three levels: the macro, meso and micro levels. Section 7.5 deals with the analysis of suppliers.

Wal-Mart: Big or Too Big?

In business, there is big and there is Wal-Mart. With $245 billion in revenues in 2002, Wal-Mart Stores Inc. is the world's largest company. It is three times the size of the number two retailer, France's Carrefour. Every week, 138 million shoppers visit Wal-Mart's 4,750 stores. In 2002, 82 percent of American households made at least one purchase at Wal-Mart.

At Wal-Mart "everyday low prices" is more than a slogan; it is the fundamental tenet of a cult masquerading as a company. Over the years, Wal-Mart has relentlessly wrung tens of billions of dollars in cost efficiencies out of the retail supply chain, passing the larger part of the savings along to shoppers in the form of bargain prices. In the United States, wherever Wal-Mart competes, average grocery prices are 14 percent lower than they are elsewhere. Needless to say, part of these savings has been realized by continuous pressure on Wal-Mart's suppliers and low wages for Wal-Mart sales clerks.

The Wal-Mart supercenter is the principal vehicle for the company's current expansion. Patterned after the European hypermarket, the supercenter is a combination supermarket and general merchandise discounter built on a colossal scale. Wal-Mart didn't introduce the supercenter to America, but it has amassed a 79 percent share of the category since it moved into food and drug retailing by opening its first supercenter store in 1988. In 2003, Wal-Mart operated 1,386 supercenters in the United States, and it is America's largest grocer, with a 19 percent market share, and its third-largest pharmacy, with 16 percent.

Wal-Mart plans to open 1,000 more supercenters in the next few years. This growth rate will boost Wal-Mart's grocery and related revenues to $162 billion from the current $82 billion, giving it control over 35 percent of U.S. food sales and 25 percent of drugstore sales.

Wal-Mart might well be both America's most admired and most hated company. "The world has never known a company with such ambition, capability and momentum," marvels a Boston Consultancy Group report. But the more size and power - Wal-Mart amasses, the greater the backlash it is stirring among competing retailers, vendors, organized labor, and community activists.

Wal-Mart controls a large and rapidly increasing share of the business done by U.S. consumer products companies: 28 percent of Dial's total sales, 24 percent of Del Monte Foods', 23 percent of Clorox's, 23 percent of Revlon's, and on down the list. Suppliers' growing dependence on Wal-Mart is "a huge issue" for manufacturers. Wal-Mart homes in on every aspect of a supplier's operation: which product gets developed, what products are made of, how they are priced, and so on. It is said that the second worst thing a manufacturer can do is sign a contract with Wal-Mart. The worst? Not sign one.

Product Category Sales Shares of Wal-Mart in Five Product Categories (2002 Data)	
Disposable diapers	32%
Hair care	30%
Toothpaste	26%
Pet food	20%
Home textiles	13%

Wal-Mart's huge advantages in buying power and efficiency have forced many rivals to close. For every Wal-Mart supercenter that opens, two other supermarkets close. As the number of supermarkets shrinks, more shoppers will have to travel farther from home. Meanwhile, the failure of hundreds of stores will cost their owners dearly and put thousands of people out of work, only some of whom will find jobs at Wal-Mart. Most likely they will be paid less: Wal-Mart is blamed sometimes for the sorry state of retail wages in the United States. Wal-Mart sales clerks—"associates" in Wal-Mart terminology—earned an average of $8.23 an hour, or $13,861 a year, in 2001. At that time, the federal poverty line for a family of three was $14,630.

Source: *Business Week,* October 6, 2003. Bianco, Anthony; Zellner, Wendy; Brady, Diane; France, Mike; Lowry, Tom; Byrnes, Nanette; Zegel, Susan; Arndt, Michael; Berner, Robert; Palmer, Ann Therese. 'Is Wal-Mart Too Powerful?', *Business Week,* 10/6/2003 Issue 3852, p 100–110

Questions

1. Which value discipline (in the system of Treacy and Wiersema, see Chapter 2) has been chosen by Wal-Mart? Explain your answer.

2. "The second worst thing a manufacturer can do is sign a contract with Wal-Mart. The worst? Not sign one." Explain this statement.

3. What is the influence of the growing size of Wal-Mart on the industry structure of toothpaste or products for hair care? Use Porter's "competitive forces" model to answer this question.

4. What do you think will be the difference in account management and strategy for a toothpaste company (e.g., Crest) when dealing with Wal-Mart as opposed to dealing with smaller pharmacy stores?

5. a. What do you think is the competitive advantage of Wal-Mart?

   b. What is the source of that competitive advantage?

7.1 GOAL AND STRUCTURE OF A DISTRIBUTION ANALYSIS

In preparation for Chapter 10, we note that in the context of using the marketing mix element of distribution, three types of decisions have to be made:

1. Choice of the distribution intensity (objective).
2. Choice of the distribution channel.
3. Management of the distribution channel.

This chapter will not discuss these decisions; instead, it will focus on providing an analysis diagram with which the necessary information can be obtained to make those decisions in as well-founded a manner as possible. In the context of this book we will limit ourselves to several main points.

A distribution analysis occurs at three levels of aggregation:

1. *Macro level*. This involves mapping out the entire distribution column both vertically (possible levels, long or short channel) and horizontally (various types of intermediate links within one level); therefore, this refers to a global distribution structure.

2. *Meso level*. This involves the following:

   • The more specific distribution structure within one type of intermediate link, for example, the distribution of power of shop chains within of supermarkets.

   • The position of brands within a single level and especially within the group of retailers (analysis of the distribution intensity). This analysis is especially important in terms of the implementation of the desired distribution intensity, as was mentioned in item 1.

3. *Micro level*. The strategies and wishes and desires of individual distributors (distributor analysis). This information is required for the implementation of the daily marketing policy toward distributors.

These levels cannot be considered separately. For example, the distribution structure has a macro component as well as a meso component. Although this distinction is useful in an analytic sense, in reality both components belong to the distribution structure. In addition, an analysis of the distribution structure at the meso level (within a single group of intermediate links) requires information about the market shares of individual distributors. This information is obtained from the distribution analysis at the micro level. In the following sections each of the three levels will be reviewed.

7.2   DISTRIBUTION ANALYSIS AT THE MACRO LEVEL

7.2.1   Dimensions of the Analysis

The analysis of the distribution structure at the macro level involves two dimensions:

1. The *number of levels* in the distribution column (vertically: the length of the channel).
2. The *type of intermediate links* within a single level, for example, within the group of retailers the distinction between supermarkets, discounters, neighborhood shops, and specialty stores or the "gray circuit" of, for example, gas stations (horizontally: the width of the channel). Insight into this issue is important for the choice of the type of intermediate links.

In regard to the length of the channel there are two possibilities:

1. *Direct delivery* to customers without the use of "intermediaries"; this includes all trade of producers on the Internet (e-commerce).
2. *Indirect delivery* that does involve intermediaries.

Direct delivery to customers is increasing because of the use of the Internet. Section 7.2.2 will discuss this further. With indirect delivery, potential intermediate links between producer and consumer include agents, importers, wholesale dealers (wholesale trade), and retailers. If a company chooses to deliver exclusively through retailers, this is called a *short channel*. In all other cases, it is called a long channel. Some of the criteria for choices in this regard are the number of final customers the company wants to serve and the type of product (e.g., shelf life and complexity).

The choice does not have to be restricted to only one channel. A *multichannel strategy* is possible as well, for example, if a company is active in both an industrial market and a consumer market or an organization delivers both through intermediate links and through direct delivery.

In the analysis, the focus is not just on the mapping out of the various possibilities but also on the importance of each type of intermediate link. For this purpose, the company needs to figure out which share of the purchases in the product category occurs through which links. In other words, the sales (in terms of money and volume) of the various types of links should be estimated. Hard data are often not available in this area, and so estimates have to be made of the importance of various links. Figure 7-1 contains the results of an analysis of the distribution structure at the macro level of the market for fresh fruit and vegetables in the United States. The figure illustrates produce markets, the channels of distribution, and their sales at each stage of the vertical marketing system in 1987 and 1997, for major industries: grower-shippers, wholesalers, retail stores, and food-service operators.

7.2.2   Elimination of Intermediaries

The use of the World Wide Web makes it relatively easy to make direct contact with customers, and direct contact enables direct trade. Trade on the Internet (e-commerce) therefore has expanded enormously and is an important component of what has been called the "new economy" since the end of the 1990s. Direct delivery to customers by manufacturers implies that intermediaries are "cut out" (*disintermediation*). That strategy fits very well within but is not required for the value strategy of customer intimacy. For example, a manufacturer of cat food may deliver cat food at a discount to a customer as it is ordered by that customer (via the Internet). If the manufacturer has a sufficiently rich database of data on cat owners, it may deliver a certain amount of cat food every few weeks or months without the customer having to place a specific order. In doing so, the manufacturer could even take into account the age of the cat and, as the cat gets older, could recommend and deliver

FIGURE 7-1   **Example of a Distribution Structure: U.S. Market for Fresh Fruits and Vegetables**

Source: http://www.ers.usda.gov/briefing/FoodMarketStructures/producemarkets.htm.

Fresh fruits and vegetables move through primary marketing channels

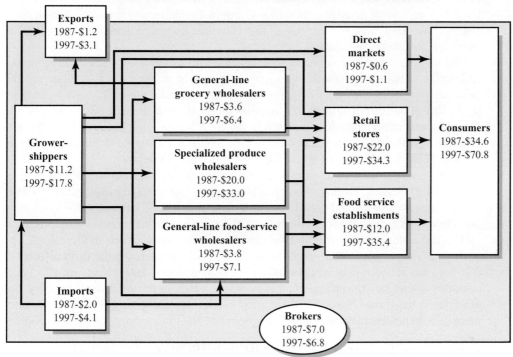

Note: All values are in billion dollars (current, not adjusted).
Sources: Bureau of the Census, Census of Wholesale Trade and Census of Retail Trade;
Blue Book, 1997: Edward W. McLaughlin and others, *Fresh Track 1999: New Dynamics of Produce Buying and Selling*, Produce Marketing Association, Newark, Deleware, 1999.

special food for older cats. Avoiding intermediaries means in principle that a manufacturer's power is increasing in relation to the retailer's.

However, e-commerce is challenging to implement for manufacturers. A manufacturer is responsible for delivery and therefore needs to set up its own *logistic system* for that purpose; the issue here is whether a sufficient volume can be attained to make it profitable. For example, it will not be profitable for the cat food manufacturer to use a car for each separate order. For this reason, manufacturers often collaborate in e-commerce. This may be a reason to collaborate with intermediaries (assembly point).

Manufacturers that produce a large assortment of products also have potential economies of scale. For example, Unilever is able to deliver to customers a wide range of products (A brands) that range from laundry detergent to rice and shampoo. If Unilever has a database with the preferences and purchasing behavior of customers, such a strategy is in principle feasible. However, another problem with disintermediation by manufacturers is the possible reaction of retailers. As a result of the large buying power of purchasing combinations, the threat of the elimination of these intermediary links may lead to undesired reactions, with the most extreme reaction being that the products of the manufacturer no longer will be placed on the shelf.

In the context of the distribution analysis, it is necessary to continue researching the possibilities and impossibilities of direct delivery to customers and to be neither too cautious nor too optimistic in the choice of strategy.

7.3 DISTRIBUTION ANALYSIS AT THE MESO LEVEL

7.3.1 Distribution Structure at the Meso Level

In the previous section, an analysis was provided of the distribution structure at the macro level. However, more detailed information is required to determine the optimal choice of a channel. We briefly describe the role of the wholesale trade and then discuss the level of individual retailers in more detail.

The *wholesale trade* is positioned between the manufacturer and the retailer, and its core function is to tailor the demand and supply of goods in markets, both qualitatively and quantitatively. In light of developments in information and communications technology (ICT) that allow manufacturers and retailers to be attuned to each other's supply and demand more easily and more intensively [electronic data interchange (EDI)], there is evidence that the wholesale trade is being eliminated. For a supplier, this means that an analysis of the added value the wholesale trade may offer is relevant.

Within a single level of intermediate links (e.g., retailers) or even within one type of intermediate links (e.g., supermarkets), it is important to understand the *distribution of power* (market shares) between individual companies and distributors. After all, this distribution also determines the importance of the individual distributors (in addition to volume and margin), and therefore it will determine the direction of marketing efforts in this regard. The analysis of the power distribution obviously should take into account the various forms of collaboration between distributors (purchasing combinations, franchising, etc.). In some countries a tendency toward concentration has occurred in the food retail industry. For example, in the United States Wal-Mart is by far the largest food retailer, with a share of more than 30 percent in some product categories (see the introductory case in this chapter).

7.3.2 Analysis of the Distribution Intensity of a Brand

The *distribution intensity of a brand* relates to the position of the brand within a single level in the distribution channel. For this reason, we consider the analysis of the distribution intensity to be an analysis at the meso level.

To determine the desired distribution intensity, the past and current distribution intensity should be analyzed. Various criteria can be used for this purpose. To measure the position within the distribution channel, typically two criteria are used:

1. *Nonweighted (numerical) distribution*. This is the percentage of shops in which the brand is available.
2. *Weighted distribution*. This is the market share in the product group of the shops in which the brand is available, in other words, the coverage of the market.

The difference between the two criteria is that the weighted distribution takes into account the size (in sales) of the shops. Shops that sell a relatively large amount from the product group count more heavily. To calculate the size of the shops where the company is represented, the following measure is used: The *selection indicator* is the average sales in the product category at the shops where the company's brand is available, divided by the average sales in the product category in all shops where brands from the product category are offered.

If the selection indicator is larger than 1, the company's brand is located in relatively large shops. The selection indicator may also be calculated by dividing the weighted distribution by the nonweighted distribution.

The criteria mentioned earlier make a statement about the distribution of a brand in the market as a whole. To measure the position of a brand in the shops where that brand is available, the following measure is used: The *sales share* is the market share of the brand within the shops where it is available (company's sales or sales divided by total sales, or sales in the product category in the shops where the brand is available).

FIGURE 7-2
Distribution Criteria

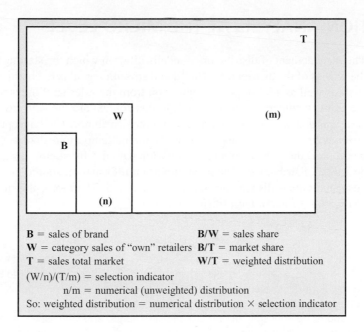

B = sales of brand   B/W = sales share
W = category sales of "own" retailers   B/T = market share
T = sales total market   W/T = weighted distribution
(W/n)/(T/m) = selection indicator
        n/m = numerical (unweighted) distribution
So: weighted distribution = numerical distribution × selection indicator

It is easy to demonstrate that the following relationships exist:

Market share = weighted distribution × sales share

Market share = nonweighted distribution × selection indicator × sales share

Another important indicator of the position of the brand in the shop is the *shelf position*. The shelf position has two important aspects: location and amount. Location (low, middle, high) cannot be quantified. Amount may be expressed in *facings*: the number of visible products. The number of facings is often related to the market share: The larger the brand is, the more facings the retailer will allocate to it. Figure 7-2 summarizes these issues schematically. We illustrate this figure and the preceding text with an example.

Suppose a brand achieves sales of $500.000 (B) in a market size of $5 million (T). The brand is located in 100 (n) among the 500 (m) shops where the product is being offered. Sales in the product category of these 100 shops are $2 million (W).

The nonweighted distribution thus is 100/500 (n/m) = 20 percent. The weighted distribution is 2 million/5 million (W/T) = 40 percent. The selection indicator is [2/100]/[5/500] ([W/n]/[T/m]) = 2. This could also be calculated by dividing 40 percent by 20 percent. The sales share is 500,000/2,000,000 (B/W) = 25 percent. The market share of the brand is 500,000/5 million (B/T) = 10 percent. This is the same as 20 percent × 2 × 25 percent.

The conclusion is that the brand has a low degree of distribution and is located especially in large shops (measured in sales within the product category). The shops where brand A is located are dependent on that brand for 25 percent of their sales in the product category.

The results of the distribution analysis are directly relevant for the use of the marketing mix. For example, if a company wants to increase the weighted distribution, it may choose to encourage retailers to include the brand in the assortment through a lot of advertising and visits by the sales staff. If the sales share is disappointing, this means that the position of the brand in the shops where it is located is weakening, for example, because of too little support in the shop. A strategy that provides more rewards to the retailer for support (push strategy) is an obvious choice. In Chapter 6 it was noted that data on the distribution of food products are available from market research agencies such as AC Nielsen.

7.4 DISTRIBUTION ANALYSIS AT THE MICRO LEVEL

The management of distributors is a daily affair in which the starting point is to respond to the wishes of the distributors. The final distribution goal is to obtain a good location on the shelf as well as a lot of positive attention from the sales staff in terms of personal sales to the final customers. Important tools in this context are the *margins* on products and *promotional activities* in collaboration with the distributor. The concept of *relationship management* has a central focus: The manufacturer attempts to realize its goals (and those of the distributor) through an optimal relationship with the distributor. Insight into the wishes and desires of distributors is the most important information source in this area. For that purpose, individual distributors must be examined. Therefore, this involves a distribution analysis at the *micro level* (distributor analysis).

CASE 7-1 *Building Relationships with Retailers*	It wasn't long ago when a Coke or Pepsi representative would show up at a local convenience store chain and, with a wad of financial promises, put together a cold vault planogram. With soft drink sales sagging, retailers, once beholden to the demanding multi-billion-dollar beverage behemoths, are pounding their chests in defiance, pressing suppliers for enhanced marketing allowances while bluntly turning aside cooler demands. "Waters and teas are catching up, and to be honest, companies like Poland Spring and Gatorade are paying good money to have prime cooler space—and I mean thousands of dollars, not chicken feed," said Kevin Noon, president of K&K Food Mart, a 10-store chain in Brockport, NY. A couple of years ago Noon slotted three cooler doors apiece for Coke and Pepsi and one door each to the noncarbonated family. Now K&K is entering into an exclusive agreement with Pepsi, meaning that Coke is relegated to a single door while Pepsi seizes 75 percent of carbonated space. **Source:** Morrison, Mitch, "Bursting the Bubble," *Convenience Store News*, May 5, 2003, p. 80.

At the most disaggregated level (sales outlets), a manufacturer may be dealing with many hundreds of "customers." By far the largest proportion of them is in one way or another involved in joint collaboration. Thus, in reality, the "salesperson" of a manufacturer (the sales manager) has to deal with a significantly lower number and often with only a few buyers.

For the purpose of organizing the analysis of a distributor it is important to determine which role the distributor actually plays for the producer. To begin with, the distributor is of course a *customer* that "resells" the product to final users. Yet in the food products industry, distributors these days increasingly are also *competitors* of manufacturers as a result of the *own brands* of those distributors (*distributor brands*).

Therefore, a distributor analysis is positioned between a customer analysis and a competitor analysis (see Chapter 6). For each distributor, insight should be obtained into the following:

1. The importance and role of the distributor.
2. The position of the manufacturer's brand at the distributor.
3. The objectives, strategy, and wishes of the distributor.
4. The strengths and weaknesses and the expected strategy of the distributor.

The Importance and the Role of the Distributor

The *importance* of a distributor may be measured by its sales in the product category. For the food products industry, relevant data can be obtained from Nielsen or GfK. For markets for durable consumer goods, the position of distributors (e.g., the position of Target in the market for appliances) should be estimated. In addition to sales, the margin is essential. For a manufacturer, the profitability of a "relationship" is ultimately what matters.

In regard to the role of a distributor, the easily answered question is whether it is only a "customer" or also a competitor. The distributor is a competitor if it carries its own brands (*distributor brands,* or *D-brands*), a situation that occurs in many markets for fast-moving consumer goods. In addition, it is important to determine the degree of freedom in brand supply for a distributor: Does the distributor have a "preferred supplier"—a manufacturer within the product category that is preferred?

The Position of the Manufacturer's Brand at the Distributor

Measures of the *position of the manufacturer's own brand* at the distributor include the shelf position, the number of facings, and the sales of the manufacturer's brand at that distributor in relation to other sales outlets and/or in relation to other distributor brands. Shelf position and facings are tools of the distributor. Another tool is the personal sale, especially in lines of business that are not related to the food products industry. All these tools have an impact on brand sales. Relatively low brand sales may indicate insufficient attention to the brand on the part of the distributor; that may indicate an inadequate marketing policy of the producer toward that distributor.

The Goals, Strategy, and Wishes of the Distributor

Objectives involve issues such as *satisfaction* of the distributor (and therefore the results until the present time) and *ambition* (limited or fast growth, growth with existing or new activities, etc.). *Strategy* here involves the implementation of the marketing strategy (*positioning* and choice of the *target audience*): On which consumers does the distributor focus? For a manufacturer, it is important to choose a distributor with a marketing strategy comparable to its own. In addition, the use of the four P's by the distributor should be examined. The "P" of product in this regard is actually related to the *wishes* of the distributor: How wide is its assortment, which product categories are in the shop with how many varieties, and what proportions of those are A brands, B brands, and distributor brands? Other relevant questions include the following: To what extent and how does the distributor implement its own communication policy? How does the distributor handle promotional campaigns? In general, to what extent is the distributor willing to collaborate with the manufacturer?

The answers to all these questions will to be provided, based mostly on observation and experiences with the relevant distributor. It may be expected that an *account manager* or another representative of the manufacturer will gain insight, through regular contacts with the buyers, into what the distributor does or does not want and how it behaves.

CASE 7-2 *Strategies of a Retailer*	Big retailers known for giant stores in suburbs are resizing stores, reformatting layouts, and remixing merchandise to make it big in the Big Apple. Home Depot recently joined Toys 'R' Us, Kmart, Best Buy, and The Container Store there in exploring ways to adapt their formulas to an urban environment. What's the appeal? High pedestrian traffic and a potential new sales growth area have become more important as suburban areas have become saturated and opportunities for expansion there have shrunk. Urban success, however, means conquering problems of tight space and high costs. But on the "if I can make it there, I'll make it anywhere" theory, as the Frank Sinatra song goes, strategies that work in dense, high-cost New York could work in other cities. **Source:** "Big-Box Stores Squeeze into Big Apple," *USA Today*, October 19, 2004, p. B3.

The Strengths and Weaknesses and the Expected Strategy of the Distributor

Finally, an attempt is made, based in part on the foregoing steps, to deduce the strengths and weaknesses as well as the expected strategy of the distributor.

In terms of the *strengths* (and weaknesses) of a distributor, two types may be distinguished: strengths that are interesting to any manufacturer (e.g., high sales per customer, friendly staff, and short waiting times at the cash register) and manufacturer-specific strengths. After all, for a manufacturer the issue is to choose a distributor that fits with the target audience and the positioning of the manufacturer's products. Characteristics of the distributor that are congruent present opportunities for the manufacturer (such as a good fresh produce department, high-quality positioning, and a large staff). Weak points of an existing distributor (e.g., low sales per customer) may be an occasion for more intensive collaboration with the manufacturer (e.g., joint promotions).

The *expected distributor strategy* also may present opportunities (or threats) for the manufacturer. Expanded support and growth of the distributor's brands may have important implications for the manufacturer. Potential options vary from strengthening the position and positioning of the manufacturer's A brands to starting to produce distributor brands.

Just as in the previous step, statements can only be qualitative in nature and assumptions probably will have to be made if insufficient information is available.

7.5   ANALYSIS OF THE SUPPLIERS

This section provides a brief introduction to the analysis of suppliers. For more extensive descriptions, the reader should refer to the literature on purchasing and business marketing.

Purchasing occurs in many areas, such as the purchasing of the following:

- Supportive goods and services (office furniture, financial services, advertising agencies, etc.).
- Means of production (labor and capital goods).
- Semimanufactured articles and raw materials.

CASE 7-3 *Analysis of Suppliers by Toyota and Honda*	Because Japanese automakers know that a lean value chain is only as strong as its weakest link, they have invested significant time and capital in developing their suppliers. In the United States, Toyota and Honda are the masters of supplier-development initiatives. When Toyota and Honda first built their U.S. assembly and engine plants, their managers quickly learned that they had to teach old-style mass producers the basics of lean manufacturing. Although U.S. companies have long sponsored company training programs for their suppliers, Honda and Toyota do not believe in conference room training. They train their suppliers according to the concept of *gemba* (Japanese for "go and see"): Training occurs on the shop floor, and transformation occurs through practice and action. Both Honda and Toyota identify significant parts of product lines and build "model lines" in the suppliers' plants. Their advisers stay until they have achieved ambitious objectives for cost, quality, and lead time. **Source:** Liker, Jeffrey K., and Yen-Chun Wu, "Japanese Automakers, U.S. Suppliers and Supply-Chain Superiority," *Sloan Management Review*, Fall 2000, p. 81–93.

A good relationship with suppliers can be a source of a competitive advantage. This applies to all types of purchasing. To a large extent, a good advertising agency determines the success of a campaign. Good housing can have an impact on staff motivation. The usefulness of qualified personnel (labor market) is evident. Good and reliable machines determine the quality of production. Certainly in the case of semifinished products and raw materials, savings in purchasing may be "channeled" to the consumer. The requirements for purchased semifinished products and raw materials depend on the chosen value strategy. A company that chooses customer leadership (*customer intimacy*) and direct delivery will require flexibility (many varieties) and reliability (timely delivery) in the deliveries. The strategy of *product leadership* requires a high and constant quality of the purchased products.

A company that chooses a low price within *operational excellence* will have a strong need for inexpensive purchasing, for example, through agreements about quantity discounts.

Whichever demands are made for whichever type of purchasing, it will be easier to comply with those demands if good *relationships* are built with the supplying companies. Therefore, an analysis of current and potential suppliers is important.

Purchasing by a company is in essence no different from purchasing by a consumer: There is a need that is satisfied through purchasing and/or acquisition. The most important differences are the following:

- In purchasing, the *need is "indirect"*: It depends on the requirements that are made of the products, which in turn depend on the final needs of the final customer.
- The purchasing process is different and more complicated: Typically, a single person is not responsible for purchasing; instead, there are *decision-making units (DMUs)*. In this situation, various people in a company are responsible for the final purchasing decisions.

In a supplier analysis, the following questions are answered:

1. Which needs within the company have to be met? The analysis of suppliers depends on the need that must be met. Therefore, an internal analysis to define that need is important.
2. Which supplier can best provide for that need? To arrive at a selection of potential suppliers, the company will have to examine the expected achievements of the suppliers in the following areas:

   - Quality: the concrete characteristics of the products.
   - Price (potential discounts, etc.).
   - Service.

The *service component* is very important in business-to-business markets and includes both components such as warranty, repair service, and reliability and additional service components such as training and information.

To be able to evaluate suppliers on these factors, information from the company's own purchasers is important: They know the market like no one else. In addition, suppliers may be asked to make "bids." This may occur through a call for tenders (e.g., construction combinations needed to create and present a building scheme), pitches (advertising agencies that need to write a campaign proposal), or normal quotes. Because *trust* plays an important role in purchasing markets, issues such as reputation, experience with suppliers, and personal contacts often are decisive in making a choice. Therefore, in a supplier analysis, these qualitative elements play an important role.

Summary

A distribution analysis is performed at the macro level, the meso level, and the micro level. At the macro level, the distribution structure is mapped out and an analysis is made of which levels are used and to what extent and how many sales are made in the category through which channels. A specific point in that regard is what the potential development in the role of direct sales on the Internet might be. The elimination of intermediary links is a way for manufacturers to avoid the increasing power of retailers. At the meso level, the power of the retailers is analyzed, along with the position of the brand at the various retailers. At the micro level, individual retailers (chains) are analyzed; an important point is to discover how the best possible relationship with the distributor can be built. For that purpose, an understanding of the distributor's goals, strategy, and wishes is required. The company's account managers are an important data source for this largely qualitative analysis. For a supplier analysis, the goal is also to build relationships. An analysis will focus on the question of which purchasing needs the company has and which supplier can best meet those needs. The company's own purchasing needs will depend on the chosen value strategy.

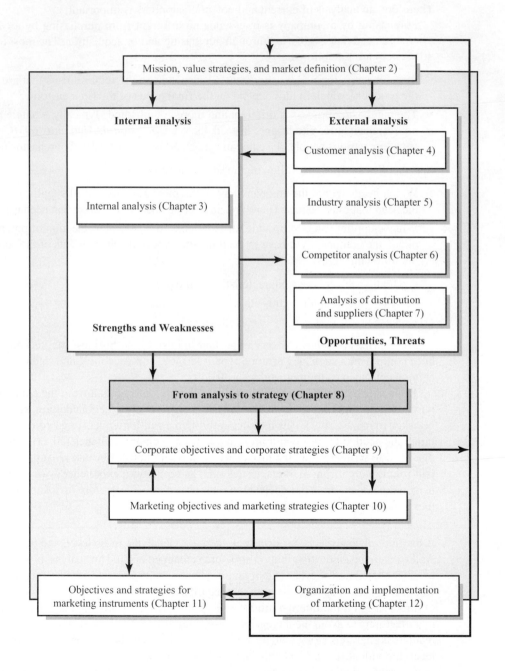

Mission, value strategies, and market definition (Chapter 2)

Internal analysis

Internal analysis (Chapter 3)

Strengths and Weaknesses

External analysis

Customer analysis (Chapter 4)

Industry analysis (Chapter 5)

Competitor analysis (Chapter 6)

Analysis of distribution and suppliers (Chapter 7)

Opportunities, Threats

From analysis to strategy (Chapter 8)

Corporate objectives and corporate strategies (Chapter 9)

Marketing objectives and marketing strategies (Chapter 10)

Objectives and strategies for marketing instruments (Chapter 11)

Organization and implementation of marketing (Chapter 12)

Chapter Eight

From Analysis to Strategy

Key Points in This Chapter

- Discuss the role of forecasting in marketing planning.
- Know the advantages and disadvantages of different forecasting methods and be able to choose the best methods in a particular situation.
- Know the steps in a SWOT analysis.
- Be able to summarize a situation analysis and discuss different value strategies and positioning options.
- Know the advantages and limitations of portfolio methods.
- Apply a portfolio method at different levels.

INTRODUCTION

In the earlier phases of the strategic planning process, an internal analysis and an external analysis were completed. Three tools discussed in this chapter can be helpful in arriving at the formulation of alternative objectives and strategies. The first tool is the use of *forecasting methods* (Section 8.1). The situation analysis is based mainly on the current situation of a brand, but what really counts are opportunities and threats in the near future. Although looking into the future may seem like using a crystal ball, applying appropriate forecasting methods makes it possible to reduce future uncertainty. The predicted issues in the internal and external environments and the company's vision about future trends are the starting point for strategy development. Two analytical tools may be used for this purpose: a *strengths, weaknesses, opportunities, and objectives (SWOT) analysis* and a *portfolio analysis*. A SWOT analysis (Section 8.2) defines strategic marketing options based on combinations of internal and external issues. The key question to be answered is what the role of the company should be within the future environment. A portfolio analysis (Section 8.3) is a tool for assessing various strategic options for different strategic business units (SBUs) or product-market combinations.

Gillette: Leader by Innovation

Gillette, the worldwide market leader in wet shaving systems, beats the competition because of its innovative power. In the laboratory of The Gillette Company in Boston, Massachusetts, dozens of test subjects shave themselves every day. The test results are analyzed and used to develop new wet shaving systems and improve existing ones. Gillette is on a continuous search for new innovations in technology, products, and markets. Pioneering innovations originate as a rule in Boston; the competition follows later.

The suggestion that one is finished developing at a given moment when it comes to razor blades does not find an audience at Gillette. "With many products you think there is nothing left to improve, but still, every time you see new models with improved characteristics. The same thing applies to razor blades: They can always be better," according to a spokesperson for Gillette. "Our strategy includes continuous investment in improvements. 'The best a man can get,' says Gillette. Such a motto has to be substantiated."

Since 2003 there has been another new shaving system from Gillette on the shelves: the Mach3Turbo. As the name suggests, it is the follow-up to the Mach3 from 1998. At first sight there seems to be little difference between the two systems, but the details make the difference. The Mach3Turbo offers so many innovative aspects that there are at least 35 patents pending on it. The three blades of the Mach3Turbo are slightly sharper and thinner than those of its predecessors; moreover, use has been made of the new antifriction technology, which ensures that shaving against the growth of the beard hairs results in less skin irritation. This is an understandable innovation, since Gillette knows from research that for 71 percent of men, shaving against the direction of beard growth is the hallmark of the ideal shaving system. Furthermore, the Lubrastrip, the microribs, and the handle of the Mach3Turbo have been adjusted.

The innovations justify, according to Gillette, the premium sales price the consumer pays: A package of four Mach3Turbo razor blades costs 10 euros in Europe, for instance. The spokesman from Gillette says: "The first reaction from many people is: 'Gosh, that's expensive. For the same money you can almost buy a crate of beer!' But look at the price per shaving turn. These razor blades last much longer than an average blade. Whoever uses Mach3Turbo will need approximately 22 razor blades per year, which is less than the average of 26 blades you use otherwise. You spend less than 60 euros for a whole year of shaving."

The Mach3Turbo was introduced in Europe at the beginning of 2003. In Gillette's home market of North America the system was on the market in March 2002. Over there it unchained a true revolution. It became Gillette's most successful line extension ever: Before the end of 2002, the Mach3Turbo was the most heavily sold shaving system in the United States, with total sales of no less than 33 percent of the total American wet shaving market, which is worth $3.4 billion. Gillette is the worldwide market leader in the wet shaving market. The brand has a very dominating position with a share of 72.5 percent in this market.

By far most buyers of the Mach3Turbo originate from the group of consumers who used the Mach3 before. A much smaller proportion will switch from another Gillette product (such as Sensor and Contour) or from another brand (such as Wilkinson Sword, Bic, and the various private labels). Although by far most Mach3Turbo users are existing customers of the company, Gillette will see the value of its market share grow substantially precisely because the new razor blades are more expensive than the existing ones. Gillette therefore always promotes the best system. However, the older shaving systems are not taken off the market. Even the Gillette Blue Silver from 1936 still exists, although the coating, blades, and packaging have been adapted through the years.

Thanks to extensive market analyses, Gillette has a reasonable insight into the choice of a shaving system by the consumer. The tendency is that more and more 18- to 25-year-olds are shaving wet. Youngsters who start shaving often choose the same system as their fathers: When the father uses SensorExcel, chances are great that the son is going to do the same thing.

The shaving market is a market with a high level of customer loyalty. Gillette of course tries to influence the beginning shaver, knowing that the initial choice of a shaving system is often a choice for life. Often there are special promotions during which youngsters 18 years old are sent a free shaving system. In the introduction year of the Mach3Turbo, that was of course the Mach3Turbo.

Another aspect of the marketing of the Mach3Turbo concerns the simultaneous launch of a new line of Gillette-Series care products. Through that action Gillette reacts to the changing view that men have of the daily shaving ritual. "Shaving is nowadays more than just gliding a razor blade over your skin," according to Gillette. "Men find the care for their skin, both before and after shaving, constantly more important. Our previous line of care products was still positioned on smell; now it is done on skin characteristics. The new line has four types: conditioning, protecting, moisture-regulating, and sensitive for sensitive skin. There are gel and foam as pre-treatment and gel, balm, and lotion as aftershave. Combined with the Mach3Turbo, you are thus talking about a total shaving concept."

Although the Mach3Turbo was brought into the market not long ago, Gillette's drive for innovation remains unchanged. In 2003 the follow-up was brought into the market: the Mach3Turbo G-Force, with an innovative handle. Soon afterward the Sensor 3 emerged, which has three independently moving razor blades and contains a Lubrastrip with aloe and vitamin E. And in 2004 America was expected to get to know the next innovation: the M3Power.

The Gillette Company: More Than Just Shaving

Markets	Shaving products, batteries, oral care
Brands	Gillette, Braun, Duracell, Oral B
Number of Users	1.2 billion worldwide
Number of Countries	200
Turnover 2002	8.45 billion dollar wordwide growth 5% comp. to 2001
Result 2002	1.21 billion dollar worldwide growth 33% comp. to 2001
Media Spending 2002	approx. 700 million dollar worldwide
Advertising Agencies	BBDO Worldwide, Ogilvy & Mather, McCann-Erickson, Lowe

---

Source: *Marketing Tribune,* March 25, 2003.

Questions

1. Give a graphic, three-dimensional representation of the business of Gillette by using the method described in Chapter 2.
2. Treacy and Wiersema distinguish between three value strategies (see Chapter 2). Which value strategy do you think Gillette has chosen? Explain your answer.
3. In this book four levels of competition are distinguished. Show per level of competition the competition for the Gillette Mach3Turbo.
4. Which segment variables do you think play a role in the marketing policy of Gillette? Explain your answer.

5. Using the information in the case, give an overview of the strong and weak points of Gillette.
6. What opportunities and threats is Gillette confronted with?
7. In which phase of the product life cycle is the wet shaving market in the primary markets of Gillette (Europe and North America)?
8. From the case description, it can be concluded more or less what the marketing target and the marketing strategy of Gillette are.
a. Describe the marketing target and the marketing strategy of Gillette.
b. Do the target and strategy chosen by Gillette fit the phase in the product life cycle in which the wet shaving market finds itself? Explain your answer.

8.1 FORECASTING METHODS

This section deals with the following topics:

- The goal and content of forecasting (Section 8.1.1).
- Different forecasting methods (Section 8.1.2).
- The pros and cons of various forecasting methods (Section 8.1.3).
- Choosing a forecasting method (Section 8.1.4).
- General recommendations for forecasting (Section 8.1.5).
- Concluding remarks about forecasting in practice (Section 8.1.6).

8.1.1 Goal and Content

One of the characteristics of strategic marketing is an orientation toward the future: Starting from the opportunities and threats expected from the environment of the organization, a course (strategy) is chosen that in principle will be followed for a longer term. In light of this orientation, it is important in the strategic planning process to make *prognoses* of a number of variables and to develop a vision of the environment (see Section 2.1.3).

This section reviews forecasting methods. We will not review in detail the "technical" issues regarding forecasting methods. The emphasis is on aspects that are important from a management perspective. For a more extensive discussion of forecasting methods, including an overview of dozens of studies of the predictive power of various methods, refer to the book by Armstrong,[1] which is the basis for this section. We will now discuss the role of forecasting in the strategic planning process.

Forecasting is especially important during the external analysis and in choosing strategies.

External Analysis

One of the characteristics of strategic marketing is that the company attempts to respond to the opportunities and threats expected from its environment. To be able to do this, it is necessary to *forecast* when certain opportunities or threats will occur. This means that during the external analysis the company should try to make prognoses of the variables from its external environment.

This process involves the following elements:

- Variables related to the customers:

  - Importance of values
  - Image of the company's brand or organization
  - Segments

- Industry factors:

  - Macroenvironmental variables
  - Aggregated market factors
  - Industry structure factors

- Factors regarding individual competitors, such as:

  - Strengths and weaknesses
  - Future behavior

A problem here is the large number of factors. It is not feasible to make prognoses for all variables from the external environment. In practice, the company should therefore limit itself to forecasting the most crucial variables. The following variables are of great importance in this regard:

- *Macroenvironmental* variables, including lifestyle trends, age distribution of the population, and economic variables such as gross national product and the consumer confidence index. These variables have a direct impact on the market size.
- The size and growth of the *potential market:* This variable determines the attractiveness of the market to an important extent; in addition, it may be used to forecast the company's sales. Then the market share needs to be forecast.
- The behavior of *competitors:* The core of the competitor analysis is the determination of threats and opportunities that result from the future strategies of competitors.

Choice of Strategy

After the internal and external analyses have been performed, strategies have to be chosen. An important criterion for strategy choice is the expected result of a strategy, especially the expected sales and profit. Forecasting sales and profit is important for three reasons:

1. The results of alternative strategies can be forecast and used as a basis for making a choice. In other words, *"what if" questions* can be answered: What happens if we choose strategy X?
2. Sales forecasts are important in determining the *budgets* for strategies.
3. Sales forecasts serve as input in a *control and evaluation* system: In a later phase, the prognoses may be compared with the actual results.

In answering the "what if" questions, the first step should be predicting what results can be expected if the *current* strategy is continued. Subsequently, the outcome of that prognosis should be compared with the objectives (*gap analysis*). If the prognosis is congruent with the objectives, the strategy does not have to be altered. Only if there is a difference should a change of course be considered.

In summary, in the strategic planning process the following five variables should be predicted:

1. Customer trends.
2. The behavior of competitors.
3. Relevant macroenvironmental variables.
4. Market size and market growth.
5. The company's sales.

CASE 8-1

The Importance of the Choice of a Forecasting Method

Albert Einstein remarked in 1932, "There is not the slightest indication that nuclear energy will ever be obtainable." When he was assistant secretary of the navy, Franklin Delano Roosevelt predicted that airplanes would never be useful in battle against a fleet of ships. There's nothing like the passage of time to make the world's smartest people look like complete idiots. Here's Coco Chanel on the miniskirt in 1966: "It's a bad joke that won't last. Not with winter coming." Why is predicting the future so difficult? After all, if history is just one thing after another, shouldn't the future be more of the same? But over and over, even our most highly educated guesses go disastrously wrong. We desperately need forecasters to narrow the infinity of plausible futures down to one or at least a manageable handful.

Source: Grossman, Lev, "Forward Thinking," *Time*, October 11, 2004, p. 36–38.

8.1.2   Overview of Forecasting Methods

Several authors provide classifications of forecasting methods.[2] When their classifications are compared, it turns out that there are important similarities. Therefore, it is not important which classification is chosen. We use the classification by Armstrong,[3] who bases his classification of forecasting methods on the way in which a prediction is created. He distinguishes two categories of forecasting methods:

1. *Objective forecasting methods.* These are methods in which the procedure that leads to a prognosis is determined exactly. The procedure is therefore reproducible and repeatable: If the procedure is repeated later, the same prediction will result. Usually the prognosis is created through a "calculation procedure." These methods are also called formal or explicit methods. There are two types of objective forecasting methods: extrapolations and causal models.

2. *Subjective forecasting methods.* These are methods in which a prediction is made "in the head" of a researcher, an expert, or another involved party. The prognosis therefore is not based on a clear, carefully described calculation procedure but is the result of a nonexplicit analytic process. If the procedure is repeated later, the result is not always the same prediction. These methods are also known as implicit or informal methods. There are two types of subjective forecasting methods: intention research (prognoses based on purchasing plans) and opinion research (forecasting based on the opinion of a number of experts).

The distinction between objective and subjective is not always the same as that between *qualitative* and *quantitative* (whether or not something can be expressed in numbers). For example, subjective forecasts may be both qualitative and quantitative: An expert might, for example, expect that sales will increase 8 percent. The "input" into the forecasting process may also be quantitative in subjective methods, for example, in the form of a number of market research reports that an expert studies before articulating her or his expectations. Using this classification, Figure 8-1 provides an overview of various specific forecasting methods and techniques. For clarification we make the following comments on Figure 8-1.

FIGURE 8-1
Overview of
Forecasting
Methods*

Objective forecasting methods

- Extrapolations
  - —Completely naive: $qv_{t+1} = q_t$
  - —Modified naive: $qv_{t+1} = q_t(1 + x\%)$ (x is determined subjectively)
  - —Moving average: $qv_{t+1} = (q_{t-4} + \cdots + q_t)/5$ (if it is a five-period progressive average)
  - —Exponentially weighted average: $qv_{t+1} = qv_t + \alpha(q_t - qv_t)$ (α = "smoothing constant" that will be determined subjectively)
  - —Regression analysis:
    - Trend extrapolation: $qv_t = a + bq_t$
    - Trend and season extrapolation: $qv_{t+1} = a + bq_t + c_1S_1 + c_2S_2 + c_3S_3$ (t = time variable; $S_{1,2,3}$ season (dummy) variables; a, b, $c_{1,2,3}$ to be determined through regression analysis)
  - —Box-Jenkins: advanced time series analysis
  - —Analogies: extrapolation with the use of comparable situation and/or test markets
- Causal
  - —Econometric, causal model: q_t = f(own marketing mix, marketing mix competitors, environmental variables) (with use of prognosis of explanatory variables to determine qv_{t+1})
  - —Leading indicators: forecasting with the use of variables that anticipate the variables to be predicted

Subjective forecasting methods

- Intentions
  - —Purchasing intention/purchasing plan research at consumers (such as new product models)
  - —Purchasing intention/purchasing plan research at organizations
  - —Role plays: intentions of subjects in imitated situation
- Opinions
  - —Consulting (through questionnaires) of experts
  - —Delphi method: experts arrive at agreement in several rounds
  - —Group discussions

General methods

- Segmentation
- Scenario analysis

*q_t = sales in period t; qv_t = predicted sales.

Extrapolation Methods

In making a prediction, extrapolation *methods* exclusively use data about the variable that the company wants to predict. This involves extrapolating patterns from the past to the future. These patterns may relate to trends and seasonal influences, for example. Aside from these "time influences," naive forecasting methods use no data about other variables that have an impact on the variable to be predicted. These methods are also called time series or mechanical techniques. Examples of extrapolation methods are trend extrapolation and methods based on an exponentially weighted average.

In addition to data from the past, data from similar situations may be used with these methods, for example, data about a similar product, a similar situation abroad, or a test market.[4] Empirical research shows that among the extrapolation methods in Figure 8-1, the method of the exponentially weighted average often leads to the best predictions in practice.[5] More complex methods such as regression analysis and Box-Jenkins do not always lead to better predictions.

Causal Methods

Causal models involve establishing (statistical) relationships between the course of the variable to be predicted (explained) and other explanatory variables. Subsequently, a prognosis of the variable to be predicted is made, based on these relationships and on assumptions about the future course of the explanatory variables. These methods can also take into account the past values of the variable to be predicted as well as time variables such as a trend and seasonal variables. The difference from naive methods is that *other variables* are included explicitly. An example of a causal forecasting method is an econometric model in which the sales of a brand are explained and predicted on the basis of the values of the company's marketing mix (price, promotion, distribution), the marketing mix of competitors, and environmental variables (such as income).

Forecasting with causal methods involves examining the relationships between the variable to be explained (e.g., sales) and the explanatory variables. Then a prediction can be made by determining the future values of the explanatory variables and then filling in the values for those variables in the model. Such a model therefore makes sense in terms of forecasting objectives only if the explanatory variables are easier to predict than is the variable to be explained. In addition, these models not only are suited for making predictions, they also have an important diagnostic function: They provide insight into the impact of other variables on, for example, sales.

Intention Research

Intention research involves asking respondents (usually a sample) to indicate their plans with regard to their own behavior. The best known example of intention research that is performed in practice is research on political voting behavior. This research is usually described inaccurately as opinion research. These polls sometimes deliver bad prognoses in practice. The biggest problems are related to nonresponse rates that make the sample less representative and the fact that people do different things than they indicate they will do. Even "exit polls" in which people who are leaving the voting booth are asked how they voted are often wrong. In the literature much research has been done about the solutions to the problems mentioned here, especially the "filling in" of data that are missing because people do not want to answer or do not know how they will vote. It has been shown that data about the parties people are considering (the consideration set) may be used to improve the predictions.[6]

Marketing applications of intention research are usually related to predicting the sales of *new products*. For this purpose, several new product forecasting methods have been developed. A simple example of such a method occurs when a company shows a group of consumers a new product and asks them if they are planning to purchase that product in the future. Based on randomly sampled answers (and, to be careful, perhaps including only respondents who indicate that they are "certain" they will purchase the product in the future), the company can make a prediction of its own sales. Such research is also called purchasing plan research or purchasing intention research. To predict market shares with this kind of panel research, the well-known *Parfitt-Collins* analysis can be applied (see Chapter 3).

An example of industrial intention research is research in which the advertising expenditures and the effect of the arrival of commercial television on the advertising revenue of other media was predicted on the basis of advertising expenditure plans of advertisers.[7]

Role plays are especially suitable for situations in which the value of the variable to be predicted is strongly dependent on the manner in which parties react to each other, in other words, when there is a high degree of interaction. Therefore, such methods are especially useful for predicting the strategies and reactions of competitors.[8]

Opinion Research

Opinion research involves asking at least one "expert" what he or she thinks will happen in a situation over which he or she has no direct influence. Therefore, it involves asking directly for a prognosis about a variable that the party concerned cannot determine. An example occurs when a manager is asked how high the sales of a brand will be in a certain period. These methods can be applied very easily. Only one or several experts need to be selected.

In Figure 8-1, two methods were mentioned that do not fall within any of the four categories of forecasting methods: segmentation methods and scenario analysis. Both methods are actually not forecasting methods in and of themselves, but they may be combined with the other methods mentioned in Figure 8-1.

Segmentation

With *segmentation,* a prediction is made not for the population or market as a whole but for separate segments. The prognoses for segments then are summed to get an estimate of the market. Examples of applications for each of the four categories of forecasting methods are:

1. Separate extrapolations by region.
2. Separate causal models for different varieties of a product.
3. Different intention research projects for different categories of consumers.
4. Different predictions of experts for lines of business within a market on which they have expertise.

An important reason for using segmentation is the expectation that different developments will occur for different segments. Another reason is to make the forecasting problem simpler. For example, it can be very difficult to predict the expected sales for a new product, but it may be easier to make prognoses for various segments of consumers, for example, consumers segregated by demographic characteristics. Especially for the purpose of predicting the market potential, segmentation methods are often practical. Figure 8-2 gives an example.

FIGURE 8-2   Segment Estimation for Predicting the Market Potential of Becel Pro-Activ

Segment	(1) Amount of Becel	(2) Becel Consumption Per Person	(3) Percent Cholesterol-Aware	(4) Expected Purchase Amount	Segment Potential (1) × (2) × (3) ×(4)
Men, single, 18–29					
Women, single, 18–29					
Men, married, 18–29					
Women, married, 18–29					
Men and women, single, 30–55					
Married, 30–55					
56 and older					
Total potential					

Scenario Analysis

In practice, developments in the environment of an organization are so uncertain that a single sales forecast cannot suffice. In such a case, *scenarios* should be defined (see Section 5.3). A scenario is a description of an environmental condition accompanied by the resulting prediction. Typically, in addition to a most likely scenario, a pessimistic scenario and an optimistic scenario are formulated. These scenarios may, for example, be related to economic conditions: a disappointing or better than expected economic development. The economic developments that fit with such scenarios can be obtained from publications of national agencies. Scenarios may also be defined in regard to the competition: The competitor does or does not react to a certain strategy.

Scenario analysis may be combined with each of the four categories of forecasting methods. Here are some examples:

1. In addition to trend extrapolation, a stronger or weaker trend may be extended.

2. In a causal model, a pessimistic value of the most uncertain explanatory variable can be inserted, for example, for the pessimistic scenario.

3. In intention research, respondents may be asked to indicate, in addition to the existing plans, what they would do if another environmental condition occurred.

4. In opinion research, experts may be asked to comment on more than one situation.

Trend impact analysis is a suitable method for predicting the effect of a certain event on a trend. This method uses opinion research to estimate the extent to which a trend extrapolation should be adjusted for important changes in the environment, such as a reaction by a competitor. Another method that can be helpful in this area is *cross-impact analysis.* This method serves to predict the way in which trends mutually influence each other. These methods are actually combinations of objective and subjective forecasting methods.[9]

Defining scenarios makes sense only if plans are made to indicate what should happen if the most likely prediction does not come true. These alternative plans are known as *contingency plans.* Such an alternative plan (a "disaster plan" if it relates to a pessimistic scenario) should indicate at which point it will be activated. For this purpose, the company should define exactly at which value of the relevant environmental variable the contingency plan will become current. For example, if the most likely situation assumed economic growth of 4 percent and the pessimistic scenario assumed 2 percent, which plan is put in effect if growth reaches 3 percent? In some organizations the contingency plans are worked out in detail and appear as an attachment to the marketing plan. However, often only global guidelines are included, and the assumption is that if another environmental condition occurs, there will be sufficient time to adjust the strategy. However, whether this is true remains to be seen. If a competitor unexpectedly turns out to be reacting, the question is whether there will not be too much delay in inventing and implementing a new strategy.

8.1.3 Advantages and Disadvantages of the Various Forecasting Methods

In the previous section, a number of forecasting methods were introduced. The question now is which method is most suitable for which situation.

A large number of criteria play a role in the choice of forecasting method. Georgoff and Murdick classify these criteria into four categories[10]:

1. *Time aspects,* such as predictive horizon, available time for making the prognosis itself, and necessity to repeat.

2. Availability of *resources* and skills such as financial resources, computers and computer knowledge, and statistical skills.

3. Characteristics regarding the *input,* such as a lot of or a little fluctuation in the variable to be predicted, sufficient quantitative data about the variable to be predicted, and any other variables.

4. Characteristics regarding the *output,* such as the required precision of the prediction and the necessity to be able to predict trend breaks.

Georgoff and Murdick show for a number of forecasting methods the extent to which they meet their criteria.

Armstrong[11] argues that the most important step in choosing a forecasting method is making the choice between an *objective* method and a *subjective* method. In this choice, two criteria play an important role:

1. The availability of quantitative data.
2. Expectations of changes in the environment: Are "turning points" (trend breaks) expected or will there be a continuation of existing trends?

Based on an analysis of a large number of empirical studies, Armstrong concludes that the predictive power of objective methods typically is greater than that of subjective methods if:

• Sufficient quantitative data are available.
• Changes may be expected in variables that can be incorporated into a model (e.g., actions by a competitor, economic developments).

Armstrong concludes that if both of these conditions are met, an objective method is preferred. However, if one or both conditions are not met, for example, if changes are expected in important variables that cannot be integrated into a model ("environmental changes" such as government decisions and quality changes), a subjective method should be chosen.

The fact that objective methods do not predict as well in the case of large environmental changes can be explained by the fact that these methods extend patterns from the past into the future. Extrapolation methods extend trends and other time movements; causal models assume that estimated relationships between variables can apply to the future. Therefore, it is not surprising that when trend breaks occur, objective methods fall short.

In regard to the choice between *extrapolation methods* and *causal models,* extrapolation methods are typically simpler and require fewer data than do causal models. In terms of the predictive power of both types of methods, Armstrong concludes that for short-term predictions (less than a year) both methods have comparable accuracy, but for longer-term prognoses causal models are preferred. The reason for this is that extrapolation methods do not take into account any changes in variables that have an impact on the variable to be predicted, whereas causal models allow changes in influencing variables to be included in the explanatory variables. For example, if the plan is to reduce the price of a product sharply, an extrapolation method would probably present too low a prediction as part of a demand prediction. However, a causal model could include the price variable and so predict the effect of a price change.

In terms of the choice between *intention research* and *opinion research,* an important practical consideration is whether there is sufficient time and money and whether the prediction has to be revised regularly. Opinion research can be performed quickly, whereas intention research is time-consuming. If time and resources are not a limitation, intention research is preferred, assuming that the specific conditions for this research have been met. The most important conditions are that the respondents (those people who make the purchasing decisions):

• Have concrete plans.
• Are accessible and able to describe their plans.

FIGURE 8-3
Choosing a
Forecasting Method

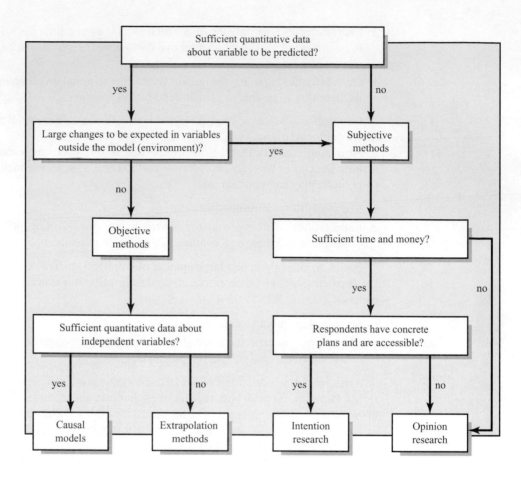

Since neither consumers nor organizations typically have concrete purchasing plans for periods longer than one year, the predictive horizon should not be too long when one is doing intention research. An important advantage of intention research is that it is based on data obtained from potential customers. In this regard it is the only forecasting method that uses a *customer orientation.* Unfortunately, a disadvantage of intention research is that often a difference exists between intentions and actual purchasing behavior. Even though respondents may indicate that they will purchase a specific new product, the actual purchase may not occur as a result of factors that cannot be explained. However, the differences between intentions and behavior may be small if the situations about which respondents are asked are *as clear as possible.* The disadvantage of opinion research is that the choice of experts is very crucial. How does one know whether someone is truly an expert?

The advantages and disadvantages mentioned in this section have been incorporated into a flow chart that can be used in making the choice of the method (Figure 8-3).

8.1.4 Forecasting Variables and the Choice of the Forecasting Method

The last section indicated which strategic variables should be predicted. Subsequently, we listed a number of general advantages and disadvantages of forecasting methods. In this section we combine these aspects by indicating which forecasting method is most suitable for which strategic variable.

The Behavior of Competitors

Subjective methods are the most suitable for predicting the behavior of competitors. The most important reason for this is the strong interaction that exists between the organization and other competitors. In addition, a great deal of qualitative data needs to be used in the forecasting, such as data about the strengths and weaknesses, objectives, and current strategies of the competitors (see also the discussion of the steps in the competitor analysis in Chapter 6).

Among the subjective methods, intention research is not suitable. After all, it is not plausible that competitors are prepared to communicate what they are planning to do. Two methods that are appropriate are[12]:

1. *Role plays*. Armstrong shows that "acting out" a market situation often produces good predictions of the potential strategies and reactions of competitors.[13]
2. *Opinion research.* Various forms of opinion research can be used. One method is to ask a number of experts from the organization to answer a series of questions about the competitors individually on paper and subsequently merge those answers. In practice there will often be agreement. If this is not the case, a group discussion may be used to attempt to come to an agreement.

Macroenvironmental Variables and Customer Trends

For a number of macroenvironmental variables such as demographic and economic trends, prognoses are made by other parties (see Chapter 5). Macroeconomic prognoses are very sensitive to assumptions about world trade. Since typically there is much uncertainty about this variable (which forms a reflection of "the economy"), often scenarios are used and predictions are adjusted regularly. Demographic developments are predicted by statistical agencies. Other variables, such as social-cultural and technological developments, are sometimes predicted by other parties (specialized institutions, individual experts). To the extent that this is not the case, the company should attempt to forecast trends by using subjective methods.

Market Size

Lehmann and Winer[14] indicate which methods for predicting the market potential can be used in which situations (Figure 8-4).

FIGURE 8-4
Possible Approaches to Estimating the Market Potential in Various Situations

Source: Lehmann and Winer (2001)

Situation	Required Data	Forecasting Method
Saturated market	Past sales Evaluation: Is an important change expected?	Extrapolation
Growing market	Past sales Evaluation: Is an important change expected from the competition?	Extrapolation with a saturation level
New industrial product	Economic circumstances Evaluation: target audience segments	Segmentation
New durable consumer product	Market segments (e.g., demographic) Intentions plus evaluations: expected degree of acceptance	Segmentation
New nondurable consumer product	Market segments (e.g., demographic) Experiments: trial and repeat purchases	New product forecasting mode

The Company's Own Sales

No general recommendation is possible for choosing a method to predict a company's sales. This depends on a large number of factors, the most important of which were mentioned in Section 8.1.2.

8.1.5 General Recommendations in Making Forecasts

The material above may create the impression that depending on the situation, a single type of forecasting method should be chosen. However, this is not recommended. A large number of empirical studies[15] show that *combining* the results of *various* forecasting methods often produces better predictions than does the use of a single method. Armstrong therefore recommends not devoting too much energy to a single method but instead devoting a little less energy to each of several methods. Lehmann and Winer provide a practical plan of steps to achieve this. They propose the following procedure for forecasting, for example, market size:

1. Place the data in a graph and make an extrapolation.
2. Specify and estimate a causal model that includes explanatory variables that:

   a. Are good predictors.
   b. Are not correlated with each other.
   c. Are simple to predict in themselves.

For a market forecast, typically general economic and demographic variables (e.g., gross national product, number of households) will be included, as well as market data (e.g., average price, total advertising expenditures).

3. Collect prognoses from "experts" through opinion research.
4. Make one's own subjective forecast based on expected changes in the future and their impact on sales.
5. Make a forecast based on segmentation: the summation of prognoses for regions, for example.

These results can be summarized as shown in Figure 8-5. In this figure, three scenarios are also included. The extent to which the predictions vary gives an indication of the uncertainty regarding the prognosis.

In creating an overview such as the one in Figure 8-5, it should be decided how a *combined* prediction can be made. After all, for a manager there is little benefit if different prognoses from different methods are presented. A lot of empirical research has been conducted into the way in which predictions should be combined.[16] The best method is to weight the prognoses on the basis of their expected accuracy. If data for this are not available (in practice, that is usually the case), it is best to allocate equal weights to the various

FIGURE 8-5
Summarizing Predictions for a Variable

Adapted from Lehmann and Winer (2001).

	Forecast		
Method	**Pessimistic**	**Most Likely**	**Optimistic**
1. Extrapolation			
2. Causal model			
3. Prediction by experts			
4. Own prediction			
5. "Bottom-up" prediction*			
Combined prediction			

*Sum of predictions of "subordinates" such as product or region managers.

FIGURE 8-6 **Presentation of Important Market Trends and Prognoses (with Unchanged Policy)**

Year	Market Size	Size of Segment A	Share in Total Market	Share in Segment A	Sales (Volume)	Sales ($1.000)	Profit ($1.000)
Past							
t − 3							
t − 2							
t − 1							
Current							
t							
Future							
t + 1							
t + 2							
t + 3							
Assumptions							

prognoses and simply take the nonweighted average. The combined prediction in Figure 8-5 would therefore be the average of the prognoses above it.

Presenting predictions for a number of variables in a marketing plan may be combined with the representation of the development in the past year. Figure 8-6 gives an example.

Finally, in presenting the prognoses, it is very important to articulate explicitly the *planning assumptions* on which the prognoses are based. This involves the assumptions that have been made regarding the following:

- Industry variables (economic, demographic, and political developments, behavior of distributors, etc.).
- Competitors (future behavior, reacting or not reacting to the company's behavior).
- Customers (Who are the customers? How do they react?).
- The organization (assumed behavior: investment decisions, use of marketing mix etc.).

Articulating these assumptions not only has the advantage that it summarizes several important preceding components of a marketing plan, it also is important in later deducing causes if the prediction does not come true. Then a check can be made whether certain assumptions have not been met. In Chapter 12 we present an example of a financial forecast of a marketing plan including assumptions.

It is therefore useful, where possible, to indicate for each assumption how sensitive the predictions are for changes in that assumption. For this purpose, a *sensitivity analysis* can be performed by "extending the calculations" about the consequences of various combinations of input values. Such a *simulation* is possible with causal methods.

8.1.6 Forecasting in Practice

Even if the right steps were chosen in the forecasting process, predictions often do not come true in practice. The saying "Predicting is difficult, especially in regard to the future" certainly applies in this case. The reasons why predictions do not come true are diverse. In Chapter 2, in the material on strategy evaluation, we outlined a framework for analyzing discrepancies between expectations and results. The question may be raised whether there is any point in making predictions. Based on the fact that in practice a large number of companies do forecasting, it appears that many organizations answer this question affirmatively. We think this is well-founded. Forecasting is a way to reduce uncertainty about the future. Although the uncertainty can never be reduced to zero, better planning can occur when a company attempts to look forward than when that activity is omitted.

8.2 SWOT ANALYSIS

A *SWOT (strengths, weaknesses, opportunities, threats)* analysis is an analysis that defines strategic options by linking strengths and weaknesses on the one hand and opportunities and threats on the other hand. A SWOT analysis therefore is different from the external and internal analyses that are being completed. Both of those analyses combined may be designated as the situation analysis. The results of the situation analysis represent the "input" into the SWOT analysis. This section deals with the following issues:

- The goal and content of the SWOT analysis (Section 8.2.1).
- Summarizing the situation analysis (Section 8.2.2).
- Choosing a value strategy (Section 8.2.3).
- Developing a marketing strategy (Section 8.2.4).
- The selection process (Section 8.2.5).
- SWOT analysis in practice (Section 8.2.6).

8.2.1 Goal and Content

First we define what we mean by strengths, weaknesses, opportunities, and threats. There is a need for a good definition because we will otherwise encounter misunderstandings when we get into specifics. We have the following three characteristics:

1. *Distinction between strengths and weakness on the one hand and opportunities and threats on the other hand.* Strengths and weaknesses are internal: They are related to the brand for which the marketing plan is made. Opportunities and threats are external: They are related to the environment and would exist even *if the brand in question did not.* Therefore, a "'good image" (measured in terms of customers) is a strength and not an opportunity despite the fact that it comes from the customer analysis.

2. *Distinction between opportunity and threat.* The distinction between an opportunity and a threat is that an opportunity is a positive development for an *unrevised policy*[17] and a threat is a negative one. We add the criterion of unrevised policy because as is often said, "There is such thing as a threat because a company can capitalize on anything." If that fundamentally correct assumption is made, there is no tenable distinction between opportunities and threats, and so it is better to use the term *issues* or *external points of attention.* Thus, we do in fact make a distinction. Therefore, an economic slump can be an opportunity for a quality product if the brand is in a position to lower the price. However, we still consider this a threat because there can be unfavorable influences in the case of an unrevised policy.

3. *Distinction between opportunities and strategies.* One difference between an opportunity and a strategy is that a strategy is something that a brand *does* and an opportunity is not. Thus, "a peanut-flavored beer developed for young people" is not an opportunity but a possible strategy. The underlying opportunity may be "expected increase in demand for specialty beers among young people." As another example, "brand rejuvenation" is not an opportunity but a reaction to the "corny image" weakness.

Finally, we sometimes use the terms *relative strength* and *relative weakness,* by which we mean that they are strong or weak not only in general but also *with respect to the competition,* that is, comparatively. Relative strengths can be determined by comparing the "absolute" strengths and weaknesses (partly derived from the internal analysis) with those of the competition (derived from the analysis of the competition).

The opportunities and threats are the result of the external analysis but should preferably be applicable to the future. The opportunities and threats are therefore detected by making *predictions* involving a number of factors in the external environment of the company (see Section 8.1).

The subsections below describe a methodology for drawing a specific connection between the "SWOTs" and the strategies devised and implemented on the basis of those SWOTs. Various authors have developed these kinds of SWOT analyses.[18] We distinguish two types: the strong analytic processes and the freer approaches. The strong analytic SWOT processes are characterized by a heavily structured step-by-step approach in which a choice of strategy is reached that is based on a wide variety of considerations and scores. One disadvantage of this method is the strong focus placed on the process, which can get in the way of the focus on thinking creatively. An advantage of the somewhat freer approach is the TOWS (or SWOT) matrix developed by Weihrich.[19] The strengths and so on are placed in a matrix, and as many different good ideas as possible are placed in each quadrant (strength/opportunity, etc.). A disadvantage of this system is that it gets cluttered, and so it becomes difficult to arrive at choices in an orderly manner. An important requirement for a selection system is that alternatives be able to be compared and contrasted with one another. But how can an idea for a new product be contrasted with an idea for a new campaign? The underlying problem here is that a method such as the SWOT matrix does not take the different strategy *levels* into account.

A SWOT analysis should meet the following requirements:

1. *It is firmly in tune with practice and has sufficient space for creative reflection.* In practice, mechanical methods are never chosen for strategy development. A situation analysis is typically carried out, but after that there never actually is a consideration of opportunities to arrive at a choice of strategy. What is done is brainstorming, delving into and understanding the results of the situation analysis, discussion, brainstorming, rethinking, more brainstorming, and so on. This approach is considered productive and also has the advantage that it can be performed by a number of people at the same time. Case 8-2 gives an example of effective strategy development at Unilever; the approach outlined there matches up well with method we have proposed.

2. *It leads to strategic decisions with sufficient focus on levels within the company.* A SWOT analysis should be truly strategic and in particular should produce ideas for the value strategy (if it is not already defined) and the marketing strategy (brand positioning). This means that the SWOT analysis must involve rethinking that is geared toward these strategic decisions and that there should not be a free brainstorming process on all possible types of tactical ideas. For instance, there is no point brainstorming ideas for communication until the brand positioning has been defined at the strategic level.

The SWOT matrix can be modified to satisfy the conditions set forth above. In this case, two modifications of the original methodology are necessary:

1. Two types of strategies are considered:

   a. *The value strategies of Treacy and Wiersema.* This choice should have been made at the company level, but if this was not done, a brand can still make choices about the method of competition: product leader, leader in low cost for the customer, or specialized in individual customer relationships. Alternatively, it can come up with an indication of what must be improved to attain a sufficient level.

   b. *The marketing strategy: target group (segment) and brand positioning.* The value strategy provides further specification of the particular target group choice (existing and new customers, background features, and lifestyle of the target group) and the brand positioning (instrumental and emotional, brand varieties).

2. Coordinating alternatives are considered "at the same time," and explicit indications are given for which strengths, weaknesses, opportunities, and threats link up with each alternative. In this context, "at the same time" means that we do not deem it necessary to consider the alternatives on the basis of their quadrant in the matrix, that is, separately for the strength-opportunity, strength-threat, weakness-opportunity, or weakness-threat quadrant. In our view, this limits creative thinking and makes it more difficult to see the mutual relationships between, for example, strengths and weakness or opportunities and threats. It also makes it difficult to narrow things down to a few alternatives, such as a maximum of three. A manager can try to amass various ideas under "umbrella options," but this produces too few coherent options.

CASE 8-2 *Strategy Development at Unilever Asia*	Tex Gunning of Unilever Foods Asia on strategy development: "We are now conducting all of our large market studies in large collective processes. The figures come back, and then we lock ourselves inside for three or four days. Then we work through all the ups and downs in this kind of process, but after that, it is also a collectively supported positioning. It can result in a lot of frustration, but you end up with a conclusion that you never could have arrived at by yourself with two other smart people. Consumers and their relationship with a brand are so complicated that a marketer can't make a go of it alone. We always get 10, 20, or 30 people in on the rethinking and the work. And we do it all over again in four months until the brand positioning is crystal clear and relevant." He gives Lipton tea as an example. "It sounds simple, but everyone sells tea in China. I've been working on it for two and a half years, and it wasn't until two week ago that we thought we really hit on it. This is what we're going to do with Lipton: Young Asians know that the future belongs to them. Those economies are so large and the political influence of the Chinese is growing so fast that the collective self-awareness is becoming infinitely large. You get a whole group of young people who want to ride that wave. Considering this, we positioned Lipton as a *bright and vital outlook on life.* That means that you have to do more than just sell tea." **Source:** T. van Vugt, 'Every marketer should go to Asia', *Tijdschrift voor Marketing,* November 2004, p. 13–16.

The rest of this section describes an approach for the SWOT analysis that is systematic and therefore guarantees that no relevant matters are overlooked but also leaves room for strategic and creative rethinking. After the *systematic* homework of the situation analysis, a more *holistic approach* must be selected for strategy development. The main phases of this approach are detailed in Figure 8-7.

8.2.2   Summary of the Situation Analysis

The situation analysis potentially produces a large list of strengths, weaknesses, opportunities, and threats. Some of those are important; others are less important. In addition, some are related to each other. To keep the subsequent analysis well organized, the situation analysis should be *summarized* into a limited number of strengths, weaknesses, opportunities, and threats. The following tips may be useful[20]:

• Include only include the most important factors ("issues"). Always limit the number to a *maximum of five* (a maximum of five strengths, five opportunities, etc.).

• *Classify* the points in order of importance.

• Ensure that sufficient *supportive evidence* is available for each point.

• Strengths and weaknesses should be *relative* to those of the competitors.

FIGURE 8-7
Steps in the SWOT Analysis

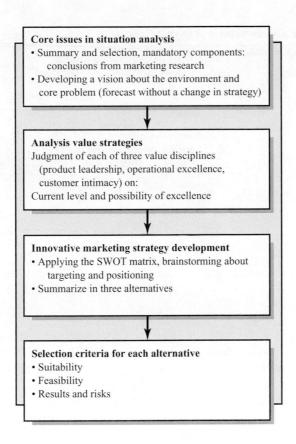

Core issues in situation analysis
• Summary and selection, mandatory components: conclusions from marketing research
• Developing a vision about the environment and core problem (forecast without a change in strategy)

Analysis value strategies
Judgment of each of three value disciplines (product leadership, operational excellence, customer intimacy) on:
Current level and possibility of excellence

Innovative marketing strategy development
• Applying the SWOT matrix, brainstorming about targeting and positioning
• Summarize in three alternatives

Selection criteria for each alternative
• Suitability
• Feasibility
• Results and risks

• Do *not mix up* strengths, weaknesses, opportunities, and threats (see the definitions in Section 8.2.1).

Therefore, the most frequently stated "issues" become the starting point for further SWOT analysis. The choice of what is relevant requires a high degree of caution and creativity. It requires caution because it may be assumed that the competition also indicates the most readily available opportunities, and the distinction may actually be in less noticeable "cues." Creativity is also important: the ability to intuit what might be an opportunity. There should be a "golden cue" for the entire SWOT process. As it is fashionable to say, a "big idea" is all it takes for a profitable strategy. That idea can often be found by listening carefully to buyers and not only paying attention to aspects that the customers like but also paying attention to what they don't like. Figure 8-8 summarizes the results of this substep.

Vision on Environment and Core Problem

After and in addition to the summary of the situation analysis, it is desirable to carry out a further reduction of the situation analysis. This facilitates the choice of what is and is not important at this point. This is actually about the development of a *vision on the environment*: a short and concise statement about what management thinks is important in the environment of the brand. We refer back to the categories in the situation analysis:

• Customer analysis
• Industry analysis
• Competitor analysis
• Distribution analysis

FIGURE 8-8 **Selection of SWOTs for a Manufacturer of Digital Cameras**

Definite Strengths and Weaknesses (SW)*	Core Issues in the Environment (Future Opportunities and Threats) (OT)*
S1 Strong position with professionals	O1 Increasing need for certainty
S2 Good in quality and innovation	O2 Decline in analog cameras
S3 Many possibilities	O3 Growing importance for consumer of advice in the shop
S4 Good relationship with retailers	O4 Increasing dissatisfaction (bad service, appliances break down)
S5 Good relationship with suppliers	O5 Cameras pay little attention to style (compare with cars)
W1 High costs and price	T1 Growing need for convenience
W2 Low market share in consumer market	T2 Aging
W3 Brand awareness relatively low	T3 Downswing
W4 Limited distribution	T4 Competitors strong in user-friendly cameras
W5 No brand extensions	T5 Competitors (e.g., Hewlett-Packard) have broader assortment (printers, personal computers, cameras, etc.)

*In total a maximum of 10 internal and 10 external items.

Each of these components is accompanied by the question: What future development or trend does the manager think is the most important? If there is a lot of uncertainty with respect to one of these components involving a development that is also considered very important, we can describe *scenarios* and then select one as the most probable scenario. For instance, suppose there is a lot of competition. We can describe two scenarios here: The competition either does or does not introduce a hefty decrease in prices. We then use this as a basis for choosing one of the two options.

Problem Conclusion and Unrevised Policy

The *performance evaluation* (part of the internal analysis; see section 3.2) provides an initial impression of where potential problems are, based on an evaluation of the strategy being followed and its results. Some examples of possible results of this are the following:

- The marketing target (such as a certain market share) of a new brand X is not achieved.
- This is due mainly to a disappointing percentage of repeat purchases.
- The cause should not be sought in the *implementation* of the planned strategy because there was an important difference between the planned implementation and the actual implementation.

This recognition of the problem is not sufficient, of course. The question remains: What are the specific causes of the disappointing results? More specifically formulated, what is the current "core marketing problem" for which the market plan must provide a solution? The answer to this question can best be given as the conclusion of the summary of the SWOTs. After all, it is in this phase that all possible relevant internal and environmental factors are analyzed, and problems are often a combination of internal and external factors. It already has already been indicated that at this point the problem conclusion was reflected in the marketing plan and even in the first chapter of the plan (see Section 1.6). A solid foundation is important for the core problem. A practical example of a core problem is that brand identity does not correspond to brand image: The brand wants to have certain associations, but the target group does not see them. This is happens a lot, sometimes more than managers realize. It is often said that a brand "is very strong because it has a great deal of familiarity." However, image is more important than familiarity. If an image is moving toward "trusted, familiar," there is the danger ("prognosis") of moving toward "corny,

FIGURE 8-9
**Development of a
Vision on the
Environment for a
Digital Camera
Manufacturer**

Situation Analysis Component	Expected Main Point
Customer analysis	Consumers will continue to demand more simplicity and user-friendliness. Alongside this development, a market for more professional users is developing.
Industry analysis	The main point is aging.
Competition analysis	The most important competition will apply itself to user-friendly cameras.
Distribution analysis	Because of the multiplicity of the supply, the customer will rely more on advice in the shop.
Internal analysis and problem	*Problem conclusion:* The current image of our brand is too strongly focused on quality and high price. *Expectation for unrevised policy:* Our position with consumers will weaken.

old-fashioned." Does the company want that? Therefore, a critical interpretation of the situation analysis is desirable.

During this phase we can also make a prediction of what is expected in the case of "unrevised policy": a prognosis of sales and profits if nothing is changed in the strategy. Of course, subjectivity plays a big role here, and the marketing plan to be developed will have to lead to better results. An advantage of this kind of marketing plan is that it emphasizes the need for change. Incidentally, this is also frequently stated within the framework of *change management:* The first step in a change management plan is to become aware of the need for change. The best way to gain awareness is to have the conviction that if the company keeps going down the same path, this will lead to disastrous or at least not prosperous results. Figure 8-9 summarizes this substep.

8.2.3 Choice of a Value Strategy

The three value disciplines of Treacy and Wiersema were discussed in Chapter 2. Every company should choose to excel in one of the three value disciplines after ensuring that a sufficient level has been attained in all three aspects (innovation, smoothly running processes, and customer orientation). The value strategy should have been defined by the time of the drafting of the marketing plan for a brand. If this is the case, we can proceed to the next planning phase.

However, it is often unclear which value strategy has been chosen. In this case, an assumption must be made as to which value strategy has been chosen or a value strategy must still be chosen.

Figure 8-10 gives an example of a possible selection method. The following must be assessed for each of the value strategies:

- *The current level.* If one of the three is at a level that is too low, this will have to be dealt with before the company considers excelling. In practice, an insufficient level of operational excellence is often a problem: The internal processes simply do not run smoothly. There are innumerable possible causes for this. The company will have to improve in this area, but this does not mean that the company chooses the operational excellence value strategy. Solving a problem is not the same thing as excellence.
- *Feasibility in excellence.* Here we can estimate whether and to what extent excellence is feasible within the time constraints. What has to happen for the company to become the best?
- *Connecting to opportunities.* Which value discipline offers the best opportunities in the environment? More specifically, what are the future desires of the client and the weaknesses of the competition?

FIGURE 8-10   **Selection Process for Value Strategy for a digital camera manufacturer***

Value Strategy	Current Level	Possibility of Excellence	Fit with Environment
1. Operational excellence	Not yet at a sufficient level.	High costs (W1) must be reduced (S2), but not to a great extent. Distribution (W4) can be increased.	Links up with B1 well (simplicity). Difficult to be better than the competition (B4).
2. Product leadership	At a sufficient level	Fits well with S2 (innovation) and S1 (professionals).	Links up with O1 (trust) well and with B4 (competition is more focused on operational excellence). But it appears that other innovations can be chosen in the future (Hewlett-Packard).
3. Customer intimacy	Customer-oriented, but not strongly one-to-one	Already achieved in distribution channel (S4) but not yet with consumers. Fits in well with our image as a specialist.	Links up with O1 and O4. Service and customer intimacy go well together. Also offers an opportunity thanks to our limited product line (W5 will be strong here) and therefore our image as a specialist.

Conclusion

Sufficient level?

- Operational excellence is still insufficient, and costs must be further reduced; only then can we start thinking about excellence.

Excellence?

- Product leadership suits us well, but quality and possibilities are found to be less important and position threatens to be difficult to defend in the future. Doubtful.
- Customer intimacy would be feasible thanks to our good relationship with distributors (get customer data via distributors according to permission marketing). Also fits in with our image as a specialist. Offers the best opportunities.

*Instead of using this approach, a manager can apply the SWOT matrix to the choice of value strategies.

8.2.4   Marketing Strategy Development

Once the situation analysis has been reduced to a few main points and the value strategy has been chosen, it is time to develop ideas for the marketing strategy. In the practice of marketing, often too little time is spent thinking about the brand image and the brand identity. It is precisely the *brand positioning* that must be the reason why people buy one brand and do not buy another. This part of the brainstorming process is therefore critical (see the example in Case 8-2).

The positioning method will end up being an extension of the chosen value strategy. If, for instance, the value strategy "product leadership" is chosen, there is not much point in considering low-price positioning. However, in this phase the company should not let itself be guided by existing preconditions such as the vision on the environment or financial constraints. In principle, any strategy is possible, even outside the current activities. It is of the utmost importance to be creative. It is important to have a "big idea."

The brainstorming phase of the SWOT analysis is crucial and requires a high level of *creativity and empathy*. The ideas the company comes up with should be as specific as possible. Thus, it does not make much sense to take on vague ideas such as "boost market share," "anticipate customer desires better," "diversify," and "reposition." At the very least, we must state exactly how the company will be able to do this. To get as many ideas as possible on potential strategies, it is advisable to hold *brainstorming sessions*. This should involve different representatives from the company, such as designers, production personnel, go-betweens (such as representatives), and upper management. These persons could first be debriefed on the results of the SWOT analysis (the most important S's, W's, O's, and T's) in order to brainstorm possible strategies.

From a marketing perspective, the positioning of the brand is an important point of discussion that must come to the fore. What is the level of brand awareness, and what are the brand associations that the target group has now? To what extent is this in line with the brand identity?

In these phases, we attempt to arrive at a few, for example, three, alternatives. "Alternatives" means that the options should really exclude each other. Otherwise, there is nothing to choose. For each alternative, we indicate in brackets the idea on which internal and external issues are based. It makes a difference whether this is based on a strength or a weakness. Strengths offer connecting points for a competitive edge, whereas weaknesses result in a defensive strategy. It does not necessarily have to be this way. A weakness can be worked out quickly by cooperating with a strong partner and thus forming the basis for an offensive strategy.

In every step, you should always be creative and interpret each signal carefully and on the basis of your own possibilities.

CASE 8-3 *Innovation in Watching Television*	It's a sad reality: Every once in a while a couch potato must turn off the tube and leave the couch. Until recently there were few television options for the potato on the go. Battery-powered portable televisions provide only snowy broadcast images, and portable video players from the likes of Creative Technology require the hassle of downloading video manually from a computer. Verizon Communications is changing all that. On February 1, 2005, it rolled out its own mobile television service, called V CAST, which lets users watch television from their cell phones in 30 U.S. metro areas for about $15 a month.

Source: Helm, Burt, "Cellular Television," *BusinessWeek,* May 16, 2005, p. 106.

Being innovative also means that *new activities* should explicitly be taken into account. In light of the fact that a situation analysis exclusively examines the existing market, this may appear strange. However, even a situation analysis may produce various signals that indicate opportunities outside the existing, analyzed market. Following the case of the manufacturer of digital cameras, examples of signals for new activities include the following:

- *Unmet needs:* needs of existing consumers to which a company cannot respond with its existing products. An analysis of complaints and problems consumers have with products can be helpful; this is the most important source for new ideas, and so it is important to listen well to consumers. It must be noted, however, that consumers will not tell you what to do; you should listen carefully and translate the information into ideas. For example, you might develop a camera with a battery indicator that works properly.
- *New consumer segments* not served now, for example, cameras for children.
- Developments in the *macroenvironment* that might have a positive effect on other markets, for example, aging, which stimulates the development of user-friendly cameras.
- The expected developments in *substitute products* within the industry factors, for example, the growth in mobile phones with a camera function, which could be a motive to become active in this market.
- What *competitors* do aside from their core activities, for example, selling copiers.

As an example of alternative marketing strategies, a brand of digital cameras, according to research, is seen as not cheap, semiprofessional, of high quality, and not very user-friendly. The question is this: Is the brand happy with this strategy? A more detailed analysis of this information reveals that a distinction must be made between three user groups: the "simple" consumer who uses a camera mainly for house, garden, and kitchen shots; the fanatical consumer who takes photographs more often and also processes them; and the professional user. The brand *image* is comparable with all three groups, but the importance of the user aspects is different. User-friendliness is most important for the simple consumer. The other two groups find quality and possibilities more important. Should the brand be changed? That depends on the desired target group and positioning. Some examples of alternative ideas are:

1. *Repositioning toward user-friendliness.* Management believes the aspect of user-friendliness will become increasingly important in the future (vision on environment). Management considers the low score in this aspect a problem. Thus far, the emphasis has always been on quality, but now user-friendliness must be incorporated into the identity and must receive more attention both in the products and in the communications.

2. *Reinforcing the quality aspect.* The competition for the position with the simple consumer is so strong and will increase to such an extent in the future that it is becoming particularly difficult to attain a leading position (vision on environment). Furthermore, our brand of cameras is not incredibly user-friendly. We choose to strengthen our position with users who are fanatics.

3. *Introduction of a user-friendly subbrand.* In the interest of profitability, the large group of consumers is of great importance. A disadvantage of alternative 1 is that the proposed repositioning of the brand may be detrimental to the image for fanatical users: User-friendliness and simplicity may not go with the idea of a top camera. This problem is diminished if a simple line of cameras is introduced as a subbrand: not a type designation, as generally occurs, but an actual subbrand.

CASE 8-4

Alternative Options for Positioning: The Identity of Lego

On its Web site the Lego brand describes its vision as follows: "Though we make toys, we are not just a toy company. Though we are famous for our product, we are defined by our philosophy. Our name comes from the combination of the Danish 'leg godt,' which means to 'play well.' In Latin it means 'I put together.' It is both our name and our nature. We believe that play is the essential ingredient in a child's growth and development. It grows the human spirit. It encourages imagination, conceptual thinking and creation." Although this vision seems clear, the Lego assortment has changed significantly from simple building blocks to technical Lego and to complete "projects" such as fire engines and Harry Potter. These extensions make Lego interesting for older children. However, the question is whether these "ready-to-make" extensions really "encourage creativity." And in the Legoland Parks one might wonder what the relation is between the classical Lego building blocks and the roller coasters. It seems that for the future several positioning options are possible: back to the core business, continuing to extend the brand, and introducing subbrands for the new products.

In addition to alternative brand identities, we can consider alternative value strategies. A SWOT matrix can be used for multiple decisions as long as we have a clear idea of the type of decision needed.

We then get an approach and result, as outlined in Figure 8-11. As was indicated in Chapter 2 in the material on the concept of market definition, if a company is considering becoming active in other markets (new activities), it may be necessary to perform an external analysis again, this time of the new market. For example, this may arise from the choice

FIGURE 8-11   **SWOT Matrix Marketing Strategy**

	O1 Increasing need for certainty O2 Decline in analog cameras O3 Growing importance for consumer of advice in the shop O4 Increasing dissatisfaction (bad service, appliances break down) O5 Cameras pay little attention to style (compare with cars)	T1 Growing need for convenience T2 Aging T3 Downswing T4 Competitors strong in user-friendly cameras T5 Competitors (e.g., Hewlett-Packard) have a broader assortment (printers, personal computers, cameras, etc.)
S1 Strong position with professionals S2 Good in quality and innovation S3 Many possibilities S4 Good relationship with retailers S5 Good relationship with suppliers W1 High costs and price W2 Low market share in consumer market W3 Brand awareness relatively low W4 Limited distribution W5 No brand extensions	Alternative marketing strategies for the next three years* • Positioning • Reposition on user-friendliness (B1, B2, S4, Z2). • Increase quality perception (K1, K4, B4, S1, S2, S5, Z1) • Introduce a user-friendly and stylish subbrand (K5, B1, B2,B5, S1, S2, S4, Z1, Z5)	

*Two applications are possible: choosing a value strategy and choosing a more specific brand identity (as in this example).

to start exporting. After the U.S. market, a second external analysis is performed of the Canadian market (see Figure 8-3).

There are two reasons to formulate a number of options explicitly instead of choosing them "all at once" for a strategy based on a situation analysis:

1. It forces the manager to consider roads other than the one already traveled.

2. If the company comes up with a single option, it is more difficult to obtain support from within the company for the "choice" (see also Chapter 12).

Obviously, each of the options must be realistic. Defining apparent possibilities has little use. Although the option "withdraw from the market" is always a possibility in theory, it typically has little value in a marketing plan in practice. In regard to the internal presentation, one might consider giving the preferred choice a central location in the marketing plan that is submitted to top management for approval and to present in the attachments one or two alternatives with explanations of why those strategies were not selected. For that matter, a rejected option may serve as a *contingency plan* ("disaster plan"): a strategy in case something goes wrong. If options have been formulated in this manner, in the last step a choice has to be made.

8.2.5   Choosing an Option

Figure 8-12 shows the three phases that may be completed during the strategy selection

Suitability

A first evaluation of the strategic options concerns the extent to which an option:

• Fits with higher strategic levels (vision, corporate strategy).

• Resolves the core problem (if that has not happened already).

• Fits with the most important *issues* in the external and internal environments.

FIGURE 8-12
Selection Process for
Strategies

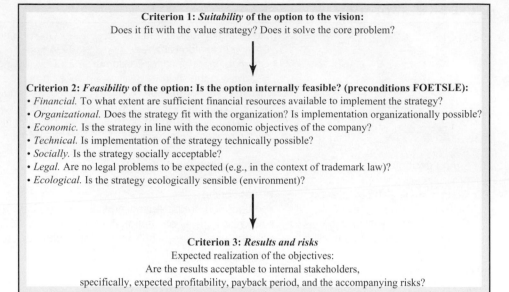

Criterion 1: *Suitability* **of the option to the vision:**
Does it fit with the value strategy? Does it solve the core problem?

Criterion 2: *Feasibility* **of the option: Is the option internally feasible? (preconditions FOETSLE):**
• *Financial.* To what extent are sufficient financial resources available to implement the strategy?
• *Organizational.* Does the strategy fit with the organization? Is implementation organizationally possible?
• *Economic.* Is the strategy in line with the economic objectives of the company?
• *Technical.* Is implementation of the strategy technically possible?
• *Socially.* Is the strategy socially acceptable?
• *Legal.* Are no legal problems to be expected (e.g., in the context of trademark law)?
• *Ecological.* Is the strategy ecologically sensible (environment)?

Criterion 3: *Results and risks*
Expected realization of the objectives:
Are the results acceptable to internal stakeholders,
specifically, expected profitability, payback period, and the accompanying risks?

For example, a company may have concluded on the basis of customer research that a market exists for significantly cheaper products. However, if the company has not chosen the value strategy of low price, offering cheaper products might not fit with the brand identity. In that case, the company therefore will not do what some customers would like it to do. This is in line with our opinion regarding the role of marketing as an intermediary between the customer and the brand (see Chapter 1).

The conclusion of the evaluation about suitability of options may be that several are satisfactory (Figure 8-13).

Feasibility

Each of the potentially suitable options is then compared to a number of internal preconditions. Evaluation based on the seven preconditions (financial, organizational, economic, technical, socially, legal, ecological, designated with the acronym FOETSLE) provides insight into the feasibility: Is it possible to implement the specific option?

Results and Risks

A choice needs to be made from the options that remain after the process of elimination that is based on these preconditions. Selection occurs on the basis of *objective variables*. These variables could be company objectives and/or marketing objectives. Company objectives typically are financial in nature (profit, cost recovery period, etc.; see Section 9.2), whereas marketing objectives often relate to sales or market share (see Section 10.1). Profit and market share are not always on the same line: With a high marketing budget, a high market share can be "bought." The issue of which type of objectives is

FIGURE 8-13
Selection of a
Marketing Strategy

	Suitability	Feasible (FOETSLE)	Expected Profit and Risk
Option 1			
Option 2			
Option 3			
Choice			

decisive depends on the internal and external situations in which the marketing plan is being written.

When market share or sales is the selection criterion, a prognosis of sales to be expected should be made for each option. Although making these predictions is a perilous undertaking, the forecasting methods described in Section 8.3 can be helpful in this area. The option with the highest expected market share will be chosen.

However, often financial considerations are decisive: The option that is expected to earn the most money is the preferred choice. A financial selection criterion implies that the profit figures for each option have to be predicted over a series of years. This means that the sales prognosis mentioned above has to be supplemented with assumptions about, for example, the required investments. In addition, the expected risk plays a large role.

Therefore, in the final option selection, an assessment has to be made involving expected revenues, risks, investments required immediately, and investments required over the long term. If financial goals are involved, often the *payback period* is used as a simple criterion: When will the immediately required investments be paid back? A manager can define a maximum for this, for example. four years.

A more advanced method for comparing alternative strategic options is *shareholder value analysis,* a method to determine the "present value" (cash value) of a strategy. The concept behind the shareholder value analysis is that a strategy may be considered an investment that will produce a certain future cash flow. The "expected shareholder value" can be determined by using discounting to calculate the expected cash flow backward to the present time. The selection criterion is therefore entirely financial in this case and in effect is related to the value a strategy has for the shareholders. After all, shareholders can choose from various possibilities in investing capital, and in principle they will choose the option with the highest present value.

An important advantage of shareholder value analysis is that a link is made between the functional areas of marketing and financing: The strategies are evaluated on the basis of financial measures.

To calculate the present value, the same formulas may be used that are employed in the investment realm. The present value of a strategy is the sum of the future cash flows converted back to the present (calculated back toward point "zero" in time), plus the residual value at the end of the duration of the strategy, also converted back to the present. To calculate the *net* present value, the investment made at point zero in time should still be subtracted. The formula is as follows:

$$\text{NPV} = \sum_{t=1}^{n} \frac{\text{CF}_t}{(1 + r)^t} - I$$

in which

NPV = net present value of a strategy

n = planning period (e.g., three or five years)

CF_t = predicted cash flow in period t (CF_n also contains the residual value of the strategy)

r = discount rate

$1/(1 + r)^t$ = discount factor

I = investment amount

The variables mentioned here are calculated as follows.

- *Cash flow.* This is calculated in the usual manner: expected annual sales times gross profit margin minus taxes, increases in fixed costs (advertising, research and development), and investments in working capital.

FIGURE 8-14 **Example of Calculation of Present Value for a Strategy**

	Current Values	Prognoses of Differences between Strategy and Unchanged Policy			Residual Value
	2005 (t = 0)	2006	2007	2008	2009 and on
Cash flow* (annual growth 10%)	100	10	21	33	46
Discount factor (r = 15%)		0.87	0.76	0.66	3.81[†]
Present value of cash flow[‡]		8.7	16.0	21.8	175.3
Total present value	222				
Investment amount	150				
Net present value of strategy	72				

*For examples of how cash flow is calculated, refer to the literature.
[†]Eternity assumption: discount factor/discount rate = .57/.15.
[‡]Cash flow in period zero (2005) until "eternity" = 100/.15.

- *Discount rate.* The average capital cost rate for the company. If a certain strategy has a relatively high risk, the discount rate may be augmented with a risk surcharge.
- *Residual value.* The value after the completion of the planning horizon. This seems difficult to determine. A possible approach is to assume that the net receipts at the end of the planning period will continue forever or will change by a certain percentage.

In choosing a certain strategy, this procedure should be performed for a situation of "unchanged policy" as well as for the options to be considered. The difference between the net present value of an option and the net present value of an unchanged policy is the value of the strategy. Figure 8-14 includes a calculation example. During the calculation, it is the easiest to assume the expected *differences* between the strategy to be considered and the "unchanged policy" all at once. Figure 8-14 is based on the assumption (prognosis) that with the strategy to be chosen (investment 150), the cash flow will increase 10 percent annually, whereas with unchanged policy a stable cash flow (of 100) is expected. In this case, the strategy should be implemented.

An advantage of the shareholder value analysis is that the financial expectations of a strategy are summarized in one indicator. This simplifies the comparison of strategies. Another advantage is that it forces the planner to make all expected revenues from and costs of strategies explicit. Setting up financial indicators is always a necessity in a marketing plan. It should be noted, however, that the reliability of the shareholder value analysis depends on the reliability of the predicted results. Therefore, it is important to follow the forecasting methods and procedures described in Section 8.1 carefully before doing shareholder value analysis.

8.2.6 SWOT Analysis in Practice

In practice, there is a tendency in some companies to solve short-term problems without considering a longer-term strategy. Therefore, these companies do not get around to choosing between options. For companies that take a longer-term perspective, internal and external analyses often are completed before objectives and strategies are chosen. In that process the strengths, weaknesses, opportunities, and threats are also considered. Nonetheless, there are few companies that regularly do a *complete and systematic SWOT analysis* that hinders the finding of the "golden needles." Figure 8-15 shows what is needed for an effective translation of a SWOT analysis into a strategy.

FIGURE 8-15
Conditions for an Effective Translation from SWOT to Strategy

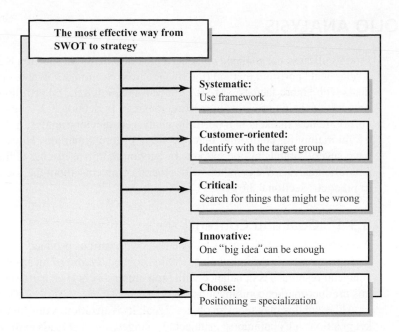

In choosing the marketing strategy, it is essential to find a *balance* between internal and external issues: between what customers need and the relative strengths (including brand identity) the firm has. This is what was defined in Chapter 1 as the core task of marketing. In marketing practice most "mistakes" are made by being too internally oriented. However, a firm does not necessarily have to "follow" the customer but can also "shape" the customer (Figure 8-16). In this process of choosing the best option, managers should think in terms of *added value.* In many markets managers are strongly price-oriented, whereas with creativity and innovation customers can be offered extra value and are willing to pay a higher price for it. Gillette in the introductory case in this chapter is a good example: Despite cheap razor blades from its competitor BIC, Gillette keeps investing in innovation and added value.

FIGURE 8-16
Following or Shaping the Customer?

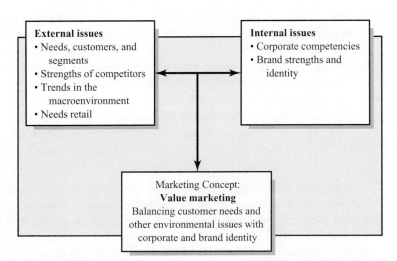

8.3 PORTFOLIO ANALYSIS

First we discuss the goal and content of portfolio methods (Section 8.3.1). Then we review a "classical" portfolio method (the BCG matrix, Section 8.3.2) and a portfolio method that deals with "more factors" (MABA analysis, Section 8.3.3). Portfolio methods in fact deal only with existing products in existing markets. In Section 8.3.4 we show how one can incorporate new markets in a portfolio analysis (trajectory analysis). Portfolio methods are useful mainly for companies that operate in different markets. However, often companies have several brands in one market. In Section 8.3.5 we discuss a "brand version" of the portfolio analysis. We conclude with several comments about the use of portfolio methods in practice (Section 8.3.6).

8.3.1 Goal and Content

A company that is active in various markets with various products should strive for balance in its product-market combinations. In this context, *balanced* means that the total use of the financial resources is in balance with (and preferably is less than) the revenues of the various product-market combinations.

Although this may seem an obvious goal, its realization is not simple. Markets and market positions are continuously subject to changes, and that leads to the consequence that the appeal made by product-market combinations to the financial resources is always changing. After all, a product that is intended to grow costs a lot of money. If the company wants to maintain a constant market share in a growing market, that also requires investments. However, a product with a large market share typically makes a lot of profit, and products in stable markets require fewer investments. Having a balanced "portfolio" of products therefore can mean that a company has products in various phases in the product life cycle, for example, a product in the introductory phase, several products in the growth phase, several in more mature markets, and several in a declining phase.

The method a company can use to achieve a balanced portfolio is to define goals for the market positions of the product-market combinations and subsequently attempt to achieve those goals by investing more or less in the various products. Portfolio methods are a tool for making a choice regarding the investments in various products. With portfolio methods, the positions of product-market combinations are represented visually in a figure or matrix in which the two axes represent approaches to the following factors:

1. *Attractiveness of the market.* The hypothesis in this case is that more should be invested in attractive (e.g., growing) markets than in unattractive markets. A reason for this is that without extra investments, the market share will decline in a growing market, partly because of the fact that the competition is typically stronger. The attractiveness of a market therefore indicates the extent to which cash is *required*.

2. *The market position of the products.* Products with a strong market position have a number of advantages in relation to smaller competitors. These advantages, such as economies of scale, cost advantages through experience effects (the so-called experience curve), better access to distribution channels, and higher awareness, lead to higher profitability. The market position therefore indicates the extent to which cash is made *available*.

Alternative investment strategies can be formulated on the basis of the visual overview of the positions of the various product-market combinations. Portfolio methods can also be used for analyzing the position of competitors and attempting to predict their future behavior on the basis of that analysis. This is especially possible if the company knows that the competitors use portfolio methods. Portfolio methods are therefore also a tool for competitor analysis.

FIGURE 8-17
Portfolio Analyses at the Company and SBU Levels

	Portfolio Analysis at the Company Level	Portfolio Analysis at the SBU Level
Goal	Tool for allocation of resources over SBUs	Tool for allocation of resources over products and brands
Dimension 1	Attractiveness of the market (e.g., market growth)	Attractiveness of the segment (e.g., segment growth)
Dimension 2	Position of SBU in market	Position of product or brand in segment

The *level within the company* at which a portfolio analysis is conducted involves two choices:

1. *Portfolio analysis at the company level.* This involves the assessment of the positions and the allocation of financial resources over strategic business units (SBUs): the choice of the company strategy (and SBU objectives). In the literature and in practice, the most attention is paid to this application.

2. *Portfolio analysis at the SBU level.* This involves the assessment of the positions and the allocation of financial resources over brands and products: the choice of the SBU strategy (and marketing objectives).

Figure 8-17 shows the differences between these applications. These two dimensions demonstrate that in a portfolio analysis, results from the external analysis and the internal analysis are linked. For this reason, the portfolio analysis is a logical sequel to a SWOT analysis. However, the relationship between the portfolio analysis and the SWOT analysis differs with the level at which the portfolio analysis is performed. In Figure 8-18 the relationship between the SWOT analysis and the portfolio analysis is depicted at the *company level.* Because a SWOT analysis is defined for a single market, a number of SWOT analyses for the same number of SBUs represent the input for the portfolio analysis. The attractiveness of the markets is the result of the industry analysis, whereas the market position of the SBUs (the collective position of the brands on a market) was examined in the internal analysis.

A portfolio analysis at the SBU level may be performed on the basis of a single SWOT analysis. In that case, the SWOT analysis should pay specific attention to the following:

- Determining the *attractiveness of the segments;* for this purpose a number of industry analyses should be performed at the segment level.
- Determining the *market position* (e.g., market shares) *within segments.*

FIGURE 8-18
Relationship between SWOT Analysis and Portfolio Analysis

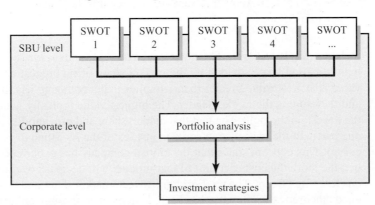

Countries may be interpreted as segments or market segments. Thus, if a company is faced with an international investment problem within a market, a portfolio analysis may be very helpful. Over time, various portfolio methods have been developed. We will review the following methods:

1. The portfolio matrix developed by the Boston Consulting Group (*the BCG matrix;* subsection 8.3.2); this is the first and most simple portfolio method, but because of its simplicity, it has the most limitations.
2. The "business screen" developed by General Electric (subsection 8.3.3).

Two other well-known portfolio methods are:

- The directional policy matrix developed by Shell. This method is no different in essential points from the portfolio model developed by General Electric and therefore will not be discussed here.[21]
- The life cycle portfolio developed by Arthur D. Little. This matrix is based on the assumption that markets (like products) have a life cycle; the dimension of market attractiveness is treated as a phase in the life cycle: embryonic, growth, saturation, decline. The position of the competition is determined qualitatively as dominant, strong, positive, fair, or weak.[22]

8.3.2   The BCG matrix

This section discusses the portfolio matrix that was developed by the Boston Consulting Group.

Content of the Matrix

Figure 8-19 shows an example of a BCG "growth share" matrix. The following two variables are placed along the axes:

1. Market growth
2. Relative market share

Market Growth   The vertical axis represents *market growth.* This axis is divided into two sections: more and less than 10 percent growth per year. The variable market growth therefore represents the attractiveness of the market. The choice of this variable derives, among other things, from the central role of market growth in the concept of the *product life cycle* (see Section 5.4.2). Another advantage of using this variable is the fact that market growth is easy to measure.

Relative Market Share   The horizontal axis represents *relative market share:* the company's market share divided by the market share of its biggest competitor. The limiting value is at 1: A value greater than 1 implies that a company has the largest market share and therefore is the market leader. The highest value typically is defined on the left, and the lowest on the right. The fact that market share and profitability are positively linked is due partly to the existence in some industries of the so-called *experience curve* (learning curve). This concept states that the more a company has experience in producing a product, the more the costs per unit of that product will decrease over time as a result of various learning effects. The relationship between market share and profit not only can be argued "theoretically" but also has been demonstrated through empirical research. The best

FIGURE 8-19
Growth-Share Matrix and Strategic Recommendations

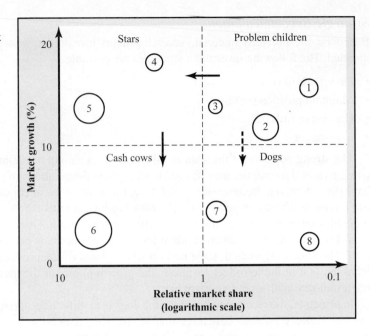

known studies in this area have been conducted with the *Profit Impact of Market Strategy (PIMS)* database: a file with financial data from a few thousand companies. One of the most remarkable results from the PIMS studies is the clear relationship between market share and return on investment (ROI).

In the BCG matrix, the SBUs are categorized by circles. It is customary to make the diameter of those circles proportional to the contribution of an SBU to the sales of the company.

Four types of products can be distinguished, depending on the placement of a product-market combination in one of the four quadrants:

1. *Stars.* These are products with a high market share in a strongly growing market. The cash resources used for and the cash resources required by these products are both high and therefore in principle are in balance. If market growth decreases, the stars may turn into cash cows.

2. *Cash cows.* These are products with a high market share in a market that is not growing very much. As a result of the strong market position, they produce many cash resources, and they require few investments because of the limited market growth.

3. *Problem children.* These products (also called "question marks" or "wild cats") have a small market share in a rapidly growing market. As the name indicates, they can create problems: They produce little but require a lot of cash resources. If they are able to strengthen their position, they can become stars and over time, when market growth decreases, cash cows.

4. *Dogs.* These are products with a low market share in a market that is growing very little. Therefore, they produce little but also require few investments. As with the stars, for these products the financial balance is even. Because many markets are saturated and by definition only one brand can be the market leader, in practice most brands can be designated as dogs.

In Figure 8-19, the most important SBUs are numbers 5 (a star) and 6 (a cash cow). In addition, the company has a medium-size star and several small problem children and dogs.

Strategic Recommendations

Based on the previous material, several general investment strategies may be recommended. The following investment strategies are possible:

- Growth (build).
- Maintain position (hold).
- Harvest or milk.
- Liquidation (terminate).

The strong positions of the stars and the cash cows should be maintained. With the cash cows, part of the revenues may be used to strengthen the positions of problem children that have the potential to become stars. Therefore, for some problem children the company will use a growth strategy financed by cash cows. No investments are made for the other problem children, and so it is a case of harvesting or liquidation. Of course, a problem in this regard is selecting the problem children for which the company perceives growth possibilities. The choice depends in large part on which phase of the product life cycle a product inhabits: Is it in the introductory phase, the growth phase, or the maturity phase? A thorough industry analysis is important here.

In principle, the recommendation for the dogs is to milk them and remove them from the market. However, if dogs have a reasonable size, they may be an important part of a company's activities. In that case, a maintenance strategy appears to be possible.

In the example, the sizable cash cow may be used to finance both stars and perhaps a problem child. The portfolio of this company appears to be relatively balanced.

Criticism

In Section 8.3.6 we will discuss the criticisms of portfolio methods in general. Here we consider several specific disadvantages of the BCG matrix. As was stated, an advantage of the BCG matrix is its great simplicity. However, that also causes disadvantages. The most important limitation that applies specifically to the BCG matrix is that for both dimensions only one variable is chosen: *relative market share* or *market growth*. Although these variables are very important for the determination of market position and market attractiveness, they form only a single underlying factor in this regard. Other underlying factors should also be considered.

To respond to this criticism, portfolio methods have been developed that take more factors into account (see the next section).

8.3.3   MABA analysis

An example of a *MABA analysis* (market attractiveness and business position assessment) is the "business screen" developed by General Electric (Figure 8-20). Instead of market growth, the vertical axis shows the *attractiveness of the market*. This variable is determined by a number of underlying industry factors, such as market size, market growth, profitability, the intensity of the competition, and the power of distributors. The attractiveness may be

FIGURE 8-20   The "Business Screen" Used by General Electric

Market Attractiveness	Competitive Position		
	Strong (Score > 3.33)	Average (1.67 < Score < 3.33)	Weak (Score < 1.67)
High (score > 3.33)	1 Invest/grow	1 Invest/grow	2 Selective investing
Average (1.67 < score < 3.33)	1 Invest/grow	2 Selective investing	3 Harvest/terminate
Low (score < 1.67)	2 Selective investing	3 Harvest/terminate	3 Harvest/terminate

Competitive Position Criteria	Weight	Value*	Score
Market share	0.10	4	0.40
Price competition power	0.05	2	0.10
Growth rate of product-market combination	0.20	3	0.60
Experience curve effects	0.10	4	0.40
Added value	0.20	5	1.00
Production equipment	0.05	2	0.10
Production capacity	0.05	2	0.10
Quality of the product	0.0	1	0.10
Sales promotion	0.05	4	0.20
Research and development	0.05	5	0.25
Labor productivity	0.05	4	0.20
Total	1.00		3.45

*1 = low; 5 = high.

determined by assigning scores to each of the underlying industry factors, weighing each of those factors on the basis of the importance management attaches to it, and calculating a total score. We provided an illustration of the manner in which this may be accomplished in the discussion of the industry analysis in section 5.5. After all, the goal of the industry analysis is to determine the attractiveness of the market. The result of the industry analysis (an attractiveness score) therefore may be used directly as the "input" for the "business screen."

Instead of the relative market share, the horizontal axis shows the *competitive position/competitive power* of the product-market combination (relative strength). This variable is also determined from scores on a number of underlying factors. An example of such a calculation appears in Figure 8-21.

Based on the scores for the factors market attractiveness and competitive power, the various product-market combinations are placed into the matrix. The axes are divided into three sections in this matrix. Therefore, there are nine possible cells (Figure 8-20). If we use the example of the market for candy bars from Section 5.6 and declare the position determination from Figure 8-21 to be applicable to that market, the attractiveness score is "average" (2.95; see Figure 5-6) and the position score is "strong" (3.45; see Figure 8-21). That means this SBU belongs in one of the cells labeled "invest/grow" in the business screen. In depicting the SBUs in Figure 8-20, the sales of the SBU may be shown through the size of the circle that designates the SBU, as in the BCG matrix.

8.3.4   Trajectory Analysis

Earlier in this chapter it was shown how the *current* set of SBUs (or products within an SBU) can be outlined with a portfolio analysis. A disadvantage of such an analysis is that it does not take into account any possible new activities. After all, for a new activity the market share is by definition zero at the starting point, and this means that it cannot be included in a portfolio analysis. To be able to consider potential new activities for a company (diversification) in a portfolio analysis, a *trajectory analysis* should be performed.[23] This includes taking the following three steps:

1. First, the *current position of the SBUs* is analyzed with a portfolio analysis. The most important question in this regard is whether the current portfolio of SBUs is balanced. In this context, questions such as the following should be answered: Are there not too many SBUs that require investments? Are there enough SBUs with positive growth perspectives?

2. Subsequently, a *prediction* should be made of the portfolio positions in the case of *unchanged policy.* This should take into account, for example, the expected growth of the various markets: Even without taking action, the portfolio position of an SBU may change if the attractiveness of the market changes. Possible actions by competitors should also be considered because they may erode the market position of the SBU. In this regard "success trajectories" and "disaster trajectories" may be detected. In terms of the BCG matrix, a success trajectory means that a problem child turns into a star through market share growth, and if the market becomes saturated, it subsequently turns into a cash cow. A disaster trajectory is the reverse and occurs if a cash cow turns into a dog through a declining market share.

Next, the results expected with unchanged policy are compared with the objectives (*divergence analysis* or gap analysis). If there is no difference, the current strategy does not require change, but if there is a difference, as is usually the case, the next planning step is taken.

3. The company determines the *desired portfolio.* For existing SBUs, the question is whether the expected positions are acceptable. For some SBUs (which top management considers promising), growth will be desired. For some SBUs in saturated markets with moderate market positions, disposal will be the best strategy. *New activities* may also be included in the desired portfolio. For example, if the expectation is that the existing markets will demonstrate little growth, perhaps new markets should be searched for to maintain a balanced portfolio.

The designation of the desired portfolio determines the development directions of the SBUs (or products), and in this process the corporate strategy is fleshed out.

8.3.5 Toward a Portfolio Method for Brands

Portfolio methods seem to be useful only for companies that are active in *different markets and/or segments.* If a company is active only in a single market (segment), the same market growth/market attractiveness applies to every product. The positions of the products in that case are all on one line, and the market dimension therefore is no longer relevant. McDonald provides an adequate resolution for this problem.[24] He recommends considering the various products as being markets and/or segments. The rationale behind this approach is that each brand and/or product has more or less its own target audience and therefore can be considered a separate "market." With this assumption (in the BCG application), the expected sales growth of the product may be placed on the first axis and the relative market share on the other axis. Figure 8-22 shows an example. In this figure, brand 2 is a small brand that has good possibilities to grow and become a star. Brand 4 appears to be a established brand with little chance to grow, and brand 1 appears to be in the last phase of the product life cycle.

Finally, we make another comment on the use of two dimensions. Both dimensions have to do with the attractiveness of a market for a brand. If there are possible new markets, then, as outlined above, a course analysis can be applied, but there is still the restriction that no focus be placed on *entry barriers:* the thresholds for entry into a market. In simple terms, there may be an extremely attractive market out there, but if there is a huge mountain in front of the market, it is still difficult to choose it. Entry barriers include access to distribution channels, a minimum level of brand familiarity, and a physical location. In this case, a somewhat less attractive market with lower thresholds may be just as attractive.

There are three dimensions of importance in the choice of a development direction for a brand[25]:

1. *Market attractiveness,* measured on the basis of features such as *expected growth of the market for the brand.* Information on this is gathered from the organizational analysis and the costumer analysis.

FIGURE 8.22
Portfolio Method for Brands with Varying Sales Growth

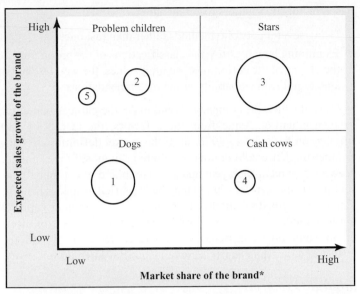

*The scaling of the axes is in conformance with normal use: from low to high. Thus, it is different from the scaling in Figure 8-19.

2. *Position of the brand in the market,* measured as market share or competitiveness (in new markets, the possibilities for attaining and maintaining a defendable competitive edge). These possibilities are estimated on the basis of the competition analysis, the customer analysis, and the internal analysis. The interconnection is produced during the SWOT analysis. This criterion produces a reciprocal relationship with the choice of the marketing strategy.

3. *For new markets, the entry barriers:* all means for penetration of the market or segment. Insight into the entry thresholds is gathered from the organizational analysis. Insight into possible means of penetration is obtained from the internal analysis.

The first two dimensions are part of a portfolio analysis. When new markets are being considered, the recommendations from a portfolio analysis must be offset against the resources needed to overcome the entry thresholds.

8.3.6   Pros and Cons of Portfolio Methods

Applying portfolio methods presents some analytical and strategic problems but also offers advantages.

Analytic Problems

Wind, Mahajan, and Swire have done empirical research on the extent to which different portfolio methods lead to different recommendations.[26] They conclude that the classification of product-market combinations in portfolio positions as "low share and low growth (dog)" or "high share and high growth (star)" depends on four factors:

1. The definition of the dimensions.
2. The rule used to divide a dimension into high versus low.
3. The weight of the underlying factors if a multiple-factor method is used.
4. The specific portfolio model.

This means, among other things, that if the chosen limit values of a dimension are changed or if different weights are chosen for the underlying factors, another classification of product-market combinations is obtained and, with it, different recommended strategies.

Based on this, the authors recommend:

- Using several portfolio methods rather than just one.
- Examining how *sensitive* the classifications of the product-market combinations are for the choice of the definitions, the limit values, the weights, and the portfolio model to be able to judge the reliability of the recommendations.

Subsequently, the company should make the choices that are the most appropriate for its own situation. Aside from these factors, the results of portfolio methods depend strongly on the *market definition*. If the market definition is changed, the positions of the product-market combinations are altered. Suppose, for example, the market for toys is growing 5 percent each year and a certain brand of computer games has a share of 7 percent in this market. This brand may be classified as a dog. However, if the relevant manufacturer redefined the market as the market for computer games, the situation might turn out to include market growth of 15 percent and a share of 30 percent. In that case, the brand would be a star. Because of the direct relationship with the market definition, the results of a portfolio analysis are quite arbitrary in nature.

Strategic Problems

Schnaars has articulated fundamental criticisms of the strategic implications of portfolio methods and especially of the BCG matrix.[27] His criticisms come down to the fact that the recommended strategies are not always truly desirable. For example, a low market share does not by definition have to lead to low profitability, particularly for companies that focus on a segment in the market (focus strategy). Markets with low growth may be interesting. In that case, companies do not milk their products or battle for market share but focus all their attention on improving quality and lowering costs.

Advantages and Applications in Practice

In terms of the *way in which* portfolio methods are used, the benefit of the models is not limited to decisions about investment strategies. In fact, in light of the analytic and strategic problems of portfolio methods outlined above, it appears undesirable to base investment decisions only on a portfolio analysis. However, portfolio methods have two additional important advantages:

1. Portfolio analyses improve the quality of strategic thinking at the SBU level.
2. At the "corporate level," portfolio analyses lead to a better understanding of the various SBUs and the product-market combinations.[28]

Therefore, portfolio methods are suitable for use as one of the diagnostic tools employed by a company and are also a very effective tool for internal *communication* within a company. Various research projects have indicated that portfolio methods are often used in practice. For example, in the early 1980s, about half of a number of top companies that were interviewed in the United States used these models.[29]

Summary

This chapter reviewed three tools that can be applied to make the step from analysis to strategy: forecasting, SWOT analysis, and portfolio analysis.

Forecasting is important at various points during the situation analysis. After all, future possibilities are especially important for the choice of strategies. There are objective and subjective forecasting methods: Objective means that predictions are calculated; with subjective methods, predictions are generated "in the head of" the person making them. Objective methods always require quantitative data, preferably time series of variables. Then a choice can be made between extrapolations and causal models. Subjective methods are purchasing intention research and opinion research (expert interviews). It is advisable to use several forecasting methods and also to define scenarios.

The SWOT analysis forms the link between the situation analysis (internal analysis and external analysis) and the strategy formation. From the results of the situation analysis (a listing of the most important strengths, weaknesses (both relative), opportunities, and threats), ideas for potential strategies are generated. It is important to do this systematically, be creative, be critical and customer-oriented, and make clear choices. Three steps are proposed:

1. The whole situation analysis is reduced to some core issues. A manager can do this by making a selection of at most 10 relevant internal and external issues. The company should explicitly formulate its vision on the environment: Which (customer) trends are considered most important in the future, and what is the core problem?
2. A value strategy is chosen (if the company has not yet done this).
3. A thorough discussion is organized about the future positioning of the brand. Using the issues from the analysis as inspiration, alternative ideas are generated. Selection is realized by applying three criteria: fit with value strategy, suitability, and expected results and risks.

Ultimately a balance has to be chosen between the needs of the customer and the brand's competencies and identity. In this process creative thinking in terms of added value is preferable to a focus on low prices.

A portfolio analysis is a tool for decisions about investments in SBUs or product-market combinations. In a portfolio analysis, the various SBUs or product-market combinations are depicted in a two-dimensional space in which one axis represents the expected cash flow (through a representation of the market position) and the other axis represents the extent to which cash flow is required (through a representation of the expected market growth). Various portfolio models exist, of which two were reviewed in this chapter: the Boston Consulting Group matrix and the business screen. Both methods require quite a few arbitrary assumptions; this means that the investment recommendations are not always as desired. For new markets also the entry barriers must be considered.

Notes

1. Armstrong, J. S. (1985), *Long-Range Forecasting: From Crystal Ball to Computer,* 2nd ed., New York: Wiley.
2. Lehmann, D. R., and R. S. Winer (2001), *Analysis for Marketing Planning,* 5th ed., New York: McGraw-Hill; Armstrong (1985), Chapter 5; Georgoff, D. M., and R. G. Murdick (1986), "Manager's Guide to Forecasting," *Harvard Business Review,* January–February 1986, pp. 110–20.
3. Armstrong (1985), Chapter 5.
4. For a further discussion of the methods mentioned here, refer to Armstrong (1985).
5. Armstrong (1985), p. 178.
6. Paap, R., E. van Nierop, H. J. van Heerde, M. Wedel, P. H. Franses, and K .J. Alsem (2005), "Considerations Sets, Intentions and the Inclusion of 'Don't Know' in a Two-Stage Model for Voter Choice," *International Journal of Forecasting* 21:53–71
7. This combination of intention research and scenario analysis is applied in predicting the effects of the arrival of commercial television in the Netherlands. See Alsem, K. J., and P. S. H. Leeflang (1994), "Predicting Advertising Expenditures Using Intention Surveys," *International Journal of Forecasting* 10:327–337.
8. Armstrong, J. S. (2002), "Assessing game theory, role playing and unaided judgment," *International Journal of Forecasting,* 18 (3), 345–352.
9. For detailed descriptions of trend and cross-impact analysis, see, e.g., Jain, S. C. (2000), *Marketing Planning and Strategy,* Cincinnati: South Western Publishing, p. 314ff.

10. Georgoff and Murdick (1986).

11. Armstrong (1985).

12. See also Singer, A. E., and R. J. Brodie (1990), "Forecasting Competitors' Actions," *International Journal of Forecasting* 6(1):75–88.

13. Armstrong (1987).

14. Lehmann and Winer (2001).

15. Armstrong (1985); Bopp, A. E. (1985), "On Combining Forecasts: Some Extensions and Results," *Management Science* 31:1492–1498; Ashton, A. H., and R. H. Ashton (1985), "Aggregating Subjective Forecasts: Some Empirical Results," *Management Science* 31:1499–1508; Gupta, S., and P. C. Wilton (1987), "Combination of Forecasts: An Extension," *Management Science* 33:356–372; Clemen, R. T. (1989), "Combining Forecasts: A Review and Annotated Bibliography," *International Journal of Forecasting* 4:559–584.

16. Lock, A. (1987), "Integrating Group Judgments in Subjective Forecasts." In *Judgmental Forecasting,* G. Wright and P. Ayton, eds., Chichester, , Wiley, Chapter 6; Ashton and Ashton (1985); Gupta and Wilson (1987); Blattberg, R. C., and S. J. Hoch (1990), "Database Models and Managerial Intuition: 50% Model + 50% Manager," *Management Science* 36:887–899.

17. This suggestion comes from Erik Kostelijk.

18. For an example, see Weihrich, H. (1982), "The TOWS Matrix—A Tool for Situational Analysis," *Long Range Planning* 15:54–6.

19. Weihrich (1982).

20. See also Dibb, S., L. Simkin, and J. Bradley (2003), *The Marketing Planning Workbook,* 3rd ed., London: Thomson Learning

21. See for a description Kerin, R. A., V. Mahajan, and P. R. Varadajan (1990), *Contemporary Perspectives on Strategic Market Planning,* Boston: Allyn & Bacon, pp. 77ff.

22. For a description, see Patel, P., and M. Younger (1978), "A Frame of Reference for Strategy Development," *Long Range Planning* 11:6–12; Arthur D. Little, Inc. (1980), A *Management System for the 1980s,* San Fransisco: Arthur D. Little; Hax, A. C., and N. S. Majluf (1984), *Strategic Management: An Integrated Perspective,* Englewood Cliffs, NJ: Prentice-Hall.

23. Kerin, Mahajan, and Varadarajan (1990), p. 53ff.

24. McDonald, M. H. B., (1990), "Some Methodological Comments on the Directional Policy Matrix," *Journal of Marketing Management* 6(1):59–68.

25. Lehmann and Winer (2001) also give these criteria, without reference to portfolio methods.

26. Wind, Y., V. Mahajan, and D. J. Swire (1983), "An Empirical Comparison of Standardized Portfolio Models," *Journal of Marketing* 47:89–99.

27. Schnaars, S. P. (1991), *Marketing Strategy: A Customer Driven Approach,* New York: Free Press.

28. Hamermesh, R. G. (1986), "Making Planning Strategic," *Harvard Business Review,* July–August, pp. 115–119.

29. Haspeslagh, P. (1982), "Portfolio Planning: Uses and Limits," *Harvard Business Review* January–February, pp. 58–72.

Part Three

Corporate Decisions and Marketing Decisions

In Part 2 the situation analysis was explained. These analyses form the basis for the decisions that are to be made (planning). This part focuses on corporate objectives and corporate strategies (Chapter 9) as well as marketing objectives and marketing strategies (Chapter 10). Decisions at this level relate to the long term and therefore are strategic in nature.

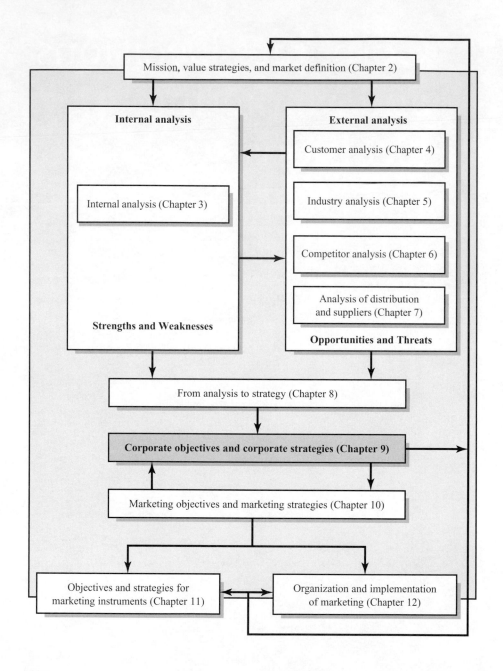

Chapter Nine

Corporate Objectives and Corporate Strategies

Key Points in This Chapter

- Know the difference between corporate strategy and marketing strategy.
- Apply a framework for corporate decision making.
- Know the different growth directions for companies.
- Know how to relate growth directions to development methods (partnering or not).

INTRODUCTION

As was discussed in Chapter 1, objectives and strategies exist at different levels within companies: the levels of the company, the strategic business unit (SBU), and the product. Brands play an important role at each of these levels. A central issue in this book is the development of a marketing plan for a brand. That can be a company, an SBU, or a product. In this chapter we assume that a company is active in different markets with different product brands. In that case there is a large difference between decisions made at the corporate level and those made at the lower brand levels. This chapter discusses the decisions that are made at the top level of the company: the corporate objective and the corporate strategy. In Chapter 10 the other types of decisions are reviewed: the marketing decisions and marketing instrument decisions. If there is no difference between the corporate level and the brand level (as with corporate brands or small companies), the decisions in this chapter and Chapter 10 are made on one level.

There is a great lack of clarity, both in practice and in the literature, about the content of the concepts of corporate objective and corporate strategy. For example, one often encounters a "mission" (*corporate mission*) instead of an objective at the point where one would expect to find the corporate objectives. In those cases, one does not encounter the designation of the corporate objective anywhere else. However, during later planning steps, corporate strategies may be encountered. In Sections 9.1 through 9.3 the planning phases are reviewed. Section 9.1 reviews the corporate mission and corporate objectives. Then we discuss the two components of the corporate strategy: the issues of "where to compete" (Section 9.2) and "with whom to compete (partnerships)" (Section 9.3).

The Samsung Way

A black-suited Agent Smith sprints down a city street. As he is felled by an acrobatic kung fu kick from Trinity, the camera pulls back to show the action taking place inside a giant floating flat-screen television: a Samsung television.

Samsung's presence in the *Matrix* trilogy is the latest step in its reincarnation as one of the world's coolest brands. Its success in a blizzard of digital gadgets and in chips has wowed consumers and scared rivals around the world. The achievement is all the more remarkable considering that just six years ago Samsung was financially crippled, its brand associated with cheap me-too televisions and microwaves. Now the company seems to be entering a new dimension. In terms of market share, Samsung is the global leader in LCD displays, DRAM chips, big-screen televisions, and microwaves. The company is number three in cell phones, MP3 players, and DVD players. In 2002, Samsung earned $5.9 billion on sales of $33.8 billion.

In 1997, the Samsung brand was weak. Although its products were comparable to those of the competition, Samsung was competing with low prices.

Eric Kim, Samsung's executive vice president of global marketing, said: "We had the technology, but without the brand we couldn't price our products the way we needed to raise our profit margins. We needed a global brand strategy. In 1997 we had 55 advertising agencies. Now we have only one: FCB. And we spend at least $400 million a year on consistent global marketing. Our central focus is on sponsoring the events relevant to our target group. A good example is *The Matrix*. That motion picture is like our brand equity: advanced, stylish, and highly digital, with a focus on young people. In 2004 the focus will be on the Olympic Games. The Olympics are an emotional event: heroic efforts and passion."

It's very difficult to change the brand equity in an existing market, but Samsung was lucky: In the late 1990s the technology started shifting from analog to digital products. In such a shift, consumers are very open to new brands. Kim says: "We became the product leader in the new digital product categories. We focus on superior design and performance. And now we can ask the price we want. For instance, in cell phones, our average prices are higher than Nokia's or Motorola's."

Samsung thinks the moment is fast arriving when it can unseat Sony Corp. as the most valuable electronics brand and the most important shaper of digital trends. "Our ambition is to be number one," says Kim. Its rivals are taking the challenge seriously.

Samsung is operating in a highly competitive market. The life cycle of much hardware is brutally short and subject to relentless commoditization. The average price of a television set has dropped 30 percent in five years; a DVD player goes for less than a quarter of its old price. The Chinese keep driving prices even lower, leveraging supercheap wages and engineering talent. Meanwhile, the Japanese are building Chinese factories to lower costs.

One of Samsung's strengths is the company's vertical business model. Samsung does not believe in outsourcing. Although the general trend is to go back to a few core competencies, Samsung remains diversified and vertically integrated: Samsung chips and displays go into the company's own digital products.

Chips and displays can make up 90 percent of the cost of most digital devices, and Samsung is the world leader in chips and displays. This gives Samsung a competitive edge in most digital products. For instance, the crystal-sharp images on Samsung's latest cell phones owe their clarity to the Samsung technology used for the displays, and Samsung produces the chips needed to power the phones.

In full control of its own supply, Samsung can customize its technology as much as possible. And Samsung often forces its own units to compete with outsiders to get the best solution.

Another ingredient is speed. Samsung says it takes an average of five months to go from new product concept to rollout, compared with 14 months in 1997.

Samsung uses its home market (South Korea) as a test market. Some 70 percent of that country's homes are wired for broadband. Twenty percent of the population buys a new cell phone every seven months. Samsung already sells a phone in Korea that allows users to download and view up to 30 minutes of video and watch live television for a fixed monthly fee. However, the Korean economy is weakening.

If Samsung has a major flaw, it may be its lack of software and content. Samsung has no plans to branch out into music, movies, and games, as Sony and Apple have done. And there lies a hazard in Samsung's vertical business model and broad product range. Samsung must keep investing heavily in research and development and new factories across its numerous product lines. Samsung has sunk $19 billion over five years into new chip facilities. Rivals simply buy the technology without tying up capital or making long-term commitments.

Source: Edwards, Cliff; Ihlwan, Moon; Engardio, Pete. *Business Week*, 6/16/2003, p 56–64.

Questions

1. According to Treacy and Wiersema (see Chapter 2), to be successful, a company has to choose a specific value discipline.

   a. Did Samsung make a deliberate choice of one of the value disciplines in and before 1997? If it did, which one? Explain your answer.

   b. Did Samsung make a deliberate choice of one of the value disciplines when the industry shifted to digital technology? If it did, which one? Explain your answer.

2. a. What is the difference between the objective and the strategy of an organization?

   b. What is Samsung's main objective, according to this case?

   c. What are the most important elements of Samsung's strategy, based on the information in this case?

3. According to the case, "Although the general trend is to go back to a few core competencies, Samsung remains diversified and vertically integrated." Do you agree with the statement that Samsung does not have core competencies? Explain your answer.

4. The industry structure can be defined by using Porter's five-forces model (see Chapter 5). Apply this model to the industry in which Samsung is competing: the world industry of digital consumer products (in a broad sense). Draw your conclusions about the attractiveness of this industry from Samsung's point of view.

5. Develop a SWOT analysis for Samsung.

6. Analyze the strategic problem with which Samsung is faced.

9.1 CORPORATE MISSION AND CORPORATE OBJECTIVES

Figure 9-1 shows the planning steps that should be taken at the corporate level. In this section we discuss the first step. This is done in two phases:

- Evaluation of the mission and vision (value strategy) (Section 9.1.1).
- Determination of corporate objectives (Section 9.1.2).

FIGURE 9-1
Planning Steps at the Corporate Level

Determination of corporate objectives (Section 9.1)

1. Evaluation of corporate mission and value strategy
2. Concrete corporate objectives

Determination of corporate strategies

3. Where to compete? Determination of desired portfolio (including new activities) and growth directions for SBUs (Section 9.2)
4. With whom to compete? Choice of internal or external growth (Section 9.3)

9.1.1 Evaluation of the Corporate Mission and Vision

In Chapter 2 we explained that the planning process starts with the determination of the corporate mission and corporate vision (including the value strategy) and the market definition for the SBU level that is partly based on those items. Although a mission is determined for a longer period, it is not inconceivable that it will have to be adjusted after a situation analysis. That way, it is possible to expand the field of activities beyond the company's own markets. Case 9-1 gives an example of a mission change.

CASE 9-1

Mission Change: Does Microsoft Overpromise?

Mission statements that include everything or overpromise do not give a clear indication of what a business is about. A lofty, unrealistic mission statement does not have great credibility. Instead, the best statements are direct and powerful. For example, in October 2002 Microsoft changed its mission statement from "To empower people through great software—any time, any place, and on any device" to "To enable people and businesses throughout the world to realize their full potential." The new mission statement is certainly broad enough, but is it realistic? Does it overpromise? Does it give any indication of what Microsoft is about? Or is it a good way of defining the mission in terms of customers' needs?

Source: myphliputil.pearsoncmg.com/student/bp_turban_introec_1/MissStmt.html-14k.

The mission says what the current status of the company is. The vision or ambition should state what the challenges are. The choice of a value strategy plays an important role in the vision. This was explained in Chapter 2. If the value strategy has not yet been chosen in this stage of the planning process, this should be done or a manager should indicate the conditions under which it will be possible to excel in a value discipline. In the discussion of the strengths, weaknesses, opportunities, and threats (SWOT) analysis in Section 8.2 we provided a framework that can be useful in the process a choosing a value strategy.

9.1.2 Corporate Objectives

The vision contains a global, long-term indication of the goals of the company. Next, the vision should be elaborated concretely into corporate objectives. Corporate objectives are often formulated for a period of one to three years. The primary objective of each company is to remain viable over the longer term. To meet this condition, a company may focus on various objectives. In choosing corporate objectives, two decisions are made:

1. What are the *most important variables* for the objectives?
2. Which *values* of the objectives do we want to achieve at what point?

Prioritizing the variables used for the objectives is an issue for top management. This involves, for example, the question of whether the company wants to emphasize market share or profit. In developing the specific content of the chosen objectives, it is important that those objectives be supported in the organization by the people who will be responsible for achieving them. This means, among other things, that the various departments of the organization should be involved in the process of creating the objectives. In making both decisions (ranking and choosing objectives), the method of the balanced scorecard (reviewed in Chapter 3) can be helpful.

9.2 CORPORATE STRATEGY: WHERE TO COMPETE

9.2.1 Components of the Corporate Strategy

Chapter 1 indicated that at every level two decisions have to be made: where to compete (markets) and how to compete (competitive advantage). At the corporate level we add a third item: with whom to compete. Thus, at the corporate level the following choices are made:

1. *Where to compete.* Choice of scope of activities: SBUs and investments per SBU.
2. *How to compete.* Choice of value strategy.
3. *With whom to compete.* Alone or in collaboration.

In this section we discuss the first component. Value strategies were discussed in Chapter 2. In Section 9.3 the third component will be reviewed.

CASE 9-2 *Corporate Strategy: Acquisitions in the Hair Care Market*	A resurgent Procter & Gamble Co. put a hurt on most of its major global competitors in some fashion, in at least some parts of the world, in the year 2003. Unilever, Colgate-Palmolive Co., Kimberly-Clark Corp., and Henkel all issued disappointing revenue and profit numbers at some point in 2003 as P&G saw its revenue grow by double-digit or high single-digit percentages. But one global rival, L'Oreal, has proved the toughest to beat. Privately, many P&Gers acknowledge that L'Oreal is the rival they respect and fear most, and with good reason. Resurgence or not, P&G lost ground to L'Oreal last year in U.S. shampoos and conditioners, cosmetics, and hair color, gaining only in skin care. Learning to compete better with L'Oreal is crucial to P&G's future, as the company has bet more than $10 billion in the last three years that it can do so. Acquisitions of the Clairol and Wella businesses put P&G in direct competition with L'Oreal in hair color and professional hair care for the first time. **Source:** Nef, Jack, "L'Oreal Proves Tough Competitor," *Advertising Age*, January 23, 2004, p. 30.

9.2.2 Portfolio of SBUs

The core of the corporate strategy is the question of where and to what extent the company wants to compete. In other words, in which markets does the company want to be active and to what extent? In effect, the issue here is the composition of the portfolio of SBUs ("markets") of the company and the importance of each of the SBUs. The method that may be useful in this task is the portfolio analysis that was discussed in Section 8.3. The advice given there is to use a portfolio analysis in combination with a path analysis in three steps:

1. Determination of the current portfolio.
2. Forecasting and evaluation of the portfolio if policy remains unchanged.
3. Determination of the desired portfolio.

In the last step, ideas about *new activities* should be considered explicitly. This cannot occur without creativity, brainstorming, and deliberations with lower management. Ideas about new activities in practice often originate from within the SBUs. In the discussion regarding the SWOT analysis (Section 8.2) we discussed the analysis of new activities at the SBU level.

The process of generating ideas for new activities in effect corresponds to the first phases of what is often referred to in the literature as the process of *new product development*. Empirical research on the success of new products has shown that often many dozens of ideas are required for just one of them to succeed. The chance of success of a new activity is larger if the new activity is attracted from the outside (for example, through acquisition; see also Section 9.3) than it is if the company decides to develop it from within.

Finally, if a company is considering entering new markets, it is probably necessary to perform a situation analysis for those markets. Thus, there is a feedback loop to the situation analysis. Only if the attractiveness of the relevant market outweighs the investments required to enter that market does a decision to enter the market make sense.

With the definition of the desired portfolio of SBUs, the *development directions* are determined. The following development directions are possible:

1. Dismantling.
2. Harvesting.
3. Maintaining position.
4. Growth in existing activities.
5. Growth in (setting up) new activities.

The first four directions apply to existing SBUs, and the last one to new activities.

Among the five growth directions mentioned, in the literature the most attention is paid to growth with existing SBUs (*expansion*) and growth with new activities (*diversification*). Within both development directions, a total of eight specific growth directions may be chosen (Figure 9-2). These growth directions are based on the well-known matrix by Ansoff[1] (Figure 9-3).

FIGURE 9-2 Growth Opportunities for a Company

Growth Direction	Customer Groups	Product*	Example of Rusk Manufacturer[†]
Growth with Existing SBUs: Expansion			
1. Market penetration	Same	Same	• Increase brand loyalty at expense of competitor (quality improvement, promotional action) • Stimulate usage by current users (advertising: rusks in yogurt) • Other segments (youth)
2. Market development	New	Same	• Other markets (industrial: cafeterias) • Geographic (exporting)
3. Product development	Same	Modification	• Modification: whole-meal rusks
4. Horizontal diversification	Same	New related or unrelated	• Related (expansion): rice waffles, knäckebröd (Swedish crackers) • Unrelated: rusk tins
Growth with New Activities: Diversification			
5. Market widening	New	Modification	• Small rusks as "toast"
6. Vertical diversification	Company becomes customer or supplier	New	• Backward: take over supplier • Forward: take over store chain
7. Concentric diversification	New	New related	• Production of cookies
8. Conglomerate diversification	New	New unrelated	• Production of candy, laundry detergent

*Relatedness may be in marketing and/or technology.
[†]Starting point: market definition is rusk manufacturer (product) for final customers and especially women (customers) for use at home (function).

FIGURE 9-3
Growth Directions in
the Matrix by Ansoff[2]

	Current Products		New Products	
Current customer groups	1	Market penetration	3–4	Product development
New customer groups	2	Market development	5–8	Diversification

Expansion

There are four types of growth direction by which a company can grow with its existing SBUs:

1. The first and most obvious way to grow is *market penetration*: increasing sales with the current products in the current markets. In a growing market, a sales increase can be obtained by maintaining market share. In stable markets, a sales increase can be achieved only if market share grows. Market penetration is usually achieved through the use of the marketing mix.

2. If market saturation occurs, management will research other growth opportunities, such as *market development*: growth by finding new customers for the current products. A well-known form of market development is geographic expansion of the market, for example, through exportation.

3. *Product development* may also be considered: new modified products in addition to or instead of the current products for the current customers.

4. A more extreme form of product development is *horizontal diversification*: new products for the existing customers (e.g., a tea manufacturer who starts producing coffee). In this case there is some synergy (both in technology and in marketing), but there is a limited spreading of risk. Another example of this form of product development is a food retailer that is also going to sell computers or mobile phones.

CASE 9-3
Market Development by Wal-Mart: Conquering the Brazilian Market

In December 2005 Wal-Mart, the largest retailer in the world, announced the acquisition of the 140 shops of the Sonae Group in Southern Brazil. With this transaction Wal-Mart has doubled the number of Wal-Mart shops in Brazil to 295. In 2004 Wal-Mart bought all 118 Brazilian shops of the retail chain Bompreco (hypermarkets, supermarkets and mini markets) from the Dutch Ahold.

Source: www.walmartfacts.com

Diversification

When a company expects that it will not be able to achieve its objectives through expansion, it may consider diversification: an exploration of new roads and areas. Four forms can be distinguished. The choice of one of these forms is determined mostly by the degree of synergy and the extent to which a company remains dependent on a limited number of activities (risk). The four forms of diversification are as follows:

1. The least extreme form of diversification is *market widening*: reaching new customer groups with modified products. This growth direction is the opposite of horizontal diversification: The "newness" is limited to such an extent that this direction in practice often is not described as diversification but as a type of expansion.

2. *Vertical diversification* (or vertical integration) means that a company takes over links that are higher (backward) or lower (forward) in the supply chain. The biggest advantage is an increase in market power: A company is less dependent on suppliers and/or customers.

3. The last two growth directions have the least synergy but the largest opportunity to spread risk. In *concentric diversification,* the company starts to bring new, related products (related in terms of technology or marketing) into the market for new customers.

4. In *conglomerate diversification* there is no synergy at all: The company brings new products into the market for new customers.

We note the following regarding the choices of growth direction in practice.

1. Be careful *with unrelated activities.* Several empirical studies have been conducted to examine the success of related versus unrelated diversification.[3] These studies indicate that the more foreign the activities are, the smaller the success usually is. The conclusion is therefore that companies should be very careful in starting up entirely new activities and that if diversification is chosen, the presence of synergy in, for example, technology or marketing is definitely preferred. The recommendation of staying within the core business of the company has to do not only with the competencies of the company but also with the way customers perceive a company. Companies with a broad range of activities are not clearly positioned and thus do not have a strong corporate brand image, and a weak brand image makes it difficult to develop relationships with customers (see Chapter 1). There is a third reason for being cautious with diversification: the danger that a company does not have a clear vision about where it wants to go, which makes it difficult to brand the company internally to employees.

2. *Perform additional SWOT analyses if diversification is considered.* If a company considers expanding its activities, this may involve another defined field of strategic activities with other market characteristics, other competitors, other customer wishes, and so on. To be active in such a different market and to find a sustainable competitive advantage, the new market should be analyzed in detail. This means in effect that an external analysis should be completed for a second time. Only after that can the actual growth direction be chosen and the next steps in the planning process be completed.

3. *The stranger the activities, the higher the decision level in the company.* If we compare the two growth directions expansion and diversification, it may be argued that the implementation of the direction of *expansion* will take place more on the *SBU level,* whereas in the case of *diversification* the involvement of management at the *corporate level* typically will be larger. For example, top management will not concern itself with the question of whether growth of an existing SBU is achieved through more intensive advertising efforts (market penetration) or by bringing improved products into the market (product development). The elaboration of the direction of expansion therefore will be determined to a great extent by the choice of the marketing strategy. However, setting up completely new activities will require so important a commitment that the decision-making process should involve high levels of the organization. This is also due to the fact that in diversification, collaboration strategies will be more likely to be considered than is the case in expansion (see the next section). An exception to this is *exportation.* Decisions about this geographic form of market development are always made at the corporate level.

The difference in decision levels does not mean that *ideas* for new activities will come primarily from top management. In practice, these ideas come both from within the SBUs and from the top of the company. Still, the innovative power of a company is determined in large part by the extent to which *top management* is open to new ideas. There are companies in which managers from an SBU left the company because of insufficient support for their new ideas and started successfully in business on their own.

9.3 CORPORATE STRATEGY: WITH WHOM TO COMPETE

"With whom to compete" refers to the choice of partners. The following subjects are dealt with in this section:

- Internal or external growth (Section 9.3.1).
- External development: competition-decreasing strategies (Section 9.3.2).
- SWOT analysis and collaboration (Section 9.3.3.).
- Collaboration in practice (Section 9.3.4).

9.3.1 Internal or External Growth

If the choice of a growth direction has been made, the next question is whether the company wants to achieve growth through its own development (internal) or through "others" (external). This decision must be made for both expansion and diversification. In both cases, the choice could be to "do it ourselves" or to "do it together with others." There are three possible *development methods*:

1. *Internal development.*
2. *External development through collaboration.* This involves various possibilities, such as joint ventures (joint interest in another company), strategic alliances (long-term collaboration agreement), and licences (approval for others to sell a company's success formula or product).
3. *External development through takeovers* (acquisitions): the "purchasing" of new activities.

Internal development is the most risky: There is no certainty about the results. In addition, it takes a long time. However, there is more flexibility: Everything is kept under the company's control. With acquisitions, the reverse is true: It can be achieved quickly, it offers a fair degree of certainty regarding the result, but it leads to a decrease in flexibility. In addition, acquisitions usually require a lot of financial resources. With external development through collaboration, the advantages and disadvantages lie between these two extremes.

In choosing the manner is which growth is to be achieved, a company should weigh the advantages and disadvantages. In general, the less a company is familiar with the market and technologies of the new product, the less it should do on its own.[4] When we translate this to the growth directions in Figure 9-2, it can be concluded that the more a company approaches the direction of "strange" activities in terms of the choice of growth direction (i.e., toward the direction of conglomerate diversification), the more the choice of a development method should lean toward external growth. Except for explicitly named exceptional situations, such as the time factor and the availability of financial resources, *expansion* should in principle be based on *internal growth,* whereas concentric and conglomerate *diversification* should be based on *acquisitions.* For horizontal and vertical diversification, internal development or external development through collaboration is recommended. Exportation is also the exception in this regard: This type of expansion can occur quickly and effectively through mergers and acquisitions of companies that are already active on site.

Because of the great importance of competition-decreasing strategies such as collaboration and acquisition, we devote attention to those issues in the following section.

9.3.2 External Development: Competition-Decreasing Strategies

In the literature about corporate strategies and marketing strategies, typically most of the attention is paid to strategies to improve the company's position at the expense of the competitors: *position-strengthening strategies* (internal development). The issue here is to claim a position in the market that is stronger than the competitor's position, that is, to "beat" the competition.

In addition to a position-strengthening strategy, a company may choose a *competition-decreasing* strategy (external development: all forms of collaboration). Examples of such strategies include the following:

- Strategies in which the concentration in markets is increased through mergers, acquisitions, and other forms of collaboration, such as purchasing combinations, franchising, and strategic alliances.
- Market agreements, for example, price agreements, agreements regarding the division of the market, and cartels.

A competition-decreasing strategy can also be a possibility if a position-strengthening strategy is not feasible: "If you can't beat them, join them." It can also be a tool to achieve a desired competitive advantage, for example, a price reduction resulting from important synergistic advantages. The choice of a competition-decreasing strategy typically has far-reaching consequences for the entire company. Therefore, decisions in this area are made at the corporate level.

A company's attention to position-strengthening strategies is also discussed in this book. A central concept in the analyses and analysis methods described in the previous chapters is the attempt to find and maintain a sustainable competitive advantage. This attempt is based on the finding that only companies with such an advantage are able to withstand the competitive forces in the industry in the long term. Without a competitive advantage, a company will achieve relatively low profitability over time. The implicit assumption here is that a company should strengthen its own position at the expense of the competitors: The goal is to be "better" than the competitors on an ongoing basis. However, there may be circumstances in which it is better to choose some type of collaboration with a competitor. These circumstances may be deduced from the situation analysis described in this book. The results of the analysis should simply be interpreted from a different perspective. Especially in the SWOT analysis, another viewpoint needs to be chosen. We now discuss this issue further.

9.3.3 SWOT Analysis and the Competition-Decreasing Strategy

In Chapter 1 and in the material on SWOT analysis in Section 8.1, we indicated that a company should search for a combination of the following:

1. A strength of its own that
2. Is a weakness for the most important competitors and that
3. Is difficult to obtain for the competitors and that
4. Is important to the customers.

This combination implies a *sustainable competitive advantage*.

A *competition-decreasing strategy* is appropriate when the first two requirements are reversed (Figure 9-4; compare with Figure 1-8):

1. The company has a weakness that is
2. A strength of one of the competitors and
3. That competitor is favorably inclined and
4. It is a response to an opportunity in the external environment and/or the issue is important to the customer.

In terms of the "favorable inclination" of the competitor, the same thing applies to the competitor that applies to the company that is seeking the initiative for collaboration: It is

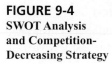

FIGURE 9-4
SWOT Analysis
and Competition-
Decreasing Strategy

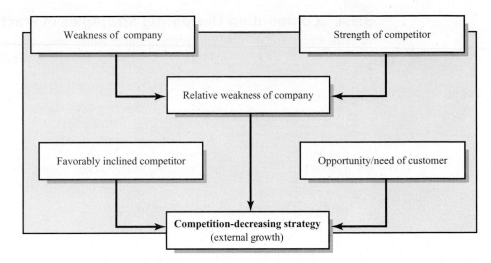

especially interesting if the other party has a strength in an area that is a weakness for the company. This means that a relative weakness of the initiating company should preferably be counterbalanced by another relative strength in relation to the competition. That means there should be a *"win-win" situation.*

CASE 9-4 *Collaboration of Boeing and IBM*	The aerospace giant Boeing is tapping Big Blue for its info-tech expertise to compete better for lucrative Pentagon contracts. As the twenty-first century unfolds, a key Pentagon initiative is the creation of network-centric operations for various war-fighting machines. For defense contractors, getting a piece of this huge technological upgrade is essential. Boeing and IBM announced a strategic partnership worth more than $2 billion in defense-related business. This teaming up underscores the aerospace company's determination to play a leading role in the military's digital age agenda. **Source:** Holmes, Stanley, "Boeing Drafts IBM for Defense Work," *BusinessWeek Online,* September 20, 2004.

This mutual dependency is especially important if there is an equal collaboration (e.g., a merger). If there is an unequal collaboration (e.g., a company that "adds" another, smaller company to its divisions through an acquisition), the requirement of a mutual advantage is less important.

An example will clarify Figure 9-4 and the relationship of the growth options described there. Suppose bank institution A has a strong position in the consumer market but a weak position in the industrial market (e.g., granting credit to companies). The company is looking for growth options and chooses market development: development of the industrial market. In principle, there are now two possibilities:

1. Internal growth: attempting to strengthen its position with companies through sales promotion; however, because of the strong position of a number of competitors in the industrial market, this appears to be a risky route that also will take a lot of time.
2. External growth.

The second option can provide bank A with a strong position immediately. To find a merger candidate, the bank analyzes the competing banks. This analysis indicates that for bank B, the reverse of the situation of bank A is true: B is strong in the industrial market but relatively weak in the consumer market. B is approached and appears willing to consider merger talks. After some time, a merger is completed and bank BA is created.

9.3.4 Competition-Decreasing Strategies in Practice

In various industries (such as the printing and graphics trade, the banking and insurance industries, and the aviation industry), there have been "merger waves" the last few years.

CASE 9-5 *Mergers and Acquisitions*	Remember the urge to merge? Quelled since 2000, it's coming back. In the last quarter of 2004, deals for U.S. companies came at a trillion-dollar-a-year pace—and more are in store. Companies are looking to mergers again to cut costs, boost efficiency, and extend their reach. Although mergers dropped off starting in 2001—a victim of recession, corporate scandals, and a sluggish stock market—the animal spirits have returned. Clearly, the rush is on. There was $250 billion worth of mergers, including assumed debt, in the last three months of 2004. That brought the year's total to $809 billion, according to Thomson Financial. Although a far cry from 1998 through 2000, when annual deal volume averaged $1.6 trillion, volume is up 49 percent over 2003. Executives at Lehman Brothers Inc. and Bank of America Corp. are prepping for a further 15 to 20 percent increase in 2005. **Source:** Coy, Peter, Emily Thornton, Michael Arndt, Brian Grow, and Andrew Park, "Shake, Rattle, and Merge," *BusinessWeek*, January 10, 2005, p. 32–35.

An important reason for the expanded use of competition-decreasing strategies is the expected increase in competition resulting from the fact that international markets are becoming increasingly open. Especially if the collaborating companies complement each other's strengths and weaknesses, the collaboration may be a better match for the competition than is either of the companies on its own. However, there are three *dangers of a merger*. First, a merged company is larger and therefore *less flexible* than a small company; this may make it more difficult to react to actual developments in the environment (e.g., an action by a competitor). Second, if the *corporate cultures* do not fit together well, there is no balanced fusion. In that case, the merger can lead to large internal problems. Third, collaboration may make it more difficult to brand the new company. In case of mergers, an important question is which *brand name* to use. Often a new *brand architecture* is needed (see Chapter 10).

Concluding Remarks: Focusing on the Core Business?

We conclude this section with some general remarks. For *product brands* the corporate strategy is indirectly relevant to the marketing plan: A corporate decision such as the investment in the brand can be affected by good internal marketing but primarily should be considered as "given." However, for *corporate brands*, as is often the case in service and business markets, corporate strategy is directly related to marketing decisions: The choice of markets partly determines the corporate positioning. Several aspects of the scope of activities of a company were discussed in this chapter. We argued that there are good reasons for being careful with diversification: It may distract from the core activities of the company and thus lead to unclear vision and positioning. However, sticking to the core business may lead to several disadvantages, among which three are important. First, if the core business is defined in product terms, it may lead to applying technologies that become redundant because of changing customer needs. This can be overcome by defining the core business in terms of customer needs (as was discussed in Chapter 2). Another issue in focusing on the core competency is the role of innovation. Innovations can be directed to serving the chosen customer needs better. A third relevant aspect is the way relatively new activities can be handled. In many cases partnering, as was discussed in section 9.3, can be helpful. Figure 9-5 summarizes these concluding remarks.

FIGURE 9-5 **Advantages of and Conditions for Focusing on the Core Business**

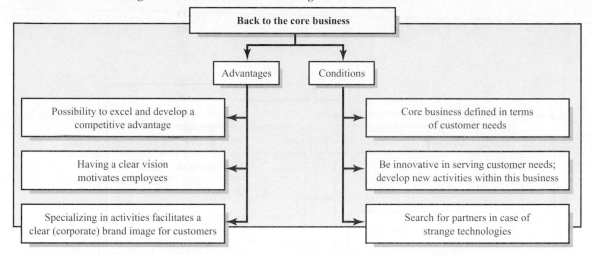

Summary

At the corporate level, the mission and vision are determined first. The main components of these decisions are determining the core business and choosing the value strategy. Based on the vision, the corporate objectives are chosen. This involves setting not only financial goals but also customer-oriented goals, internal goals, and innovation goals (the balanced scorecard discussed in Chapter 3). Subsequently, it should be determined where (in which markets) the company wants to compete: the portfolio of SBUs and the desired development for each SBU. A company may grow with its existing SBUs (expansion); the possibilities then are market penetration, market development, product development, and diversification. Growth can also be achieved with new products and services (diversification); this may occur through market widening through vertical diversification, concentric diversification, or conglomerate diversification. The managers of a brand can influence corporate decisions through the internal marketing of a plan (see Chapter 12).

At the corporate level, a decision needs to be made about with whom the competition will occur: alone or in collaboration with others. Since growth occurs more rapidly and carries fewer risks if it occurs through collaboration or merger, there is an increasing trend toward mergers. The current merger waves are also related to the desire for internationalization.

Finally, it is recommended that companies be careful about broadening their activities. From a customer point of view, it is more effective if the core business is defined in terms of customer needs and if innovation is applied for developing better ways of meeting those needs.

Notes

1. Ansoff, H. I. (1957), 'Strategies for Diversification', *Harvard Business Review,* vol. 35, September–October, p. 113–124.

2. Ansoff (1957)

3. For example, Porter, M. E. (1987), "From Competitive Advantage to Corporate Strategy," *Harvard Business Review,* May–June, pp. 43–59, analyzed 2,021 acquisitions of 33 strongly diversified companies in the period 1950–1980. More than half the acquisitions had ended by 1986, whereas in fact 74 percent of the 931 unrelated acquisitions had been ended.

4. Roberts, E. B., and C. A. Berry (1985), "Entering New Businesses: Selecting Strategies for Success," *Sloan Management Review,* Spring 1985, pp. 3–17, recommend this on the basis of experience and theory.

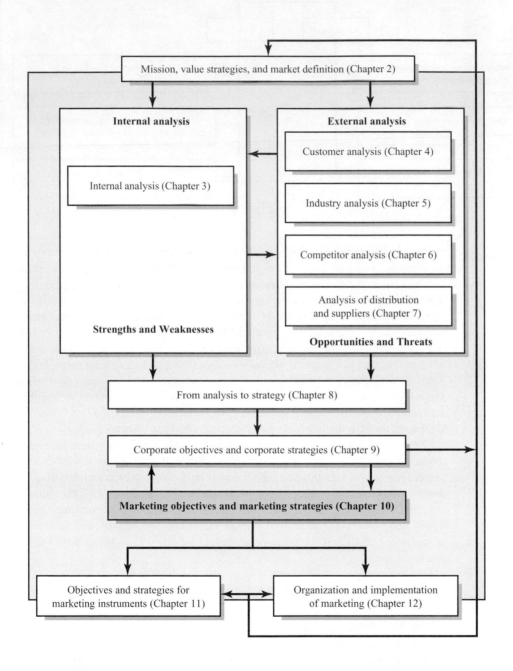

Chapter **Ten**

Marketing Objectives and Marketing Strategies

Key Points in This Chapter

- Know how to formulate marketing objectives.
- Apply methods for targeting customers.
- Know the principles of and methods for positioning.
- Know the role of the brand.
- Know how to choose a brand name and brand design.
- Apply guidelines for managing brands over products (extensions), internationally, and over time (crisis management).

INTRODUCTION

In Chapter 1, the hierarchy of objectives and strategies in a company was illustrated. In Chapter 9, the first two phases in that hierarchy were reviewed more closely:

1. Corporate objectives
2. Corporate strategies

The results of these steps include the choice of markets in which the company wants to be active, that is, the answer to the question of *where to compete*. This chapter reviews the two subsequent phases:

3. Marketing objectives
4. Marketing strategies

These phases specifically provide an answer to the question of *how to compete*. Chapter 11 is devoted to the following phases:

5. Marketing mix objectives
6. Marketing mix strategies

These phases represent the elaboration of the issue of how to compete.

In the context of the marketing strategies, a central concept is that positioning should be based on a sustainable competitive advantage. Marketing plays a central role in finding and achieving such an advantage: Searching for a sustainable competitive advantage requires a careful analysis of the market and the competitors (market research), whereas its achievement depends to an important degree on the use of the marketing mix, such as

FIGURE 10-1
Market Segmentation, Targeting, and Positioning

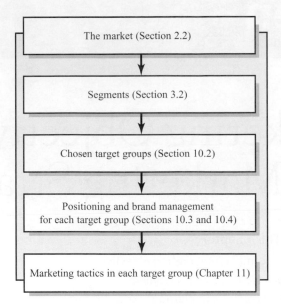

product and communication. To achieve marketing strategies, strategies for other functional areas in a company should be formulated, such as strategies for purchasing, production, and logistics. After all, the choice of a sustainable competitive advantage is so important that there may be consequences for the entire company or strategic business unit (SBU).

Section 10.1 reviews the marketing objectives, after which Sections 10.2 through 10.4 are devoted to the following components of the marketing strategy: choice of target group (10.2), brands and brand positioning (10.3), and brand management (10.4). Figure 10-1 shows the relationship between these subjects.

Dasani Withdraws from the European Market

Bottled water is a booming business. Annual sales are rising about 20 percent per year in the United States and in Europe. As a result of the health trend, bottled water is becoming more important to consumers.

Aquafina is the best-selling water brand in the United States. Dasani is the second most popular brand in the United States. It was introduced in the United States in 1999. Dasani is bottled by the Coca-Cola Company. Pepsico is the owner of Aquafina.

The main competitors in Europe are Nestlé (with brands such as Vittel, Perrier, and San Pellegrino), Danone (Evian), and San Benedetto. These three companies account for about 50 percent of the European market.

However, when introducing Dasani in the European market, the Coca-Cola Company had to confront more than these competitors. It had to face a totally different view on what bottled water is supposed to be.

In the United States, Aquafina and Dasani are produced from tap water. The process is described in detail on Dasani's Web site: "To create Dasani, Coca-Cola bottlers start with the local water supply, which is then filtered for purity using a state-of-the-art process called reverse osmosis. The purified water is then enhanced with a special blend of minerals for a pure, fresh taste."

Bottled water from the tap, which is fully accepted by consumers in the United States, is a curious concept to Europeans. The European consumer is used to bottled water from natural sources, not to bottled water from the tap. Purity should come from Mother Nature, not from a state-of-the-art process called reverse osmosis.

The Coca-Cola Company wanted to use the United Kingdom as the first step in introducing Dasani in Europe. Dasani was introduced in the United Kingdom at the beginning of 2004.

When Dasani was introduced in the United Kingdom, problems were bound to happen. The concept was strange to the consumer, and legal requirements did the rest.

Calcium is a legal requirement in all bottled water products in the United Kingdom, including Dasani. To deliver the required calcium Dasani added calcium chloride into the product, but the calcium chloride that was used was contaminated with a small amount of calcium bromide. During the reverse osmosis, a chemical reaction happened in which the calcium bromide was transformed into bromate at a level that slightly exceeded British legal standards.

Although there was no health risk, the Coca-Cola Company withdrew Dasani from the United Kingdom. The planned introduction of Dasani to Germany and France was postponed indefinitely.

The European reaction to the introduction of Dasani can be illustrated with two BBC news stories. The first is dated March 1, 2004; the second was published after the withdrawal of the brand on March 24, 2004.

Soft Drink Is Purified Tap Water

March 1, 2004—Soft drink giant Coca-Cola has admitted it is selling purified tap water in a bottle.

It says the source for its new Dasani bottled water is the mains supply at its factory in Kent. The company says Dasani is "as pure as bottled water gets" due to a "highly sophisticated purification process." But the U.K. water industry is worried that the marketing of the product implies tap water is impure, which experts say is not the case.

Coca-Cola is investing £7 million in launching Dasani, which has become the second most popular bottled water in the United States following its launch there in 1999. Marketing for the product says it goes through four stages of production before it is bottled, starting with being passed through three separate filters. Coca-Cola says "reverse osmosis," "a technique perfected by NASA to purify fluids on spacecraft," is then used to filter the water further before minerals are added to "enhance the pure taste." Finally, "ozone" is injected to keep the water sterile, the company says.

But water industry representatives say consumers do not need to buy Dasani to get "excellent-quality, healthy water." Barrie Clarke, spokesman for the suppliers' representative Water UK, said: "We don't think there are any impurities in tap water. If people like the bottle, the convenience, the style, then fine, but I don't think that is the way they are marketing this product. Tap water is pure, and that's the opinion of the drinking water inspectorate, which carries out three million checks a year."

Judith Snyder, brand public relations manager for Dasani, confirmed that "municipal" water supplies were used but said the source was "irrelevant" because it "doesn't affect the end result." She said: "We would never say tap water isn't drinkable. It's just that Dasani is as pure as water can get—there are different levels of purity."

Source: BBC news story, March 1, 2004.

Dasani U.K. Delay Cans Europe Sales

March 24, 2004—Coca-Cola has put off plans to sell its Dasani water in Europe following a contamination scandal that forced it to pull 500,000 bottles off U.K. shelves.

The company has also canned the idea of reintroducing the product to the United Kingdom. Dasani disappeared from the shops in mid-March after it was found to have illegal levels of bromate.

Coca-Cola said it has "full confidence" in Dasani despite the setback, which followed news that Dasani was no more than treated and purified tap water.

The problems mean that a planned launch in France—seen as a key market—and Germany is now on hold. And a U.K. relaunch is certainly off the cards for the moment, although it may come back in the future.

The company, however, is optimistic that the early problems can be overcome. "Dasani is a proven success story in other parts of the world, and we see no reason why it could not be so in Europe," it said. "But now is not the right time to bring it back to the market." Analysts tend to agree, adding that the brand already may be too battered for a British revival.

Dasani is a curious brew that is made from mains water at a factory in Sidcup, Kent. Coca-Cola says that after being passed through a "highly sophisticated purification process," the drink is "as pure as bottled water gets."

Bromate, meanwhile, is described by the Food Stan-dards Agency as "a chemical that could cause an increased cancer risk as a result of long-term exposure." In a statement last week, Coca-Cola said the contamination had been initially caused by its regular practice of adding calcium to Dasani. In this case, the calcium "did not meet our quality standards," the company admitted. As a result, bromate went on to be formed during the manufacturing processes. Although there were no immediate safety fears, Coca-Cola decided on the recall. The product's bromate levels were twice the legal limit in the United Kingdom but were below Europe's higher limit.

Source: BBC news story, March 24, 2004.

Sources: www.dasani.com; BBC news stories, March 1 and March 24, 2004.

Questions

1. Which elements from the macroenvironment caused the failure of Dasani in the United Kingdom? Give a short explanation of your answer.
2. Which growth strategy (Ansoff, see Chapter 9) was used by the Coca-Cola Company when it began the introduction of Dasani in Europe? Explain your answer briefly.
3. In marketing, the concept of brand equity is very important.

    a. Describe what brand equity is.
    b Describe the brand equity of Dasani in the United Kingdom.

4. In your opinion, which mistakes were made by the management of Dasani in introducing the brand in the European market? Explain your answer.
5. Would you recommend a reintroduction of Dasani into the European market?

    a. If yes, which marketing strategy would you propose?
    b. If no, why not?

6. If the Coca Cola Company considers a reintroduction of Dasani in the United Kingdom, should it use the Dasani brand name or introduce the product under a different brand name? Explain your answer.

10.1 MARKETING OBJECTIVES

As was indicated in Chapter 1, marketing objectives are objectives for which the functional area of marketing may be held primarily responsible. These objectives may be formulated on different levels: at the company, business unit, or product level. In practice, marketing objectives occur most frequently at the product level. Marketing objectives are expressed in measures that relate to the following:

1. Market share or sales.
2. Profit.

Examples include the following:

- Sales of brand X should increase 10 percent next year.
- After the introduction of brand Y, in three years a market share of 10 percent and a profit of 1 million euros should be achieved. The loss in year 1 may not exceed 0.5 million euros, and in the second year a profit of 0.5 million euros should be achieved.

A problem in defining objectives that are related to *both* types of measures is that there is often a contrast between market share and profit. After all, investments are required to obtain a high market share, such as high expenditures for sales promotion or price reductions. Therefore, if there is more than one objective, a priority should be indicated: What is the primary objective, and what is the secondary objective?

The responsibility for the choice of the marketing objectives for products lies at the SBU level. Therefore, this is the core of the *SBU strategy*: the desired position of brands or products within an SBU. The choice of marketing objectives depends, among other things, on the following factors:

1. *The attractiveness of segments.* Because brands and products in principle are linked to segments in a market, the choice of the SBU strategy and product (marketing) objectives is determined partly by the segmentation analysis: In which segments can growth be expected? A portfolio analysis for segments is a tool for choosing objectives, just as it is at the company level.
2. *Phase in the product life cycle.* The industry analysis provides information in this area. In the introductory phase and the growth phase of a product, the most important objective typically is *growth* in market share and sales. As the product moves more into the maturity phase, *profitability* becomes more important, partly to recover the costs of investments made in earlier periods. In the saturation phase, competition typically is strong and the emphasis is on achieving and maintaining *market share*. In the declining phase, harvesting strategies often are appropriate and objectives such as *profit* and "cash flow" are chosen.
3. *The competition.* The competitor analysis provides information on the goals and objectives of competitors. If the most important competitors emphasize profit objectives, there may be room for a higher market share. If there is a tough battle for market share, achieving a high market share does not appear feasible and perhaps the objective should be more focused on profit.
4. *Company objectives and company strategies.* As was indicated earlier, product objectives are determined to an important extent by the company-level decisions we have discussed.
5. *Financial resources.* The internal analysis provides insight into issues such as the available resources in the company and the SBU for the product. If those resources are limited, achieving a high market share will be difficult.

6. *Long-term objectives*. If there are long-term objectives, they will have an influence on the short-term objectives. For example, if a company has objectives for long-term profit, the short-term focus may be on obtaining market share that may lead to profit in later years. In general, a short-term objective should fit into a time line that leads toward a long-term objective.

10.2 SEGMENTATION AND CHOICE OF A TARGET GROUP

This section deals with the following topics:

- The importance of segmentation (Section 10.2.1).
- The steps to be taken in segmenting and targeting (Section 10.2.2);
- The evaluation of market segments (Section 10.2.3).
- The selection of market segments (Section 10.2.4).
- Customer intimacy and loyalty programs (a segmentation strategy) (Section 10.2.5).

10.2.1 Importance of Segmentation

The definition of the market, followed by the choice of the company strategy, has determined items such as which products the company wants to make for which customers (markets), for example, "clothing for women." Although this means that the target group already has been determined to an important extent in the choice of the company strategy, several more specific choices about the target group should be made during the formulation of the *marketing strategy,* such as the following:

- Does the company want to approach the entire market with a single product or with different products and varieties?
- Does the company want to attempt to reach the entire market or emphasize several segments or even only a single segment?
- Can the chosen segments be categorized by general characteristics (age, income, etc.) and by situation-specific characteristics (product usage)?

These questions are all related to *segmentation*: Should the customers be split into groups? If they should, which positioning should be chosen for each segment? The segmentation decision therefore is a closer, more specific interpretation of the choice of a target group: In the company strategy, this choice is made on a global level; in the marketing strategy, on a specific level. The most important reason for splitting the market into groups is that different people may have different preferences, and this may lead to higher profitability than would be the case if different groups were approached with the same strategy. Whether segmentation is useful depends on the size of the segments and the higher costs associated with the use of different strategies.

A "different strategy" in theory means a difference in one or more of the four P's: product, price, promotion, and place. In practice, segmentation almost always involves differences in the "supply" (product). After all, product changes allow a company to respond to specific needs. For example, a manufacturer can bring several different brands of laundry detergent onto the market with several varieties within each brand.

It is not inconceivable to approach different segments with a single product, but this should be done with, for example, different advertising campaigns. For example, a newspaper could recommend its fashion columns in women's magazines while promoting its sport attachments in men's magazines. However, a disadvantage of attempting to present different characteristics of a single product to different segments is that the product will have an unclear image in the market, in other words, no clear positioning. Without clear positioning, the company will not have a clear competitive advantage. Thus, if a company discovers segments with different needs in a market, in practice segmentation will mean a different product (or product variety), perhaps supplemented with the use of another price and/or promotion and/or distribution. In other words, segmentation has direct consequences for product decisions and *assortment decisions*: Does the company offer the market a single product or a line of different products?

Aside from assortment decisions, segmentation may have consequences for the rest of the marketing mix. Examples include the following:

- *Variety only in product.* Many laundry detergent manufacturers bring different varieties into the market (with or without colorfastness, liquid or solid, etc.) that do not differ or hardly differ in price and are not always subject to different advertising.
- *Variety in product and price.* A car manufacturer may bring various types into the market without doing separate advertising for the different varieties.
- *Variety in product, price, and promotion.* The car manufacturer may use different advertising campaigns, such as advertising on a specific television station for the cheaper models and in a glossy magazine for the more expensive ones.
- *Variation in all four elements of the marketing mix.* A manufacturer of baby clothing produces more expensive and cheaper clothing, advertises separately for those varieties, and distributes the expensive clothing through baby specialty stores and the cheaper clothing through warehouses and lower-price textile stores.

10.2.2 Steps to be Taken

Several steps need to be taken in choosing target groups on the basis of segments. Figure 10-2 shows the *STP-steps: segmenting, targeting, and positioning. Market segmentation* involves dividing the market into buyers groups that may require different products and different marketing mix strategies. For this purpose, the company first identifies ways to divide the market into segments and then creates a "profile" for each segment: a description that is based on general and situation-specific characteristics. The second step is choosing *market target groups*: defining the characteristics to be used as a basis for determining the attractiveness of each segment and choosing which segments the company wants to enter. The third step is *product positioning*: finding a clear "place" for the product in the minds of the customers and in relation to the competitors.

The steps in market segmentation were discussed in Chapter 4. This section reviews the choice of target groups, and Section 10.3 discusses the choice of the brand positioning.

FIGURE 10-2
Steps for Market Segmentation, Determination of Target Groups, and Positioning

Market segmentation (Section 4.2: Segmentation research)

1. Identifying segmentation variables and segmenting the market
2. Developing profiles per segment

Market target groups (Section 10.2: Segmentation and choice of a target group)

3. Evaluating the attractiveness per segment
4. Selecting the segments

Brand positioning (Section 10.3: Positioning managing a brand identity)

5. Identifying potential positioning concepts for each chosen segment
6. Choosing, developing, and communicating the chosen positioning concept

10.2.3   Evaluation of the Market Segments

After different potential segments have been identified and described, a choice has to be made: Which segments will the company focus on? In other words, what are the target groups in the market? This choice problem is comparable to the problem of choosing investment levels for SBUs (see Chapter 9). For the process of making investment decisions for SBUs, a company can take the following two steps:

1. Performing situation analyses and SWOT (strengths, weaknesses, opportunities, and threats) analyses for the markets in which the various SBUs are active. For example, a manufacturer of animal food analyzes the markets and SBUs of fodder, dog food, and cat food. These analyses are conducted within the SBUs, for example, under the responsibility of the marketing managers.

2. Communicating the results of the SWOT analyses as well as the tentative plans of the SBUs to top management. Within top management, investment decisions can be made per market or SBU, based on items such as a portfolio analysis.

The problem of choosing *products* can be handled in a similar fashion, but at a lower level in the company. This requires the assumption that a segment (group of customers) corresponds to a product category. With that assumption (segment equals product group), the following two steps can be taken:

1. Within an SBU, perform a situation analysis and a SWOT analysis for each *segment;* for example, within the dog food market, perform analyses for the segments of dry standard food, wet (canned) standard food, luxury food (small cans), and other food (chews, etc.). For each segment, items such as attractiveness can be examined by listing the factors that were mentioned in Chapter 5 (industry analysis), such as segment size, segment growth, and industry structural factors according to the model of Porter. For example, the conclusion might be that the standard food segments are becoming less attractive because of increasing competition but that the luxury food segment appears to be attractive because of limited competition and high margins. Such segment analyses may be the responsibility of, for example, product (or "brand") managers. It is important to look not only at segment growth but also at the competition. A declining segment may be attractive if competitors stop serving that segment.

2. Perform a portfolio analysis for those *segments* in which a company is already active and an analysis of the attractiveness of new segments. The criteria for the evaluation are:

   • Relationship with objectives.

   • Possibilities and resources of the company to achieve success in the segment.

   • Possibility for creating a competitive advantage in the segment.

10.2.4   Selection of the Market Segments

This process involves three potential *segmentation strategies*:

1. *Concentrated marketing (focus/niche strategy).* This entails choosing a single segment in the market. The advantage of this strategy may be that there is little competition in that segment. The disadvantage is the high risk: The company is dependent on only a single group of buyers.

2. *Selective marketing.* This entails selecting several segments. The advantage of this strategy in comparison with concentrated targeting is lower risk through spreading of activities. An example would be car manufacturers with types that differ in price.

3. *Complete market coverage.* This means that a company attempts to serve all customer groups. This may be achieved by bringing a large number of different brands and/or products into the market. Examples include IBM in the computer market, Philips in the market for household appliances, and Unilever in the market for "yellow fats." This strategy is possible only for large companies. Another possibility is to bring one or several products onto the market that are aimed at a broad target group, such as Coca-Cola. A risk of complete market coverage with one brand is the absence of focused brand-positioning and thus the lack of brand identity.

The naming of the segmentation strategy depends on the market definition (see Section 2.3). For example, if a car manufacturer uses a broad market definition (e.g., the car market) and chooses a single segment in that market, it might be called a niche strategy. If that manufacturer chooses a narrow market definition (e.g., top-quality cars) and explicitly maintains that definition in its situation analysis, it would count as complete market coverage.

In marketing practice, selective targeting seems to be the most common strategy: It may provide a balance between "gambling on one number" and "having no clear identity" (Case 10-1). The ultimate choice of target groups also depends on the branding strategy (Section 10.4) since it may be easier to serve different segments by using subbrands.

CASE 10-1 *Targeting a Business Market: IQ Corporation Goes from Me-Too to Me-Two*	The Dutch Biotechnology company IQ Products BV is developing and marketing products for flow cytometry, a technique used in medical research and diagnostics. The products in question are proteins (antibodies) designed to recognize specific structures on human (or animal) cells. The field is very broad and highly competitive, and intellectual property rights play little to no role; it is clearly a me-too market. Recently, IQ has moved away from trying to approach this market in total and has decided to focus strongly on two segments within it: perinatal and transplantation-associated research and diagnostics. By specifically targeting these segments, IQ has identified new customers, has been able to set up strategic collaborations, has been able to generate segment-specific products and intellectual property (IP), and, most important, was able to realize 15 percent growth in 2004 in a market where going for 5 percent growth once was considered ambitious.

In the literature on segmentation, three other strategies are often discussed: concentrated, differentiated, and undifferentiated marketing. *Concentrated marketing* corresponds to the first strategy that was mentioned above.

Differentiated marketing means complete market coverage with different strategies for different segments. *Undifferentiated marketing* is the choice to cover the whole market with a single strategy. However, this book uses a different classification of segmentation strategies. First, in the other approach mentioned here, the option of choosing *several* segments is lacking. For that option we introduce the term *selective marketing*. Second, we consider the choice to avoid approaching segments with different strategies (undifferentiated marketing) not to be a segmentation strategy. After all, this means that a company does use segmenting but subsequently ignores differences in the needs of the different segments. In effect, this is a choice to omit a segmentation strategy.

The opposite strategy is also not advisable: segmenting too much. Some companies fault themselves for applying *oversegmentation*: too many brands for too many segments. For example, Unilever sharply cut its portfolio of brands (Case 10-2). The question is whether this is wise for Unilever. It is well known that in general, customers strongly follow the lead of brands. Brands have their own images and customer groups, and if a brand disappears, it will be easier for smaller companies to conquer part of the market. The question is whether the short-term thinking of many managers can create problems in the long run.

CASE 10-2
Killing Off the Brands

In early 2000, Unilever announced it would dispose of no fewer than 1,200 of its 1,600 brands. Unilever has three reasons for this. The first is that many of its brands are "local": limited to a single country. For a group that wants to operate in an international market, it is much easier to do so with international brands. A second reason is the contribution to sales and profit. The seven best brands of Unilever (such as Magnum) are responsible for three-quarters of the sales, whereas the thousand badly operating products contribute only 8 percent. In short, it is too expensive to continue maintaining all those brands. A third reason involves the supermarkets. The retail sector is not happy with having many brands: That creates a lot of the same products, costs shelf space, and is impractical with certain actions (special price sales).

10.2.5 Customer Intimacy and Loyalty Programs

After target groups have been chosen, the next issue is whether the target group should be approached as a whole or one on one. In Section 4.5 we paid attention to obtaining data from individual customers (after approval: *permission marketing*) and to the selection of the most profitable customers. To strengthen the bond with the most important customers, a choice can be made to use *loyalty programs*.[1] These are programs in which the marketing mix is used in such a way that customers are directly rewarded for loyalty to the brand. This is a tool for the seller to increase the *bond* between the customer and the brand and reduce the chance that the customer will switch to a competitor. For this purpose, the organization requires a database with individual customer data. As was indicated in Section 4.5, this also requires *permission marketing*: A customer has to give permission for the seller to start a direct relationship with him or her. The next step may be that the seller actually starts *rewarding loyalty*: gives a reward for brand loyalty. We include this with the concept of loyalty programs, but not the practice of approaching customers directly and "processing" them (database marketing).

CASE 10-3
Loyalty Program

There has been a lot of activity in the area of retail loyalty programs. However, although the goals of these initiatives are simple—learn about the customer and keep him or her coming back—finding successful means of implementation has become a huge challenge. Retailers with successful programs have learned a few tricks. They make the customer feel special, they offer a tangible incentive, and they do it in a way that is too invisible to make the shopper feel like a white laboratory rat. Also, they do not overtly railroad the customer into joining something. In 2001 one of the newest, most sophisticated programs was at Target, the first major retailer to move into the smart card market. In a partnership with VISA, Target launched a chip-embedded card that can be used in Target and other stores. The card tracks purchases and singles out customers for certain discounts. A frequent purchaser of, for example, pet food may instantaneously receive 20 percent off at the register. Furthermore, every time the card is used, it creates a branding impression.

Source: Stankvich, Debby Garbato, "Establishing Fidelity in Loyalty Programs," *Retail Merchandiser*, August 2001, p. 4.

Before a loyalty program can be started, individual customer data are required. A *customer card* is the most widely used tool for this purpose. A customer card may be provided for free or for a fee. *Free cards* have the advantage of high participation but have low involvement. For a *paid customer card* (becoming a "member"), the reverse is true. In both cases, customers should be rewarded with, for example, discounts, early notice of special actions, and/or a magazine or journal. Another way to get individual data is through the Internet. On the Web site of Pampers, for example, customers can provide code numbers of Pampers packages and thus collect points for presents (the "Pampers Gifts to Grow Rewards Program").

Although rewards such as a magazine for "members" are often described as being a component of a loyalty program, this practice does not involve true *rewarding of loyalty* but instead merely the use of tools that the seller may rely on in attempting to *build* customer loyalty. A real loyalty program exists only when loyalty is truly rewarded; on the basis of demonstrable brand loyalty (determined with a specific measure), a customer is offered a reward of some kind (in the form of a specific interpretation of the marketing mix). In practice, the following measures are used for customer loyalty:

- *How long* someone is a paying customer: the length of the brand "membership." This measure is often used for magazines: The longer someone has a subscription, the more attractive discounts can be used. This is also used frequently with "clubs" (whether or not in the nonprofit area); the longer the membership, the lower the price.
- The *cumulative purchasing amount,* such as the *frequent flyer* program of KLM with which points are collected. The "stamp cards" of retailers are another example. In this regard the customer card can be used as a tool to register purchases. If the data are used subsequently to provide rewards to loyal customers, it is indeed a loyalty program.

The rewards may relate to each of the four elements of the marketing mix:

1. *Product:* free premiums (extras), service in the form of advice, maintenance, and so on.
2. *Price:* discount on new purchases, accessories, and so on. This is the form of reward used most frequently in loyalty programs.
3. *Place:* home delivery for loyal customers.
4. *Communication:* A magazine can be a reward for brand loyalty if nonloyal customers have to pay for it and loyal customers do not have to pay or can pay less. Specific information based on the purchasing behavior of customers may also be a reward for loyalty.

Figure 10-3 summarizes the essence of a loyalty program. In practice, loyalty programs for individual brands do not occur very often. Many sellers are merely at the point of registering Name-Address-Residence (NAR) data on customers and offering discounts to customers without basing a distinction on the extent to which someone is a customer. More frequently occurring are savings programs for a number of brands collectively. A well-known example is Airmiles, in which points ("air miles") are collected from various sellers that may be used to obtain not only air travel but also various products for free. A disadvantage of collective savings programs is that there is not a strong link with loyalty to a specific brand. This is an argument for programs for individual brands. In addition, it seems important that the reward not be too indirect and not be complicated to collect.

FIGURE 10-3
Characteristics of a Real Loyalty Program

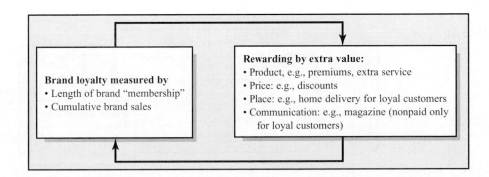

Brand loyalty measured by
- Length of brand "membership"
- Cumulative brand sales

Rewarding by extra value:
- Product, e.g., premiums, extra service
- Price: e.g., discounts
- Place: e.g., home delivery for loyal customers
- Communication: e.g., magazine (nonpaid only for loyal customers)

10.3   POSITIONING: MANAGING A BRAND IDENTITY

First we outline the goal and structure of branding and positioning (Section 10.3.1). In Section 10.3.2 we define several concepts that are important in branding: brands, brand levels, brand values, and positioning strategies. Then we go into two so-called brand elements: developing a brand name (Section 10.3.3) and the role of design and a logo (Section 10.3.4). In this section and in Section 10.4 we use the work of Keller, who has developed a measurable brand equity model to analyze, build, and manage brands.[2]

10.3.1   Building Customer-Oriented Brand Value

Various authors[3] have emphasized the importance of a strong and consistent brand image. In this regard, a lot of attention has been paid to the concept of *brand equity*. There are many definitions of the concept of brand equity (brand value). We compare two definitions: the one of Rust and the one of Keller. Rust[4] divides *customer equity* into three components:

- *Value equity*: the "instrumental" value from using the product.
- *Brand equity*: the added emotional value of the brand to the product.
- *Retention equity*: the loyalty of the customer to the brand.

Within this definition, the brand equity component is limited to the "emotional" value of the brand name. Keller[5] defines brand equity from the view point of the *customer*. According to Keller, *customer-based brand equity* is the effect brand knowledge has on the manner in which consumers react to the marketing of a brand. Therefore, positive brand equity means that consumer reactions to, for example, advertisements and price changes will be more favorable if the consumers know the brand better. The source of brand equity is therefore *brand knowledge*. This consists of *brand awareness* and *brand associations*. Brands should strive to attain high brand familiaxity, but also and above all, strong, unique, and favorable brand associations must be achieved (Figure 10-4).

The connection Keller posits between the brand and the consumer is evident: It concerns attaining brand knowledge in many facets in the target group. This in turn concerns the associations that are relevant for the target group and unique with respect to the competition.

The definition of brand equity of Rust is fundamentally different from the definition of Keller. Rust limits brand equity to "emotional value," whereas Keller sees all associations, whether instrumental or emotional, as part of brand equity. It seems that the Keller definition encompasses both the value and the brand equity of Rust. We follow the definition of Keller, since in our view the brand concept represents the necessity of having a *strong reputation*. Case 10-4 shows that a strong brand equity can be either instrumental (the retailer Aldi, low price) or emotional (Porsche).

FIGURE 10-4
Strong Brand Equity

Source: Keller (2003).

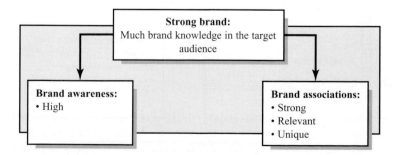

Brand personality — identity
Brand positioning — Mind share   Brand
                                        Process: Intentional shaping
                                                 of perceptions

Brand positioning Results is the image
              Promotions Should tell a Brand Story

Chapter 10 *Marketing Objectives and Marketing Strategies* **227**

CASE 10-4

Different Ways of Having High Brand Equity

For six years, the results of the Annual Reputation Quotiënt (RQ) of research institute Harris have been published in *The Wall Street Journal*. This annual survey measures the reputations of the most visible companies in a country., including companies in the airline, oil/energy, automotive, technology, financial services, and retail sectors. Each company is evaluated by adults (18+) who are randomly selected based on their familiarity with the company. Respondents rate companies on 20 attributes in six key dimensions:

- Products & Services
- Financial Performance
- Workplace Environment
- Social Responsibility
- Vision & Leadership
- Emotional Appeal

In 2004 German people loved the cheap supermarket stores of Aldi as well as the car brands Porsche and Audi the most. The top brands are especially strong in reliability, which is what Germans appreciate. Aldi also has the advantage of a good reputation: This retailer offers many good-quality products for a low price. Despite the low service level, consumers seem to like the way Aldi treats its customers.

Source: Harris Interactive & Reputation Institute, http://www.harrisinteractive.com/services/rqarchive.asp

The familiarity of the brand is important for a customer relationship. The personality the brand wants to have is called the *identity*. *Positioning* means that a brand attempts to capture a place in the "mind of the customer" with its identity. The result of positioning is called the *image*: the brand image that the target group actually has. In the last few years positioning has become increasingly difficult. A strong increase in the various media (such as television stations), the advance of new media such as the Internet and mobile telephones, an increase in the number of brands and varieties, a decrease in the true differences between products, and an enormous increase in communication pressure have all occurred over the last 10 years, and this has had repercussions for the consumer.

Consumers have become more fickle: They have become moment consumers who have completely different preferences from one moment to the next. They have also become more individualistic, paying less attention to the environment and charting their own course. In addition, they are less interested in products and services and make less of an effort to collect information about products during the purchasing process. They rely much more on whether a brand is well known (knowledge); they try products they know (behavior: trial purchase), and if they like those products (attitude, experience), they keep buying them out of habit (behavior: repeat purchase).

The process that is described here is the *low-involvement* behavior of consumers. In the past, many consumers often had a *high involvement* with products: People were strongly interested in the product and were prepared to go to a lot of trouble to make a purchase (such as collecting information beforehand and weighing alternatives). They therefore completed all the phases of the classic consumer decision-making process in sequence: information collection, weighing of alternatives, determination of preference, purchase. These days it is much more a case of low involvement. The purchasing process now takes the following course: familiarity, purchase, evaluation after purchase. If the product does not disappoint, it is followed by repeat purchases that sometimes lead to conscious brand loyalty but often lead only to *habit purchases*. In the final purchasing decision, *recognition* often plays an important role. In this process, the consumer increasingly uses "memory cues"; mnemonic aids or handles that are easily dug up from memory. Often these are the primary associations

FIGURE 10-5
The Communication Spiral

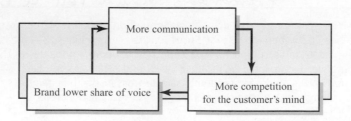

the consumer has with the brand or the advertising for the brand (e.g., a color, word, picture, or person).

Because of these developments, obtaining a "mind position" with the consumer is becoming more necessary.[6] However, because of increasing competition and communication pressure, it is becoming increasingly difficult for sellers to do that. In the last few years, the consequences of this problem seem to be that sellers are only increasing the communication pressure. This process has been called the *communication spiral* (Figure 10-5).

The problem in the communication spiral is the misperception that positioning should be achieved mostly through *communication*. In reality, reputation is determined much more by what a brand *actually does*. A brand can build its image by truly satisfying customers and through the way that satisfaction happens. That does not mean that communication is no longer important. Chapter 1 indicated that an important factor in a bond with a customer is that a brand be familiar to a client and have an image that is comfortable for the target group.

10.3.2 Brand Levels, Brand Attributes, and Positioning Strategies

Four concepts are relevant to consider before brand decisions can be made: brands, brand levels, brand attributes, and positioning strategies.

Brands

What is a brand? A *brand* may be defined from the supply-side perspective (the company) and from the demand-side perspective (the customer). The supply-oriented definition of a brand is "a name, designation, sign, symbol, design, or combination thereof intended to *identify the products and services* of a supplier and distinguish them from competing products and services."[7] A brand can also be defined from the perspective of a customer: A brand is a *set of associations* linked to a name, mark, or symbol. This definition stresses the *consequence* of the use of a brand and is applied in this book. A brand is much like a *reputation*. Not only products and services are brands, but also shops, shop formulas, people, places, organizations, ideas, and events.

CASE 10-5
Personal Branding

It's not a night with Ben Affleck or a most frequently requested video, but for plenty of J. Lo wannabes, zipping on one of the star's $130 velour track suits is as close as they get to wearing celebrity skin. After a bumpy start in 2001, Jennifer Lopez's flirty, teen-oriented clothing line rebounded in 2002, topping $65 million in sales. Now her perfume, GLOW by J. Lo, is the best-selling fragrance at Macy's. Lopez wasn't the first music star to lure her fans to retail—her ex-boyfriend, hip-hop artist and producer P. Diddy, is behind the high-end Sean John menswear line. Many other stars are angling for a spot on the racks: Celine Dion (with COTY perfume, which reflects the singer's romantic image), Eminem with the sportswear label SHADY, rapper-actor Ice-T with ICEWEAR, rapper Eve with the clothing line FETISH, and No Doubt vocalist Gwen Stefani with a denim-heavy line called LAMB, for example.

Source: Winters, Rebecca, "You Heard the Album, Now Buy the Jeans," *Time,* February 3, 2003, p. 51.

Brands fulfill different functions for customers:

1. *Identification*. Brands make products and services recognizable.
2. *Trust and quality*. The customer knows what to expect and where it comes from, and there are no risks.
3. *Symbolic function*. By purchasing brands, people show who they are or what they want.

Although consumers will not easily admit to researchers that they are strongly influenced by brands during purchasing decisions, research shows that this is the case. The most striking forms of evidence in this regard are blind taste tests. For example, in research by de Chernatony and Knox,[8] 51 percent preferred Pepsi and 44 percent preferred Coca-Cola. When the tasters were told what they had been drinking, only 23 percent preferred Pepsi and 65 percent preferred Coca-Cola.

Brand Levels

Brands and brand names exist at different levels. Figure 10-6 gives an overview with examples. *The corporate level* refers to the supplier of the brand. A supplier sometimes is part of a larger group. A company may choose to use or not use the group name in terms of positioning. In the insurance industry these days, it is clear that group names are increasingly being used as a source of trust. This is related to the idea that consumers increasingly consider it important to know who is behind the brand and how that entity behaves (in social terms). A good reputation and a good corporate image are therefore very important.

A *family brand* is a brand that is used for various product categories. A family brand may be different from the corporate brand.

An *individual brand* is limited to a product category. The emphasis in this book is on the individual brand. An individual brand has its own image and its own target group.

The lowest brand level indicates the *type of product* (item or variety).

This classification into levels is arbitrary. For example, the distinction between type and individual brand is often difficult to make. In the car industry some brands work with type numbers (Peugeot 501, Mercedes A), but these numbers may also be considered individual brands. For example, there is a great difference between a Mercedes A (small) and a Mercedes D (large). In the same industry "real" individual brand names are increasingly being used (Renault Mégane, Twingo).

Brands can decide to use several brand levels at a time, for example, by using a corporate brand as support for an individual brand or the other way around: an individual brand with a variety. When a company uses two brand levels, the main brand is the *primary brand* and the "lower" brand is the *subbrand*. Making choices about using brand levels is called the *brand architecture* or *brand portfolio*. Using one brand name is called *mono branding*;

FIGURE 10-6
Brand Levels

Level	Fast-Moving Consumer Goods	Durable Consumer Goods	Services
Company brand (corporate brand)	Procter & Gamble	Volkswagen	ING Group
Family brand (umbrella brand)	Crest	Volkswagen	ING Financial services
Individual brand	Crest toothpaste	Volkswagen Passat	ING Direct
Type of variety	Crest Sesame Street Kids' Cavity Protection	Passat 2.0T Value Edition	Orange Home Loans

combining two names, *dual branding*. In marketing practice, especially in service markets, we often see dual branding: showing the "sender" of a brand (endorsing). Unilever is applying endorsing: On every product from Unilever, the Unilever logo is shown. An advantage of this is that it makes brands more reliable: A product is coming from a reliable manufacturer. Another advantage of dual branding is "cross-selling": the possibility of communicating from a manufacturer to customers about several brands.

Brands can also decide to cooperate with other brands. If both brands continue to exist in this form of cooperation, it is called *cobranding*. The advantage of cobranding is that brands can make use of each other's strengths. Empirical research shows that in cobranding situations the weaker brand gets more of an advantage from cobranding than does the stronger brand.[9] A specific form of cobranding is *ingredient branding*. This occurs when a brand communicates as part of another brand, for example, "Intel inside."

CASE 10-6

Cobranding of Car Manufacturers with Bose

Porsche and Mercedes-Benz (DCX) have been trumpeting Bose stereo systems to bolster their own tony brands for a while now, and they could soon turn to Bose to supply a truly high-quality ride. Company founder and chairman Amar Bose is ready to unveil what he believes is a revolutionary road-handling suspension system. Working in Bose's favor is the fact that auto engineers have a great deal of respect for the company and its founder. Marketers at auto companies also know the power of a strong brand. They could make a case for adopting Bose's technology and then touting it in advertising and even inside the vehicle. Lesser automotive brands fighting for street credibility, such as Suzuki, Mitsubishi, and Kia, could also see a boost in image from cobranding with Bose. A recent study by J.D. Power & Associates shows that Bose is the brand consumers most often link with superior sound quality in cars. Thus, if Bose's idea has merit, automakers will be all ears.

Source: Kiley, David, "Can Bose Tame Rhythms of the Road?" *Business Week Online,* July 23, 2004.

Brand Attributes

There are two meanings of *brand value*:

1. *Brand values* are the intended brand *personality attributes,* such as friendly, feminine, or honest.

2. The *brand value* (without an "s") means the *financial value* of the brand. Measuring the financial value of a brand is important in, for example, acquisitions of brands.[10]

We will now discuss brand values (attributes). As was mentioned earlier, Keller (2003) defines brand equity from the perspective of the customer and emphasizes the sources of brand equity. In his *customer-based brand equity* model, brand awareness and brand associations are the sources of brand equity. The focus is on achieving knowledge effects. The tools to achieve this knowledge in the target group are the fixed *brand elements* such as brand name and logo, the four elements of the *marketing mix* (product, price, place, and communication),[11] and so-called *secondary associations* such as linking the company name to the brand (*endorsing*), linking with a completely different brand (*cobranding*), and linking to events (see Section 10.4.5). A brand should strive to attain high awareness and achieve in the target consumers' minds associations that are strong, relevant, and unique (Figure 10-7). The result of strong sources of brand equity includes brand loyalty. Aaker[12] also developed a brand equity model that is often used and that contains components similar to those in Keller's model: brand awareness, brand associations, perceived quality (a specific association), brand loyalty, and other elements, such as patents.

Positioning requires choosing a specific brand value (attribute). The chosen brand value should fit with what customers consider important: Customer values and brand values

FIGURE 10-7   **Building Customer-Based Brand Equity**

Source: Adapted from Keller (2003).

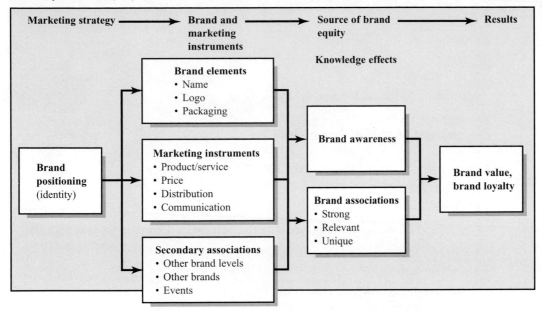

should correspond. There are several enumerations of *brand (personality) characteristics* in the literature. A well-known list of attributes is that of Rokeach,[13] who makes a distinction between *terminal ("end") values* (what someone considers important "in life," such as an exciting life, happiness, friendship) and *"instrumental" values* (personality characteristics such as ambition, clean, honest, responsible) (Figure 10-8). The distinction between those two categories is difficult to make. Figure 10-9 contains three different classifications.

FIGURE 10-8
Values According to Rokeach

Source: Rokeach (1973).

End Values	Personality Characteristics*
A comfortable life	Ambitious
An exciting life	Broad-minded
A sense of accomplishment	Capable
A world at peace	Cheerful
A world of beauty	Clean
Equality	Courageous
Family security	Forgiving
Freedom	Helpful
Happiness	Honest
Inner harmony	Imaginative
Mature love	Independent
National security	Intelligent
Pleasure	Logical
Salvation	Loving
Self-respect	Obedient
Social recognition	Polite
True friendship	Responsible
Wisdom	Self-controlled

*Called instrumental values by Rokeach.

FIGURE 10-9
Positioning
Characteristics

Positioning based on the classic needs hierarchy of Maslow

- Physical needs
- Safety
- Social
- Status
- Self-actualization

Positioning Based on Marketing Mix

- Product
- Service
- Price
- Personnel
- Distribution
- Image (communication)

Positioning based on brand personality characteristics according to Aaker (1997)

- Sincerity (down-to-earth, honest, wholesome, cheerful)
- Exciting (daring, spirited, imaginative, up to date)
- Competence (reliable, intelligent, successful) ·
- Sophistication (upper-class, charming)
- Ruggedness (outdoorsy, tough)

The oldest classification is the well-known needs hierarchy of *Maslow*. A brand can choose at which needs level it wants to distinguish itself. In a section on differentiation strategies, Kotler[14] uses a classification based more or less on the *marketing mix*. Jennifer Aaker did research into the personalities of brands.[15] Using extensive empirical research, she found that the brand personality characteristics may be organized into the five factors mentioned in Figure 10-9.[16] The classification by Aaker may be seen as an elaboration of distinction in the area of image.

Positioning Strategies

The word *positioning* that has been used several times in this book was emphasized by Ries and Trout in their classic book *Positioning: The Battle for Your Mind*.[17] The title indicates the message of the book: The goal of positioning is to capture a place for the brand in the mind of the target group. The primary focus therefore is on perceptions and not really on products. Positioning is striving to create a perception in the mind of the target group. The final result (the achieved image) is the brand image. An image may be both functional and psychosocial. The desired image is the positioning (also designated as the brand identity, the proposition, or even the "strategy"). Obviously, the goal is that image and positioning will correspond. Figure 10-10 illustrates what positioning is by depicting the *positioning triangle*: A central concept in positioning is *the selection of those "values" (characteristics, consequences, and final values)* for which:

- The *target group* considers them important.
- The *organization* or brand is strong in that area.
- The *competitors* are less strong in that area.

FIGURE 10-10
The Positioning Triangle

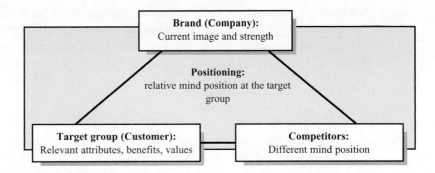

In the choice of positioning, four strategies can be followed in theory. These strategies are based on the *means-end chain* of meanings. Figure 10-11 shows this chain as well as the potential positioning strategies.

Informational Positioning Informational positioning involves an emphasis on communicating a tangible advantage of using a brand, perhaps connected to a physical characteristic of the product ("reason why"). For example, Freedent sugar-free chewing gum prevents stomach acid and damage to the teeth (benefit) because it has a pH-reducing effect (functional characteristic). This positioning strategy is often used for new products (e.g., Philips wide-screen television) and products with a problem-solving character (e.g., laundry detergents, dishwashing detergents, lime deposit cleaners). Informational positioning is particularly effective when there are clear differences between brands, in short, when brands have or are able to claim a USP (unique selling position). In light of the fact that brands increasingly look like one another, effective application of informational positioning is becoming more difficult.[18]

Transformational Positioning In this strategy (also called lifestyle or image positioning), the emphasis is on communicating values, perhaps linked to product advantages. As mentioned earlier, values are issues the consumer considers important in life, a type of ideal. Examples are being healthy, caring for children, living responsibly, enjoying oneself, convenience, being

FIGURE 10-11 Positioning Strategies

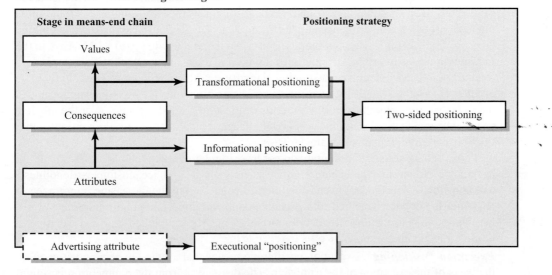

good to others, and making a career for oneself. An example is Starbucks coffee. In this kind of positioning, often it is not the values that are shown but various possessions and forms of behavior of the consumer. The values are the binding element in this regard. The choice alternative (brand) is placed in an environment that is clearly dominated by certain values. The consumer asks himself or herself: Am I such a person or do I want to be such a person? If the answer is yes, the brand may be considered for purchase.

In this type of positioning, psychosocial aspects play a large role. This strategy is often used for products that are purchased for pleasure (such as soft drinks and beer), products that hardly differ from each other (such as cigarettes), and products in which characteristics do not play a role (such as perfume). In general, transformational positioning is difficult to achieve for new products: It takes a lot of time and money to build up a psychosocial image. Maintaining this type of positioning also requires persistence. Yet transformational positioning is quite popular. The reason for this is that products are starting to look more alike in terms of their functional characteristics. This means that distinctions based on abstract image characteristics, especially those created through communication, are becoming an obvious alternative.

CASE 10-7 *Transformational Positioning*	**New Kmart Image Campaign Revives the Value Message** In 2002 the Michigan-based retail store Kmart Corp. tried to adopt a new brand image by positioning itself as a store that understands family values in an attempt to strike an emotional chord with shoppers and to emerge from bankruptcy. The corporate branding campaign was aimed at focusing on how the retailer appreciates values that are important in shoppers lives, such as putting family first and showing an appreciation for money and practicality. "Kmart, the Stuff of Life" was the branding message used by Kmart in all its commercials. The branding message was the culmination of 18 months of research, including focus groups, into how shoppers viewed Kmart. Kmart's difficulty in clearly differentiating itself has long been an issue that analysts have painted to as one factor leading to its financial troubles. **Source:** Howell, Debbie, "New Kmart Image Campaign Revives the Value Message," *Retailing Today,* March 11, 2002, p. 3.

Two-sided Positioning   This type of positioning relies on the entire means-end chain: The product advantages are linked both to the *functional product characteristics* and to the *values* of the consumer. An example is Apple, which distinguishes itself through user-friendliness but also through an impertinent character. Many other lines of business also try to combine "reason" and "feeling." Think of brands such as Apple, McDonald's, and KLM. Also, in the fast-moving consumer goods branch it may be noticed that brands that for many years strongly relied on functional positioning (laundry detergents, diapers, feminine hygiene products, etc.) increasingly are working on building a brand personality. Since many brands have chosen to position themselves in terms of lifestyle-related variables over the last few years, it seems that a development is taking place that includes renewed attention to distinctions based on functional characteristics.

Those "characteristics" definitely do not have to relate only to the physical product but also may be found in added characteristics such as service, advice, customer-friendliness, and knowing the customer. This development is connected to the increasing importance of customer loyalty, for which customer satisfaction is an important condition. Since awareness and ability to identify are also important, it may be concluded that two-sided positioning in general appears to be effective.

Execution Positioning   Execution positioning means that a brand is being positioned on the basis of the execution of the campaign. The distinction from the competition is sought mostly or partly from an *advertising characteristic*. In effect this is not truly a case of positioning, since advertising associations rather than brand associations are created. The brand or product is linked to a unique element or symbol in the communication (the color blue for Pepsi Cola, the apple for Apple). This strategy may be chosen with or without a link to a phase in the means-end chain. Both may produce a successful strategy, especially if this technique is applied consistently over time. A familiar advertising characteristic may be a handy "cue" for consumers to dig up the brand name from memory when standing in front of a store shelf. In general, execution positioning is most effective when it is linked to a concrete and abstract characteristic of the brand, that is, in combination with one of the other three positioning strategies. Conversely, each of the other three positioning strategies can be more effective when there is a familiar advertising characteristic. A good example of this is the cowboy of Marlboro.

Conclusions A successful brand is a brand that is familiar and for which the target group has strong, relevant, and unique associations. Those associations are preferably both concrete (in a broad sense, this also includes service aspects) and abstract; the entire means-end chain (or customer value hierarchy) is used. Consistent use of an advertising characteristic increases awareness in that regard. Different brand levels may be used in positioning. The positioning of subdivisions of brands (varieties) often is concrete. In contrast, the positioning of corporate brands (divisions or group level) often is abstract.

Positioning Statement If a brand positioning has been chosen, the entire package may be summarized in a positioning statement: within the category ____ brand A will be better for target group ____ than competitor B for goal ____ (usage goal) because it ____ (advantage, benefit). This is demonstrated through ____ (characteristic) and leads to the brand personality ____ (final value).

The brand's positioning is the basis for the brand elements and the marketing mix. We will now deal with the brand elements brand name and logo and design. These elements are the intellectual property of a company and can be registered and protected.

10.3.3 Developing a Brand Name

"The most important marketing decision you can make is what name you give to your product," according to Trout and Rivkin.[19] "The most important" might be an overstatement, but it is definitely important and underappreciated. In many situations, the brand name is already determined. But sometimes, as in the case of introductions, there is a new brand name to be chosen. Mergers and takeovers entail name changes, and so the question of what name or names should be used arises here. Despite its vast importance, the choice of a name is often poorly thought out in practice. Two dangers in choosing the "wrong" name are as follows:

1. It is difficult to link the desired associations with the name.
2. The name turns out to be legally invalid.

Associations and the Name

The brand name is the main bearer of identity. In fact, the same thing applies to people: A person's name gives you a good idea of his or her character. This character (brand personality) is typically learned along with the name over the course of time. One could say that a name does not have a "charge" at birth; the charge develops over time. One could also say that each association must be learned for each name; this is partly true. Names may also have meaning built into them. Similarly, it is true for people that a name such as Carol, for instance, has different associations than does a name such as Elizabeth. These are also learned associations that have to do with a parent. This is precisely the case for brands. The amount of effort required to attach certain associations to a brand name depends on the type of name. One can distinguish between the following types of brand names:

1. Functional names
2. Meaning names
3. Abstract names
4. Abbreviations or numbers

Functional Names   Examples of functional names are the University of Groningen, the *Journal of Marketing,* the *Northern Gazette,* and BBC 2. It is possible to link a distinctive character to the name in this category. Functional distinctions are not a big problem, but emotional characteristics ("higher brand values") are more difficult. A special category of functional names includes questions, sentences, and specific promotions such as www.iwantacheaperloan.us.

Meaning Names   Examples of meaning names are Apple, Jaguar, and Diesel. The advantage of this type of name is that it has a meaning immediately. However, this can also be considered a disadvantage because it may be more difficult to give it a different association later. Apple has shown that this can be done: No one thinks about an apple when he or she thinks of the brand even though the name and the logo are still literally an apple.

Abstract Names   Examples of abstract names are Heineken, Achmea, Ola, and Sony. This is the most common category. This type is also the best suited for taking on its own charge. Initially, the names do not mean anything (they are new words), but after a while the target group begins to associate the name with something.

Abbreviations or Numbers   Examples are KLM, HP, TNT, and 501. These names work similarly to the way functional names work: It is difficult to create emotional distinctiveness. Another disadvantage is confusion: Abbreviations are easily confused with each other, for example, KPN (telecom) and the paper manufacturer KNP. Companies considering a name that is longer than two words must take into account the fact that people will abbreviate it even though the company does not. This may be a reason to keep the name short.

The choice of a name type is also dependent on the "brand strategy": which levels are used. Variations are almost always functional or designated with an abbreviation or number and often are abstract (Peugeot 306, Canon Powershot G3).

CASE 10-8 *More Meaning in Brand Names*	Every company wants a name that stands out from the crowd, a catchy handle that will remain fresh and memorable over time. Yet such names are hard to find, especially because of naming trends. Although the giddy 1990s were all about quirky names (Yahoo, Google, Fogdog) or trademark-proof monikers concocted from scratch (Novartis, Aventis, Lycos), tastes have shifted amid the uncertainties of the new millennium. Today's style is to build corporate identity around words that have real meaning. The new names are all about purity, clarity, and organicism. For example, the company Rivet helps companies tag financial data, and so the name functions as an effective metaphor for what the firm actually does. Similarly, Silk (soy milk), Method (home products), Blackboard (school software), and Smartwater (beverages) are new names that are simple and make intuitive sense. There's a trend toward meaning in words. When it comes down to evocative words versus straightforward names, straightforward will win in testing every time.

Source: Frankel, Alex, "The New Science of Naming," *Business 2.0,* December 2004, p. 53–55.

The same thing applies to coming up with a brand name for developing an advertising campaign: First, a briefing must be drafted with the following major points: the vision on the environment, the product, the target group, and the brand positioning. If these points need clarification, it is not yet time to be considering a name. The reason for this is that a carefully considered name may come with certain built-in associations. These associations may come from the sound, length, and other phonetic properties (how it sounds, e.g., Italian). However, spontaneous associations can also be achieved by choosing an abstract name that still has a link with another meaning. In current practice, it is quite common to choose a name in between an abstract and a meaning name, for example, CompliMints (see also Case 10-8).

There are three ways to come up with a new name:

- *Invent it yourself.* This is the quickest and least expensive method but typically produces the worst names. The problem is that managers often cannot step outside themselves and may have trouble imagining how the name will go over with the customer.

- *Hold a competition among personnel and/or customers.* The biggest advantage here is that a foundation is created for the name or name change. Personnel and customers must learn to accept and spread the name, and so it is wise not to surprise them with it. The disadvantage is that only obvious, bad names come out of the box. You can hold a contest, but it should be explicitly stated that it is not guaranteed that one of those names will be used; they will be submitted to a professional agency for assessment, for instance.

- *Use a brand name agency.* There are a few agencies that specialize in this service. Enlisting the services of an agency is typically the preferable course of action, possibly in combination with a contest.

CASE 10-9 *Changing the Name*	Companies that bear the name "tsunami" are considering change. One example is a small software company called Tsunami Research, which is seeking a replacement name. The name is now linked with the deaths of thousands, and this association may have possible long-term effects. The company now faces the high costs of rebranding itself. **Source:** Bounds, Gwendolyn, "Brands Bearing Name 'Tsunami' Ponder Change," *Wall Street Journal,* Eastern Edition. January 18, 2005, p. B1–B3.

Working Methodology of a Brand Name Agency   A brand name agency usually takes the following steps:

1. Request a briefing from the client. There must be complete clarity with respect to various strategic decisions in addition to brand levels and use in other countries.

2. Come up with a large number (approximately 50) of names. These names are submitted to the client. The agency learns from the feedback what appeals to the client and what does not. This may also include names from a contest.

3. Submission of a smaller quantity, including old and new names. Using the same process, an attempt is made to narrow the list to three names.

4. Test the three names with the target group. This is not necessary, but it is recommended if quick acceptance is important to the manager.

5. Conduct a connotation and legal study of the three names. A *connotation study* attempts to determine whether a name creates undesired associations in another country. For instance, a detergent was introduced to the market in Spain that denoted the Spanish word for a whore. A *legal study* attempts to determine whether the names are already in use elsewhere (and are registered) and, for instance, whether the corresponding Web site is still available. For domain names, registration is a common problem. Sometimes large

companies have to fight in court for their domain names. For example, Kraft won a legal battle about the domain name milka.fr from the French couturier Milka Budimir and the Chinese Olympic Committee won a battle from a smart person who registered beijng2008.org.[20]

6. Selection of the name by the client.

10.3.4 Design and Logo

Because the design and logo are strongly related to brand positioning, we discuss these elements not under the marketing instrument product in Chapter 11 but in this chapter on marketing strategy. *Design* relates to the design of all external appearance forms of the brand: the *logo* (form, color, etc.), brand signs, and packaging. Since these product elements are directly linked to the brand, they are important carriers of the brand personality. A logo should be an extension of the brand personality. A good example is the logo of the Rabobank: a person in the middle of a circle who portrays the positioning of the Rabobank: "you as customer have a central place and we as bank are located in the middle of society." However, in the case of more abstract logos a manager should be aware of the spontaneous associations a logo has. In practice, logos are often dealt with too lightly. Often it is said that a certain logo "is outdated" or "not appealing enough" and that the "house style" therefore should be modified. Then a new logo is designed, and if the management likes the new logo, a new house style is born. However, this approach ignores the function of the logo as the carrier of the brand personality. A new logo can be designed only after a discussion has taken place about the brand personality: What does the brand or company want to represent? A similar issue applies to brand signs.

CASE 10-10 *The Beckham Logo*	David Beckham has agreed to extend his relationship with the sportswear giant Adidas for another four years. So what clinched the deal? What do you give the man who has everything? His own logo, of course, capturing Becks as he runs up to take one of his famous free kicks with his arm outstretched. The design is the epitome of what great logos are all about. It's simple, powerful, and instantly recognizable. Its success is in the moment that it captures, using just a few strokes. To take a human being and turn him into an unmistakable icon is a great achievement. In the same way that in the late 1980s and early 1990s Michael Jordan's Jumpman logo and number 23 jersey became synonymous with the Nike brand, Adidas hopes the Beckham logo will have as powerful an effect.

Source: Piggy Lines, "Design Choice/Adidas Beckham Logo," *Marketing (UK)*, March 18, 2004, p. 10.

Brand signs are symbols, colors, spelling, and the like, that are "own" to the brand, for example, the special way in which the name Coca-Cola is written or the color "canary yellow" associated with Post-It from 3M. Brand signs are, just like logos, strongly connected to the brand personality. For example, colors have their own radiation: Blue is perceived as mild, red as lively and fierce. Colors are important for the brand and for varieties. For example, colors play an important role in the recognition of coffee varieties (red brand, gold brand, silver brand, etc.). Packaging obviously plays a functional role but also has strongly communicative one. The packaging design therefore has a relationship with the brand and subbrands.

Registration and Legal Considerations

From a legal perspective, virtually all visible distinguishing characteristics of brands (names, logos, symbols, colors, and packaging forms) are considered "brands" on their own and may be registered as such within the framework of trademark law. Because of the strong associative role of brand names and signs, it is indeed important for companies to register them. Without registration a competitor can easily misuse the brand signs of another company. For registration, the registration office [in Europe, the Office of Harmonization for the Internal Market (OHIM)] strongly looks at the *distinctive power* of a brand sign. For example, the color combination yellow-blue of the Swedish Ikea was judged to have too little distinctive power to be registered as a "brand." The same holds for the names "Super Champion" for computer games and "Fitline" for clothes. Philips successfully registered the form and varieties of this form of its coffee machine Senseo.[21]

Some long-existing brand names are so successful that people start to use them as *category names* (for example, Luxaflex, aspirin, spa). A risk of using a brand name as category name is that it loses its distinctive power and cannot be legally protected.

10.4 MANAGING BRAND VALUES

Brand values have to be managed:

- Over time (consistency and crisis management).
- Over products and varieties (extensions).
- Over countries.

We discuss these issues in Section 10.4.1 through Section 10.4.3 We then conclude this chapter with a short review of brand "mismanagement" (Section 10.4.4) and a short discussion of events (Section 10.4.5).

10.4.1 Brand Values over Time

Obtaining strong brand associations with the target group takes time. Awareness and consistency have a strengthening effect in this area. Consistency plays a role on two levels:

1. At the level of the chosen *positioning*.
2. At the level of *execution* of the communication.

At the first level, consistency is essential. A chosen positioning should be maintained for a long time (consistent over time) and should be carried out in all communication expressions (consistency among communication instruments: *integrated communication*). Sudden changes in positioning lead to confusion and a lack of credibility. Maintaining positioning for a long time seems incompatible with the desire for regular *innovation* of brands, but this does not have to be the case. Sharpening and shifts in emphasis are always possible as long as the core message (proposition) is not changed too much (see Case 10-11).

CASE 10-11 *Positioning of CNN*	Upon its launch in 1981, CNN positioned itself to consumers and cable affiliates through a succinct, benefit-oriented tagline that summarized the essence of the programming. "Around the World in 30 Minutes" strategically and creatively positioned the network's programming format. Committed to its new positioning, CNN's *Headline News* infused the tagline into all marketing efforts for many years, including consumer print and cross-channel cable advertising. Through a combination of consumer communication and brand extensions within the cable industry, *Headline News's* tagline made a lasting impression in the minds of consumers and industry professionals alike. The longevity of "Around the World in 30 Minutes" helped solidify a space as one of cable marketing's most durable campaigns. The essence of this tagline has been the underpinning of *Headline News* for almost 20 years. "Around the World in 30 Minutes" told viewers that *Headline News* would deliver comprehensive, fast-paced news suited to their busy lives.

Source: "CNN Headline News' 'Around the World in 30 Minutes,'" *Cablevision,* July 23, 2001, p. 72.

At the level of execution, consistency has advantages and disadvantages. One advantage at this level is awareness: A constant advertising characteristic, preferably linked to a brand value, increases awareness. A disadvantage of consistency in execution is a lessening of attention. It is obvious that new, original advertising grabs more attention than does well-known advertising. Research[22] has shown that regular changes in execution lead to positive effects on market share. The big danger of innovative communication is that it may distract from the brand. The impression is that among all commercials, for more than 50 percent no brand name or the wrong name is remembered. Without a link to the brand, communication is by definition not effective. The recommendation therefore is that changes in execution may be effective as long as a clear and natural *link with the brand* is made.

Another aspect of managing brands over time is dealing with a *crisis*. True stories include beer bottles that were discovered to contain pieces of glass, cat food that killed cats, spinach with poison, and an insurance company that distributed sex films instead of informational films. Failing to respond adequately to such a crisis is very damaging to trust in a brand and in a company and therefore is damaging to brand equity (and brand value).

CASE 10-12 *Crisis Handling by Tylenol*	It was a crime that forever changed the way we buy over-the-counter medications. In 1982 seven people in the Chicago area died after taking Tylenol capsules that had been randomly laced with cyanide. No one was ever charged with the murders. However, James Lewis was released from prison in 1995 after serving 13 years of a 20-year sentence for trying to extort $1 million from Johnson & Johnson, Tylenol's parent company. About a month after the deaths, Lewis wrote Johnson & Johnson demanding money or he'd strike again. As a result of the case, regulations were adopted that require tamper-resistant packaging. The crime cost Tylenol's makers $100 million for the recall of 31 million capsules. Johnson & Johnson decided to stop all Tylenol advertising until several weeks after the seven deaths. In December 1982 the company aired "You can trust us" commercials that received high visibility. Tylenol finished third in top-of-mind awareness of all advertising behind Coca-Cola and Burger King that month.

Source: Howard, Lucy, and Carla Koehl, "Release in the Tylenol Case," *Newsweek,* October 23, 1995; "'Trust Us' Tylenol Ads Working," *Advertising Age,* December 6, 1999, p. 77.

The characteristics of successful crisis management are *speed, openness, and responsibility*. The longer a company waits with communication, the more speculation occurs, and the more vague a company is and/or the more it places the blame on others, the more suspect it becomes. Figure 10-12 gives several tangible guidelines for good crisis management.[23] The goal of crisis management is to use open communication to build a foundation for restoration of trust in the brand and the company after the crisis. A threat such as a crisis, if adequately handled, may even strengthen the brand (see Case 10-12).

10.4.2 Managing of Brands over Products

Many companies have a tendency to "hang" new products under existing brands (extensions). In doing this, they hope to address other customer needs and to have the success of the brand rub off on the new product. There are two types of extensions:

1. *Category extensions.* Under an existing brand name ("parent brand"), a company brings new products onto the market outside the category of the parent brand; for example, a manufacturer of watches brings cars onto the market.
2. *Line extensions.* These are assortment expansions under an existing brand within the same category as the parent or flagship brand; this involves the introduction of varieties (flavors, forms, package sizes, etc.).

FIGURE 10-12
Guidelines for Crisis
Management

Crisis preparation

- Have a team of experts (lawyers, doctors, etc.) available.
- Prepare a crisis plan (including making a single person responsible for contact with the media).

Crisis management

- As fast as possible (after the first relevant information has arrived) present a statement externally (press, retail, competitors, etc.) but also internally (staff). The information supply should be under the company's control as much as possible.
- Open communication and no shifting the blame to someone else.
- If the crisis is serious, enact a "recall" (calling back products).
- Stop all current marketing communications of the brand.
- Be accessible for complaints with, for example, a free 800 number and via e-mail and the Internet.
- If applicable, pay compensation to victims.
- Have a "renewed" product available as soon as possible.

The major type of new product introductions is extensions, of which line extensions constitute the majority.

Ries and Trout argue that extensions are fundamentally objectionable since broadening a brand may confuse consumers and weaken a brand's image.[24] This is indeed a serious risk of (category) extensions, but we do not want to take the argument that far. Much research has been performed on the success of extensions that has shown that under certain conditions, extensions can indeed be successful. An important finding is that in the eyes of the target group, the extension should *fit* with the parent brand: There should be a logical fit between the extension and the brand.[25] For example, the extension BIC perfume in addition to BIC pens turned out not to be a success; the extension 7-Up Ice Cola (a clear cola from 7-Up) was not successful for the same reason. Research, however, shows that the perceived fit between a parent brand and an extension can be improved by *communication*.[26]

There is a relationship between the positioning strategy and the possibility for extensions. Brands with *informational positioning* are more strongly linked to the product than are brands with transformational positioning and have *less room for extensions*. In practice there is the temptation to bring many extensions onto the market, yet from the perspective of maintaining the brand image (and also for the "parent brand"), this often is not wise.

Managers considering brand extensions should thus ask the right questions[27]:

1. How is the parent brand *currently positioned*?
2. Will consumers understand the *logic* for the extension? Which elements of the positioning are extended?
3. Is the positioning element that is extended *relevant* in the new extension category?
4. If there is no logical fit, can *communication* help lead consumers to such an understanding?
5. What is the *impact* of the extension on the parent and other existing extensions?

To answer these questions, appropriate market research and continuous monitoring of effects (tracking) are necessary (see Chapter 4). If this is done and if companies introduce extensions step by step and facilitate perceptions of fit, extension strategies can be very profitable (Figure 10-13).

FIGURE 10-13
Guidelines for Brand Extensions

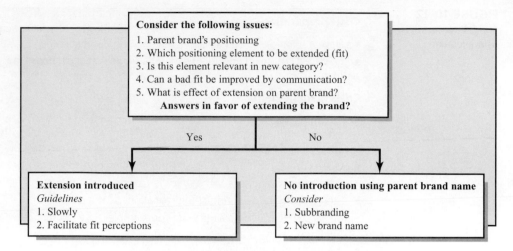

If research indicates that an extension is too risky, a manager might consider choosing another brand portfolio strategy: introducing the new product by using a new brand name or applying subbranding.

10.4.3 Managing of Brands over Countries

The *internationalization* of business is occurring very quickly. Retail businesses, producers, and service providers are developing into multinationals. Through mergers and acquisitions, companies seek reinforcement from each other, and local brands (brands limited to a single country) increasingly are becoming part of international groups that subsequently use those brands for a global brand strategy. Consumers are also becoming increasingly international, both physically (traveling) and from the home base (television, Internet).

In light of these developments, the question is how far an international brand should go in the standardization of the marketing communication. An advantage of having the same communication in all countries is efficiency and consistency. A disadvantage is that differences between countries are not taken into account. Four international advertising strategies can be distinguished[28]:

1. *Global strategy*. This strategy uses the same positioning, the same creative concept ("campaign idea"), and the same execution in each country. This strategy is used by, for example, Coca-Cola, Marlboro, Levi's and Carlsberg beer ('probably the best beer in the world').

2. *Adaptation strategy*. This involves adapting only the execution, usually in the form of a translation (dubbed or produced again). This strategy is used by, for example, Philips and KLM. This strategy requires a high degree of coordination between company divisions and communication consulting firms in the various countries. This may be difficult because the local companies and agencies usually prefer more autonomy since they know the local market better.

3. *Differentiation strategy*. With this strategy, the central message of the campaign (the proposition) already has been determined but the implementation of the communication is delegated to the countries. The advantage of locally imagined creative concepts is that they take into account the cultural differences between countries. McDonald's, Pepsi Cola, and all brands of Procter & Gamble use this strategy.

4. *Local strategy*. In this strategy, nothing is standardized, but a positioning, a concept, and execution are chosen for each country: "Think globally, act locally." Many Japanese brands use this strategy. Also, brands such as Heineken appear to have chosen this strategy: In the United States this brand has a very different positioning (top-quality import beer) than it does in the Netherlands (beer for everyone).

The choice about the degree of standardization depends on issues that include the nature of the products and the differences in preferences, purchasing behavior, and values between countries. A balance must be found between the necessity of a consistent international brand policy and the differences in customer values between countries.

10.4.4 Pitfalls in Brand Management

We conclude this section by discussing a number of pitfalls in brand management (Figure 10-14). The "mortal sins in brand management" mentioned in this figure are mostly related to *short-term thinking* in practice. Managers are often held accountable for financial annual returns, and sales promotion actions (which may undermine the brand personality) can be used to achieve high sales in the short term.

Another natural inclination of brand managers (and communication consultancy firms) is to do "*something new,*" such as a new campaign (with prizes that may be won) and new introductions. These practices are often in conflict with the long-term thinking that is required for brand management. Managers should be held more accountable for the components of brand equity than for money.

10.4.5 Experience Branding

The previous sections demonstrated that brands need to make a clear choice of what they represent: What is the central brand value? To translate those values into more concrete meanings for the customers, a company may choose to make customers more involved with the brand by providing them with *experiences*. In this process, the *involvement* of the customer with the brand is in effect actively strengthened. In this context, Pine[29] indicates that after the age of the products and subsequently the age of providing services, the age of the experience economy has arrived. According to Pine, companies should actively involve the customer with the brand by creating experiences. Experience branding may be implemented through various elements of the marketing mix and various media. The Internet can also play an important role here. Examples include inviting people to compose their products on their own via the Internet, letting people play games on the Internet, providing free advice and answering questions via telephone or the Internet, sponsoring events, organizing an event (see Case 10-13), offering customers a cup of coffee in the shop (retail), and placing a jumping tent in front of the children's clothing shop. The desired experience and

FIGURE 10-14
Brand
Mismanagement

Source: Achenbaum, A. A.
(1992), *"The Mismanagement
of Brand Equity,"* ARF
Fifth Annual Advertising
and Promotion Wokshop,
February 1, 1992, ARF.

1. Too many products and extensions
2. Too many price reductions
3. Financial demands of retailers
4. Weak brand organization, for example, inexperienced or insufficiently supported management
5. Short-term orientation
6. Too much emphasis on advertising activity and too much partiality for television advertising
7. Marketing planning that is oriented too much to the past
8. Unreliable market research

the intensity of the experience along with the choice of the marketing mix elements and the media depend on the brand value and the type of customer. Therefore, to do this well, clear choices have to be made. In practice this is often a problem because managers and directors usually do not want to choose. Yet customers need familiarity before they start to feel involved with something.

CASE 10-13 *Experience Branding at Heineken*	The brand managers at Heineken seem to have strange case of a split personality. On the one hand, Heineken does not know which brand identity it wants to choose and four advertising agencies are asked to provide ideas; on the other hand, the experience marketing surrounding this brand appeared to receive a new impulse with the opening of the Heineken Music Hall on the Arena Boulevard in Amsterdam in March 2001. But according to Karen Williams of Heineken, the hall is not intended primarily for organizing the company's own events: "We wanted to connect our name with the music hall since Heineken does a lot in music and this was a good opportunity to expand that sponsoring." Therefore, Heineken sees the music hall mostly as a sponsoring object and so appears unable in either its normal branding or its experience marketing to make clear choices. Sjaak Vink, director of the advertising consulting agency HetStormt, said: "My advice would be to make a choice who you want to be and then be consistent in your communication." **Source:** *Nieuws Tribune,* January 25, 2001, and February 8, 2001.

Summary

Marketing objectives usually are expressed in terms of sales or market share. The choice of a target group and brand positioning forms the core of the marketing strategy. Target groups may be chosen after research has been performed into which target group is the most attractive, based on the segmentation research described in Chapter 4. It should also be determined whether the target group will be approached as a single entity or one on one. In the latter case, loyalty programs may be used to strengthen the bond. A brand positioning must be chosen for the identified target group. In light of the enormous amount of commercial signals consumers are bombarded with, this phase is crucial. Companies should decide at which brand level and to what extent they want to profile themselves: corporate level, umbrella brand, individual brand or variety, or a combination. Subsequently, a choice must be made at which level (informational or transformational) changes in positioning may be required. In that case, an alternative brand positioning must be formulated: In this regard various classifications of values may be used, for example, a simple classification based on the marketing mix or on the image level based on brand personalities. Finally, a focused positioning is chosen, for which internal feasibility and consistency over time are preconditions. The central brand value is the basis for choosing the brand name, design, logo, and other brand elements. These elements should have a natural link with the brand meaning and should have enough distinctive power to be registered. Brand values should be managed over time (consistency and open crisis communication), products (extensions should fit with the parent brand), and countries (think globally, act locally). If the basic image of the brand has been determined, decisions need to be made about the extent to which experience marketing will be used.

Notes

1. Dowling, G. R., and M. Uncles (1997), "Do Customer Loyalty Programs Really Work?" *Sloan Management Review* 38:71–82.

2. Keller, K. L. (2003), *Strategic Brand Management: Building, Measuring and Managing Brand Equity,* 2nd ed., Upper Saddle River, NJ: Prentice-Hall.

3. Ries, A., and J. Trout (1981), *Positioning: The Battle for Your Mind,* New York: McGraw-Hill; Kapferer, J. N. (1998), *Strategic Brand Management: Creating and Sustaining Brand Equity*

Long Term, 2nd ed., London: Kogan Page; Aaker, D. A. (1991), *Managing Brand Equity: Capitalizing on the Value of a Brand Name,* New York: Free Press; Aaker, D. A. (1995), *Building Strong Brands,* New York: Free Press. More recently, the Kellogg School of Management devoted a book to branding: Tybout, A. M., and T. Calkins, eds. (2005), *Kellog on Branding,* Hoboken, NJ: Wiley.

4. Rust, R., and V. Zeithaml (2000) *Driving Customer Equity: How Lifetime Customer Value Is Reshaping Corporate Strategy,* New York, Free Press.

5. Keller, K. L. (1993), "Conceptualizing, Measuring and Managing Customer-Based Brand Equity," *Journal of Marketing* 57:1–22; Keller (2003).

6. Ries and Trout (1981).

7. Keller (2003).

8. De Chernatony, L., and S. Knox (1990), "How an Appreciation of Consumer Behaviour Can Help in Product Testing," *Journal of Market Research Society* 33(3):333.

9. Simonin, B. L., and J. A. Ruth (1998), "Is a Company Known by the Company It Keeps? Assessing the Spillover Effects of Brands Alliances on Consumer Brand Attitudes," *Journal of Marketing Research* 35(1):30–42.

10. In regard to measuring financial brand value, refer to Keller (2003), Chapter 9.

11. Yoo, B., N. Donthu, and S. Lee (2000), "An Examination of Selected Marketing Mix Elements and Brand Equity," *Journal of the Academy of Marketing Science* 28(2):195–211.

12. Aaker (1991, 1995).

13. Rokeach, M. (1973) *The Nature of Human Values.* New York: Free Press; see also The Rokeach Value Survey. In: Chapter 3, of O. Bearden, R. G. Netemeyer, eds. (1999), *Handbook of Marketing Scales: Multi-Item Measures for Marketing and Consumer Behavior Research,* Tousand Oaks, CA: Sage, 2nd edition, p. 121.

14. Kotler Ph, and K. L. Keller (2005), *Marketing Management,* 12th ed., Upper Saddle River, NJPearson, Prentice-Hall, p. 318ff. In this latest edition price is not mentioned as differentiation variable.

15. Aaker, J. (1997), "Dimensions of Measuring Brand Personality," *Journal of Marketing Research* 34:347–356.

16. The Aaker framework has been criticized in Austin, J. R., J. A. Siguaw, and A. S. Mattila (2003), "A Re-Examination of the Generalizability of the Aaker Brand Personality Measurement Framework," *Journal of Strategic Marketing* 11:77–92; Azoulay, A., and J. N. Kapferer (2003), "Do Brand Personality Scales Really Measure Brand Personality?" *Brand Management* 11:143–155.

17. Ries and Trout (1981).

18. Carpenter, G. S., R. Glazer, and K. Nakamoto (1994), "Meaningful Brands from Meaningless Differentiation: The Dependence on Irrelevant Attributes," *Journal of Marketing Research* 31:339–350.

19. Trout, J., and S. Rivkin (1996), *The New Positioning,* New York: McGraw-Hill.

20. Shield Mark quarterly newsletter, December 2005 (Shield Mark is an international consultancy office for brand protection issues).

21. Shield Mark, December 2005.

22. Lodish, L. M., M. M. Abraham, J. Livelsberger, B. Lubetkin, B. Richardson, and M. E. Stevens (1995), "How T.V. Advertising Works: A Meta-Analysis of 389 Real World Split Cable T.V. Advertising Experiments," *Journal of Marketing Research* 32:125–139

23. For an extensive discussion, refer to Seymour, M., and S. Moore (2000), *Effective Crisis Management,* Trowbridge, UK: Cromwell Press.

24. Ries and Trout (1981).

25. Aaker, D. A., and K. L. Keller (1990), "Consumer Evaluations of Brand Extensions," *Journal of Marketing* 54:27–41; Reddy, S. K., S. L. Holak, and S. Bhat (1994), "To Extend or Not to Extend: Success Determinants of Line Extensions," *Journal of Marketing Research* 31:243–262;

Kirmani, A., S. Sood, and S. Bridges (1999), "The Ownership Effect in Consumer Responses to Brand Line Stretches," *Journal of Marketing Research* 63(1):88–101

26. Lane, V. R. (2000), "The Impact of Ad Repetition and Ad Content on Consumer Perceptions of Incongruent Extensions," *Journal of Marketing* 64:80–91.

27. These questions and recommendations are based partly on Braig, B. M., and A. M. Tybout, "Brand Extensions." In: *Kellogg on Branding,* A. M. Tybout and T. Calkins, eds., NJ: Wiley, Chapter 5.

28. Floor, K., and F. van Raaij (2002), *Marketing-Communicatiestrategie* (Marketing communication strategy), Groningen, Netherlands: Wolters Noordhoff.

29. Pine, B. J. (1999), *The Experience Economy: Work Is Theatre and Every Business a Stage,* Boston: Harvard Business School Press.

Part **Four**

Implementation

11. Objectives and Strategies for Marketing Instruments
12. Organization and Implementation of Marketing

After the discussion of the situation analysis in Part 2, corporate and marketing objectives and strategies were reviewed in Part 3. These decisions are strategic in nature and in principle are related to a time frame longer than a single year. Chapter 10 stated explicitly that brand decisions require a long-term vision. Part 4 will focus on the implementation of strategic decisions. We distinguish two phases in the implementation: the elaboration of strategies into tactical marketing decisions and then their execution. The elaboration of strategies in marketing tactics is related to the use of the four P's: product, price, place, and promotion. This is the subject of Chapter 11. Chapter 12 discusses guidelines for execution and focuses on aspects of the organization of marketing, personnel management, and practical planning tips.

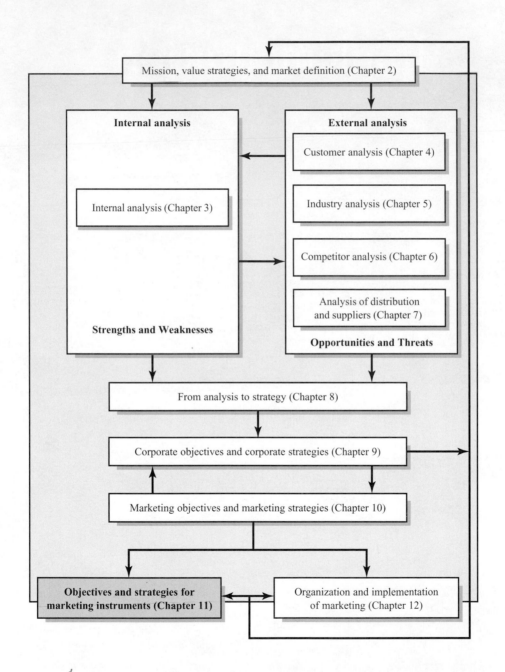

Chapter **Eleven**

Objectives and Strategies for Marketing Instruments

[handwritten: Relationship between Strategy + 4 Ps]

Key Points in This Chapter

- See the relationships between a choosen value strategy, the marketing strategy, and decisions about the marketing instruments, product, price, channels, and communication.
- Know how to formulate objectives for marketing instruments.
- Know which kind of decisions have to be made with each marketing instrument.
- Know the steps in the communication planning process.
- Be able to apply the main guidelines in communication: customer, choose, creative, and check.

INTRODUCTION

Chapter 10 provided an answer to the question: How are we going to compete with the brand? We paid attention to choosing the target audience and the brand positioning on the basis of the value strategy and the competitive advantage the company pursues. The brand elements (name and logo) also were dealt with. The marketing strategy provides the direction for the marketing mix. If a manufacturer of dog food has decided to focus on high-quality food (*product leadership*), the four elements of the marketing mix could be used as follows:

1. *Product.* Goal: quality product. Strategy: quality food in an exclusive and smaller package with a classy name.
2. *Price.* Goal: price perception: high price in relation to regular dog food. Strategy: price setting based on the market: higher price than regular dog food.
3. *Channels.* Goal: within half a year a nonweighted distribution spread of 95 percent in pet specialty stores and 70 percent in other retail businesses. Strategy: high margin for retailers.
4. *Communication.* Advertising goal: within one year an assisted name awareness of 90 percent among people with a dog. Strategy: Television advertising with the message "If you

FIGURE 11-1
From Vision to the Four P's

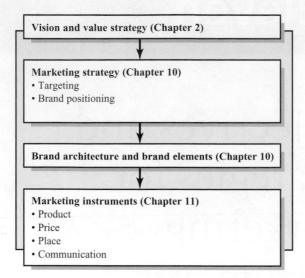

truly love your dog, you give it _____." In addition, advertising in women's magazines. Action goal: generate 40 percent "trial" within half a year. Strategy: an introductory discount of $1.

Figure 11-1 shows the hierarchy of decisions within a company. In this chapter we pay attention to the use of the marketing mix. In the framework of this book, the review of the four P's has been limited to a brief overview.[1] First, we discuss the marketing mix objectives in general (Section 11.1). Next, in Sections 11.2 through 11.5, we discuss all possible decisions that need to be made for each of the four elements of the marketing mix. In light of the important role of communication in building brand and customer loyalty, Section 11.5, which reviews marketing communication, contains the most extensive discussion and has been set up as much as possible in accordance with prevailing marketing practice. Finally, in Section 11.6 we discuss the relationship between the four P's and the Internet and also pay attention to the choice of the value strategy (Chapter 2), the marketing strategy (Chapter 10), and decisions about the marketing mix elements.

For each element of the marketing mix two types of decisions have to be made:

1. Objectives.
2. Tactics (operational decisions): decisions for the short term (one year or less).

The Boss of Boss

In 1923 the company Hugo Boss was founded by the German Hugo Boss. The company occupied itself mainly with the production of overalls. However, through time that changed drastically. Today Hugo Boss is known primarily as a lifestyle brand.

Hugo Boss is listed on the German stock exchange. Since 1991 shares of the company have been mostly in the hands of the Italian textile group Marzotto. In 1999 the company sold around 750 million euros worth of clothing. More than 60 percent of sales are now made outside Germany.

The brands Hugo, Boss, and Baldessarini were brought to the market in 1993. The company switched in this way from one brand, Boss, to three brands. Hugo Boss is the umbrella brand that comes up with, for example, art sponsoring.

In the terminology of Hugo Boss (citing from the corporate profile of Hugo Boss):

The HUGO BOSS Group

HUGO BOSS is fashion. HUGO BOSS is lifestyle. HUGO BOSS is success. Three brands make HUGO BOSS one of the world's leading fashion groups: BOSS, HUGO and BALDESSARINI.

BOSS

BOSS is successful. International. Dynamic. Modern. BOSS is cosmopolitan. A lifestyle merging business and sports. For men and, starting this year, for women worldwide.

HUGO

HUGO is trend. HUGO is young. An unconventional lifestyle for the upbeat scene. HUGO Man and Woman—different and avantgarde.

BALDESSARINI

Sophisticated luxury. Elegant exclusivity. BALDESSARINI reflects the life and style of St. Moritz, Portofino and Monaco. The finest quality for discerning dressers.

Strategy

Our brands form our Group, and our Group forms the umbrella for our brands. HUGO BOSS implements stringent design and quality standards to produce superior products that deliver value for money. And HUGO BOSS is growing on a global scale. With brands for men and women.

Fashion and Brand Image: The Collections

Fashion and brand image are synonymous at HUGO BOSS: our brand and fashion positionings are identical. All the brand collections adhere to a lifestyle philosophy: in addition to the core range of tailored clothing, sportswear and accessories, HUGO BOSS also offers non-textile products such as eyewear, fragrances, watches, shoes and leather goods. The ever-present brand signature is distinctive in each of the three collections.

Boss is for the businessman. Hugo is for the young, more fashionable man. Peter Littmann, the boss of Boss, once translated this as "not the type of man a mother would like as a son-in-law." Baldessarini is for the elite: expensive, Italian, and quite snobby.

"Hugo Boss grew in the yuppie years," says Littmann, "because it was macho and Wall Street. But the zeitgeist changes. We had to do something. We had to go from the uniform brand to the more individual and split-up brands of the 1990s. We had two alternatives there. Either you do everything very precisely, as we Germans prefer. You take your time, perform market research, and make no mistakes. Or you choose the other option. Move quickly, and then only 80 percent turns out well. That 80 percent was good enough for us. The biggest problem was how we could achieve the proper distribution for the three brands. Shopkeepers didn't understand the brand concept that quickly either. They wanted to sell everything and thought that Hugo was a cheap product line extension of Boss.

"We had to decide which brand fitted which shop concept. When you're in a hurry, this doesn't always go right. You take retailers that are not the right ones, because they have the wrong customers."

The products of Hugo Boss are being brought onto the market in two ways. Part of the sales is realized through the "normal" retail business, which receives its products from the wholesaler. Hugo Boss defines its sales outlets based on a careful selection: After all, the sales outlet has to suit the image of Hugo Boss.

With the three brands, however, the "mono-brand stores" came into being. Based on a franchising formula for each of the three brands, specific shops are designed: the Hugo shop, the Boss shop, and the Baldessarini shop. The franchise takers of these shops all have the same shop design. They obtain their products directly from Hugo Boss: There is no longer a wholesaler in between. The whole assortment can be directed better in the "Hugo Boss shops." The shops have the function of a "flagship store": Other retailers can see there how the brands of Hugo Boss are to be positioned in the market. It shows that everywhere where there is a shop being opened, sales of Hugo Boss in the other distribution outlets rise as well. The visibility of the brand and the image are improved.

"It's difficult to distinguish between brands," Littmann continues. "Fashion is difficult to distinguish. You don't want to separate the brands too far apart, because it is after all one Hugo Boss. You segment by choosing your media. Hugo appears in different magazines than does Baldessarini or Boss. When you're a Hugo customer, you probably won't even see the other advertisements." Littmann wants to address target groups he could not have reached with one brand. Moreover, through this approach the main brand also gets new blood, he thinks. It is surprising, though, that nothing has been done with price segmentation. A more expensive brand did emerge, but not a cheaper brand. Littmann did not want people to be attracted to Hugo because of the price. It had to be about lifestyle: Hugo attracts a completely different customer than does Boss or Baldessarini.

Hugo Boss uses a wide variety of instruments for marketing communication. For an impression of these instruments, it is worth citing the corporate profile once more:

Marketing Communications

Marketing communications comprise a central element of the HUGO BOSS strategy. Their goal is to charge the brands with emotional meaning, transforming them into sensual experiences.

Advertising

Advertising campaigns visualize our brands. For every one of the HUGO BOSS brands, a global advertising campaign is developed each season in cooperation with top photographers and renowned art directors. The campaign motifs are used in print and poster advertising. TV commercials promote the HUGO BOSS fragrances.

Sponsoring

Sponsoring emotionalizes our brands. Our Formula One activities have infused the BOSS brand with positive values such as dynamism and success, as have golf and tennis. Cultural sponsoring enriches the HUGO BOSS brands, adding the dimensions of aestheticism and the arts.

Events

Events sensualize our brands. Appealing to all the senses, they conceptualize the brand experience. Fashion shows and Shop openings are ideal vehicles for energizing target groups.

Public Relations

Public Relations communicate our brands. Product PR, film & VIP wardrobing, plus interviews with designers, bring the brands to life.

Trade Marketing

Trade Marketing dramatizes our brands. Visual merchandising, sales workshops and dealer events offer a palpable presentation of the brand lifestyles.

"The question of where the limit of the Hugo Boss brand is, is difficult to answer," according to Littmann. "By now the Boss brand also contains perfumes and shoes. A watch is on its way. But how strong is the brand? What are its competencies? We do have an answer to that. The Hugo Boss brand is strong in everything a man can wear on his body. Therefore, there is no furniture or crockery. Perfume and shoes: yes. I also don't believe in products that, as in the 1980s, get surplus value just by sticking a name on them. They have to be products that are legitimate, that have the right to carry the name Boss. Honestly speaking, we kind of reached the end of the possibilities.

"We have to search now in another direction. For example, we have Boss glasses. Why not also for Hugo? We've started with perfumes at Boss and now also have a Hugo perfume. This we can refine further."

Since 1999 a completely different direction has been added to the assortment: Products for women also have been brought into the market under the Hugo Boss brands.

Source: *Adformatie* October 17, 1996; corporate profile from Hugo Boss, www.hugoboss.com.

Questions

1. a. Which segment strategy does Hugo Boss use? Explain your answer.

   b. Do you think there is a question of oversegmentation? Explain your answer.

2. Which value strategy (Treacy and Wiersema, see chapter 2) do you think is used by Hugo Boss? Explain your answer.

3. With the introduction of the brands Hugo and Baldessarini, was it a matter of a decision on the marketing level or on the instrument level? Explain your answer.

4. a. What are the two sources of brand equity (brand value)?

   b. Describe the brand equity of Hugo Boss.

   c. Describe the brand equity (brand value) of Boss. Do you think the brand value of Boss is different from the brand value of Hugo Boss? Explain your answer.

5. Aaker distinguishes five "basic characteristics" for the personality of a brand (see Section 10.3).

   a. Which five characteristics are they?

   b. Which characteristics are central for Hugo Boss?

   c. From this point of view do you think it is wise to position the brands of Hugo Boss toward women? Explain your answer.

6. Describe the brand policy of Hugo Boss.

   a. In the book four brand levels are distinguished. Name these brand levels for Hugo Boss, based on the information in this case.

   b. Explain why Hugo Boss has chosen this brand policy.

7. In the book category extensions and line extensions are discussed.

   a. Which type of extension is applied to the brand Boss? Explain your answer.

   b. Do you think the policy that is carried out for the brand Boss with respect to extensions is wise? Explain your answer.

8. a. Describe a situation in which clothing is a shopping good, a situation in which clothing is a specialty good, and a situation in which clothing is a convenience good.

   b. In which of these categories would a customer place the clothing of Hugo Boss? What are the consequences for the distribution intensity of Hugo Boss? Explain your answer.

9. In practice, manufacturers often use a combination of push and pull strategies. How are push and/or pull strategies being used by Hugo Boss?

10. How can electronic data interchange be applied in the relationship between Hugo Boss and the Hugo Boss shops?

11. In the book a number of marketing communication instruments are distinguished. Which instruments are, and which ones are not, used by Hugo Boss?

12. Hugo Boss expects a synergy effect between the marketing communication instruments that are being deployed: advertising visualizing, sponsoring emotionalizing, and so on. Do you think there is a question of real synergy and therefore real integration of the instruments used by Hugo Boss? Explain your answer.

13. Communication goals can be connected to brand name awareness, brand associations, and trial purchases.

   a. In which of these three categories do you think the communication goal for the Hugo Boss brands belongs? Explain your answer.

   b. Formulate a measurable communication goal for Boss.

   c. How would you measure whether your goal is being achieved?

14. How could Hugo Boss use the Internet to influence the market?

11.1 OBJECTIVES FOR THE MARKETING MIX

A *goal* (objective) is a *desired effect.* In practice, however, often no objectives are formulated for the marketing mix. A likely reason for this was given earlier in this book: The choice of the marketing strategy determines the marketing mix strategies to a large extent, and this may mean that people consider it less important to formulate separate objectives. Another reason may be that people find it difficult to formulate objectives for certain elements. An objective for an element should meet the requirement that a direct link can be made with the relevant decisions about that element. In other words, a measure should be chosen that can be used to measure the effect. The measure "sales" cannot always be chosen: It is not easy to determine the separate effect of, for example, a product change or an advertising campaign on sales.

An important disadvantage of omitting marketing instrument objectives is that it cannot be determined whether the various instruments have been effective. After all, without a formulated objective, it has not been determined what should be measured (e.g., for advertising, is it memory of the message, brand awareness, knowledge of product characteristics?) and it also has not been determined at what level of a variable effectiveness would occur (is it brand awareness of 50 percent or 80 percent?). This is an important problem, especially for communication. Both in the literature and in practice, a lot of attention is paid to the question of the effectiveness of advertising. For companies, this issue is important for the purpose of making future advertising decisions, and it is also relevant to discussions about the manner in which advertising agencies should be paid.

Therefore, on the level of the marketing mix, formulating objectives in combination with the measurement of results is a logical step in the planning process.

CASE 11-1 *Communication Objectives in Marketing Practice*	Despite being ranked the third most important marketing function (behind direct response and interactive efforts), events often are mismanaged. Just 36 percent of chief marketing officers say events are tightly integrated with other marketing functions. Only 46 percent say they consistently measure event effectiveness against overall marketing goals.
	Source: "Marketing Strategy: S&MM Pulse," *Sales & Marketing Management,* May 2005, p. 12.

To formulate marketing mix objectives, the same four requirements apply that apply to company and marketing objectives: They need to contain a *time frame,* be formulated *quantitatively,* be *ambitious,* and be *realistic.* However, it is difficult to meet all these requirements for some marketing mix elements. We now discuss potential objectives for each of the four elements of the marketing mix; we also review the decisions that have to be made.

11.2 PRODUCT DECISIONS

A product is an item that is offered in a market to satisfy a specific need. A product may be physical (a good such as a car) but also may be a service (a hairdresser), people (politics), places (vacation country), organizations (an employment agency), or an idea ("a good environment starts with you").

11.2.1 Objective

The objective of the instrument product is formulated at the level of individual products. The *product objective* can be defined as follows[2]: "*Product quality:* the degree to which the characteristics of the product connect with the wishes and desires of customers in the target audience." In other words, the objective is the extent to which a product is a solution for the "problems" of customers.

The concept of "quality" in this formulation has a different meaning than it does in daily usage. In daily usage, a high quality means that a product possesses certain positively evaluated characteristics to a high degree (and also typically has a high price); an example would be a Volvo with a high degree of safety, durability, luxury, and so on. However, in the product objective, a high quality may also apply to a product that has certain characteristics only to a limited extent. This is the case if the target audience does not consider those characteristics very important. For example, a Lada may be a very good fit with the wishes of certain buyers (who do not consider safety and luxury to be important but price to be very important) and as such have a high "quality."

The question is whether this objective meets the requirement of being able to quantify it. Although it may not appear easy to quantify the concept of quality as it is defined here, it is possible. For example, a company might indicate in the product objective what percent of the customers in the target audience having a satisfaction score of at least a 6 on a 10-point scale is desired. Such an objective can be formulated for the entire product. The wording of a question in that regard might be: "Could you indicate with a score the extent to which the Lada you bought meets your wishes?" A similar line of questioning may be chosen for individual product characteristics.

Another quantifiable product objective might be in the area of *complaints:* A specific maximum number or percentage of complaints could be formulated as the objective.

FIGURE 11-2
Product Decisions

> *Objective:*
>
> - In terms of "quality"
>
> *Decisions:* Levels:
>
> 1. Product mix decisions (company strategy)
> 2. Product group decisions and brand decisions (marketing strategy)
> 3. Product element decisions
>
>   - Composition of the product and choice of varieties
>   - Design: logo, brand signs
>   - Packaging
>   - Service provision

11.2.2 Decisions

Product decisions are made at various *levels* in the company (Figure 11-2). We now elaborate on the types of decisions mentioned in Figure 11-2.

Product Mix Decisions

Decisions at this level relate to the composition of the product mix (or the assortment) and therefore to the investments in strategic business units (SBUs) and product lines (introduction, growth, maintenance, harvest, elimination). Such decisions are made at the company level and are included in the formulation of the *company strategy* (see Chapter 9).

Product Group Decisions and Brand Decisions

Decisions at this level are related to the composition of the product group, that is, to the introduction, growth, and elimination of brands and/or products. The choice of the number of brands or products within a product group is determined to a large extent by the marketing strategy: the choice of the target audience and the desired positioning. After all, if the company wants to serve several segments, each with its own positioning, it may be do this with different brands or products. Connected to this issue is brand management: the choice of brand names, potential line extensions, and so on. Decisions about the composition of a product line and brand policy therefore correspond to a large degree to the *marketing strategy* and are made at a minimum at the SBU level.

Product Element Decisions

This relates to decisions about *individual* brands or products. Only these decisions may be considered *element decisions* in regard to the product, and they typically are the responsibility of a "product or brand manager." These decisions include the following:

1. The brand elements: name, logo, and design.
2. Product development and product improvements.
3. Packaging.
4. Service level.

Brand Elements: Name, Logo, and Design   These decisions are strongly related to the brand and are described in Chapter 10 (marketing strategy).

Composition of the Product and Product Improvements   This involves questions such as the following: What characteristics should make up the product (functional and symbolic)? To what extent should each characteristic be present? Which varieties should be chosen? This decision therefore involves "technical" product development: the transformation of the product idea into a concrete product. Small product changes (product modifications such as taste alterations) are also included with composition decisions. In addition to decisions about the physical characteristics of a product, decisions about the "added" characteristics are important, including the symbolic characteristics. All these decisions are closely related to the chosen brand positioning and in principle were determined at that stage.

Packaging   The packaging has typically been mostly "technical/functional" in nature: Packaging serves as protection for the product and as such is of essential importance in the logistical trajectory (transport, storage, etc.). However, the increasing importance of positioning and brand policy has led to the process by which a second function of packaging is becoming increasingly important: the *communicative* function. Especially because of the increase in impulse shopping behavior, the external appearance of a product is playing an ever larger role. This applies not only to fast-moving consumer good such as chips and shampoo but also to the packaging of durable consumer goods such as household appliances. As a result of the communicative role, packaging design has a relationship with the brand and subbrands.

CASE 11-2 *Packaging and Colors*	Designers must keep up with color trends. Fashion, home decor, the auto industry, and the entertainment business lead the trends, especially with kids and teens. For example, the *Harry Potter* movies resulted in purple becoming an accepted color and *Shrek* made green popular. **Source:** Parlin, Sandy, "Colors That Motivate," *Beverage Industry*, June 2003, p. 52–54.

Service Provision   Each product may be perceived as a service. In the context of building customer loyalty, it is desirable to bring about higher customer satisfaction through forms of service provision. This involves not just requested service provision such as giving warranties and processing complaints; it also involves unsolicited service provision with the eventual goal of exceeding the expectations of the customer. For example, a detergent brand can provide advice on the Internet about cleaning.

11.3 PRICE DECISIONS

The price is a characteristic of a product (see Figure 11-3). Therefore, the marketing mix element of price cannot be considered separately from the element of product. If the company alters the physical characteristics of the product, this almost automatically will have consequences for the price. There is also a direct relationship with positioning: A quality image often is related to a high price. Conversely, many consumers use price as an indicator of quality: A high price indicates high quality.

11.3.1 Objective

The primary objective of using a price is obviously to generate and preferably maximize revenues. However, in a marketing context this objective is not specific enough. For example,

FIGURE 11-3
Price Decisions

Objective: In terms of "price perception" ***Decisions:*** 1. Price policy 2. Price strategies 3. Determination of the price

a problem is that sales are determined by many other factors. In that case, using the objective of "turnover" or "profit" for the element of price is not useful. After all, it is impossible or hardly possible to determine the impact of only the price on turnover. Turnover and profit measures are therefore important mostly as marketing objectives (see Chapter 9).

A measure that is influenced directly by the price and can be used as *price objective* is *price perception:* What attitude does the company want the target audience to assume about the highness of the price of the product?[3]

There are different ways to measure price perception. One method involves presenting consumers with a series of different prices for a certain product and asking at which prices they start to perceive the product as being cheap or expensive and at which prices they perceive it as being too cheap or too expensive. If one uses this measurement method, the price objective might, for example, be that the company wants to choose a price at which a maximum of 10 percent of the people in the target audience will perceive the product as being "expensive or too expensive." It is possible to calculate such a price by using the line of questioning presented here; the price that consumers considered the most normal can also be calculated, as well as the acceptable price range.

If the company wants to position the product in relation to a specific competitor, that competitor may be named explicitly in the objective and the price perception measure. A price objective then might be that the company wants a certain percentage of the target audience to know that the product is 10 eurocents cheaper than the competing product.

11.3.2 Decisions

The following decisions may be included in the price decisions:

1. Price policy.
2. Price strategies.
3. Determination of the price.

Price policy

Price policy involves the description of *policy rules* in relation to price. The goal is to create a framework of parameters that the various decision makers in a company can use to make price decisions. In the price policy, items such as the following are determined:

- The relation of the price to that of *competitors*.
- Rules about any *reactions* to price changes by competitors.
- The extent to which price *promotions* are used.

Price strategies

Price strategies involve long-term decisions about the price. These strategies concretely involve decisions regarding the following:

- The pricing of products in a *product line* (e.g., the choice of the price difference between types of video cameras of a single brand or between different types of packaging of one laundry detergent).
- Price agreements with *distributors*: recommended retail price, minimum price, and so on.
- *New products:* using a *skimming strategy* or a *penetration strategy.* In *skimming,* the company begins with a high price and then gradually drops that price over time. This strategy serves to recover the development costs quickly and is often used for durable consumer goods such as DVD players and video cameras. With a *penetration* strategy, the company starts with a low price that is increased over time. This strategy has the goal of

quickly achieving a high market share and is often used for nondurable consumer goods, for example, the introduction of a new snack.

- *Existing products:* price increase, price decrease, maintaining the price: Decisions about these issues depend on, among other things, the phase of the product life cycle the product is in.

CASE 11-3 *Pricing in the Insurance Market*	Good news for good drivers: State Farm Mutual Automobile Insurance is rethinking the way it prices policies. The nation's largest auto insurer is converting to the "tiered pricing" model that was adopted in the 1990s by its top competitors, Allstate and Progressive. Sophisticated data-mining techniques enable insurers to be much more precise in assessing the risks of individual drivers. Allstate, for instance, used to have just three main pricing categories: preferred, standard, and nonstandard. Tiered pricing usually translates into lower coverage rates for better drivers. That's one reason State Farm has been losing ground to its competitors as drivers shop around. The company wrote 39.5 million auto insurance policies in 2004, down 200,000 from the year before. That marked a second year of decline for State Farm. Number three Progressive, meanwhile, increased the number of policies it wrote last year by 7 percent. Clearly, it was time for a tune-up at State Farm.

Source: Beuce, Dan, and Adrienne Carter, "A Good Neighbor Gets Better," *BusinessWeek*, June 20, 2005, p. 16.

Determination of the Price

After the price policy and the price strategy have been formulated, the highness of the price should be determined. The definitive price determination is determined by the following elements:

- The *costs* (source: internal analysis).
- The *market:* What is the status of the price knowledge, price perception, and price sensitivity of the final customers?
- The prices of the *competitors.*
- The price policy and the price *strategies.*
- Other factors, such as psychological *price borders* ($199 instead of $200).

There are various methods for researching the price sensitivity of products, including the following five:

1. *Causal models.* This involves analyzing time series of sales and price (and other elements of the marketing mix) with the aid of regression analysis: A researcher tries to find relationships between variables by applying statistical methods. This is the only method that uses actual behavior. All the other forms may be seen as types of experimental research.
2. *Conjoint measurement (see also Section 4.4).* Respondents are asked to arrange a number of "products" (combinations of characteristics, including, e.g., the price) in order of preference; this is followed by a subsequent calculation of which characteristics are the most important. This can also indicate the influence of price changes on the preference.
3. *The Gabor-Granger method.* This method uses a number of direct questions about purchasing decisions and prices to determine the price sensitivity curve of a product.
4. *The brand-price trade-off (BPTO) method.* In this method, respondents have to choose from several brands at certain prices, after which the price of the chosen brand is increased and the respondent has to make a new choice, after which the price of that brand is increased, and so on. Based on the various choices the respondents

make, it is possible to calculate preference shares (a type of market share) of the brands at various prices, which in turn measures price sensitivity.

5. *Price acceptance research.* This involves asking people which prices they consider cheap, expensive, too cheap, or too expensive, after which an acceptable price range can be determined.

Among these methods, the last one is the most simple. A disadvantage of this method, as with the Gabor-Granger method and the BPTO method, is that respondents are asked more or less directly to indicate the price sensitivity. Such a strong focus on the price apart from other product characteristics may have an impact on the reliability of the results. Conjoint measurement does not have that disadvantage, since it approaches the choice method of consumers closely without placing the emphasis on a single characteristic such as the price. Causal models have the advantage of measuring real behavior but can be used only for markets with sufficient data (especially food products). Conjoint measurements may be used for all product categories.

11.4   CHANNEL DECISIONS

Channels (or the distribution) form the physical connection between the company and the final users of the product. The decisions that need to be made regarding the distribution are related to the choice and management of the distribution channels. Decisions related to logistics are also very important from a marketing perspective, but we do not include them with the marketing decisions. In this section we discuss decisions relating to the distribution channels (*channel management*).

Having a good distribution is very important and may even produce a sustainable competitive advantage. For example, the global and very intensive distribution of Coca-Cola is a clear competitive advantage for this product. Even in remote locations in the Himalayas, Coca-Cola is for sale. However, a "good" distribution does not have to be an intensive one. This depends on the product and the target audience. A durable good needs to be offered in fewer places than does a nondurable good. In addition, more exclusive products can be offered in fewer places than are "normal" products. The reason for this is that customers are prepared to make more of an effort to purchase certain products than they are for other products. For distribution there is a direct relationship with the marketing strategy and other elements of the marketing mix. The distribution decisions (Figure 11-4) receive input to a large extent from the distribution analysis discussed in Chapter 7.

FIGURE 11-4
**Distribution
Decisions***

Objective:

- In terms of "availability"

Decisions:

Determining preference for distribution channels
- Number of channels
- Length of channel
- Type of intermediate links
- Intensity
- Shelf position

Management of the distribution channels:
- Push and/or pull strategy
- Collaboration

*We do not include logistic decisions with marketing mix decisions.

11.4.1 Objective

The *objective of the element of distribution* is stated in terms of *availability*[4]: "To what extent and where should the product be available so that those in the target audience are able to obtain it?"

As was indicated earlier, the answer to this question depends to a large extent on the marketing objectives and strategies.

CASE 11-4 *Coca Cola Opened a New Bottling Plant in Somalia*	Coca Cola typically employs intensive distribution to make the product globally available. In 2004 Coca Cola has opened a new bottling plant in the Somali capital Mogadishu, for door-to-door distribution. It is the largest single investment in the country since central government collapsed 13 years before, and is a sign of growing business confidence. More than 500 people attended the opening of the Coca-Cola plant, whose forerunner was destroyed in the early 90s. The absence of a central government and continuing lawlessness in Somalia has, until now, deterred investors. The old Coke plant was destroyed at the beginning of the country's civil war. But the relative calm of the last few years has encouraged Somalis living overseas to put more money back into the country. **Source:** Grant Ferrett, 'Coca Cola makes Somalia return', *BBC News*, 6 July 2004, http://news.bbc.co.uk/1/hi/world/africa/3865595.stm

Availability consists of two elements: quantitative (the extent to which) and qualitative (where). The quantitative element may be measured on the basis of the *nonweighted or weighted distribution;* also, visibility on the shelf is measurable. An example of a distribution objective is: "With our brand B, we want to increase the weighted distribution from 80 percent to 90 percent within one year." For a manufacturer of A brands, a distribution of 100 percent is not feasible, since some price-oriented store chains do not include A brands in their assortment.

11.4.2 Decisions

Two types of distribution decisions must be made.

Determination of Preference for Distribution Channels

A company should first determine what the "ideal" distribution picture looks like. Whether this is possible depends partly on the management strategies that will be used in the second step in regard to the distribution channels. In designing the *optimal distribution structure,* five elements are relevant:

1. *The number of channels.* Especially if a company serves different markets, a choice of several channels is possible. For example, a drinks manufacturer may supply the hospitality industry via the wholesale liquor trade, whereas a food products retailer is supplied with its products via the food products wholesale business. An insurance company may choose more than one channel: direct delivery to customers, via insurance brokers, via banks, and via employers. The Internet has made it easier for customers to order directly from the supplier, and therefore it offers important perspectives for manufacturers for direct sales outside retail (*disintermediation;* see Section 7.2.2 and Case 11-5). In this regard, two types of suppliers may be distinguished: companies that already existed and now also deliver via the Internet (retailers, insurance companies, travel agents, book sellers) and companies that are exclusively involved with e-commerce such as Amazon.com and Dell). Since the rise of Internet, the use of more than one channel and thus *multi channel management* has become of vital importance.

CASE 11-5
Online Shopping Hit New Highs in 2005

Holiday shoppers spent more online in 2005 than they did in 2004, continuing to steal market share steadily from brick-and-mortar shops, according to a report released last week by Goldman Sachs, Nielsen/NetRatings, and Harris Interactive. Holiday shoppers in the United States spent $30.1 billion from late October until December 23, a 30 percent increase over the 2004 holiday season, according to the report, which surveyed 8,600 shoppers in the United States. Online spending made up 27 percent of total spending during the holidays, up from 16 percent four years ago. Brick-and-mortar shops attracted 68 percent of holiday spending this year, down from 72 percent last year, the report found.

This was a good season for computer hardware and peripherals, with online sales in that sector growing 126 percent to $4.8 billion in spending. But clothes were still the most popular item bought online during the season, with spending reaching $5.3 billion in that segment, according to the report. Consumers spent less online on toys and video games this year, with the category sinking 9 percent compared with 2004. The study also found that consumer satisfaction with online shopping is slowly creeping up, with 64 percent of those surveyed saying they were satisfied with their experience, compared with 61 percent in 2004.

Source: *PCWorld*, January 3, 2006, http://www.pcworld.com/news/article/0,aid,124146,00.asp.

2. *The number of levels, or the length of the channel.* Several intermediate links are possible between the company and the final customers: representatives, agents, importers, wholesalers, and retailers.

3. *The types of intermediate links.* A food products manufacturer should choose within the group of retailers, for example, supermarkets, discounters, neighborhood shops, and specialty stores.

4. *The intensity of an intermediate link.* There are three possibilities in this regard: *intensive distribution* (as large a number of distribution points as possible), *selective distribution* (a limited number of distribution points), and *exclusive distribution* (in a certain region only a single distributor). The intensity decision depends particularly on the type of product that is being offered. In this context, a distinction is made between three types of products:

   a. *Convenience goods.* These are products consumers will take little trouble to purchase. Examples are almost all food products. These products should in principle be distributed intensively.

   b. *Shopping goods.* The consumer is prepared to make an effort (travel time, collection of information) to purchase this kind of product. This mostly involves higher-priced products such as furniture and clothing. Such products require a selective distribution.

   c. *Specialty goods.* These are products with a very high attractive value to the customer. The customer therefore is prepared to make great efforts to purchase them. Examples are exclusive cars and warehouses with a strong attraction (de Bijenkorf, Ikea). These "products" can succeed with an exclusive distribution.

5. *The shelf position.* The position of a brand on the shelf and the number of *facings* (visuable units of the product) may have an important impact on the purchasing opportunity. The optimal place on the shelf depends on issues such as the positioning in relation to competitors that was determined in the marketing strategy.

Management of the Distribution Channels

If an "ideal" channel has been designed, the next step is an attempt to achieve the established objectives. Since distribution channels consist of companies and people that typically are not under the company's control, strategies need to be chosen for that purpose. This also applies if the company wants to make changes in the existing distribution channel. As a result of the strong concentration in the food retail business in some countries, manufacturers of food products have two target audiences: the distributors and the final customers. In principle, two distribution strategies may be used:

1. *A push strategy.* With this strategy, the company tries to "push" the product through the channel. Tools that may be used for this include trade margins and trade discounts and the efforts of the sales staff.
2. *A pull strategy.* With this strategy, the company tries to "pull" the product through the channel because an important demand for the product is created at the consumer level. The most important tools here are advertising and promotional actions.

In current practice, push and pull strategies are used in combination: It is important to establish a strategy toward the distributors and also to strengthen and maintain a consumer need. In this area, there is an increasing amount of *collaboration* between manufacturers and distributors. The interests of distributors and manufacturers also are parallel to a large extent: obtaining the highest sales (and profit) possible from the final customers. These objectives can be achieved better through a collective and therefore synchronized effort rather than without consultation. If the distributor is not sufficiently involved in the planning of, for example, a promotional action of the manufacturer, there is a chance that the distributor will run out of stock.

A manufacturer should therefore see the intermediate links as *collaboration partners;* this leads to a collective effort, and the distribution structure becomes an effective competition tool. In lines of business in which the power of distributors is concentrated (such as the food industry), *account management* is often chosen: an organizational structure that holds individual people at the manufacturer responsible for the relationship with and sales to a single customer (an "account," e.g., Wal-Mart). The relevant account managers then take over some responsibilities from the "classic" sales managers (sales staff, representatives). In the food industry, the collaboration with distributors is so advanced that some manufacturers attune their decisions about the breadth of a product group (such as new product introductions and their timing) to the wishes of the distributor. This is called *category management.*

The essence of category management is that both the manufacturer and the retailer no longer think in terms of brand and products but instead consider the interest and profit of product groups as a whole. In addition, they need to consider each other's interests. Category management implies that that the manufacturer and the retailer *jointly* determine and manage the assortment within a product category. The planning of promotional actions is also increasingly attuned to the wishes of distributors. In general, promotions (if paid for by the manufacturer) are an important tool for distributors, especially if the promotions are made exclusively with the distributor. Another thing that increasingly occurs in practice is that suppliers and their customers (such as manufacturers and distributors) attune their logistic processes to each other. *Electronic data interchange (EDI)* may be used for this purpose. EDI is a system in which the computers of companies that are trading with each other are connected so that those companies can exchange documents electronically. Since the data of suppliers and customers regarding, for example, office supplies are linked, the computer of a customer can keep the inventory stocked without further interference from a person by "independently" ordering office supplies at the computer of the supplier. The supplier then can independently send the invoice to the computer of the customer. Finally, the computer of the customer can independently send a payment order to, for example, the bank. Thus, whereas in the past an entire department kept inventories, wrote and sent orders, and arranged payments, now one computer directed by a single employee can do the same amount of work. The use of EDI therefore can lead to important cost savings.

Finally, the most far-reaching collaboration between a manufacturer and a distributor in which all the issues mentioned above play a role (both category management and EDI) is called *efficient consumer response (ECR).* In this strategy, the wishes of the final customers are responded to as efficiently as possible through collaboration between the manufacturer and the distributor. Typically, the following decisions are synchronized:

- *Breadth of the assortment* (e.g., number of varieties) of the manufacturer and the retailer (category management).
- *Production and distribution* of the manufacturer with the inventories and orders at the distributor (synchronization of production and logistics: *product replenishment*).
- *Promotional actions.*

11.5   MARKETING COMMUNICATION

The "P" of promotion consists of communication and "actions" (promotions). *Communication* then involves informing and convincing the target audience of certain characteristics of the brand; thus, it has not only short-term goals but also *long-term goals.* "Actions" (*sales promotion*) refer to all short-term efforts to achieve more sales by making temporary changes in the four P's. To connect with daily usage, we use marketing communication as an umbrella concept that includes *all tools.* We call the steps that have to be taken to arrive at the execution of the marketing communication the *communication planning process.* Figure 11-5 gives an overview of the steps taken in the communication planning process. We assume that an advertiser" wants to communicate about its brand and brings in a communication agency in this process.

The advertiser has the primary task of choosing a communication target audience and proposition (message) and determining the communication goals and a corresponding budget. In practice, the actual "imagining" and elaboration of the communication expressions and the selection of the media are delegated to a communication consulting agency (also called an advertising agency). Ideally, the advertiser will to perform the measurement of results afterward.

FIGURE 11-5
Steps in the Communication Planning Process

Tasks of the advertiser
1. Determination of the target audience (Section 11.5.1)
2. Selection of a proposition (Section 11.5.2)
3. Communication objectives and communication budget (Section 11.5.3)
4. Briefing for the communication consulting agency (Section 11.5.4)
Tasks for the communication consulting agency
5. Creation and execution (Section 11.5.5)
6. Pretesting (Section 11.5.6)
7. Communication resources and media (Section 11.5.7)
Task of the advertiser
8. Brand tracking and advertising tracking and effect research (Section 11.5.8)

CASE 11-6
How to Promote the U.S. Army

"Your son is looking for guidance on one of the biggest decisions he'll ever make. This is not time to find yourself at a loss for words. Make it a two-way conversation; get the facts. Todaysmilitary.com." Directed at the parents and strongly Web-driven, these are the main characteristics of the new 2005 marketing campaign of the U.S. Army. The commercials and advertisements don't show action scenes from the army but stimulate parents to discuss opportunities to let their kids do useful and paid work in the army. All advertisements lead to the Internet, where people can find relevant information. Clarke Caywood, professor of marketing at Northwestern University in Chicago, says: "The army knows very well how to make an integrated marketing campaign. They show up at sports matches, in shopping centers, and you can win an iPOD if you provide your adress.The only problem is that people just don't want the 'product.' I tested the slogan 'Your turn' with my students, and they all shouted 'To die.'"

Source: Taps, Freek (2006), 'It's up to the soldiers' mother now', *Tijdschrift voor Marketing*, January 2006, pp. 38–41.

11.5.1   Determination of the Target Audience

The first step to be taken by the advertiser is to define the *communication target audience:* To whom do we want to tell something? The communication target audience does not have to correspond to the marketing target audience (see Section 10.2). Often the communication target audience is broader: Not only the potential buyers should be reached but also the most important influencing groups. In this context, it is relevant to know who plays which role within a household in the purchasing process of a product category (initiator, decision maker, etc.). For example, in toys the mother or father is the final decision maker, and women have a large input into the brand choice for cars. Older people often let themselves be guided by the opinions of their children and grandchildren for certain purchases. Another item that plays a role is whether the goal is to hold on to users or to attract new buyers.

The communication target audience should be described with as much detail as possible so that the advertising agency has as much information as it can have for the development of the campaign. The best results are obtained by describing the target audience as an *individual* based on three categories of dimensions (Figure 11-6).[5]

Strategic dimensions are dimensions that are related to the actual use of the brand or product. For example, an important choice is whether the manager wants to communicate

FIGURE 11-6
Dimensions for Formulating the Communication Target Audience

1. Strategic dimensions: brand use

- Users or nonusers
- Trial purchases, habit purchases, brand loyalty
- Preference for our brand or for that of the competitor

2. Creative dimensions: relationship between brand and user

- How, when, and where does the target audience use the product?
- What does the brand mean to the target audience?
- What is important to the target audience?
- What are the current brand associations?

3. Media dimensions: users' profile or "brand personality"

- What is the demographic and socioeconomic profile?
- What is the "lifestyle" (including media consumption)?

mostly with users or with nonusers. *Creative dimensions* are dimensions that in effect relate to customer values: the "reasons" for brand use. These dimensions give the creative types at the advertising agency an impression of the relationship between the target audience and the brand. The so-called *media dimensions* refer to the general characteristics of the target audience (independent of the brand): "hard" background variables such as age and income class as well as qualitative variables such as habits, hobbies, and interests ("lifestyle"). These dimensions are important in the creative process: What kind of person is the average user? This is closely related to the brand personality: An average user can also be described by describing the brand as a person. The second use for media dimensions is related to the formulation of communication objectives and the execution of media planning. For both steps it is desirable to describe the target audience in measurable terms.

11.5.2 Proposition

The *proposition* is the message of the communication: What does the brand or product provide to the consumer to make his or her life a little easier or richer or to solve a problem? The proposition proceeds from the positioning that has been chosen for the brand and is in effect the *simplified-language version of the promise* that is being made. In Section 10.3 we formulated a positioning statement: *Within the category ____ brand A will be better for target audience ____ than competitor B for goal ____ (usage goal) because it ____ (advantage, benefit). This is demonstrated through ____ (characteristic) and leads to the brand personality ____ (final value).* The proposition may be deduced from this type of positioning. Many designations for the choice of the proposition are used in practice, such as "advertising strategy," "copy strategy," and "creative strategy." The last designation incorrectly creates the assumption that the proposition has to be created by the advertising agency.

In practice, choosing a proposition is a challenging process. A positioning or proposition is often too broad: A brand wants to excel in too many elements, and the relevant managers want to say as much as possible in the communication. However, in communication, it is essential to be clear and therefore to *focus on a single message*. In selecting the core message, it is important to reason strongly from the perspective of the target audience. In effect, only two questions need to be asked:

1. How does the target audience perceive our brand now (*image*)?
2. How do we want them to perceive our brand (*identity*)?

When image and identity correspond, there is no communication problem. However, if there are differences, it is the role of communication to adjust the image. The way in which both questions are elaborated depends on the level of customer values that is important in the product category: Is the main focus on instrumental values (physical product characteristics) or on final values (abstract product characteristics)? We now review both situations.

Instrumental Values

Instrumental values are very important in "problem-solving" product categories such as laundry detergents and feminine hygiene products. If there is a difference between "what the target audience currently thinks (e.g., competitive brand Y removes potato peels better)" and "what the target audience should think (e.g., brand X removes potato peels better)," this gap can be resolved through communication (a campaign that shows that potato peels are removed).

This method is suitable for adjusting instrumental values but less suitable for adjusting abstract values. The reason for this is that an abstract image cannot easily be adjusted with communication since a brand cannot suddenly start portraying a different personality (consistency; see Section 10.3.4).

FIGURE 11-7
Measurement of
Results and Effect
Research

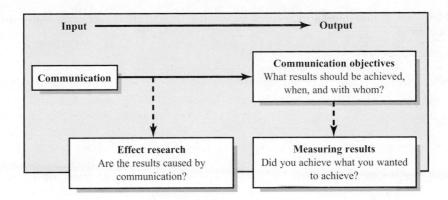

Abstract Values

To develop a proposition in which *abstract values* play an important role, the technique of *perceptual mapping* is often used (see Chapter 3). In such depictions it is easy to represent a "desired position" (identity) and therefore include the way the company wants to adjust the image. The fact that this is possible only on a limited scale implies that only *limited movements* are feasible in such image pictures.

11.5.3   Communication Objectives and Communication Budget

A communication objective is a desired communication effect. Communication objectives are a tool for the communication planning process. If the requirements for useful objectives are met (Specific, Measurable, Ambitious, Realistic, Timed: SMART), communication objectives are the standards that can be used to evaluate whether a campaign has been successful. *Communication objectives* therefore are very closely related to the *measurement of results.* Conversely, measuring results has little value if no objectives have been formulated. Thus, the measurement of results means that a measurement is taken of the extent to which the objectives have been achieved. To make it plausible that the measured results have actually been "caused" by the communication, *effect research* should be performed in addition to the measurement of results. Effect research generally involves a search for a *causal relationship* between an "input variable" (in this case communication) and an output variable (communication goal). Figure 11-7 summarizes these issues.

Although formulating goals and measuring results are necessary from a planning perspective, in practice this is done infrequently. Usually objectives are mentioned, but they are often not quantitative. Sometimes quantitative "advertising goals" are formulated, but they often appear to be related to coverage. Although coverage is a required condition to achieve real effects, coverage goals in themselves cannot be interpreted as effect objectives. Examples of true communication (effect) objectives include advertising awareness, brand awareness, and brand associations.

Choice of Communication Objectives

In choosing communication objectives, the question is "What do we want to achieve for whom and when?" We have already discussed the "for whom" question. We now discuss the question "What do we want to achieve?"

A goal of communication will always be to achieve more sales, make more profit, attract more visitors, and so forth. Yet goals such as market share are not suitable as a communication objective, since those types of items are determined by many factors besides communication. Sales variables may be mentioned as objectives in communication, but then

FIGURE 11-8 Communication Objectives and Measurable Variables (In This Figure, "Advertising" may be Read as "Communication")

Source: Adapted from Franzen (1998).

Advertising Input

A. Characteristics of the advertisement (campaign)
   Choice of media
- Rough drafts, creative execution variables
- Physical variables (length of advertising spot, format, color, etc.)

B. Advertising expenditures

   Confrontation (exposure) and reach
- Volume: millimeters, seconds
- Expenditures: money (share of voice: spending share)
- Reach: absolute or relative [e.g. gross rating points (GRPs): percent viewing figures]
- Contact frequency

Output on the Individual Level: Communication Objectives

C. Advertising responses
- Advertising attention
- Advertising appreciation (likability)
- Advertising awareness

D. Brand responses
- Brand awareness [top-of-mind awareness (TOMA), spontaneous, aided]
- Brand associations (strength, relevance/importance, distinctiveness)

E. Brand behavior responses
- Purchasing intention
- Trial purchases
- Brand loyalty* and repeat purchases*

Output at Market Level

F. Market responses*
- Sales
- Market share

*Not communication objectives but marketing objectives.

they should be marketing objectives. "True" communication objectives are deduced from the marketing goals.

Various diagrams are presented in the literature for the purpose of selecting variables that may be used as communication goals. Most of them are based on the classic *hierarchy of communication effects:* knowledge (*cognition*), feeling (*affection*), and behavior (*conation*). Quantifying these knowledge, feeling, and behavior effects is very useful, although recent research shows that a *hierarchy* of effects cannot be demonstrated.[6] Another disadvantage of classifications that are based on hierarchical models is that no explicit relationship is established with the input: the communication itself. A diagram that actually does this is the so-called 'Advertising Response Matrix' of Franzen,[7] which is shown in Figure 11-8.

The Advertising Response Matrix indicates that in effectiveness research (and therefore also in the formulation of objectives) three levels should be distinguished:

1. Advertising *input.*
2. *Output* at the *individual* level.
3. *Effects* at the *market* level.

The *advertising input* level represents the communication effort. It consists of a qualitative component (category A: the characteristics of the campaign) and a quantitative component (category B: the weight of the campaign). Qualitative aspects are the substantive characteristics of the campaign (e.g., in advertising at McDonald's a menu or Big Mac in the picture or not, using humor or not) and the physical variables (the length of the advertising spot, using outdoor advertising or not, etc.). Quantitative aspects are the efforts expressed in terms of volume (number of seconds) or money (e.g., the advertising budget portion *share of voice;* McDonald's share in total fast-food advertising expenditures is 50 percent) or the achieved coverage [e.g., *gross rating points* (GRPs): percent viewing figures; a campaign of McDonald's has been shown, for example, 20 times in one month with an average viewing figure of 10 percent and produced 200 GRPs; if the average number of times people have seen the spot was, for example, four (average *contact frequency* of four), the net coverage is $200/4 = 50$ percent].

CASE 11-7 *TiVo as an* *Opportunity*	TiVo is making friends with the very medium it became famous for helping people avoid: the 30-second commercial. And now that TiVo and Comcast are officially paired, it's expected that the two will devise more ways to make room for marketers. Comcast CEO Brian Roberts revealed at the recent National Cable and Telecommunications Association show that the team plans to develop a system to insert relevant and targeted ads into programming that's being played back at another time. **Source:** Whitney, Daisy, "TiVo a Problem? No, Ad Solution," *Advertising Age,* June 6, 2005, p. S4.

The second level is a representation of *individual responses,* that is, the responses of people from the target audience that the company has to measure itself through market research. These responses consist of three main groups:

1. *Psychological advertising respon*ses. These are reactions to a single advertisement, such as the appreciation (*likability;* the percentage that enjoyed a particular commercial by McDonald's) and reactions to a series of advertisements such as advertising awareness (e.g., the percentage of people from the target audience who know that McDonald's has a campaign with soccer teams that are visiting McDonald's).

2. *Psychological brand responses.* This is brand awareness (already very high for McDonald's) and brand associations (percentage of people from the target audience who know that McDonald's offers a soccer menu, percentage of people who consider McDonald's to be child-friendly, etc.).

3. *Brand behavior responses.* These are behavioral intentions with regard to the brand (percentage that expects to be visiting McDonald's within one week), trial purchases, and information behavior, purchasing behavior, usage behavior, and brand loyalty (e.g., percentage that indicates recommending McDonald's to friends).

The third level consists of the aggregated effects at the *market level.* This refers to the size and strength of the brand preference in the market, the sales, the market share, the price elasticity, the profit margin, and the cash flow. Both at this level and at the second level the issue is the effects over time: direct effects (after a single advertisement), short-term effects (within one year), and long-term effects (after one year).

In terms of the Advertising Response Matrix, market response (sales, category F) is the most important goal that needs to be achieved. However, this is a marketing objective. Individual purchasing behavior (category E) is also a marketing objective. An exception to this is *trial:* Trial purchases are influenced mostly by communication and thus may be considered communication goals. The clearest communication objectives are represented under category D: brand awareness and brand associations. The reason for this is that these objectives are influenced primarily by communication. A second reason is that these are also the sources of *brand equity,* according to Keller.[8] In addition, the advertising responses might be presented as communication objectives except for the fact that this is

FIGURE 11-9   Communication Objectives for a Brand

	Total		Target Audience A		Target Audience B	
	1/1/06 (Current)	1/1/07 (Plan)	1/1/06 (Current)	1/1/07 (Plan)	1/1/06 (Current)	1/1/07 (Plan)
Aided advertising recall	__%	__%	__%	__%	__%	__%
Top of mind brand awareness (TOMA)	__%	__%	__%	__%	__%	__%
Percent of people who associate (aided) brand with "adventurous"	__%	__%	__%	__%	__%	__%
Percent of people who consider brand at purchase	__%	__%	__%	__%	__%	__%
Percent of people who purchase brand for the first time (trial)	__%	__%	__%	__%	__%	__%

never sufficient: Communication is a tool to achieve something with the brand. However, advertising responses are very important in *pretesting:* testing beforehand how an advertisement or commercial comes across to people in the target audience.

In summary, the middle part of the Advertising Response Matrix (categories C, D, and E, with the exception of brand loyalty and repeat purchases) contains all possible communications objectives. Which variables are chosen from this range depends on where the largest bottlenecks are. At this point the "classic hierarchical advertising models" are useful. The oldest model is the *AIDA model*: attention, interest, desire, action. If spontaneous brand awareness is low, there may have to be a campaign to increase it. If the price image is unfavorable, improvement in this regard may be necessary. If the desire is doing well but the trial purchases are not, planning an action is conceivable. Research in combination with the desired proposition will therefore be the basis for the choice of the specific communication objectives. Each campaign will also have a marketing objective, and it is therefore conceivable to incorporate the marketing objective into a communication plan.

To meet the requirements for objectives, the objective should be quantified and should contain a time designation. Examples are as follows:

- Within half a year, 80 percent of our target audience (women over age 30) should have heard of our brand at some time (*aided brand recall*).

- Within one year, the percentage of the 4 million households with a washing machine that identifies brand X as a low-foaming laundry detergent that is effective in cleaning laundry should increase from 10 percent to 40 percent.

- By October 1 of next year, 70 percent of our target audience should have purchased the product at least once, and the average report mark that the "trial purchasers" give our product at a minimum should be equal to that of our competitor Q (combined objective).

If a company has different target audiences, the objectives may be summarized as they are in Figure 11-9. This figure also shows that to measure the progress and success of a campaign, a measurement of the variables for the objectives should be taken both beforehand (zero measure) and afterward.

Budget Determination

After the communication objectives have been determined, the available *budget* is determined. These steps are closely linked: Ambitious objectives cost a lot of money. In practice, various methods are used to determine the communication budget. The most common methods are the following:

1. A percentage of turnover (last year's sales or expected sales).
2. Closing entry: what the company can afford.
3. Comparable share to that of competitor.
4. Based on objectives and tasks.

The disadvantages of the first two methods are that reverse reasoning is applied: The turnover determines the sales promotion instead of the opposite. This leads to *cyclical budgeting*. Moreover, the budget then is not based on opportunities in the market and the specific required promotion of products. A disadvantage of the third method is that it is uncertain whether the competition is doing well. A company is better off looking at its own resources, opportunities, and objectives. Budgeting based on *objectives and tasks* therefore is the best method: What do we want to achieve, and how much does that cost? For that purpose, items such as desired coverage should be determined and the number of required contacts per consumer should be reached. Since the link between objectives other than coverage and budget is not always easy to indicate, this will require making assumptions about effectiveness on the basis of past experience.

In this phase the budget usually is a tentative budget. Depending on the concrete plans that are developed in later phases (e.g., by the advertising agency), the budget often will be modified. In addition, sometimes the advertiser already has made a global allocation for resources, for example, for advertising, consumer promotions, and trade promotions.

11.5.4 Briefing and Requirements for Communication

Earlier in this chapter we indicated that an advertising agency almost always is engaged in elaborating the campaign development and media choice. In presenting the assignment, a *briefing* is used: a (brief) description of what is expected of the communication consulting agency. The marketing or brand manager is primarily responsible for this process. After consultation and deliberation with the advertising agency, the agency should declare its agreement with the briefing. The components of a briefing are briefly listed in Figure 11-10. A lot of information for the briefing may be obtained from the marketing plan.

FIGURE 11-10
Components of an Advertising Briefing

Marketing background

1. What it is about: company and brand or product
2. Environment: summary of SWOT analysis and key problem

Campaign goal

3. Communication target audience
4. Promise and proof
5. Brand personality
6. Measurable communication goal and budget

Preconditions

7. Media and resources
8. Other preconditions (e.g., style and time planning)

In an introductory section, a description is provided of the company, the *brand* or product, the characteristics, technical data, and so forth. There follows a reproduction of the *objectives* and an elaboration of the *other P's:* product, price, place, and promotion/communication (to the extent that they have been determined already). A description of the strengths, weaknesses, opportunities, and threats (*SWOT*) analysis provides the framework within which the campaign is developed. The perceptions of the target group are very important. The *core problem* often has to do with the difference between image and identity. For the competition, the central focus is the content of their communication, the media allocation, and the budget. The media behavior of the competitors may sometimes be analyzed by the agency on the basis of advertising expenditure figures (see Section 6.7). Components 1 and 2 form the marketing background of the campaign. Components 3 through 6 are the core of the briefing. First, the communication *target audience* is described, for example, based on the dimensions mentioned in Section 10.2. Component 4 is the focused *proposition* (with any evidence), and component 5 contains the *brand personality.* Then there is the *communication* goal: What does the manager want to achieve with that target audience, and how much money is available (draft *budget*)? The budget mentioned in the briefing sometimes may be modified on the basis of the creative ideas of the agency.

In the component *media and resources,* the wishes of the advertiser are indicated in relation to any other promotional tools [e.g., direct marketing (DM), Internet] and the media choice. Some advertisers determine a budget allocation for this (e.g., division print/television); others do it qualitatively or delegate it entirely to the agency.

The last component contains the other preconditions within which the campaign has to be developed, such as necessary elements in the advertising expressions (house style and layout), whether or not to use humor, and legal regulations. In this component the time planning is also described.

A *clear and well-defined briefing* is very important for the advertising agency. Advertising agencies often complain that advertisers do not know how to write good briefings. The biggest problem is that advertisers cannot or do not make a choice. They want too much. This leads to briefings that are broad and therefore vague. A vague briefing means insufficient direction, which means the advertising agency can go in any direction with the campaign and brand consistency is no longer feasible. The disadvantage of this is that the campaign may go in a different direction different from what was planned originally, and there is also a risk that afterward a lot more work may need to be done if certain designs are rejected by the advertiser. A good advertising agency will therefore refuse to approve a briefing that has not been completed.

At this point, the task of the client is finished and the baton is passed to the advertising firm. Figure 11-11 indicates the requirements the brand communication must meet. The requirements are along the lines of those for the SWOT analysis but are tailored more to communication.

1. *The perception of the customer is number one.* Communication serves to teach the target group something, and so we must know what the target group thinks about the brand (image). Often this is not in line with what the brand wants (identity).
2. *Choose a core value.* Too much communication is the same as no communication. In an environment in which people are overloaded with information, we can be happy if they remember a single thing about our brand. What word should this be? All managers should force themselves to name a single word or sentence with which the brand will be associated.

FIGURE 11-11
Requirements
for Effective
Communication

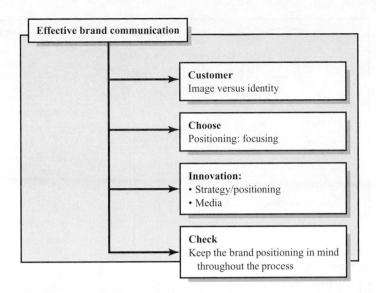

3. *Be innovative.* This goes both for the positioning and for the media mix. Another reason is the overload of information: Try to "rise above the ground level" and find out how to reach target group.

4. *Check everything about the positioning.* After the briefing, agencies are called in, along with other people in the organization, and it takes a while before everything is thought out and implemented. Throughout this process, the manager in charge of communication should check everything related to and based on the positioning.

11.5.5 Creation and Execution

Creation

Creation involves inventing a "fun" way to sell the message to the target audience. The central idea is called the *concept. Execution* is the elaboration of that method and the development of the campaign. We now discuss both elements. In advertising agencies, usually two people are involved with the creative process: a *copywriter* (text writer) and an *art director* (designer). Sometimes one of them thinks of the idea, and sometimes it is a joint effort. Few tools are available for the invention of a creative idea. Creation has been called a "handicraft." A creative type needs to have a "feel" for it. One creative type is also different from another. Some advertising agencies are well known for their surprising, innovative campaigns, yet that is not appropriate for every brand. Geursen[9] has developed a "model" that can be used in the process of creation (Figure 11-12).

Creation starts with considering "something of the brand" ("Nike shoes are fast"). This "something" should ideally be invented by the advertiser (proposition), and if it is not, the creative type will think of something about the brand. Most often, an advertiser comes up with many "unique selling points" of the brand and the agency then has to choose one on which to focus. Agencies have commented that this is simplest when the brand actually has something to say, for example, something new. Research on television advertising[10] has shown that the effect is the strongest when a brand has something new to announce. If there is no instrumental message, a search can be made for something more abstract (transformational positioning): an element of the brand personality. The creative type subsequently ponders the way in which that can be communicated. The creative idea may be an illustration, a piece of text, a parallel ("a greyhound is fast"), an incident, and so on, that can logically be

FIGURE 11-12
Creation is Making One Thing Big

Source: based on Geursen (1990)

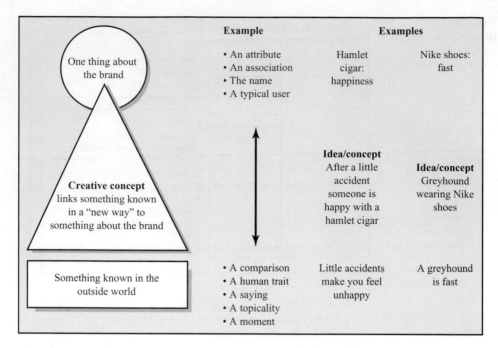

linked to the message and the brand. From this central idea (concept) the campaign is developed (such as a picture of a greyhound with sneakers) and the "something" of the brand is communicated in an enlarged fashion (hence the triangle). Figure 11-13 lists the requirements for creative ideas.

The requirement for entertaining advertising is supported by research. The *likability of the ad* in general has a positive connection with higher effects on the *brand values*. Entertaining advertising also leads to less zapping.

The requirements of a logical fit with the brand and message and distinctiveness are related to *brand recognition*. Simplicity is necessary because in consumer markets, communication must be simple. The broader applicability is related to *brand consistency*. Good creative ideas form an essential component of the brand and lead to better recognition and memory of the brand. Ideas that can be developed to go beyond a single campaign into a campaign that will run for years are 'worth their weight in gold'.[11] Case 11-8 gives an example of such an enduring concept.

CASE 11-8	An example of a brand that elaborated on the same creative idea for more than 30 years is British Hamlet cigars. The concept (advertising idea) was the accident around the corner: Something went wrong for someone, but by lighting a Hamlet cigar after the incident, the person still developed a satisfied feeling. With the supportive slogan "Happiness is a cigar called Hamlet, the mild cigar" and always the same music, both an instrumental value (light) and especially a final value (happiness) were communicated; therefore, this was a two-sided positioning. In the years 1961–1994 the company made endless variations on this theme (after that time television advertising for tobacco products was outlawed), and the Hamlet campaign won many prizes with famous commercials such as "man in photo booth" and "free kick in soccer" and was a successful cigar brand for many years.
Sustaining an Advertising Concept for a Long Time: Hamlet Cigars	

In practice, the following problems occur with creative ideas:

- *The creative idea lacks a natural link with the brand or the product category*. This is one of the biggest shortcomings of creative ideas. To be noticed in the enormous amount of

FIGURE 11-13
Requirements for a Good Creative Concept

- It leads to entertaining advertising.
- It fits logically with the brand.
- It fits logically with the message.
- It is distinctive.
- It is simple.
- It can be applied through various media.
- It may be applied as variations on a theme over time and therefore can be milked for a long time.

communication expressions, agencies continually come up with "creative" approaches. This makes advertising entertaining, and commercials may hold people's attention. However, the lack of a logical link with the brand leads to a situation in which the advertising is remembered but not the brand. In that case, advertising is by definition not effective. For example, a viewer who watches a television commercial in which a dog with dirty paws walks into the kitchen and a child dries the dog with a towel would not automatically think of candy bars.

- *Good creative ideas are thrown out because of imagined "wear-out."* The true cause of this problem often is a change in managers or advertising agencies. Continuing for a long time with a creative idea requires a long-term vision (see Case 11-8).
- *Creative ideas are not distinctive.* In this case the idea is actually no longer creative but, more important, no longer unique for the brand. This is also a cause of advertising confusion.

Execution

The creative concept has to be executed, or, put differently, translated into pictures and words. This book does not give guidelines on this issue. The reader should refer to two excellent chapters (creative tactics and creative execution) in the book of Percy and Elliot.[12] We do note, however, that the growing availability of *eye movement and eye fixation data* (see Section 11.5.6) has allowed very interesting research on these topics. For example, a recent analysis[13] of 1,363 print advertisements tested with the infrared eye-tracking methodology on more than 3,600 consumers showed that the pictorial is superior in capturing attention, independent of its size. The text element best captures attention in direct proportion to its surface size. The brand element most effectively transfers attention to the other elements.

11.5.6   Pretesting

There are three forms of pretesting:

1. Qualitative testing of a design for an advertising expression: *concept test*.
2. Qualitative testing of a fully developed advertising expression: *qualitative pretest*.
3. Quantitative testing of a fully developed advertising expression: *quantitative pretest*.

Concept Test

In the consultation between the advertising agency and the advertiser there is usually a moment at which a design for an advertising expression (based on the "creative idea") is submitted for approval to the advertiser. In print advertising the concept is then an advertising sketch, and for television advertising a *storyboard* is made: drawings of all the scenes with corresponding indications of the audio support (music and text) that is planned. In this phase it may be desirable to ask several consumers for feedback on the design. This could involve questions regarding intelligibility and attractiveness. An advantage of concept testing is that after that stage, it is still relatively easy and cheap to make changes. A disadvantage is that the final expression is different from the concept. Especially in television advertising this is a problem: A commercial including music, editing, and so on, may produce completely different feelings than does a storyboard.

CASE 11-9 *Concept Testing:* *How Unilever's* *Television* *Advertising for* *the U.S. Market* *Is Prepared and* *Tested*	Unilever has a diagnostic technique that lets the company reedit mediocre ads into great ones. Unilever works with Albuquerque, New Mexico–based Ameritest/CY Research to find out what target audiences think about the company's ads. After determining that an ad's concept has a flawed execution, Unilever engages "the Spielberg variables"—that is, adding the style and storytelling methods used in feature films to the ad. Part of the process is to deconstruct the ad into frames to identify flaws at narrative inflection points and then construct a "flow of attention" or "flow of emotion" graph. The important brand information should appear at these peak attention points. Creative changes can then be made to achieve a superior effect. **Source:** Kastenholz, John, "The Spielberg Variables," *Harvard Business Review,* April 2005, p. 16

Qualitative Pretest

A test similar to a concept test may be performed with a ready-made expression. An advantage is that the actual expression is being tested and the respondents therefore receive a faithful image of the advertising. A disadvantage is the high costs of modifications.

Quantitative Pretest

Quantitative pretests have the following goals:

- To obtain insight into the expected effects of an advertising expression.
- To obtain insight into which components of an expression receive the most attention.

Expected Effects   The most direct way to do quantitative pretesting is to ask a group of respondents to give their opinion about an advertisement with the aid of closed questions (e.g., with so-called *Likert scales*: scales with opposite values at either end, for example, very unclear . . . very clear or completely disagree . . . completely agree). This way of pretesting is used by Procter & Gamble (see Case 11-10).

Aside from questions about the advertisement to be tested, questions may be posed about the brand, for example, the brand personality. In this way a quantitative pretest can easily be used to perform a "zero measurement" of the variables included in the objectives.

CASE 11-10 *Quantitative* *pretesting at* *Procter &* *Gamble*	Procter & Gamble is one of the largest advertisers. Procter is a real television advertiser: More than 90 percent of its advertising budget goes for TV advertising. Given the enormous investments, it is no wonder that P&G makes sure to pretest the majority of its commercials. The pretesting focuses on three factors: persuasiveness/credibility, uniqueness/distinctiveness, and trial intention. By doing this pretesting for many brands for many years, P&G has compiled a large data file with pretest results. That database also contains the results after the closure of a campaign. By comparing the pretest and the actual results of brands within product categories, P&G gets a detailed insight into the predictive power of pretests. Based on these experiences, standards have been developed that a commercial must meet in a pretest in order to be approved.

Measuring Attention with Eye Movement Data

Verify is an organization that can perform quantitative pretests. With the aid of special mirrors in "laboratory circumstances," the *eye movements of respondents* who watch advertisements in magazines, on television, and so forth, are documented. With these data it may be detected which components of the expression are watched the most, how long the expression as a whole is watched, and what the influence of the "environment" of the expression (the context, such as editorial pages in a magazine) is. The scores are compared with those of competitors and with the medium as a whole. Verify measures *attention,* which is not a communication-effect objective, though it is a condition for achieving communication effects.

Limitations and Use of Pretesting

Pretests have two important limitations:

1. *No actual circumstances.* Pretests can be conducted only in research circumstances. The issue here is whether respondents in "laboratory conditions" will behave in the same manner at home. A danger is that if respondents know why they are included, advertising expressions will receive too much attention.
2. *Bad predictive value.* Research by Lodish and associates[14] demonstrated that the results of quantitative pretests are poor predictors of achieved brand equity and market shares. The results of pretests therefore should not be used in absolute terms, especially not in comparative terms.

In light of these limitations, the question may be raised whether pretesting has any value. The simple answer is that it does. Research by Lodish and associates[15] into the long-term effects of television commercials shows that if commercials do not have an effect in the short term, they also do not have an effect in the long term. This implies that it is important from the very beginning to measure the results of a campaign and compare them with the starting situation. If no short-term effects can be detected, action should be taken.

11.5.7 Media Selection

In this book we make a distinction between three levels of communication instruments:

1. Brand elements (name, design, and logo).
2. Communication instruments such as advertising and sales promotion.
3. Media such as television and magazines.

The brand elements are discussed in Chapter 10. Communication tools and media are discussed in this section. The distinction between communication tools and media is not entirely clear at all points. For example, the Internet is a medium but also is a separate instrument. Sponsoring is strongly related to outdoor advertising. As a result of the mutual relationships between communication instruments and media, sometimes the collective term *media resources* is used.

A company has a multitude of communication instruments at its disposal to stimulate customers to purchase its products. Figure 11-14 gives an overview. We make a distinction between "fixed" brand elements and other communication resources.

We now analyze the communication instruments listed in Figure 11-14 and then the media.

FIGURE 11-14
Marketing
Communication
Instruments

Brand elements

1. Brand name (see Chapter 10)
2. Design and logo (see Chapter 10)
3. Packaging (see Section 11.2)

Communication instruments

1. Advertising
2. In-store communication
3. Personal selling
4. Direct marketing communication (Internet, mail, mobile telephones)
5. Public relations
6. Experience communication (sponsoring, events)
7. Promotions

Media

1. Print
   - Newspapers (paid and unpaid)
   - Magazines
   - Door-to-door papers
2. Airwaves
   - Television
   - Radio
3. Cinema
4. Outdoor advertising (bus shelter, billboards, advertising on buses and trains)
5. Direct mail (addressed or unaddressed)
6. Internet/computers ("e-communication")
7. Mobile telephone technology ("m-communication")
8. Various and alternative media

1. *Advertising.* Advertising includes every paid form of nonpersonal presentation and promotion of ideas, goods, or services by an identified sponsor. Examples are magazine and television advertising, cinema commercials, and outdoor advertising (billboards, bus shelters, etc.).

2. *In-store communication.* In-store communication (also called *merchandising)* is the collective description for marketing communication in and around a store. The most important instruments and media are store arrangement, article presentation, display, and personal selling (discussed separately below). As a result of the increase in impulse purchasing behavior (low involvement), the importance of store communication has increased. Advertising and in-store communication together form *mass selling.*

3. *Personal selling.* Personal selling is an oral presentation in a discussion with one or more potential customers to generate sales. Examples are representatives, product presentations, company days, exhibitions, and shows.

4. *Direct-marketing communication. Direct marketing* is a form of marketing that is aimed at obtaining and maintaining a structural, direct relationship between the

supplier and the customer. Direct marketing communication is one-to-one communication that is used for this purpose. The forms most frequently applied are communication via the Internet, promotional messages sent directly to people (direct mail), and telephone sales.

5. *A component of public relations (PR).* PR refers to the systematic promotion of mutual understanding between a company and its public groups. The goal is the creation and maintenance of a positive image in the public groups (customers, employees, suppliers, capital suppliers, shareholders, the government, and the general public). The tools of public relations include press releases, publicity, annual reports, sponsoring, and sponsored media (e.g., magazines of retailers).

   PR is aimed at target audiences both outside and within the company. Although it is difficult to include internal PR with marketing, let alone with sales promotion, there is an overlap in activities. Marketing PR entails informing the company about its brands and products and is applied on occasions such as the introduction of new products. In the case of "calamities" PR is important (see the material on crisis communication in Section 10.4).

6. *Experience communication (sponsoring and events).* In sponsoring, the sponsor provides money, goods, services, or know-how to the party that is being sponsored, which in turn contributes to the achievement of the communication objectives of the sponsor. Sponsoring is a thematic communication instrument that can be used both for marketing communication and for corporate communication. Sponsoring has received a lot of attention in the last few years. Among all sponsoring revenues, the majority (70 percent) goes for sports sponsoring. *Events* may be organized by the company or may be sponsored (see Case 11-11). The advantage of organizing on one's own is that the brand can be made completely into an "experience." In Section 10.4.5 we noted that other instruments and media, such as the Internet, may be used to create experiences for customers.

7. *Promotions (sales promotion).* This includes all short-term actions directly targeted towards stimulating sales. There are three types of promotions[16]:

   a. *Consumer promotions.* These are promotions by manufacturers aimed at final customers, such as discount actions, money-back actions, and "premium" actions (a temporary free gift with purchase); these actions are sometimes supported by in-store communications paid for by the manufacturer, such as special article presentations (*displays*).

   b. *Retailer promotions.* These are promotions of the retail trade toward the consumer, such as discount actions (paid for by the retailer).

   c. *Trade promotions.* These are actions of the manufacturer aimed at the retail trade, such as competitions for the highest sales or temporarily providing bonuses.

CASE 11-11 *Sponsoring*	Racing fans weren't the only ones riveted to the corporate logo–covered NASCAR racers in 2005's Daytona 500: Wall Street has picked up on the huge popularity of auto racing and is rewarding companies that are connected with it. Companies such as Ford Motor, General Mills, and Georgia-Pacific have enjoyed big returns on the stock market after announcing that they are sponsoring a NASCAR team, according to a study of 24 sponsors. Researchers found that the companies had mean gains in stock market value of more than $300 million the two days after the announcement.

Source: "NASCAR Sponsorship Revs Stocks' Engines," *USA Today,* February 21, 2005.

The total communication budget should be divided over these communication instruments, after which each instrument is elaborated in detail and executed. The weight each of the instruments receives is determined by the following:

- *The specific characteristics of each instrument.* Advertising is impersonal but flexible and reaches a large audience. Personal selling is very effective but is expensive and therefore can be used only for a limited number of customers. Direct marketing communication has the advantage that a relationship with a customer may be built up, but it is more expensive than advertising and requires an actual database. "Public relations" may be very effective in certain situations (e.g., with a new product introduction) because of its high credibility. Sponsoring may strengthen the image with certain groups, but it also has risks (e.g., sports sponsoring). Exhibitions and shows may be a supplementary instrument in some branches. Promotions are effective in the short term but do not build up preferences in the long term.

- *The type of product or market.* For companies that are active in consumer markets, advertising is usually the most important tool to stimulate sales. After advertising, promotional actions are the next most important in consumer markets. A tool that is becoming increasingly important is direct marketing communication. In industrial markets, in which not the customers but other companies are the final consumers, the most important promotional tool is personal selling. In industrial markets, advertising is increasingly being used, even on television.

- *The choice of a push or a pull strategy* (see Section 11.3). A push strategy requires strong personal selling and actions aimed at the trade. A pull strategy involves advertising and promotions aimed at the final customers.

- *The phase in the purchasing process in which the most important problems are located.* In the first phases of the purchasing process, that is, to achieve the communications objectives, the tools of advertising and public relations are usually the most effective. Personal selling and promotions are the most effective in the later phases in the purchasing process: convincing and stimulating to purchase (sales objectives).

- *The phase in the product life cycle.* In the introductory phase, awareness should be built up through advertising and publicity. Trial purchases may be stimulated through promotions. Personal selling is aimed at obtaining a high distribution. In the growth phase, the use of all instruments can be decreased. In the maturity and saturation phases, all instruments become more important again. In the declining phase, consumer actions become relatively important.

Media

The choice of the media strategy is of vital importance for at least two reasons:

1. The largest part of the communication budget goes to media.
2. Getting attention in the growing "clutter" is becoming more difficult. For this reason creativity and innovation are important for the media strategy too.

The choice of the media strategy is closely linked to the development of the campaign. Some concepts are appropriate exclusively for television, and others primarily for print (see Figure 11-14). In practice, usually a combination of media is chosen. Factors that determine the media choice include the following:

- *Coverage.* Which medium can we use to reach the target audience as efficiently as possible?

- *Communication ability.* Suitability of the medium to the message: Is an explanation required? Does an "atmosphere" need to be created? Is the message mostly *thematic* (informative) or action-oriented?
- *Contact frequency.* How often can we reach the target audience through the medium?
- *Costs.* What are the costs per 1,000 readers reached (print) or per percent viewing figures [gross rating points (GRPs): television and radio], and what are the total costs?

Because creativity in media is essential for success, there is a growing interest in *alternative media* such as "game advertising," floor advertising, and video screens. These media normally are complementary to "classical" media.

CASE 11-12 *Alternative Media*	In several cities across the United States, flat video screens have been installed in bar and restaurant restrooms, allowing spots to be shown while customers take care of business. EK3 Technologies, based in London, Ontario, developed the system, in which ads are digitally programmed to run on the screens, called Nbox displays, 24 hours a day. The first Nbox displays began appearing in Toronto two years ago. They have since spread to Atlanta, Boston, and Los Angeles. Clients that have used the technology to advertise include Budweiser, Pontiac, and Fox Sports Net. So far, the reactions have been mainly positive. **Source:** Anderson, Mae, "Toilet Targets," *Adweek,* Midwest Edition, September 30, 2002, p. 38.

A number of the communication resources and media described here have undergone many changes recently.

Sales Promotion

In the last few years, there has been a shift in consumer markets from advertising to promotions; increasingly, companies are choosing to stimulate sales in the short term. The causes of this include a greater acceptance in companies of the instrument of promotions, more pressure on product managers to achieve higher sales, and increased competition: more brands that are starting to look like each other. Another factor may be that the availability of more data and more detailed data (scanning) makes it easier to measure the effects of promotions.

Three comments about the use of promotions follow:

1. Frequent use of promotions may have *negative consequences for brand equity in the long run:* Consumers start to doubt the quality and get used to brand switching. Therefore, it is recommended to use mostly value-adding promotions and fewer price discounts. Another recommendation is to have a promotion fit as much as possible with the brand, for example, by offering extras that fit logically with the brand.
2. Effect research into promotions shows that *promotions are often not profitable for manufacturers.*[17] Often there is a sales peak during the promotion, but afterward the sales are typically lower (hoarding by consumers), and promotions do not always lead to effects that are favorable for the manufacturer, such as increased sales in relation to the competition and extra consumption. Another market effect is that competitors often react to each other's price promotions, thus decreasing the mutual market share effects.
3. Retailers are often not happy with actions because they lead to *irregularities in demand* and therefore make extra demands on logistics, inventory, and administration.

Some of these effects are summarized in Figure 11-15, which depicts the so-called *price promotion doom loop.* Generally speaking, this circle shows the risk of a short-term (cash) orientation of companies instead of a long-term brand and customer orientation.

FIGURE 11-15
Price Promotion
Doom Loop

Source: Calkins, T. (2005),
"The Challenge of Branding."
In Alice M. Tybout and Tim
Calkins (eds), *Kellogg on
Branding*, Hoboken, NJ: Wiley.

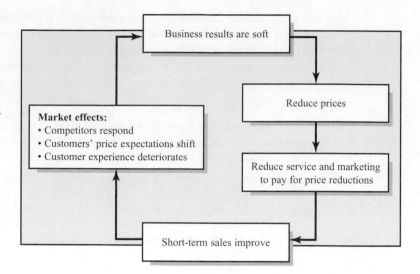

Television

In many countries the number of television channels has increased greatly. For advertisers this has advantages and disadvantages. Among the advantages of increased competition in the television advertising market are the *broader possibilities* (more advertising time, combination commercials, and more flexibility). A potential advantage is that the specific target audiences that watch specific channels can be reached better, but this can occur only when channels profile themselves sufficiently. Among the disadvantages of the increase in the number of channels are *dispersion* (it is very difficult to reach a large part of the audience) and *irritation* (caused by increased amounts of advertising). The second factor is leading a lot of advertisers to use more *nonspot advertising,* that is, communication on television in ways other than commercials, for example, through program sponsoring or *product placement* (the visible presence of a product in a program). Other issues in television advertising are *increasing zapping behavior* and growing technological *possibilities to skip commercials.* Advertisers are choosing to use more advertising via media other than television, for example, the Internet (see Case 11-13).

CASE 11-13

The 30-Second Advertisement Starts to Look Obsolete

A 30-second spot in the Super Bowl, the most frequently watched television program in the United States, sells for more than $2 million. Meanwhile, a staggering $128.7 million was spent on political ads in last year's race for the White House. Yet it's somewhat ironic that the monolithic U.S. television networks that have provided so much of the world's most popular TV content (*Friends, The Simpsons, Frasier*) are confronting a plethora of problems. First, cable shows seem to be attracting more quality audiences. Second, personal video recorders such as TiVo are becoming more popular in the United States. Last but not least, clients are starting to demand ideas that extend beyond the 30-second TV ad. There are glimmers of hope. Reality shows such *The Apprentice* and *Survivor* attract big audiences, and *Desperate Housewives* was the undisputed hit series of 2004. One thing is for sure, however. The Internet is claiming more ad dollars than ever, and advertisers have fallen in love with its accountability. It claims 5.1 percent of all ad spending, more than cinema and outdoor combined.

Source: *US,* Campaign (UK), March 11, 2005, Supplement, p. 38.

The Internet

Another important development has been the advance of the Internet. The penetration of the Internet is increasing very rapidly worldwide. The Internet potentially offers suppliers important opportunities to come into contact with customers directly and on a global scale. The penetration of the Internet is strongest among youth, but adults and even elderly people are increasingly "Internetting." In modern countries a majority of people regularly use the Internet to seek product information. The number of transactions on the Internet is increasing but is perhaps bounded by concerns about privacy. Privacy seems to be an important limitation to any expectation of large-scale transactions through this medium. However, this does not hold true for banking transactions: The Internet is commonly used for banking. Thus, if paying systems continue to become safer, it may be expected that the use of Internet for transactions (*e-commerce*) will continue to grow rapidly. For advertisers an advantage of Internet is its *accountability*: It is relatively easy to measure some effects, such as effective reach. The Internet can be used as an advertising medium (on the Web sites of "others") or as a company's own communication and transaction channel (a company's own Web site). Both applications are developing rapidly. A recent development (2005) is the enormous growth of *weblogs*. Every five months the number of weblogs is doubling, and research showed that at the end 2005, 10 percent of online customers weekly participated in a weblog. Thus, news increasingly is spread via weblogs instead of via television or newspapers. Weblogs thus increase the communication and negotiation power of customers (see Section 5.5.2). This makes it important for marketers to follow the customer and create value by stimulating *communities*. Managers have to give up control to gain control. In Section 11.6 we pay more attention to the Internet.

CASE 11-14 *How Youths Communicate*	Adults have long claimed that youths speak a different language. Whatever they speak, today's North American online young consumers age 12 to 21 communicate in a wide variety of ways. An overwhelming 95 percent use instant messaging (IM), own their own mobile phones, or have a broadband connection at home, and more than one-third have all three. Compared with adults, these young consumers exhibit starkly different behaviors and attitudes about mobile phones. But younger Internet users are not enamored only with the virtual: In most cases they prefer face-to-face communications to IM, e-mail, phone calls, and text messaging. **Source:** Study by Forrester Research, October 2005; summary on http://www.forrester.com/Research/Document/Excerpt/0,7211,37052,00.html.

Integrated Communication

In the use of each of the media instruments mentioned earlier, the concept of integrated communication plays a central role. This concept is related to two levels, and for both levels guidance is provided from the perspective of the brand:

1. *Integration of the communication instruments.* To achieve an optimal results with the various instruments, it is important to synchronize the instruments. In this way, as clear an image of the company and its products as possible should be communicated to the environment. This means that the following should be synchronized: the content of advertising messages, the content of communication via the Internet, and the information provided by the contact staff. The last item is often a problem in practice: In external communication a certain brand personality may be "portrayed" (e.g., "you are the central focus for us"), but if that promise does not come true at the first telephone contact because of long waiting times and less than friendly telephone operators, the

company loses credibility. Oddly, especially with many service providers, the harmonization of external and internal communication leaves a lot to be desired.

2. *Integration within each of the communication instruments,* for example, within advertising the synchronization of the various media (television, newspapers, Internet, etc.). An example relates to the synchronization of thematic advertising for an insurance company through television commercials with the sales activities via newspapers.

The guidance of the communication instruments and media occurs completely from the perspective of the brand: All communication expressions must contribute to the desired brand personality.

CASE 11-15
Integrated Communication at IBM

As vice president of worldwide integrated marketing communications for IBM Corp., Lisa Baird is responsible for all strategic brand, product, and services advertising at IBM as well as media, direct, interactive, events, and sponsorships. In 2004, Baird was the driving force behind the "On Demand" campaign for IBM through television spots, print, online, direct, events, and other media. Baird said that one of the challenges is that IBM targets C-level executives who consume many different media. "Our clients are global travelers at multinational corporations, so we try to engage them in innovative ways and develop truly global programs." For example, in 2004, IBM teamed up with CNN on a global broadcast partnership, sponsored the U.S. Open tennis tournament, and used streaming media on sites such as CNN.com and ESPN.com to communicate with business and information technology audiences. Baird said another one of her challenges is to test all marketing messages rigorously to make sure they are accomplishing IBM's communications goals and are seamless across all media.

Source: Maddox, Kate, "IBM Makes the Most of Many Media," *B to B,* October 25, 2004, p. 10.

11.5.8   Brand Tracking, Advertising Tracking, and Effect Research

After all plans have been executed, it should be determined whether the objectives have been achieved. For this purpose, measurements should be made of the variables of the objectives (*measurement of results*). Let us suppose that such measurements have occurred beforehand as well. The optimal way of measuring results is to repeat those measurements not just once but periodically. If sufficient measurements of the variables of objectives are available, the next step may be to perform *effect research:* Which developments in the variables of the objectives can be attributed to communication?

Measurement of Results

As was indicated earlier, the Advertising Response Matrix is a tool for choosing communication goals. That means that this matrix may also be used for measuring results. Figure 11-16 shows which data sources are available to obtain insight into the various components of the matrix.

Measurements of advertising expenditures (B1) are available at agencies such as Nielsen Media Research. Coverage figures (B2) are collected in many countries by various organizations (see Case 11-16).

CASE 11-16
Competition in the Market for Media Reserach

Frank Maggio, the irrepressible new owner of ErinMedia, a fledgling television research firm in Bradenton, Florida, is out to swipe business from Nielsen Media Research. Maggio says he vows to grab 60 percent of Nielsen's business in five years. To divine the ratings that guide how advertisers spend $72 billion a year on television spots, Nielsen makes national projections of numbers taken from a sample of 8,000 homes. Those homes are equipped with "people meter" monitors that track the shows viewers watch. To peg ratings in some local markets, it relies on hand-scrawled diaries. It's Dark Ages stuff, Maggio scoffs. Today viewers can have a hundred channels or more to watch, making diaries a joke, and cable boxes make it possible to track the detailed viewing habits of millions of homes rather than relying on a mere sample. Whereas Nielsen typically publishes viewing data in 15-minute blocks, ErinMedia can offer it by the second, showing when people zap away from one ad but stick around for another.

Source: Fass, Allisson, "TiVo This Story," *Forbes,* July 4, 2005, p. 58.

Category C contains items such as pretesting, which was discussed in Section 11.5.6. Advertising tracking and *brand tracking* (category D) means that advertising responses and brand responses are measured *continuously and consistently.* Those responses are related to awareness and associations. Brand tracking therefore continuously measures the sources of brand equity, which immediately indicates the advantages of tracking. *Tracking* (also called monitoring) is a diagnosis instrument for the brand; it is in a way a "brand thermometer." If one of the measured variables "scores" worse, immediately a check should be made to see what may be causing that. Another advantage of tracking is that if time series become available over time, there are possibilities for performing effect research.

Category E relates to the purchasing behavior of individuals. On this issue, data for markets for fast-moving consumer goods are collected by GfK through a consumer panel (see also Section 4.7). Another way to collect these data is through a company's own customer database, assuming the customers are willing to provide their Name, Address, Residence data at the time of purchase; this also can be done if transactions are conducted via the Internet (e-commerce). Even then the purchases made at competitors are unknown.

FIGURE 11-16
Communication Objectives and Information Sources*

Source: Adapted from Franzen.[18]

Advertising input

A. 1. Characteristics of the advertisement (campaign)
   - Company's own evaluation and judgment by experts
2. Choice of media
   - Company's own measurements and data (BBC)
B. 1. Advertising expenditures
   - Nielsen Media Research
2. Confrontation (exposure) and reach
   - Various agencies
   - Single-source research

Output on the individual level

C. Advertising responses
   - Pretesting
   - Advertising tracking

D. Brand responses
   - Brand-tracking instruments (monitoring)

E. Brand behavior responses
   - GfK consumer panel
   - Single-source research

Output at the market level

F. Market responses
   - Nielsen and GfK store panels

*In this matrix, "communication" could be substituted for "advertising." However, some factors for communication instruments apart from advertising are more difficult to measure.

Single-source research means that within a panel of households, for each individual household ("single source") it is documented what that household purchases (this occurs through *home scanning*; the consumers scan bar codes of products at home with a hand scanner) as well as what television programs the members of the household watch. Since per household the viewing behavior (category B2) and purchasing behavior (category E) are known, single-source research is particularly suitable for effect research. Category F relates to sales data (marketing objectives). The supplier has data regarding its own brand in its own files. Sales of competing brands may be obtained from AC Nielsen, IRI or GfK for markets of fast moving consumer goods, and for some other markets.(see Section 4.7).

Effect Research

Earlier in this chapter we described methods and sources for measuring both the input and the output of communication activities. To know whether there are causal connections between the two, additional research methods should be applied. These methods can be classified into two categories:

1. *Causal models*
2. *Experiments*

In these two categories, only experiments provide a pure insight into causal relationships.

Causal Models   *Causal models* are used to determine whether there are relationships between various factors. In terms of the Advertising Response Matrix, several applications are possible. The best-known application is the one in which a relationship is made between B and F in Figure 11-16: whether advertising has an impact on sales. In doing this, it is important to include not only advertising expenditures as an explanatory variable but also other marketing mix elements, such as price and distribution. When all relevant elements of the marketing mix are included, it may be determined whether the sales are influenced by the advertising expenditures. If that is the case and there is a reasonable presumption of a causal link, it is confirmed that the advertising was "effective" in the sense of being connected to the sales.

In addition to the connection between advertising expenditures and sales, the relationship between advertising expenditures (category B2) and brand equity (category D) can be examined. For this purpose there should be time series available for the sources of brand equity, for example, brand awareness. If a company uses brand tracking, it will have those time series.

A third application of causal models is to examine the relationship between brand equity (category D) and sales (category F). In that case, as many explanatory variables as possible should be included. Such research indicates which components of brand equity (e.g., a specific image aspect) contribute to the achievement of sales and to what degree.

Experiments   An *experiment* involves varying the "input variable" (e.g., television advertising expenditures, the creative expression, the time allocation of the advertising budget, a store display or not) across groups of consumers and then measuring the extent to which this leads to differences in the variable of the objective (e.g., certain brand associations or sales) for those groups. If care is taken that both groups of consumers are comparable and are exposed in a comparable way to all other influences, differences in the "output variable" (result) can be attributed completely to the "input variable" (cause). Experiments have the advantage in comparison to causal models that they:

- Are suitable for demonstrating *true causal relationships;* experiments are actually the only way to do reliable research on the relationship between communication and sales.
- Are not dependent on the availability of time series of variables and therefore can be used in *all product categories* beyond fmcg's.

Experiments are used regularly in marketing science. An example is a study by Lodish[19] of the long-term effects of television advertising. To research that issue, those authors exposed a research group to additional television advertising for one year. During and after that year the purchases of the research group were documented, as well as those of a control group that had been exposed to less television advertising during the research year. After the research year, the advertising pressure was the same for both groups. The measurements of purchases during the research year and the two subsequent years showed the following:

- If TV advertising has an effect in the current year, that effect will double in the two subsequent years.
- If TV advertising has no effect in the current year, there will be no effect subsequently.

In marketing practice, experiments are not used very frequently. A reason for this may be that managers are hesitant to deviate from their preference policy in the area of, for example, communication. For example, it is conceivable that it will be difficult to use an experiment to persuade an advertiser that is convinced of the benefit of television advertising to allocate part of the television budget to the magazine advertising it considers less effective. However, such an experiment could provide support for the advertiser's assumption about the effectiveness of television advertising (or the reverse, which would be equally important to know). Another barrier relates to the implementation. The reliability of an experiment depends on its structure, and a thorough preparation and a well-considered "design" therefore are necessary.[20]

Split-cable research is a specific application of experiments. This type of research uses single-source data and involves two separate target audiences that are brought into contact with television advertising in different ways (e.g., a difference in advertising pressure); the research focuses on determining the differences in purchasing that may result.[21] This kind of research currently can be implemented in only few countries because single-source data are not available in every country.

We conclude this section about communication with a few final remarks. In comparison to expenditures on advertising, companies spend only a little on *communication research.* It appears that people prefer to increase the media pressure rather than allocating a portion of the budget for effect research. Apparently, the benefit of research is not sufficiently appreciated. It might be a task for marketing science to demonstrate the added value of applied research. The following arguments might be used:

- Planning cannot occur if objectives have not been set and the results of communication are not measured subsequently. Without planning, providing direction is also difficult.
- In practice it is often argued that it is impossible to determine the separate effect of communication because so many other factors also have an influence on sales. However, earlier in this chapter we described methods (causal models and experiments) that can be used to determine the separate effect of communication.

- It is also often argued that even when it is known whether a campaign succeeded, it still is not known why the communication succeeded, and therefore it is also not known what should be done differently in the future. In this context it is often said: "We know that half the communication expenditures are effective, but we do not know which half." This remark is an argument for doing more experimentation, since experiments can be used to examine the effect of each form of input, including, for example, two different creative expressions, such as a more informational versus a transformational communication expression.

11.6 VALUE STRATEGIES, BRANDING, AND THE INTERNET

11.6.1 Introduction

Chapters 2, 9, and 10, along with this chapter, paid attention to how a brand can compete. Consecutively, we reviewed value strategies, other corporate strategies, brands and positioning, and the marketing mix. In this section we discuss how these concepts can be applied to brands that use the medium of the Internet. Case 11-17 shows that the high penetration of Internet makes this an interesting medium for advertisers.

CASE 11-17 *Penetration of the Internet, 2005*	The penetration of the Internet in modern countries is about two of every three households, as the table below shows.

Country	Penetration of Internet, %
New Zealand	78
Sweden	75
United States	69
Australia	68
Norway	68
Netherlands	66
South Korea	65
Canada	63
United Kingdom	63
Japan	61
Germany	57
Top 30*	65
Rest of the world	8
World total	15

Source: http://www.internetworldstats.com/top25.htm (updated November 21, 2005). ©Copyright 2001–2005, Miniwatts International, Ltd. All rights reserved.

*Including other top 30 countries (penetration above 50 percent) not mentioned here.

The Internet can be used in two ways:

1. A Web site of the brand.
2. Advertising on other Web sites.

The most interesting issue is the first application. That is the case because a company's own Web site has, from a marketing point of view, very interesting characteristics:

- The Internet is a two-way medium and is suitable for *customized communication* and transactions and thus for *building relationships*.
- The Internet (a Web site) is a medium that is fully owned by the brand; actually, a Web site is a *privately owned channel*. Some people predict that customers in the near future

will all have their own "television channels" by, for example, putting their own video clips on their Web sites.

- The use of the Internet is very *widespread,* especially among youngsters, who are the adults of tomorrow.

Thus, although the Internet hype of the 1990s is far in the past, the use of the Internet for advertising is worth being revived. We will treat the question "How can a brand compete over the Internet?" from the perspective of each of the three value strategies (Section 11.6.2, customer intimacy; Section 11.6.3, product leadership; Section 11.6.4, operational excellence) and subsequently show how the translation can occur toward brand levels, positioning, and the marketing mix. We end this section with some conclusions and a future perspective.

11.6.2 Customer Intimacy and the Internet

Value Strategy

The value strategy of customer intimacy appears to be an obvious way for brands to provide customer values through the Internet. After all, on the Internet a brand has direct contact with a customer. Yet customer intimacy requires more than that. The choice of this strategy means that the supplier chooses to take individual customer wishes into account and therefore in one way or another provides "tailored" products and services. This strategy in theory makes it possible to perform *mass customization:* delivering products that are made to order for each customer.[22]

This requires that the supplier know the customer and therefore know his or her preferences. This requires a current database that includes, in addition to NAR data, data on information search behavior and purchasing behavior. The customer must be prepared to "log in" under a certain name on the site of the supplier. In doing this, the customer expects that he or she will be recognized and that "made-to-order" transactions can be performed. This requires that the design of the Web site include a personal welcome page and preferably also personal offers that fit with the preferences of the customer and reward loyalty. In this value strategy, it should be possible to make real personal contact with the organization.

Implementing customer intimacy through the Internet requires *a very advanced database* and a flexible supply of product and service delivery. A clear example of a brand that chose this strategy is Amazon.com. When you log in on Amazon, the site knows your preferences and informs you about new titles that might be interesting to you. More and more brands offer customers possibilities to "make" their own products and buy them; it is possible to construct one's own Barbie doll on the Internet and have Levi's made to order or design one's own Toyota Scion. Another well-known example is Dell, which enables customers to put together their own personal computers over the Internet. However, making one's own product is not customer intimacy but only a first step, since the company does not necessarily keep the customer's preferences.

Brand Levels and Positioning

For brands that choose customer intimacy, trust plays an important role. Customers consciously enter into a relationship and place great importance on privacy. For brand levels, this means that a brand needs to position itself as an identifiable supplier. Thus, the *corporate brand level* may play an important role in that regard. Another advantage of the use of this brand level is that the supplier may use *cross-selling.* For example, Unilever could offer different products to the customer if the company pursues customer intimacy for certain SBUs.

The positioning can be two-sided: The central benefit could be that the brand offers products made to order for a "reasonable" price, in short, that it truly is close to the customer.

CASE 11-18
Customized Communication at Starwood Hotels

It seems that the effective days of e-mail are ending, even in high-end businesses. Take, for example, the case of Starwood Hotels & Resorts Worldwide. This lodging brand sent an e-mail to its married male customers with the tagline "Share a Weekend with Your Girlfriend at Westin." Marketing mavens, take note: This not what is meant by customer intimacy. That refers to the fact that you should know who your customers are and use information you gather about them intelligently, as if you were the corner store operator who knows everyone coming through the door.

Source: Steinert-Threlkeld, Tom, "You've Got Mail: But Check with Your Wife," *Baseline*, January 2005, p. 1.

Marketing Mix

It has been said that for brands on the Internet, the implementation of the four P's should take place very differently than it did in the days of the classic manner. Figure 11-17 shows this. The implementation of the marketing mix should be much more *customer-oriented:* Products are made to order; in setting the price, the question of what the customer is prepared to pay plays a much bigger role (including through auctions, negotiations, etc., for example, priceline.com); distribution may occur physically or through the Internet; and communication should place much more emphasis on a *dialogue* than on a monologue. In addition, the role of the brand is not limited to communication but is important in each contact with the customer.

Figure 11-17 assumes that each brand operates according to these new possibilities, yet that depends on the chosen value strategy. If we return to the value strategy of customer intimacy, many of the principles of the new interpretation of the marketing mix apply. Both producing and delivering products made to order and two-sided communication are important.

FIGURE 11-17   **Marketing Instruments in "Normal" Marketing and Customer Intimacy**

Source: Adapted from the Gronsted Group.

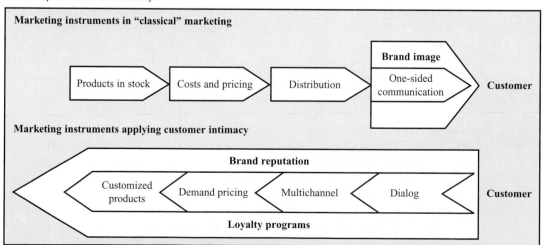

11.6.3   Product Leadership and the Internet

Value Strategy

The value strategy of *product leadership* means that the supplier is the first with innovations and in effect continuously leads the way in the product category. Another possibility is being the "brand leader": the best in emotional positioning. The added value of the Internet at the level of this value strategy does not appear to be very large for most products and services, with the exception of products that can be delivered physically through the Internet, such as software, news products, clipping service, and magazines. Innovative products and services may be offered both in the classical way and through the Internet. However, added value is possible in the area of positioning and communication.

CASE 11-19 *The Internet in Product Leadership*	Not that long ago, Fleetwood Enterprises Inc. was in the recreational vehicle industry the unquestioned leader in product innovation, invariably the first to market with features that made buyers reach for their checkbooks. But in the mid-1990s, as the company grew to nearly $3 billion in sales, the pace of product innovation slowed. When the company's market share began to stall, Fleetwood management in 1999 ordered an overhaul of the company's entire product development process to speed new designs to market. The changes included the deployment of new collaborative design software. The software products foster collaboration across departments such as engineering and manufacturing as well as with external suppliers and customers early in the design loop. The result: Fleetwood is back in the product innovation driver's seat. One challenge, however, is to establish confidence in Internet security, since Web-based design collaboration means you're sharing highly confidential intellectual property. **Source:** Stackpole, Beth, "Innovation in the Fast Lane," *eWeek*, July 23, 2001.

Brand Levels and Positioning

The positioning of a brand with this value strategy might be that the brand profiles itself as the "specialist" in the relevant category. Because the brand is leading the way, it may be assumed that the brand is very expert. In terms of brand personality, a value such as competence can be a good fit. In this case, the corporate brand plays a role as well. Customers like to know who that innovator is.

Marketing Mix

An elaboration in terms of the marketing mix might be that the brand keeps customers as informed as possible of new products and developments. In this regard, the supplier could also provide advice to customers with questions without that advice being directly related to sales (e.g., service). The brand might also use a well-organized Web site to help customers as much as possible in the information search process or with problems in the category and also to refer customers to places where even more relevant information is available.

An example of a company that uses this strategy is Pampers. The site Pampers.com provides much relevant information for parents with babies: results of polls (what size family do you want? etc.), frequently asked questions and answers from experts (when should my baby speak sentences of more then two words?), the possibility of posing one's own question to the expert panel or comminicating with other parents (community), and the possibility of participating in a real loyalty program ("Pampers gift certificates": collecting points by filling in bar codes and then receiving gifts for the baby).

With this value strategy, the added value of the Internet appears to be communication and service.

11.6.4 Operational Excellence and the Internet

Value Strategy and Positioning

The value strategy of operational excellence implies that a supplier chooses to deliver convenience and/or a low price (positioning with distribution or price). In both areas, the Internet may provide added value.

CASE 11-20 *The Internet and Operational Excellence*	Royal Resorts has implemented an e-commerce engine that provides real-time transactional capabilities. For the first time, consumers can not only view a property but pinpoint the specific unit and week of ownership they desire and then make the purchase online in a completely self-service transaction. Through www.royalresortscancun.com, Royal has introduced true e-commerce functionality for its active sales initiatives at the Royal Sands, a 340-villa resort in Cancún, Mexico. Maximizing Internet sales is taken seriously at Royal; it offers a 10 percent discount for units purchased over the Internet, which is an important way to motivate buyer behavior and demonstrate to consumers the benefits of self-service and the efficiencies of e-commerce. This way, customers are seen as an integrated part of the supply chain and an essential link to optimize operations. **Source:** Brown, William J., "A Web-Based Sales Lesson," *Lodging Hospitality,* September 1, 2002, p. 18.

Marketing Mix

In terms of Figure 11-17, the marketing mix elements of price and distribution play a role here. The potential added value of the Internet in the area of *convenience* is that products may be delivered to the home. This is an important reason for the growth in e-commerce. E-commerce requires excellent distribution. For some products, home delivery implies that people have to be home, which is often contrary to the wish for convenience. This problem might be solved if homes were equipped with cooled boxes that could be opened from the inside and the outside (as is already the case sometimes in the United States). Competing through the Internet with a low price is feasible for brands that are able to save costs. An obvious cost saving for a brand applying e-commerce is that no distributor is used (disintermediation). However, that is countered by additional logistic costs. Another potential cost saving is in the purchasing: Brands that can reach large groups of customers may achieve purchasing discounts. Some brands already incorporate this by indicating that a certain product is being offered for a certain price assuming that a certain number of buyers are prepared to buy it. The reverse also happens: customers who join together via the Internet and extract price discounts from suppliers.

11.6.5 Conclusions and Future Perspective

Value Strategies and the Internet

In this book the concept of thinking in terms of customer values plays a large role. The Internet can also play a role in this area. The extent to which the Internet does this depends on the chosen value strategy of the brand. The strongest added value of the Internet seems to be for the following value strategies:

- *Customer intimacy*. With this value strategy, the Internet provides good opportunities for a brand that positions itself in terms of the product (made to order), distribution (home delivery), and communication (two-sided).
- *Operational excellence*. With this value strategy, a brand on the Internet may attempt to gain a competitive advantage with price or distribution.

- *Product leadership*. With this value strategy, a brand will position itself with the marketing mix element of product, and the added value of the Internet lies in supplementary services and communication.

Future Perspective

Although it is difficult to look into the future, we end this chapter with a subjective perspective. In regard to the environment, we expect the "clutter" to continue to grow: The quantity and diversity of communication will continue to increase along with the number of competing products and services. This will lead to several trends among the customers. First, their expectations will rise and it will thus be more difficult to fullfill their needs. Take a look at how current youths are living in comparison with the way the youths of the previous generation lived. Second, for customers it will be increasingly difficult to make the best choices. Third, in this dynamic world customers will value convenience more. Fourth, they will demand honesty and openness.

How should companies react to this? The clear anwer to this question is that companies that really listen to their customers and help them solve their problems will win the game. Regarding the three value strategies, it looks as if *customer intimacy* will best fit the anticipated needs. If a company really knows the individual needs and perceptions of its customers and is able to deliver customized products and services, this may meet the need for convenience, trust, and real satisfaction better than do the strategies of product leadership and operational excellence. Some elements of the product leadership strategy could and should be combined with this: regularly improving products and services based on research on customers and building a clear brand reputation.

In regard to communication channels, there can be a shift from classical media advertising (television, print, outdoor) to customized communication through the Internet, enabling a company to provide advice and participate in communities. In addition, investments are needed in building databases and keeping them up to date, based on a permission marketing principle.

Summary

On the basis of the chosen target audience and positioning, decisions are made about the elements of the marketing mix. Product decisions relate to decisions about the choice of varieties, the design, and the service. As a result of the necessity to pursue customer satisfaction, competitive advantages based on products and services are very important. Price decisions relate to the interpretation of the price policy, price strategies (such as skimming and penetration), and price determination. Because price is often seen as an indicator of quality and therefore is directly related to brand positioning, it is often said that these days too much attention is paid to price actions. Distribution decisions relate to the choice of channels and the management of channels. With the rise of Internet multichannel management has become of vital importance.

In the communication planning process, an advertiser should determine the target audience, the proposition, and the communication objectives as well as the communication budget. Communication objectives should be specific and measurable and may relate to brand awareness (knowledge), brand associations (attitude), and purchasing intention (behavior). The choice of the objectives depends on where problems are located (image versus identity) and on the chosen proposition. Based on a clear and focused briefing, the communication consulting agency develops a creative concept that may be pretested with a target audience.

The best creative ideas are ideas that are strongly linked to the brand, entertaining, distinctive, simple, and applicable in many variations. The message may be communicated through an increasing range of media. Growth may be observed in the use of sales promotions for consumers and the trade (with the risk of getting into a price promotion doom loop), experience communication, and direct communication via the Internet. Advertising via television has also been increasing but zapping behavior and equipment enabling *customized* TV watching may hinder spot advertising and might stimulate non-spot advertising. In building a strong, relevant, and unique brand image, communication remains a very important tool, and therefore brands will need to apply the various media in a creative and integrated fashion. Innovation is needed to be heard within the 'clutter'. The Internet is a normal part of the integrated communication mix but offers special opportunities to support the value strategy of customer intimacy. In addition, advertisers should continuously and consistently measure factors such as advertising knowledge and attitude toward advertising, brand knowledge, and customer satisfaction. If such a measurement of results produces time series, causal models can be used to examine if and why communication has been effective. Also, experiments may be used to examine the effects of communication. In summary, brand communication is most effective under the following four conditions: Always apply the customers' perspective, be innovative in positioning and media, choose one brand value, and continuously check whether everything adds to the brand positioning. Chapter 12 discusses the organization and implementation of, among other things, communication.

Notes

1. For a more extensive description, refer to Kotler, Ph., and K. L. Keller (2005), *Marketing Management,* 12th ed., Upper Saddle River, NJ: Pearson.
2. Leeflang, P. S. H. (2003), *Marketing,* Groningen, Netherlands: Wolters Noordhoff, p. 326.
3. Leeflang (2003), p. 410.
4. Leeflang (2003), p. 375.
5. Adapted from Franzen, G. (1984), *Mensen, produkten en reclame: een handboek* (People, products and advertising: a handbook). Alphen aan den Rijn, Netherlands: Samsom.
6. Vakratsas, D., and T. Ambler (1999), "How Advertising Works: What Do We Really Know?" *Journal of Marketing.*63:26–43
7. Franzen, G. (1998), *Merken en Reclame* (Brands and advertising), Netherlands: Kluwer Bedrijfsinformatie.
8. Keller, K. L. (2003), *Strategic Brand Management: Building, Measuring and Managing Brand Equity,* 2nd ed.,Upper Saddle River, NJ: Prentice-Hall.
9. Geursen, G. (1990), *Een hazewind op gympen* (A greyhound in sport shoes), Leiden, Netherlands: Stenfert Kroese.
10. Lodish, L. M., M. M. Abraham, J. Livelsberger, B. Lubetkin, B. Richardson, and M. E. Stevens (1995a), "How T.V. Advertising Works: A Meta-Analysis of 389 Real World Split Cable T.V. Advertising Experiments," *Journal of Marketing Research* 32:125–139.
11. White, R. (1993), *Advertising: What It Is and How It Works,* 3rd ed, London: McGraw Hill.
12. Percy, L., and R. Elliot (2005), *Strategic Advertising Management,* 2nd ed., New York, Oxford University Press, Chapters 11 and 12.
13. Pieters, F. G. M., and M. Wedel (2004). "Attention Capture and Transfer in Advertising: Brand, Pictorial and Text Size Effects," *Journal of Marketing* 68:36–50.
14. Lodish et al. (1995a).
15. Lodish, Leonard M., Magid M. Abraham, Jeanne Livelsberger, Beth Lubetkin, Bruce Richardson, and Mary Ellen Stevens (1995b), "A Summary of Fifty-Five In-Market Experimental Estimates of the Long-Term Effect of TV Advertising," *Marketing Science* 14:G133–G140.
16. Blattberg, R. C., and S. A. Neslin (1990), *Sales Promotion: Concepts, Methods and Strategies,* Englewood Cliffs, NJ: Prentice-Hall.

17. Heerde, H. J., S. Gupta, and D. R. Wittink (2003), "Is 75% of the Sales Promotion Dump Due to Brand Switching? No, Only 33% Is," *Journal of Marketing Research* 40:481–491.

18. Franzen (1998).

19. Lodish et al. (1995b).

20. For a further discussion of this topic, refer to Malhotra, N. K. (2004), *Marketing Research: An Applied Orientation,* 4th ed., Upper Saddle River, NJ: Pearson.

21. The previously mentioned research studies by Lodish (1995a and 1995b) on short-term and long-term effects of television advertising were based on split-cable research.

22. Pine, B. J. (1993), *Mass Customization: The New Frontier in Business Competition,* Boston: Harvard Business School Press. See also Broekhuizen, T. L. J., and K. J. Alsem (2004), "Success Factors for Mass Customization: A Conceptual Model," *Journal of Market Focused Management* 5:309–330.

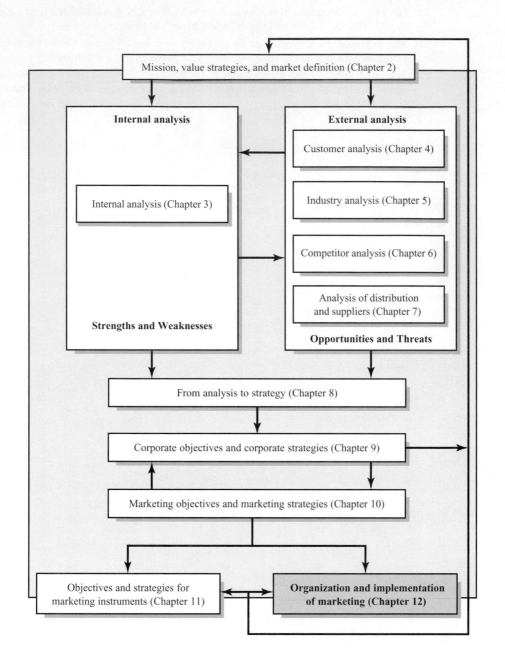

Mission, value strategies, and market definition (Chapter 2)

Internal analysis

Internal analysis (Chapter 3)

Strengths and Weaknesses

External analysis

Customer analysis (Chapter 4)

Industry analysis (Chapter 5)

Competitor analysis (Chapter 6)

Analysis of distribution and suppliers (Chapter 7)

Opportunities and Threats

From analysis to strategy (Chapter 8)

Corporate objectives and corporate strategies (Chapter 9)

Marketing objectives and marketing strategies (Chapter 10)

Objectives and strategies for marketing instruments (Chapter 11)

Organization and implementation of marketing (Chapter 12)

Organization and Implementation of Marketing

Key Points in This Chapter

- Know how to organize marketing and communication in a market-oriented organization.
- Know what motivates people in an organization.
- Know how to stimulate innovation.
- Be able to sell a marketing plan.
- Know the main pitfalls in planning.

INTRODUCTION

Chapters 2 through 11 detailed the various phases of the process of strategic marketing planning. Chapter 2 began with the vision and the identification of market boundaries. Chapters 3 through 8 were dedicated to the internal analysis and the external analysis. Chapters 9 through 11 were about planning (decisions). At least of equal importance is everything a company has to do to implement the plans properly: the organization and the implementation (execution). A marketing plan can be successful only if the people involved in the implementation (often the entire organization) are motivated to implement the task.

This final chapter is dedicated to the organization and implementation of marketing. First, Section 12.1 will discuss the organization of marketing and communication. Next, Section 12.2 will deal with team building and stimulating motivation in general within organizations, including incentives. Section 12.3 is about securing a foundation for a marketing plan, including making a financial performance timeline. Section 12.4 provides guidelines for the implementation of the planning.

We complete the book with a set of 11 tips for strategic marketing.

Nokia: Connecting People

We live in a world in which a growing part of our personal communication takes place through the use of wireless media such as mobile phones.

In 2003 the market for mobile phones grew strongly worldwide. This was largely a result of growth in markets such as India, Russia, and Brazil. In countries with a high penetration of mobile phones, there has been a growing shift in demand for equipment with more extensive uses (e.g., photo or video applications).

The market volume in 2003 was about 471 million units sold, a growth of 16 percent over the 405 million units sold in 2002. The growth was 20 percent in Europe, the Middle East, and Africa; 15 percent in the Asia-Pacific region; and 13 percent in North and South America.

Mobile telephony is changing from a medium for spoken communication to new "data-driven" applications in the area of multimedia applications both in the consumer market and in the business-to-business market. As proof of this growing demand for advanced products and services, in 2003 sales of mobile phones with a camera were for the first time higher than sales of digital cameras.

The worldwide demand for mobile phones with a camera is particularly strong in Asia, especially in Japan and Korea. Also, mobile phones get continuously more computer-like features, and phones with color screens are becoming much more common.

Competition in the market for mobile phones is based on control of the complete value chain. The market grows, and so constant investments are needed by the manufacturers in the key areas, such as branding, logistics, and product development. The mobile market is dominated by companies such as Nokia, Motorola, Sony Ericsson, and Samsung.

Nokia

Nokia is the world leader in mobile communication. Nokia says the following about this: "Nokia dedicates itself to enhancing people's lives and productivity by providing easy-to-use and secure products like mobile phones, and solutions for imaging, games, media, mobile network operators and businesses."

Since January 1, 2004, Nokia has adjusted its organizational structure to make it connect better to the strategy. The new structure has four business groups:

- Mobile telephony.
- Multimedia: products with functions such as imaging, games, music, media, and a wide variety of other attractive content.
- Networks: network infrastructure, service platforms, and related services for network operators and service providers.
- Enterprise solutions: mobile solutions that help companies mobilize their staff (also at a distance) but at the same time guarantee the security and reliability of the network.

Net Sales per Business Group (Fourth Quarter 2003)	Euro (Million)	Percent
Nokia mobile telephony	7,009	80
Nokia networks	1,706	19
Nokia other activities	108	1
Nokia Group	**8,789**	**100**

Nokia's organizational structure also has three horizontal departments. "Customer and Market Operations" contains Nokia's sales and marketing organization and production, logistics, and purchasing. "Technology Platforms" delivers the technology for Nokia's business groups and customers.

"Nokia Research Centre" is a crucial factor for the development of future products and services from Nokia. In close cooperation with all business groups, the Research Centre supports the activities of Nokia in the following areas:

- Development of new concepts, technologies, and applications.
- Development of breakthrough technology for the products of the future.
- A breeding ground for the development of new ideas.

Nokia believes that effective research and development is essential for the company to be able to compete in the market for mobile communication in the future. The following figure shows the organizational structure of Nokia.

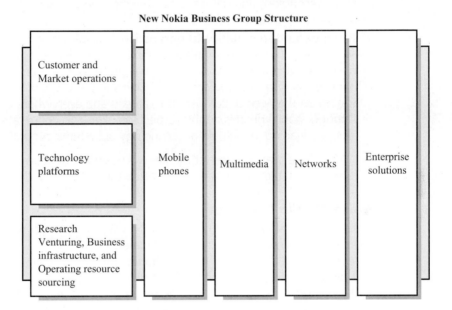

New Nokia Business Group Structure

Nokia's Business Strategy

Nokia has formulated its business strategy explicity: "We want to make use of our leading position by continuously tapping new segments in the mobile market. For this we choose the segments which we believe will grow fast, or faster than the average growth in the mobile market. From a historical point of view, this expansion to such segments in the first phases of their product life cycle has led to the situation that Nokia could position itself as one of the leading players in mobile communication. Through this Nokia has had an important influence on how we nowadays make use of mobile communication. Since this is also our goal for the future, we have formulated the following three strategies:

- **Expand mobile voice:** We believe that there are many opportunities for growth on the mobile market, and we plan to focus our central attention on this in the future as well. We think in this case above all of markets with a low percentage of mobile connections, compared to the size of the total population, of geographical environments where it is more cost-effective to build a mobile infrastructure than a fixed network, or of densely populated areas where factors such as bad living conditions or theft will lead to a preference for wireless solutions. We also want to focus on markets where the need for network capacity grows because the mobile network operators stimulate the switch from fixed to mobile networks.

- **Drive consumer mobile multimedia:** We plan to identify and explore new opportunities in the market with regard to products as well as servicing. We expect in this respect that new chances will evolve when several technologies will be combined, especially in the area of consumer multimedia. Our strategy is to discover and to identify the fastest growing segments in multimedia applications for the consumer market and to generate—in a profitable way—income through this. We want to do this by anticipating new consumer needs in this area and by developing innovative products and services. In the near future we will focus on visual technology and games, areas in which we already have developed a number of products.

- **Bring extended mobility to enterprise:** We want to explore the profitable segments in the business market by means of products and services from which businesses and individual employees will profit. Here we are thinking about handsets and tailor-made communication solutions. We will do that by concentrating on the need of companies to always and everywhere be contactable through mobile phones. In this respect we expect to cooperate with partners who are leading in the field of technology or systems integration.

"We believe that our three strategies will position our activities positively when the different digital techniques are brought together."

Nokia Mobile Telephony

Nokia mobile telephony is the world's largest producer of mobile phones. Nokia's product portfolio covers all consumer segments.

When the functionality of mobile phones shifts from voice-centered to integration with visual media, entertainment, and business applications, new markets with an enormous growth potential will emerge. In 2002 Nokia's market share rose for the fifth consecutive year, reaching a worldwide proportion of 38 percent.

The strategy of Nokia mobile telephony contains the following three spearheads:

- Differentiation of product supply. In 2002 Nokia launched a total of 34 new products with extra features in the fields of image, multimedia, mobile games, and ring tones. Fourteen of the new mobile phones had color screens and multimedia options. This stresses the growing importance of these new applications for Nokia's product portfolio.

- Thanks to Nokia's strong brand equity, segmentation is the basis of the company's success. For a long time Nokia has been capable of finding niches in the market for mobile phones, from price-sensitive consumers to fashion-oriented teenagers. Nokia strives to offer the perfect mobile solution for every segment.

- Excellence in execution. Nokia sees its experience and efficient way of operating as a key competency that offers the company more and more of an advantage with regard to the competition. Nokia has learned to offer new ideas and technologies in a customer-oriented way, at the right moment, and in the right amount. A short "time to market" is essential for success in the market for mobile phones.

Source: Nokia, www.nokia.com, March 28, 2004.

Questions

1. Give a graphic display of the market definition of Nokia with the aid of a diagram (see Section 2.3).
2. Treacy and Wiersema distinguish three value strategies (chapter 3). Judging from the information in this case, has Nokia made a choice for one of these value strategies? Explain your answer.
3. Give an example of a useful application of portfolio analysis (Section 8.3) by Nokia.
4. Place each of the three business strategies in the growth matrix of Ansoff (Section 9.2).
5. Construct a balanced scorecard (Section 3.1) for the strategic business unit (SBU) "Nokia mobile telephony." Use the information from the case but make your own assumptions when the information in the case is not sufficient.

12.1 ORGANIZATION OF MARKETING AND COMMUNICATION

In many companies, there has been a marked fall-off in the influence, stature and significance of the corporate marketing department[1]. Today, marketing is often less of a corporate function and more a diaspora of skills and capabilities spread across the organization. By itself, the disintegration of the marketing center is not a cause for concern, but the decline of core marketing competence certainly is. This, in combination with the turbulent environment of companies such as more demanding customers makes it more important then ever to properly incorporate marketing within an organization.

The most important condition for marketing is having a strong *market orientation*. The issue then becomes what the infrastructure of the organization should be like in the context of this condition. Another organizational issue is the departments with which marketing must collaborate the most to be able to implement strategies effectively. We now examine both of these issues. We start by discussing the organization of marketing. Then we focus on the organization of communication because the instrument of communication determines the brand image to a considerable extent.

12.1.1 Organization of Marketing

The question to be answered here is how and where a marketing department fits into an organization. However, before addressing this question, it is important to state that having a marketing department does not mean that an organization is customer-oriented. If interest in the desires of the customer is limited to the marketing department, there is something wrong. Customer orientation concerns the *entire organization*. The reverse also applies: A customer-oriented organization does not necessarily have to have a marketing department. Especially in smaller companies, there is often no marketing department, but this kind of company may in fact be customer-oriented.

CASE 12-1 *Organization of Marketing*	Marketing rarely has direct representation on boards of directors. As a result, many long-term marketing and brand strategies have withered on the vine because of inadequate resources or corporate commitment that fluctuates with each quarterly income statement. Most boards include a chief financial officer and one or two "industry people" with backgrounds in operations. Rarely does one see a vice president of sales or chief marketing officer at the table. Think about it: Every board has an audit committee, but have you ever heard of a customer

or market committee? Why not? Most boards are self-propagating: New candidates usually are selected by existing (read "not marketing") members. Even when nominated, marketers are rarely selected.

Source: Wong, Ken, "One Rung Shy of Leadership?" *Marketing,* May 16, 2005, p. 9.

Forms of Organization

To know how marketing activities should be organized within a company, it is important to establish what those activities are. This includes all activities that concern the analysis of the environment (*analysis*), the making of marketing decisions and the drafting of a marketing plan (*planning*), the implementation of the decisions that are made (*implementation*), and the checking and evaluation of the results (*control*). The most important choices regarding these decisions are the choice of markets and target groups and the distinguishing power. All these marketing activities show that there must be a direct link between marketing and upper management. Moreover, marketing must be "on equal terms" with departments such as finance, personnel, and research and development. This is the case because marketing decisions can be implemented only in close cooperation with other "functions" within a company.

How can marketing be organized? The following are the main options:

1. *Functional* organization.
2. *Product* organization.
3. *Customer-oriented* organization and account management.
4. *Regional* organization.

We now explain each of these options.

Many companies opt for an organizational form in which the various basic functions are fulfilled by separate departments. In this case, a company may have a purchasing department, a production department, a personnel department, a finance department, and a *marketing department.* The marketing department may include tasks (and subdepartments) such as market research, sales, product development, and communication. An organization in which the tasks of the employees are grouped on the basis of company functions is called a functional organization. A division based on functions is the most common and is a simple system. The disadvantage is that no one is responsible for a particular product or particular customer groups (segments).

Companies with different products or brands often opt for the *product management* or "brand management" system. Separate managers are appointed who are responsible for a certain product (e.g., the diapers) or a certain brand (e.g., Pampers). Managers in these positions must collaborate extensively with each other within the company to be able to set up all the activities they want to undertake related to their brand (e.g., innovation, price setting, research) in a well-coordinated way.

Another way to organize the marketing function is as a *customer-oriented organization*: a division according to markets or customer groups. This kind of division is particularly useful if a company is clearly servicing different target groups, such as consumers and organizations (business markets).

The *account management system* is a variation of the customer-oriented organization. An account manager is a person who is responsible for a client (account). This system is increasingly common among food manufacturers that often have only a few clients (distributors: food retailers) that are all quite large. The task of the account manager is to ensure that the relationship with the distributor remains optimal.

FIGURE 12-1
Customer-Oriented
Organization in
Combination with
Brand Management

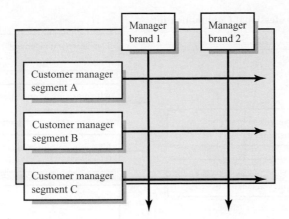

A fourth form is the *regional organization*, in which separate managers are responsible for the turnover in regions (parts of a country, countries, or combinations of countries and/or parts of the world).

Toward a Customer-Oriented Organization

Forms of a "brand management" organization are both useful and logical in many companies. It is handy if there is one manager and one group of people responsible for a brand. The danger is that too much focus is placed on the brand and/or product and too little is placed on the customer. It is sometimes said that "brand management is dead." This does not mean that brands are not important but rather that a strong organizational focus exclusively on brands is not wise. Because of the vast importance of customer-oriented business, it is important that another form of a buyer-oriented organizational form always be chosen as well. An example could be a consumer variant of account management: the appointment of a customer manager within the company who is responsible for a certain target group (e.g., young people). This manager knows the target group well and tries to promote its interests within the company. The goal is *not* to sell as much as possible. A customer manager is not a salesperson but certainly is suited to coordinate *complaint settlements*. If there are different target groups, there can be different customer managers. If this system is combined with a brand management system, the customer managers will negotiate regularly with the various brand managers to ensure that the target group is served in the best possible way. With a customer manager, the company brings the customer in house, as it were (Figure 12-1).

In practice, one of the forms outlined in the figure may not used; instead, there are combinations. In these cases, the *formal organization* (the structure) becomes more complicated. Therefore, the importance of good *informal organization* increases. Informal organization concerns the rules of conduct within a company that are not established formally but are customarily followed. Examples include "dropping in on each other" and drinking coffee together. Informal communication in an organization is very important for the ability to react quickly. Organizations that work only according to established hierarchical systems are often not very flexible and are not able to react quickly to changes in the environment.

12.1.2 Organization of Communication

All forms of communication of a brand (or company or product) influence the brand image for the target group. A strong and positive reputation is very important for success. This can be achieved only with communication that is organized and implemented professionally. Chapter 11 stated that agencies must be contracted for the development of a

FIGURE 12-2 **Factors that Promote Professional Communication**

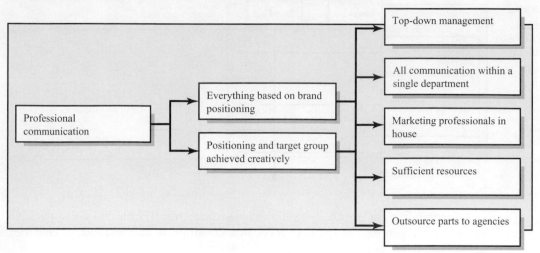

campaign. Creative communication and creative and efficient media planning require independent expertise. However, this does not negate the fact that the responsibility for communication lies entirely with the brand and that there is still a huge amount of communication to be done and arranged by the brand.

There are two major preconditions:

1. A *clear image* should be communicated consistently.
2. This image should be communicated in a *creative way* that *fits* with the brand.

These preconditions can be satisfied only if upper management emphasizes their importance and is therefore prepared to accept their consequences.

The following factors are important in fulfilling these preconditions (see Figure 12-2):

1. *Management from the top of the organization.* The image to be communicated is determined in the vision on brand positioning. This is a matter for upper management. The "leader" of the company plays an important role in communication, but many others participate as well. This can lead to a consistent image only if an intrinsic top-down management system is already in place. Therefore, there must always be a "hotline" between the head of communications and the head of the company. The head of communications can also take on the job of *"reputation watchdog"*[2] (see also Case 11-15). For instance, if there is a crisis situation (e.g., poison, unsafe products, personal scandals), it should be dealt with quickly and adequately.

2. *Continuous fine-tuning of all forms of communication.* In light of the previous point, all forms of communication must be well attuned to each other. In large companies, there generally should be different departments and persons who are concerned with communication (public relations, sponsoring, advertising, design, personal sales, direct marketing, personnel, etc.), and the primary danger is that they will work counter to each other and go their own ways. Organizations often decide to choose another logo without bringing that choice in line with the brand positioning, or a different image may be given in personnel advertisements than is used in advertising. Optimal alignment can be achieved if all communications activities are organized in one large department. In this department, the specializations mentioned above can be defined and the heads of those subdepartments can regularly confer and drop in on one another and on the head

FIGURE 12-3
Organization of
Communication
within a Company

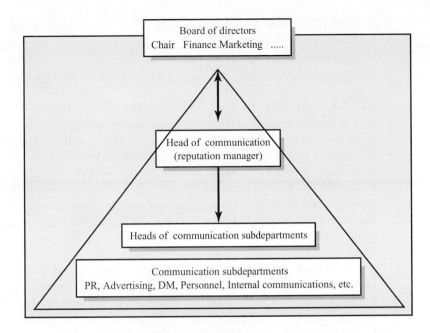

of communication. This, in combination with the previous point, provides a picture like the one in Figure 12-3.

3. *Personnel with marketing and communication knowledge.* A great deal of knowledge is needed for professional communication, and so people have to be taken on for this purpose. It is sometimes thought that only people originating from the relevant sector (financial services, universities, health care, etc.) are in a position to run these marketing and communication departments. This misconception leads to the idea that only people with an understanding of that market will work in communication. This has two big disadvantages: The people in question often have little understanding of marketing, and they lack a fresh external perspective. A good communication strategy can ensure good communication in every market and for any company.

4. *Sufficient support and resources.* It takes time and thus money to change images. One-time communication or only a bit of communication is too little. Being modest doesn't help either: Even with a good product, word-of-mouth advertisement and public relations unfortunately do not get the job done today. The competition will do more and do it more professionally. You may be the best, but if nobody knows that, you have a problem.

5. *Support from professional communication agencies.* As was stated above, even with good communication knowledge in-house, assistance from agencies is often required. Matters related to communication that can be outsourced include creation (translation of brand positioning into communication), media planning (both through a communication consultancy bureau), brand name development (name agencies), and design (design firms).

12.2   CUSTOMER ORIENTATION AND MOTIVATION

This section deals with the following subjects:

- The importance of motivation and innovation (Section 12.2.1);
- Vision (Section 12.2.2).
- Leadership (Section 12.2.3).

- Open communication (Section 12.2.4).
- Shared goals (Section 12.2.5).
- Stimulating innovation (Section 12.2.6).
- Customer-oriented rewarding with the balanced scorecard (Section 12.2.7).

12.2.1 Importance of Motivation and Innovation

A good implementation of a strategy is essential for success. Managers can make excellent plans, but a plan will be effective only after a good implementation, and that implementation is done by the employees. Employees perform best when they are motivated, that is, when they are proud of working for their organization. A generally accepted starting point for getting employees motivated is *team building.* Implementation will be succesful if the organization operates as a team of people working on *shared goals.* Therefore, a good implementation requires motivated and involved staff that is impressed with the necessity of marketing and customer-oriented thinking and also has good relationships with other functional areas within the company.[3]

In this book we have argued that supplying customer values and maintaining a brand identity are increasingly important for every organization. True customer orientation can be achieved only when everyone in the organization feels connected to the customer. In addition, the people in the organization need to portray the brand identity of the organization. In short, these days more than ever, the people in an organization are the sources of its success. Two aspects of the human factor are crucial in this respect:

1. Motivation is required for a good implementation.
2. Learning and renewal are required to receive input from the entire organization to provide customer values even better.

If any change in strategy will have to be implemented within an organization (e.g., operate in a more market-oriented fashion), the implementation of that change will have to start with the people: It is not without reason that the factor of personnel is often called the *fifth P of marketing.* As a result, it can be concluded that the marketing function and the personnel function in organizations should collaborate strongly (see Case 12-2) or should be integrated.[4]

CASE 12-2 *Motivation of* *Employees at* *Nordstrom*	Seattle-based Nordstrom Inc. is an example of a company that has made frontline employees the focus of its business strategy. It presents its organizational structure as a pyramid with not the CEO but Nordstrom shoppers at the top. The idea is that customers are dictating the company's strategy, and it is frontline workers who are crucial to serving their needs. Store salespeople are paid higher than average salaries to attract top workers, whereas managers earn relatively less. The company promotes heavily from within, giving preference to those who have sold on the retail floor and understand the challenges faced there. Nordstrom marketers want to define their company by its personalized service, and to achieve this, they put their money into motivating the frontliners.

Source: McMaster, Nick, "Incentive-Powered Marketing," *Potentials,* November 2002.

The importance of the personnel seems logical, yet it is not always emphasized strongly. In the literature and in the practice of strategic management the triad of "strategy, structure, people" often is mentioned; this means that after the choice of a strategy has been made, a suitable organizational structure is set up, after which the focus is on the completion of the personnel policy. In our view, the sequence of these steps should be altered to "strategy, people, structure": There is a group of people who are responsible for the execution of the strategy, and those people should be optimally motivated to tackle the task. Then they are surrounded by and supported with a structure that, among other things, should serve to motivate them optimally. The following section outlines several instruments that may be useful in that regard.

12.2.2 Vision

In Chapter 2 the focus was on the mission of the organization. An important element in that area is the vision of top management about where the organization "wants to go" in the next few years: What is the positioning or the added value of the company? This vision typically builds on the core competencies of the organization. If the vision is transmitted in a credible and convincing way to the personnel and is supported and shared by them, the vision forms an important tool for motivating a group of people and providing a direction for taking action. A common vision is generally seen as the most important direction for a team. Peters refers to the "WOW! factor,"[5] in which a vision requires that top management dare to choose and therefore also dare to choose goals it does not want to achieve. A vision may also contain the brand positioning.

12.2.3 Leadership

If there is a motivated vision, it should be communicated via all channels externally but also internally. Personnel must know where the company is going. *Leadership* plays a key role here. The figurehead of the company or the brand should spread the message clearly and internally, and certainly the leader must be the *inspirer*. He or she can use every opportunity to do this. Think of a leader of a political party. The motto for this is: "Keep it simple and repeat it." "Visions" that are too complex are not clear, and the effects of learning will be attained only after sufficient repetition.

Ideally, the leader should also be a "people manager," someone who stays close to the personnel, shows that he or she understands them, and knows what matters. The reason for this is that otherwise the "boss" ends up being detached from the personnel and there is a risk that the personnel will separate itself from upper management, for example, during changes. It also stimulates open and honest communication, which is important for stimulating creativity and innovation within the organization.

12.2.4 Open Communication

Research shows that marketing implementation is more successful if leaders create an organizational culture that is characterized by *open communication* between personnel and managers. Conversely, it has been shown that bad internal communication in an organization is one of the most important reasons for bad implementation. Two forms of internal communication play a role: communication between top management and employees and communication among employees. A leader should provide a good example and pay attention to individual personnel. Another principle is that people should be used as much as possible on the basis of their strengths. Therefore, it is important in terms of motivating people to understand the characteristics of individual people and then engage them as much as possible on the basis of those characteristics.

Another important issue is informing personnel about policy measures. Top management should try to be close to the personnel and therefore not regularly announce one-sided top-down measures. A problem that might develop in this regard is that the organization will be less battle-ready: Endless deliberations and democratic processes may make it impossible to lead an organization and become a barrier to prompt action. However, that does not have to be the case. Obviously, top management should also be able to execute unpopular measures. However, when that happens with a direct and open information supply, the foundation for support is increased. In this regard, a parallel may be made with the recommendations in this book for crisis management (see Section 10.4.1).

12.2.5 Shared Goals

The development of *shared, measurable goals* is an important instrument for team building. The goals of an organization flow from the vision of top management. Both the vision and the goals should be supported by all the people in the organization: *Shared values and goals* are the glue that makes people within an organization a team.[6] Organizations that do not have measurable goals therefore should make an attempt to formulate them.

Typically, a top-down approach does not work well in this regard. People usually do not like having something imposed on them from above. The intent should be to involve all personnel in the formulation of goals. A bottom-up approach might be considered in which groups of two brainstorm goals, after which those groups are joined together into groups of four that have to come to agreement about goals and the like. Such processes are typically guided by professional agencies. The chosen goals can be used in the measurement of performance.

12.2.6 Stimulating Innovation

The guidelines described here are related to *doing things right* (implementation), but it is also very important to continuously wonder whether the company is *doing the right things*. This implies that a company has to be innovative. A company should try to receive as many inputs for renewal and improvement as possible from within the organization but also from outside. This is also related to customer orientation: It is important to foresee as well as possible—and better than the competitor—what customer future needs are. Market research can help in getting ideas for innovation, but will mostly not be enough. This is because a customer mostly is not able to come up with new ('future') needs. So, innovation should also be stimulated from the 'supply side' (such as research and development). For innovation *managing knowledge* is essential: Knowledge should be developed, maintained, and shared as much as possible. Knowledge management involves:

- The development and updating of knowledge and skills.
- Stimulating and maintaining a culture of learning and innovation (among other things through a little hierarchy and a lot of freedom).

Knowledge management therefore does not refer only to good information systems. Knowledge management has two tracks:

1. An "*IT track*": the development of excellent information technology.
2. A *human track*: stimulating learning within the organization.

The use of the human track means that the organization has a willingness to learn. Freedom and independence are prerequisites for such an environment. It is inevitable that mistakes will be made, but people learn from mistakes, and so this has to be accepted. Several of the instruments mentioned earlier may help stimulate a learning environment, for example, rewards for new ideas.

Informal consultation is also indispensable. In effect this is a form of internal communication: communication between employees. This information exchange should also take place between functional departments in an organization, for example, between marketing and production or between sales and research and development. All information about customers, competitors, and other relevant issues should be exchanged. This fits with the concept of market-orientation described in Chapter 1: customer orientation, competitor orientation, and interfunctional decision making, and information exchange.

12.2.7   Customer-Oriented Rewarding with the Balanced Scorecard

The organizational goals can become a part of the reward systems for employees. People's motivation is strengthened only when it is translated to individual goals. Therefore, tasks and individual goals must be deduced from the measurable goals for the entire organization. This also occurs in consultations between employees and managers. The individual goals then become in part the basis for rewards for the staff. The balanced scorecard discussed in Chapter 3 works well here. We can choose to reward motivation and customer orientation. These are two separate fields in the balanced scorecard. If a manager has achieved a target, this means a higher reward. The targets selected and their completion depend on the value strategy that has been selected. It should also be kept in mind that people may appreciate different prizes (financial, a large office, a nice car, etc.). This system can stimulate the creation of a more customer-oriented attitude that pays for itself over time through increased sales and profit.

12.3   SELLING THE PLAN: INTERNAL MARKETING

Even if an organization already has team spirit, strong motivation, and pride, it is necessary to enlist support for each marketing plan. Support is needed for three *internal target groups:* other departments (functional areas) such as personnel and research and development (feasibility plan), upper management (make sure money is brought in to implement the plan), and employees (for the implementation). The main point is to bring the plan to the person, in short, to sell the plan. Everyone in the company is a person, and people are responsive to arguments and a good story.

Managers who make plans have been known to complain that upper management does not have any money for their great ideas. Discontented, they ask themselves how they "can carry out marketing with almost no money." This answer is that they were evidently not in a position to sell the plan well internally. If a plan is really good and is sold internally in an attractive manner, the money will be there. There is always money for a good plan. All that is necessary is to convince upper management that the plan will pay for itself. The internal selling of the "product" marketing plan is called *internal marketing.*[7] In big companies, upper management often has various plans under review for which a limited budget is divided. The idea is to sell your plan better than others in the company sell theirs.

12.3.1   Performance Projection of the Plan

The first thing the plan should show is that the marketing objectives will be achieved. This implies that marketing expenditures will be paid back in an acceptable time frame and/or that profit will increase, depending on the performance objectives. A challenging goal of an increase in market share of 15 points will demand a higher marketing budget than will an increase of 5 points. Thus, it is critical to make a credible performance time line.[8] Figure 12-4 provides an example.

Figure 12-4 shows the predicted performance of a high-priced personal computer (PC). The main marketing objective of this brand is to increase market share (in terms of revenue) from 2.2 percent in 2005 to 2.5 percent in 2008. Market growth is predicted to slow from 20 percent to 14 percent in those years. The underlying marketing strategy is that the brand will focus on the advantages of having a PC at home in combination with a laptop and that Orange has the unique selling proposition that the communication between these computers is the most reliable among all brands. This decision is accompanied by a large campaign in 2006: The marketing budget increases from $15 million in 2005 ("current") to $25 million

FIGURE 12-4   **Example of a Marketing Performance Plan for the Personal Computer Brand Orange**

	Current	Projected		
	2005	2006	2007	2008
Market size (units, 1000)	17,930	21,157	24,543	27,979
Market growth (percent)	20,3	18	16	14
Market share (%)	2,1	2,2	2,3	2,4
Sales (units, 1000)	377	465	564	671
Market size ($million)	17,571	19,888	22,579	25,181
Market share	2,2	2,3	2,4	2,5
Sales revenues ($million)	387	457	542	630
Sales growth (percent)	8,0	18,3	18,5	16,2
Mean market price ($)	980	940	920	900
Mean price of Orange ($)	1027	983	960	938
Number of customers (1000)	270	300	330	360
Revenue per customer	1432	1525	1642	1749
Percent margin (excluding marketing)	15	15	15	15
Gross profit (millions, excluding marketing)	**58**	**69**	**81**	**94**
Marketing budget ($million)	**15**	**25**	**20**	**20**
Net profit ($million)	**43**	**44**	**61**	**74**

Assumptions:
Customers will value the innovative communication between Orange laptops and personal computers.
Competitors will not be able to develop a comparable communication technique.

in 2006. It is projected that sales per customer can increase since more customers will buy a PC and a laptop in one transaction. Net profit will be stable in 2006 but will increase in 2007 and 2008.

Making "wonderful" estimates such as those in Figure 12-4 is not enough; the main thing is they should be credible. The next section discusses factors that should accompany financial projections.

12.3.2   Succes Factors for Internal Marketing

The following factors increase a plan's chances of acceptance (Figure 12-5):

1. *Convincing reasons why the plan will succeed.* For an upper-level manager, only one thing counts: being convinced of the predicted success. What is the creative discovery, the innovation, the *consumer need* that makes the plan so good?

2. *Good base of support.* Every plan claims that it will pay for itself in no time, but upper management knows that there is always uncertainty with respect to the future. The most convincing plans are those which have the strongest base of support. Research plays a key role here. It is powerful to assert that 75 percent purchasing intent was attained on the basis of research rather than on the basis of your own estimation. It is also more honest to indicate explicitly the assumptions of the plan than to have upper management find them out during the discussion. That will make them suspicious.

3. *Show the alternatives that were not chosen.* Many managers have a tendency to present a single idea without showing why alternatives were not chosen. A disadvantage of this is that it puts upper management on the spot. There are no choices apart from yes or no.

FIGURE 12-5
Effective Internal Marketing

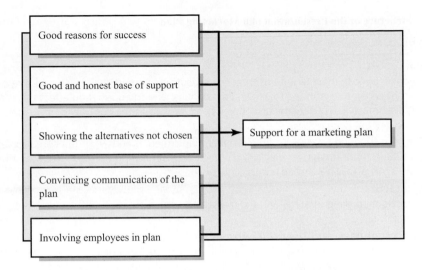

If a comparative perspective is used, the listener can help decide, as it were. This boosts your chances of acceptance. "Unrevised policy" is always an available alternative, and it definitely helps if you can forecast what "disastrous" results will occur if this alternative is chosen.

4. *Convincing presentation of the plan.* A convincing method of internal communication of the plan helps enormously: videos, Web sites, oral presentations—anything goes. Some companies are very strong in this area: As soon as a certain idea has the necessary internal base of support, a whole battery of creative tools is put into action to achieve that goal. Figure 12-6 gives guidelines for the oral presentation of a plan. It is important to tell a convincing story in a short period of time. This means that the arrangement of the presentation does not have to follow "scientific standards" such as slowly and meticulously building up to a conclusion. This kind of arrangement is generally considered boring by managers and is therefore not suitable for selling a plan.

5. *Involving internal target groups in the process.* If other internal target groups are involved in the development of the plan, this will increase the chances of acceptance as well as cooperation and motivation during the implementation phase. This "involvement" can vary from participation in decision making to keeping up to date (communication). The advantage is that coworkers do not feel ambushed later and can have the feeling of being coresponsible.

One might have the impression that upper management will be "disobliging" and that it will be very difficult to get it to extend its support. This is not the case. The interests of everyone in the company are the same: collectively deliver good performance and thus (for the most part) earn money. Of course upper management is critical to all plans within a company, but the board must also extend a lot of support to marketing plans. This involves not only money but also attention, information, and the active stimulation of the making of the plan. Upper management must also recognize that not every plan will pay for itself in no time. Especially for brand investments such as advertising, it is not always sufficient to demonstrate that an investment will quickly produce profits. It takes time to build up a brand, just as it does to win loyal customers. Upper management and other investors (such as shareholders) should therefore not always work from a short-term perspective (as with sales promotions) but take a long-term perspective (as with thematic communication).

FIGURE 12-6 **Structure of the Presentation of a Marketing Plan**

Source: Cohen, W. A. (1998), *The Marketing Plan*, 2nd ed., New York: Wiley.

1. Introduction

In the introduction, the most important items from the executive summary may be shared: the core of the plan, the opportunity that is being responded to, expected revenues, and the budget. In effect this is a short summary beforehand that also immediately gets the attention of and stimulates the curiosity of management.

2. Why this plan will succeed

This part contains the situation analysis and the research performed. It ends with the core problem and the most important opportunities and threats, as well as the objectives. The most important message of this part of the presentation is why this plan will succeed (while others fail).

3. Strategy and tactics

This part contains the marketing strategy and the marketing implementation of the plans (such as the communication plan).

4. Assumptions, prognoses, and financial information

This part contains all assumptions (required to be able to discuss uncertainties and risk), the relevant prognoses, the project planning, the profit and loss pictures, and how much money is required and when.

5. Conclusions

Here the most important opportunity is repeated: why the plan will succeed, the required money, and the expected return on investment.

12.4 PLANNING GUIDELINES

We now give a few guidelines for the eventual implementation of these plans.

Trigger

A plan will be more successful if it has a "trigger": someone who feels that she or he is in charge of the plan.

Tasks

It is important that people know what is expected of them. Therefore, the formulation of clear tasks is vital. In relation to the targets, agreements must be reached about who is responsible for what. The marketing plan should also indicate in detail what is expected of each person.

Interim Measurements

A marketing plan is normally drafted once a year. Typically, there is also an annual measurement of the results. However, interim measurements are recommended to enable timely adjustments. For instance, customer analyses can be conducted almost continuously. Customer satisfaction studies, advertising, and brand tracking should be a normal part of the monitoring. This approach requires extensive data collection and therefore an information system that is adapted to this process. In practice, it seems important to appoint a single person to be in charge of keeping the necessary information up to date.

Good Process Evaluation

If the measurements show that the goals have not been reached, a good process evaluation is important. A thorough process evaluation is necessary to avoid altering a strategy or product that is essentially good;the problem is related not to the product but to the implementation. In this context, four possible combinations of strategy (good/not good) and implementation (good/not good) can be distinguished (Figure 12-7).

FIGURE 12-7   **Strategy and Implementation: Problem Diagnosis**

Source: Bonoma, T. V. (1984), "Making Your Strategy Work," *Harvard Business Review* 62:67–76.

Implementation		Strategy	
		Good	**Bad**
	Good	Success Objectives for growth, market share, and profit are achieved.	**Rescue or ruin** Good implementation may soften bad strategy and allow management some time to make corrections, but a good implementation of a bad strategy may speed the decline.
	Bad	Problems Bad implementation disguises good strategy: Management may conclude that the strategy is not good.	**Failure** Cause of failure is difficult to determine because bad strategy is masked by bad implementation.

In the most positive situation, strategy and implementation are both good. In all other cases, the diagnosis of disappointing results is a challenge. If both are bad, it is a failure in any case, but it is unclear whether it is related to the strategy because it was not implemented well. However, if the strategy is good but is implemented badly or vice versa, a risky situation develops. With a bad implementation of an excellent strategy, there is a risk that management may conclude that the strategy is not good. If the strategy is changed unnecessarily, the company moves to the cell at the bottom right in Figure 12-7, where it becomes a failure. With a good implementation of a bad strategy, there are two possibilities. If management concludes that the strategy is not good and alters it, there is still a chance for success (a move to the left in Figure 12-7). However, if management does nothing, a good implementation of a bad strategy will lead to "ruin." In following the results of the chosen strategies, explicit attention should be paid to the question of whether the chosen strategy was implemented well. Only after that step should any changes be made in the strategy itself.

Flexibility

Finally, we advise against implementing the overall plan too rigidly. Marketing planning must not lead to a bureaucratic budgeting and prognosis system. It also should not lead to only once-a-year thinking about the strategy. Strategic choices have to be made continously. Furthermore, flexibility and room for creativity should be monitored and safeguarded. Balance must be achieved between strong control of the system and freedom to innovate.

Differences among Companies

For all the guidelines given above, there are differences between large and small companies. In small companies, the owner/director is usually very much involved in marketing and planning and there are not many other people in the organization involved in the planning process. In this case, the degree of formulation of the planning and the extent of the marketing plan may be more limited than they are in large companies.

12.5   CONCLUDING TIPS FOR STRATEGIC MARKETING

In this last section of the book we present some concluding remarks. The main part of the book is devoted to describing strategic marketing as a process. In doing this in practice two problems may arise: 'technical' problems (how to do it exactly) and strategic problems

FIGURE 12-8   **Eleven Tips for Strategic Marketing**

1. **Customer**	Think about everything concerning the psychology of the customer; demonstrate empathy for the customers. Help them solve their problems, such as lack of time and stress[9].
2. **Choice**	For building relationships a clear brand image is needed. Dare to choose: "specialize."
3. **Systematic**	Analyze yourself, the environment, and the customer systematically.
4. **Critical**	Be critical and future-oriented because a small problem today can be a ticking time bomb for tomorrow's success.
5. **Vision**	Choose a value strategy as a vision that works to motivate and direct.
6. **Creative**	Be innovative; think outside the box. One "big idea" can be enough.
7. **Patience**	Do not focus on the short term: Building brand reputation and customer loyalty takes time
8. **Customer loyalty**	Reward loyalty from the customer with concrete advantages (true loyalty programs).
9. **Personnel**	Do not pay managers only for profit and market share but also for customer loyalty.
10. **Check**	Check all activities for the brand positioning: brand name, design, communication, and so on. A funny commercial with poor brand recollection is bad.
11. **Organize**	Make sure there is marketing knowledge in the company and that communication is managed from the top of the organization ("reputation manager"). Also consider appointing customer managers.

(what choices to be made). Technical problems can only be overcome by trial and error and by giving an own interpretation to the guidelines in this book. Remember: there is no truth.

Strategic problems in the end are more serious. The main thing is to strongly emphasize the customer. There are some other tips too. Figure 12-8 provides a number of tips for effective strategic marketing.

CASE 12-3

Starbucks Is Successful through Service

The success of the coffee chain Starbucks is so large that there are games in which you have to guess whose postal code has the highest Starbucks density. Postal code 10020 (midtown Manhattan) scores quite high with 179 Starbucks stores. The long-term goal of Starbucks is to increase the number of stores from 7000 to 30,000 in the United States. The enormous success of Starbucks cannot be attributed to promotion, since there is hardly any advertising for this brand. It is mainly the quality of the service that is responsible for the success. With a good feel for what customers want and by introducing the right services (for example, the possibility of burning one's own CDs), Starbucks demonstrates that success should start with a good product and a good service.

Source: Viktor Frölke, 'Starbucks transforms coffee into a marketing concept', *NRC Handelsblad*, January 12, 2006, p. 16.

The final case in the book (Case 12-3) is devoted to Starbucks, a company that shows that marketing success is not caused by communication but by listening well to customers and translating their needs into innovative products and services.

We believe our set of 11 guidelines will leave the competition in the dust.

Summary

Successful implementation of a customer-oriented strategy requires a good organization and places high demands on marketing and on the people in an organization. The introduction of a customer management system has the advantage that the customer is brought in-house, so to speak. For communication, it is important that this process be managed and coordinated from the top of the company or the brand. A motivated team is in the best position to implement any strategy. A clear vision, a leader who is an inspirer and a people manager, collective goals, open internal communication, an open learning environment, and customer-oriented rewards stimulate team building. A marketing plan must be sold internally to obtain as much support as possible and the necessary resources. The plan should be financially sound, clearly indicate why it will succeed, be grounded in research, and be contrasted with alternatives such as unrevised policy. All other departments should be involved in the development of the plan. Finally, creative internal marketing must be introduced for the plan: the internal selling and presentation of the plan, for example, to upper management. Customer orientation is also stimulated by targeted rewards. This can be combined with the use of the balanced scorecard. The attainment of customer and innovation targets means extra rewards. Successful implementation of a plan is facilitated if there is a "trigger" for the plan, personal tasks are clearly indicated, and there are not only annual but also interim measurements of targets. If a target is not reached, a good process evaluation is needed: Is it because of the strategy or because of the implementation? If adjustments are needed, flexibility is needed to leave room for innovation.

Notes

1. Webster, jr., F.E., A.J. Malter, S. Ganesan (2005), 'The Decline and Dispersion of Marketing Competence,' *Sloan Management Review,* 46 (4), 35–43.

2. Alsop, R. J. (2004), *The 18 Immutable Laws of Corporate Reputation,* New York: Free Press.

3. See also McDonald, M. (2002), *Marketing Plans,* 5th ed., Oxford, UK: Butterworth-Heinemann.

4. Glassman, M., and B. McAfee (1992), "Integrating the Personnel and Marketing Functions: The Challenge of the 1990s," *Business Horizons* 35:52–59

5. Peters, T. (1994), *The Pursuit of WOW!* New York: Vintage.

6. Howard, R. (1990), "Values Make the Company: An Interview with Robert Haas," *Harvard Business Review* 68:144; Katzenbach, J. R., and D. K. Smith (1993), "The Discipline of Teams," *Harvard Business Review,* March-April, pp. 111–120.

7. Piercy N., and N. Morgan (1991), "Internal Marketing—The Missing Half of the Marketing Programme," *Long Range Planning* 24(2):82–93.

8. For a strongly financially driven marketing planning approach, see Best, R. J. (2004), *Market-Based Management,* 3rd ed., Upper Saddle River, NJ: Pearson.

9. Cristol, S.M., P. Sealey, (2000), *Simplicity Marketing,* New York: The Free Press.

Index